THE JUS

The Justice Facade

Trials of Transition in Cambodia

ALEXANDER LABAN HINTON

OXFORD

UNIVERSITY PRESS

OXFORD

UNIVERSITY PRESS

Great Clarendon Street, Oxford, OX2 6DP,
United Kingdom

Oxford University Press is a department of the University of Oxford.
It furthers the University's objective of excellence in research, scholarship,
and education by publishing worldwide. Oxford is a registered trade mark of
Oxford University Press in the UK and in certain other countries

First Edition published in 2018

Impression: 1

Published in the United States of America by Oxford University Press
198 Madison Avenue, New York, NY 10016, United States of America

British Library Cataloguing in Publication Data
Data available

Library of Congress Control Number: 2017958197

ISBN 978–0–19–882095–6 (pbk)
ISBN 978–0–19–882094–9 (hbk)

Printed and bound by
CPI Group (UK) Ltd, Croydon, CR0 4YY

For my Father, Ladson,
and Mother, Darlene, in loving memory

Acknowledgments

Many people have helped make possible this book which, along with its companion volume *Man or Monster? The Trial of a Khmer Rouge Torturer*, has been in process for almost a decade. Indeed, the research in Cambodia for these two volumes, which began in 2008 and continues into the present, has involved over three hundred interviews with individuals ranging from court officials and civil parties to rural villagers—as well as participant observation, documentary and archival research, and attendance at numerous Khmer Rouge Tribunal outreach activities and ECCC trial sessions.

I'd like to recognize my family first and foremost. My wife, Nicole, read multiple drafts of the manuscript. She and our daughters, Meridian and Arcadia, patiently supported me while I worked on the book and traveled to Cambodia for research. I appreciate their love as well as that of my parents, my father Ladson and late mother Darlene, to whom this book is dedicated. I'd also like to acknowledge my other family members, including my brothers, Laddie and Devon, and their families, Susan, Carolee, Kendra, Dev, Carina, and Mika, as well as my in-laws, Peter, Jacki, Alissa, David, and Josh.

I'm also lucky to have an amazing group of colleagues at the Rutgers Center for the Study of Genocide and Human Rights (CGHR), including the other members of the CGHR Executive Committee, Nela Navarro and Stephen Eric Bronner, and previously Tom LaPointe. Thank you!

While in Cambodia, Youk Chhang and his staff at the Documentation Center of Cambodia (DC-Cam) provided a "home away from home." Youk also offered his time to answer many questions about his experiences and DC-Cam's outreach work, which is the focus of a chapter. I'd also like to thank Youk for permission to use several images from the DC-Cam/SRI archive. Thanks also to my other colleagues and students at CGHR and Rutgers, including the Division of Global Affairs and Department of Sociology and Anthropology. Rutgers University (FASN, GAIA, and the Research Council) also provided sabbatical time and grants to help support this research, as did the United States Institute of Peace (the ideas and conclusions in the book are, of course, my own and do not necessarily reflect the view of the USIP).

The ideas in this book were first presented at the Institute for Advanced Study in Princeton, where I was fortunate to spend time while also working on *Man or Monster?* It was an ideal space in so many ways. Throughout, Didier Fassin offered encouragement and support, which I greatly appreciate. I'd also like to thank the other faculty in the School of Social Sciences, Joan Scott, Michael Walzer, and Danielle Allen, and the other Fellows, particularly Jens Meierhenrich, Kimberly Theidon, and Jarret Zigon.

More recently, I have been fortune to work with my editor at Oxford, Merel Alstein, her colleague Natasha Flemming, James Baird, Dipak Durairaj, Jack Webb, and the other members of the OUP production and marketing teams who helped with this manuscript. I received very helpful reviews, which helped me revise and strengthen the manuscript considerably. Their support and efforts are greatly appreciated.

I have also received useful feedback at different talks I have given at different academic and professional institutions. I'd like to thank the audiences for their remarks and the hosts, including the participants in the "Rethinking Peace Studies" initiative, for providing me with a venue to present ideas.

Many other people provided support, encouragement, and suggestions during the course of this project. I'd like to thank Samphors Huy for her research assistance. The late Reach Sambath and his colleagues Dim Sovannarom, Pheatra Neth and Lars Olsen from the ECCC Public Affairs office also greatly facilitated my research.

In addition, I'd like to thank Jeremiah Alberg, Joyce Apsel, Kurt Bredenberg, David Chandler, Terith Chy, John Ciorciari, Jean-Marc Coicaud, Lawrence Douglas, Khamboly Dy, Craig Etcheson, Kok-Thy Eng, Daniel Feierstein, Mark Goodale, Paul Hastings, Vannak Huy, Helen Jarvis, Judy Ledgerwood, Michelle Lipinski, Sophat Morm, Dirk Moses, Charles Nuckolls, Robert Paul, Clement Price, Sreyneath Poole, Joanna Regulska, Steven Riskin, Tony Robben, Robert Ruffini, Fatily Sa, Victoria Sanford, Sirik Savina, Giorgio Shani, Bradd Shore, Sorya Sim, Greg Stanton, Ernesto Verdeja, Dawn Wilson, Andrew Woolford, and Carol Worthman. Great thanks are also owed to Mark Urken and Louis Harrison. My apologies to the many other deserving people I have inadvertently left off this brief list.

Finally, I'd like to thank the individuals who spoke to me, often for hours at a time, during interviews and conversations. Of particular note are those appearing in this book, including Bou Meng, Vannath Chea, Sophea Im, Kassie Neou, Lao Mong Hay, Chum Mey, Neth Phally, Theary Seng, Thun Saray, "Suon," Nou Va, and the late Reach Sambath and Vann Nath. Thank you.

Note: Minor portions of two essays that have appeared elsewhere are included in this book:

Hinton, Alexander Laban. 2014. "Justice and Time at the Khmer Rouge Tribunal: In Memory of Vann Nath, Painter and S-21 Survivor." *Genocide Studies and Prevention* 8(2): 7–17.

Hinton, Alexander Laban. 2013. "Transitional Justice Time: Uncle San, Aunty Yan, and Outreach at the Khmer Rouge Tribunal." In *Genocide and Mass Atrocities in Asia: Legacies and Prevention*, edited by Deborah Meyersen and Annie Pohlman, 86–98. New York: Routledge.

Contents

PART I VORTICES

PART II TURBULENCE

PART III EDDIES

List of Illustrations

Introduction

Chapter 2

Preamble II

Chapter 4

Chapter 5

Chapter 6

Preamble III

Chapter 9

List of Abbreviations

ADHOC	Cambodian Human Rights and Development Association
CA	KID Citizen Advisors
CIHR	Cambodian Institute of Human Rights
CJR	Center for Justice and Reconciliation
CPK	Communist Party of Kampuchea
CPP	Cambodian People's Party
CSD	Center for Social Development
DC-Cam	Documentation Center of Cambodia
DED	German Development Service
DK	Democratic Kampuchea (period of Khmer Rouge rule)
ECCC	Extraordinary Chambers in the Courts of Cambodia
ETGE	DC-Cam "ECCC Tour and Genocide Education"
EU	European Union
HRC	UNTAC Human Rights Component
ICC	International Criminal Court
ICTJ	International Center for Transitional Justice
ICTR	International Criminal Tribunal for Rwanda
ICTY	International Criminal Tribunal for the former Yugoslavia
KAS	Konrad-Adenauer Stiftung
KID	Khmer Institute of Democracy
KPNLF	Khmer People's National Liberation Front
KRT	Khmer Rouge Tribunal
LDP	Living Documents Program (DC-Cam)
NGO	Non-Governmental Organization
OCIJ	Office of the Co-Investigating Judges
OCP	Office of the Co-Prosecutors
OSJI	Open Society Justice Initiative
PAS	Public Affairs Section
PPA	Paris Peace Agreement
PRK	People's Republic of Kampuchea
PRT	People's Revolutionary Tribunal
PTC	Pre-Trial Chamber
PTSD	Post-Traumatic Stress Disorder
SCSL	Special Court for Sierra Leone
SNC	Supreme National Council
SOC	State of Cambodia
TPO	Transcultural Psychosocial Organization
UNTAC	United Nations Transitional Authority in Cambodia
VIF	Victim Information Form
VSS	Victims Support Section (formerly VU)
VU	Victims Unit (later Victims Support Section)

Table of Cases

Table of Legislation

Table of Instruments

Preface

Uncle San and the Khmer Rouge Tribunal

Uncle San's eyes are closed.

He dozes in a dirty white hammock knotted to the trunk of a tree, thick roots sunk deep into the ground. He clasps his hands behind his head, his lips curled into a frown. Uncle San dreams, nightmares of violence and suffering, memories from the past. While sitting on a raised platform and sipping tea in his rural Cambodian village, Uncle San explains what happened.

"Hello, my name is San," he begins, a checkered yellow Cambodian scarf slung over his right shoulder. "I am 64 years of age, and I live in a village in Siem Reap province. I have lived in this village since I was young, but during the Khmer Rouge Regime I was forced to live in another area."

Uncle San's nightmares, it is clear, are anchored to a moment in time, Democratic Kampuchea (DK), the period when the Khmer Rouge—a group of Marxist-Leninist, Maoist-inspired revolutionaries led by Pol Pot—ruled Cambodia. After a long civil war, the Khmer Rouge took power on April 17, 1975, and began launching a "Super Great Leap Forward" that would surpass all other communist revolutions, including that of their close socialist ally, China.[1]

One of their first acts was to immediately rusticate the urban population, often under the pretext that the United States, which was allied to the Khmer Republic, the regime the Khmer Rouge overthrew, was going to bomb the cities. Throughout Cambodia, the roads swelled with crowds of people as the urbanites were dispersed into the countryside. Later, the Khmer Rouge continued the population movements, relocating Cambodians to more distant areas where they lived in cooperatives. Uncle San and his fellow villagers were among those forced to abandon their homes.

In the cooperatives they found that almost everything was communal: oxen and plows to till the paddy fields, rice distributed at meals, thoughts and emotions shared during self-criticism sessions, and hard labor exerted to harvest crops and build the infrastructure that would transform DK into an unprecedented communist state. The ideal did not match the realities on the ground, leading to hardship, suffering, and mass death.

Uncle San vividly remembers the moments that still haunt his dreams. "During the Khmer Rouge Regime," he recollects, "I was forced to plant rice all day long."

---

[1] On DK, see Chandler 1999; Hinton 2005; Kiernan 2008.

The Justice Facade: Trials of Transition in Cambodia. Alexander Laban Hinton. © Alexander Laban Hinton, 2018. Published 2018 by Oxford University Press.

The hard labor, carried out as part of a struggle to "build and defend" the revolution, could extend into the night and was all the more taxing because the villagers often received minimal food rations. Some began to steal, Uncle San among them, an infraction that could lead to death. "Once," he illustrates, "I took a crab from the field and was beaten for doing so. I remember the mistreatment of monks, hard work, poor food, tortures and killings," including blindfolded villagers being executed and kicked into mass graves.

By the time of its downfall on January 6, 1979, the DK regime's policies, ranging from collectivization and forced labor to increasingly frequent purges of suspected enemies, had resulted in the death of roughly a quarter of Cambodia's eight million inhabitants due to starvation, overwork, malnutrition, or execution. When Uncle San returned to his village at the end of DK, he found "my home was destroyed. What makes me most sad is that all of my family members were killed."

"Since then," Uncle San explains, "I have bad dreams every night about what happened."

"Usually," he adds, "I try not to think about the past by spending my time planting rice, going to the pagoda, and chatting with my neighbors," including his next door neighbor, Aunty Yan, who Uncle San has known "since I was a child. Her family was killed during the Khmer Rouge Regime. We often eat rice and drink tea together." For almost thirty years, Uncle San has remained tangled in this violent past, afflicted by trauma, unable to move forward.

Then one day in 2008, the possibility of justice arrived. He tells the story.

Like many Cambodians, Uncle San has often sought relief from the past through a traditional practice, lighting incense for the spirits of the dead. Uncle San lives in a wooden house commonly found in Cambodian villages, a single story structure raised by piles from the ground, to which the house is connected by a ladder. The steps are firm but narrow, the ascent steep.

Just off the entrance is a shelf holding a small incense bowl placed next to two photographs of dead relatives. He often stands before the photos, three sticks of incense in hand—representing the Buddha, the wisdom of dhamma he preached, and the monastic order the Buddha established—and prays for the souls of those who died during DK.

"One day, I was praying for my dead family," Uncle San says, when "Aunty Yan told me that there was going to be a special meeting in the village about the Khmer Rouge," one conducted by a Citizen Advisor from the Khmer Institute of Democracy (KID), a Cambodian non-governmental organization. "I was interested about this meeting," Uncle San recalled, "and other villagers seemed curious about it too."

At the gathering, the KID's Citizen Advisor informed Uncle San, Aunty Yan, and the other villagers about the creation of the Khmer Rouge Tribunal (KRT), an international hybrid court officially called the Extraordinary Chambers in the Courts of Cambodia (ECCC). "This was the first time I and the other villagers learned about it," Uncle San remarks. The Citizen Advisor apprised the villagers that the KRT, which was being held in Cambodia's capital, Phnom Penh, "was established through an agreement signed by the Royal Government of Cambodia and the UN in 2003. It includes participation from international and national staff. The goal of the agreement is to seek justice, national reconciliation, stability, peace, and security in Cambodia."

In the days following the meeting, Uncle San talked with Aunty Yan about the tribunal as they drank tea together. Aunty Yan, who lives in a wooden house with a concrete bottom level, is somewhat wealthier than Uncle San. Every day, Aunty Yan would sit on a raised platform in front of her house, listening to radio programming about the KRT. Because of her greater knowledge about the tribunal, Aunty Yan told Uncle San more about the KRT, including the possibility of victim participation. "Aunty Yan taught me that victims can submit a complaint to the court," Uncle San recalled. "She showed me the complaint form and taught me how to fill it out. I think I want to!"

First, however, they wanted to see the court, which is open to the public and offers free bus service from the court's information center in Phnom Penh. When Uncle San and Aunty Yan arrived there, they boarded a modern bus—painted blue and white, the court colors, and adorned with the court logo—and drove to the ECCC compound, located on the outskirts of the capital.

To enter the court, the bus had to cross a checkpoint, guarded and blocked by an iron gate. As the bus was being cleared by security, Uncle San, Aunty Yan, and the other passengers glimpsed the main court building, labeled by a large sign reading, in Khmer, English, and French, "Court Room." Just beyond, the roof of another building, this one with traditional Cambodian spires, rose up, seeming to merge with the spare modern court building.

Then the gates were pulled back, the villagers allowed to pass. The bus parked and the driver opened the doors, enabling Uncle San and the others to walk along a path to the packed courtroom, where a trial was taking place.

"It was big and beautiful," Uncle San says. "We sat in chairs, and were given head phones to listen to what the judges and other parties were saying in the court. We observed that all people were interested in the hearing, especially the accused person." But Uncle San emphasizes, "I didn't understand *who* was being accused of being criminals." So, during a break, he asked Aunty Yan to explain.

"Which members of the Khmer Rouge will the court bring to trial?" Uncle San inquires.

"The KRT will only try the senior leaders of the Khmer Rouge and those most responsible for committing serious crimes committed during the Khmer Rouge Regime dating from April 17, 1975 to January 6, 1979," Aunty Yan replies. Pol Pot died in 1998 but his deputy Nuon Chea and others still might be tried.

Uncle San thinks back to an execution he had glimpsed, a Khmer Rouge cadre dressed in black clubbing a man, an ordinary villager just like Uncle San, in the back of the head and dumping his body in a mass grave filled with the skulls and bones of the victims.

"Why only those Khmer Rouge?" Uncle San follows up.

"The court officials say that it's because the goal of the KRT is to seek justice, national reconciliation, stability, peace and security in Cambodia," Aunty Yan answers and then adds, "trying all the Khmer Rouge would not fulfill this goal."

Uncle San considers her remarks, imagining how the executioner must have attended a meeting where a Khmer Rouge boss, black Mao-cap on his head and red scarf around his neck, had ordered, "Comrades, you must smash the enemy to bits until none of them remain."

As they talk in front of the court, Aunty Yan explains that "a group of people in the courtroom sitting behind representatives are civil parties," or those who had "submitted an application to the court and was accepted by the judges. They directly take part in the trials or take part through their representatives."

Uncle San thinks of the different parties inside the courtroom, including both Cambodians and foreigners. The judges, dressed in red robes, sit in the back. The defense lawyers and defendant sit to their front left, the prosecutors to their right next to the civil party lawyers. Behind them, ordinary Cambodians, just like Uncle San, sit in chairs, many wearing colorful traditional scarves.

Then Uncle San makes a decision. He will seek more information at the office of the KRT's Victims Unit, which had recently been set up to assist victims who wanted to participate in the proceedings. The office is very modern, with a large desk and cushioned chairs, a water cooler, a photocopy machine, a computer screen, and a file cabinet, the drawers shut tight. One drawer is labeled "secret."

On the wall, there are three official ECCC posters, each of which highlights key aspects of the hybrid court and includes the court's logo and slogan, "Moving forward through justice." One, focused on the raised hands of a line of judges, centers on text that reads, "Every decision must have the support of both Cambodian and International Judges." Just below, in smaller print, the poster states, "Both Cambodian and International standards of law must be upheld."

A bit later, the head of the Victims Unit, a Cambodian woman with shoulder-length hair and formal dress, sits down at her desk opposite Uncle San. "The Head of the Victims Unit at the KRT told me," Uncle San says, "that I can be a civil party if I fill out the form and the judges accept my application based on several conditions of the law." The woman smiles as she shows Uncle San one of the forms, explaining to him how to fill it out. "If I am a civil party," Uncle San adds, "I have the right to participate in all of the court proceedings, plus a right to request collective and moral reparations."

"The next day," Uncle San continues, "Aunty Yan, myself, and a few other villagers met for tea." With half a dozen neighbors, young and old, gathered around them, Uncle San and Aunty Yan describe the court, how justice works, the defendant, and possible reparations, such as a traditional memorial stupa or a water well. "We talked for a long time about the KRT and the future of Cambodia," Uncle San says. "We agreed that the establishment of the KRT is very good to seek justice for victims. The trials can find the truth and give us relief from the past."

Afterward, Uncle San retreats to his hammock to rest. Tucking his yellow scarf behind his head, Uncle San dozes. His mind fills with images of his village transformed with fancy houses, electricity, smooth new streets, and a large factory in the distance.

"Then," Uncle San finishes, "I slept the whole night with no bad dreams."

Who is Uncle San? He is a figment of the transitional justice imaginary, a piece of the justice facade, though one that shows cracks, suggesting more than first meets the eye.

Introduction

The Transitional Justice Imaginary

What is the point of holding international tribunals in places like Cambodia?

Uncle San gives an answer: justice. He stresses the benefits, including "national reconciliation, stability, peace, and security." At least these are the goals stated in the thirty-four-page graphic booklet, "Uncle San, Aunty Yan, and the KRT," which features Uncle San and was produced in 2008 by the Khmer Institute of Democracy (KID), the non-governmental organization (NGO) mentioned in the preface.

Indeed, the entire preface is based on this KID Khmer Rouge Tribunal (KRT) booklet, the pages of which are divided by visual representations accompanied by, on the opposite pages, explanatory text. The booklet was created to explain the possibilities of victim participation to rural Cambodian victims of the Khmer Rouge, a small piece of a larger Extraordinary Chambers in the Courts of Cambodia (ECCC) outreach effort.

"Uncle San, Aunty Yan, and the KRT" provides an initial ethnographic grounding to introduce the arguments in this book, the literatures with which it is in conversation, and the key concepts that, like the Uncle San narrative itself, run through it. These include: the transitional justice imaginary, the justice facade (particular manifestations of this imaginary), and phenomenological transitional justice, or the way transitional justice is lived, experienced, practiced, and translated.

By transitional justice, I refer to an assemblage of discourses, institutions, capital flows, technologies, practices, and people devoted to providing redress for mass human rights violations and enabling a transformation of a society from this violent past to a better future. While the genealogy of the field of transitional justice is complicated,[1] it is usually described as beginning at one of two temporal markers, even if related precedents or precursors are sometimes acknowledged. In one set of genealogies, transitional justice begins in the late 1980s with the end of the Cold War and Latin American attempts to deal with the past as places like Argentina and Chile (and subsequently Eastern European countries) transitioned to democracy.[2] It was around this time that, as the post-Cold War "new world order" and possibilities of human rights and peacebuilding were being asserted, the word "transitional justice" was coined.

---

[1] Recent overviews of the field include: Arthur 2009; Lawther, Moffett, and Jacobs 2017; Sharp 2013; Simic 2017. See also the Transitional Justice Database bibliographies (http://tjdbproject.com).

[2] Arthur 2009. See also Hinton 2010b; UN 2008.

The term began to be widely used to refer to criminal tribunals, truth and reconciliation commissions, memorialization efforts, and institutional reforms that provide redress and a sense of justice enabling post-conflict countries to transition from troubled pasts to better futures.[3] By so doing, transitional justice mechanisms were said to prevent recurrence, educate affected communities, "combat impunity," promote reconciliation, advance the "rule of law," and reveal "the truth"—discourses that circulated widely at the ECCC in a variety of contexts, including everyday conversations, formal documents like the 2003 Agreement to hold the ECCC, outreach initiatives, and texts like the Uncle San booklet.

Other narratives, particularly those focusing on legal accountability and trials, push the date further back to efforts just after World War II, when tribunals were established to try the leaders of Nazi Germany and Japan.[4] Indeed, legal justice has emerged as the preeminent modality of transitional justice, even if it has been critiqued by some scholars who note the limitations of trials and argue for the benefits of other sorts of transitional justice mechanisms more focused on social repair.[5]

If the "better future" of transitional justice is conceptualized in different ways (for example, as peace, reconciliation, good governance, rule of law), it is most often framed in terms of democratic liberalism, an idea around which these other ideas often cluster. I refer to this "classic" view of transitional justice as the "transitional justice imaginary."[6] In this imaginary, transitional justice is envisioned as a teleological transformation from a state of authoritarianism to one of liberal democratic being.

While widespread and even predominant,[7] particularly during the early history of transitional justice (thus the "classic" moniker I use above), this imaginary is not the only transitional justice discourse that circulates. Indeed, there is increasing attention being paid to alternative visions of transitional justice, such as understandings of transitional justice framed primarily as reparative or restorative, including those that are more open, context-sensitive, and attuned to other issues. Accordingly, the transitional justice imaginary is variably invoked depending on the person, time, and context.

The transitional justice imaginary itself comes in stronger and weaker forms. And it has a loose structure centered around its core assumption of a teleological transformation from authoritarianism to liberal democracy and a set of secondary assumptions—again more or less (or not at all) present and, when present, manifest to greater or lesser extents—including utopianism, progressivism, universalism, essentialism, globalism, and facadism.

This is a problem. The transitional justice imaginary is, I would argue, an impossible vision, a utopian vision that is always "to come," to use Derrida's phrasing,[8] and

---

[3] On the origins and history of transitional justice, see Arthur 2009; Elster 2004; Sharp 2013; Teitel 2003.

[4] Teitel 2003. For longer genealogies of transitional justice, see Bass 2001 and Elster 2004.

[5] McEvoy 2007; Fletcher and Weinstein 2002.   [6] Hinton 2013.

[7] See Arthur 2009; Franzki and Olarte 2014; Hinton 2010a; Sharp 2015; Teitel 2015.

[8] Derrida 1992.

doomed to fail. This imaginary is also dangerous, potentially masking power and diverting attention from geopolitical interest, domestic manipulations, and structural violence. In addition, it has effects, asserting particular forms of subjectivity and ways of being in the world while obscuring others.

Nevertheless, this imaginary circulates widely, finding expression in different sites and contexts, including the narrative of the Uncle San booklet. I refer to such concrete manifestations of the transitional justice imaginary as the "justice facade," a metaphor emphasizing that the transitional justice imaginary provides a distanced and surface-level view that masks power and the complexities of everyday experience.

Only once we have recognized this justice facade and the naturalized assumptions of the transitional justice imaginary that inform it, may we begin to more deeply understand what takes place in transitional justice encounters—and whether or not they have much of a point. Along these lines, the second part of this introduction offers a dynamic phenomenological approach to transitional justice, one focused on discourse, power, and the complexities of everyday experience where "justice in transition" takes place and tribunals like the ECCC may or may not become meaningful and spark the imagination. Indeed, this process of "justice in translation" and the everyday is the primary focus of this book.

And when these measures are meaningful, as this book will show, the meanings may diverge sharply from those naturalized by the transitional justice imaginary. In the end, instead of a utopian "better future," transitional justice might be best viewed as providing new possibilities to spark the imagination and social relations in societies emerging from difficult pasts. This may be as basic as the ability to forget the past, to share coffee or tea with neighbors who were once enemies, or to rebalance one's relationship to the spirits of the dead—while *not* achieving an end state of liberal democracy.

The remainder of this introduction discusses these conceptual points, which frame the arguments in the book. In doing so, this introduction draws extensively on the Uncle San booklet and two other texts—a landmark 2004 UN Secretary-General report on "The Rule of Law and Transitional Justice" and Kathryn Sikkink's influential book, *The Justice Cascade*[9]—and related literatures in which the key assumptions of the transitional justice imaginary are manifest.

I begin by discussing the utopian roots of the transitional justice imaginary before turning to look at how this imaginary emerged in the 1980s and early 1990s and some of its other aspects (manifest to varying extents) including its progressivism, teleology, universalism, essentialism, globalism, and facadism. My introduction concludes with a discussion of how a discursively-informed phenomenological approach to transitional justice helps us break down the naturalized assumptions masked by the justice facade and more deeply consider the meaning of peacebuilding and transitional justice measures like the ECCC.

---

[9] KID 2008; Sikkink 2011; UN Secretary-General 2004.

The Utopian Imaginary

To ask "what is the point?" is to ask a question about a place of contact and the related movement that ensues. On the one hand, "point" is etymologically related to the root, *peuk*, meaning "to prick," a piercing or puncture produced by, for example, the sharp end ("point") of a sword. It suggests contact, rupture, and effect.[10] On the other hand, this "effect" suggests "a point," as in "an end aimed at, an aim, an object," one with a "purpose," "completion," and a "zenith."[11]

If the transitional justice imaginary has such "a point" (teleological transformation to liberal democracy), it is one that has a genealogy and that is nested within a larger "utopian imaginary." The roots of this utopian imaginary range far and wide. Plato presented a famous early version in his design for good public life in *The Republic*. Sir Thomas More's *Utopia* provided another.[12] Both involved an idealized end if leaving questions about the means by which to realize this aspiration.

Aspiration, in turn, refers to "the action of desiring and striving for something." The term is etymologically related to the Latin word *aspirare*, which connotes breath, respiration, and spirit, including the idea of divine invigoration ("the breath of god") that moves one in the name of a higher purpose ("inspiration").[13] An aspiration therefore suggests the desire for something "higher," an upward movement suggested by a tertiary association with a rising (a "spire"). In its modern manifestations during and after the Enlightenment, this aspiration of the utopian imaginary has been frequently framed in terms of progress.

While the idea of utopian progress has a long and complicated history, the aspiration of the transitional justice imaginary has a specific set of connotations, ones deeply informed by Enlightenment conceptions about the betterment of the human condition through the application of the scientific method, secularism, and reason. Often these ideas coalesced around "stage theories" of progress, which held that societies advanced through an upward movement from lower ("savagery," "barbarism," "primitivism") to higher states of development culminating in its "point," the attainment of "civilization" with such corollaries as complexity, science, and rationality.[14] This scalar theory was also potentially an ideological justification that could be used to legitimate colonial projects such as the "white man's burden" to uplift more "primitive" peoples.

Along these lines, the utopian imaginary favors abstraction, the universal, and the bird's-eye view, refusing the messiness of particularity with an idealized order and design in mind. In the modern world and its post-Enlightenment aftermaths, it has inspired grand experiments in social engineering, ones that have too often ended in tragedy and failure as particular individuals are sorted into different "types" that do and do not belong—thereby legitimating the elimination of contaminating others who threaten the pure, utopian order. The French Revolution provided an early example,

---

[10] "Point" and "Prick," *Shorter OED* 2007.   [11] "Point," *Shorter OED* 2007.
[12] More 2003; Plato 2013.   [13] "Aspiration," *Shorter OED* 2007.
[14] See Adams 1998.

with violence legitimated in the name of an idealized new political order. The utopian imaginaries of later socialist revolutionary regimes sometimes led to even greater violence and even genocide in places like Soviet Russia, Maoist China—and Cambodia under the Khmer Rouge. Other examples abound, including Nazi Germany.[15]

If some of the most extreme examples of the catastrophic failures of the utopian imaginary have taken place under those sorts of regimes that have been called—to use Arendt's phrasing—totalitarian,[16] the utopian imaginary has also inspired liberal democratic efforts that, if not leading to mass death and suffering, have gone awry, sometimes with devastating consequences, in other cases with disastrous failure.[17] Often, the utopian aspirations and stage theory assumptions of these efforts are masked, as has been the case with variants of modernization and democratization theory as well as development, human rights, and peacebuilding projects, all of which are related to the transitional justice imaginary.

Recognizing such spectacular failures inspired by the utopian imaginary does not lead to the conclusion that "there is no point" to efforts at betterment, of course. The key issue is to consider what went wrong and to see if there are different "points" to consider that may be obscured by the utopian imaginary's bird's-eye view—a perspective shared by the transitional justice imaginary. This book argues that one path forward in this regard is to answer the question "what is the point" from an experience-near perspective, one that is grounded in the semiotic systems and discursive regimes mediating lived experience. In doing so, I join other scholars who have argued for casting attention in this direction, including James Scott's invocation of the Greek concept of *mētis* (or "practical knowledge" in contrast to formal knowledge and "high-modernist thought"), Clifford Geertz's notions of "the experience-near" (versus the "experience-distant" gaze, including that of law), and Hannah Arendt's focus on "common sense" (versus the totalizing "ideological supersense").[18]

Working in this tradition, my book argues for a phenomenological approach to transitional justice that refocuses attention on lived experience. The transitional justice imaginary, like related democratization, peacebuilding, human rights, and development imaginaries, implicitly or explicitly asserts "the point" of transitional justice, progress culminating in liberal democracy. Such discourses, I argue, create a justice facade masking the lived experience of transitional justice and what "the point" is as seen from this phenomenological perspective—one that may be open-ended, varied, and offering possibility that may (or may not) catalyze the imagination (but not in a teleological manner that assumes a predetermined, progressive utopian end).

This argument builds on my previous study of the ECCC, *Man or Monster? The Trial of a Khmer Rouge Torturer*, which argues for greater attention to taken-for-granted and naturalized articulations—"the banality of everyday thought"—and what they redact amidst the "thick frames of power."[19] Similarly, I am here calling for an unpacking of transitional justice imaginary and all that is backgrounded and edited out, including, as is often the case with international justice, such lived

---

[15] Bauman 1989; Scott 1998.   [16] Arendt 1973.   [17] Scott 1998.
[18] Arendt 1973; Geertz 1985; Scott 1998.   [19] Hinton 2016.

experience and practice. And, as I discuss throughout and in the book's conclusion ("Justice in Translation"), a focus on lived experience and practice also recenters attention on a key and underexplored issue in transitional justice, how it is "translated." Given the genealogy, aims, and assumptions they share with transitional justice, the arguments of this book bear directly on topics such as peacebuilding, development studies, and human rights.

The Transitional Justice Imaginary

"Moving forward through justice"

—ECCC motto

Transitional justice emerged at a paradoxical moment in the late 1980s. On the one hand, a number of twentieth-century paradigms and master narratives, including Marxist-Leninism, modernization theory, and development, which share the utopian imaginary's idea of stage transition (even if they vary in terms of its precise beginning and end as well as the exact sequence, stage characteristics, catalyzing conditions ["dialectics"], and mechanisms of "progress") had been discredited or were being heavily critiqued.[20]

On the other hand, at this time there was a new optimism about the possibility of human progress with the end of the Cold War, the overthrow of socialist and authoritarian regimes, and the rise of the human rights regime. These trends gave rise to utopian proclamations about a "Third Wave of Democratization" and even "The End of History," signifying the failure of communism and ascendancy of the highest stage of political being, liberal democracy.[21] There were hopes for a "new world order," an idea famously invoked by George Bush in 1991 to refer to the sudden and rapid spread of freedom, international peace, the rule of law, human rights, and democratization.

This new liberal order would be catalyzed in part by humanitarian intervention and peacebuilding projects, signaled by UN Secretary-General Boutros Boutros-Ghali's landmark report, "An Agenda for Peace."[22] This document stated that, with the end of the Cold War, "we have entered a time of global transition" that, if challenged by "fierce new assertions of nationalism and sovereignty," offered an opportunity to fulfill the long-delayed ambitions of the UN Charter as "Authoritarian regimes have given way to more democratic forces," including those "seeking more open forms of economic policy."[23] It laid out a vision for a new post-Cold War series of international peacebuilding interventions, one of the first of which took place in Cambodia.

Teleological transformation

It was in this context and from these diverse strands of influence that "transitional justice" was formulated. Focusing on a series of conferences that took place between

---

[20] Edelman and Haugerud 2005; Ferguson 1990.
[21] Huntington 1991; Fukuyama 1989.   [22] Boutros-Ghali 1992.   [23] Ibid.

1988 and 1994, with particular focus on a ground-breaking November 1988 Aspen Institute conference, in which a number of activists, engaged scholars, lawyers, diplomats, and practitioners who would become key figures in the transitional justice field met, Paige Arthur has traced how the idea of transitional justice was fashioned at this time.[24]

How, the participants asked, might a society confront a violent and repressive past? If their deliberations were particularly informed by the Latin American experience, especially Argentina and Chile, the participants also grappled with the related experiences of countries in Asia, Africa, and Europe. Their wide-ranging discussions took place as grand narratives of structural change were being eclipsed and a new, utopian human rights vision was ascendant.[25]

While there were diverse points of view, much of the discussion centered on the issue of democratic transition facilitated by justice mechanisms that would both provide redress and catalyze change. This idea had been partly envisioned by a group of Latin American and U.S. scholars participating in a project on transition that led to the 1986 publication *Transitions from Authoritarian Rule*.[26] Instead of focusing on long-term structural change, this group argued that democratic transition could be catalyzed by short-term technical and legal change driven by elite actor agency. Such actors would fashion a new beginning characterized by liberal democratic ideals, participatory citizenship, rule of law, human rights, and equality.[27]

These ideas informed the transitional justice imaginary that would emerge at the Aspen Institute and later conferences. By the time of the publication of Neil Kritz's landmark 1995 volume, *Transitional Justice: How Emerging Democracies Reckon with Former Regimes*, the term was coined and the (regressive) beginning and (progressive) end of transitional justice becoming self-evident and directly spelled out: authoritarianism and democracy.[28]

While it was possible to envision attempts to deal with the past in different ways (redress, restorative justice, social justice), the dominant transitional justice imaginary that emerged was characterized by teleological transformation (the "two t's of transitional justice") driven by an aspiration for human progress of a particular sort, a utopian dream of creating liberal democratic, human rights-infused being—a goal it often shares, as noted above, with related endeavors such as human rights activism, development agendas, humanitarianism, and peacebuilding.

This "classic" vision of transitional justice, with teleological transformation at its core, would proliferate across a variety of contexts and become increasingly institutionalized in places ranging from the United Nations to the International Center for Transitional Justice to the ECCC. If such institutions are at times informed by alternative and more contemporary visions of transitional justice, the "classic" transitional justice imaginary still circulates widely and often in a naturalized and taken-for-granted manner.

---

[24] The next two paragraphs draw directly from Arthur's 2009 genealogy.
[25] See Moyn 2012.   [26] O'Donnell and Schmitter 1986; see Arthur 2009, 343–48.
[27] See Ibid., 347.   [28] Kritz 1995.

Figure 1 Uncle San dozing with no more bad dreams. "Uncle San, Aunty Yan, and the KRT," p. 33. *Reprinted by permission of the Khmer Institute of Democracy.*

Progressivism

The progressivism of the transitional justice imaginary, more strongly expressed in evolutionist terms, is evident in discourses and practices at transitional justice sites like the ECCC. The KID booklet, which ends with a dream, is again illustrative in this regard. The last graphic (Figure 1) in the booklet depicts Uncle San lying in a hammock, resting contentedly, his eyes closed. A thought bubble shows us his dream of the Cambodia to come, one with modern homes (highlighted by the contrast with the traditional thatch houses where Uncle San now lives and that appear in the background), electricity, well-being, and industry, a signifier of the capitalism and a market-driven economy that can take place in the "stability, peace, and security" of the new Cambodia.

This future, in which, the accompanying text tells us, Uncle San sleeps "the whole night with no bad dreams," is contrasted with the start of the booklet, which includes a parallel frame in which Uncle San dozes uneasily, troubled by nightmares from the Khmer Rouge past. In between stands international justice, symbolized by Uncle San's visit to the ECCC, the mechanism of his transformation.

Here, in just a few pages, we find a clear manifestation of the transitional justice imaginary and the progressivist aspiration that infuses it. This idea is captured by the ECCC's motto, "Moving forward through justice," an idea that directly suggests the meaning of progress, as in a "forward or onward movement toward a destination," including "development toward a better, more complete, or more modern condition."[29] The Uncle San booklet is informed by this aspiration for an idealized end in this sense of upward movement and development toward modernity, as illustrated by the concluding dream bubble, with its imaginary "destination" of modernization. In this sense, it is more than idealistic (the pursuit of ideals, even if ones that are unrealistic) but a futuristic state of liberal democratic being that is utopian (striving for a radically different, visionary new state) and constructed by the contrast to a dystopian opposite (the violence, authoritarianism, and suffering manifest in Uncle San's initial dreams).

The progressivism of the transitional justice imaginary can also be seen in academic accounts, including genealogies that assume rough early beginnings that come together in a swelling flow of global justice. This idea, which is widespread and both implicit and explicit in discourses about transitional justice, is exemplified by Kathryn Sikkink's notion of "the justice cascade."[30]

Drawing on her riverine metaphor, Sikkink argues that this "cascade" has been catalyzed by two "streams" and a "streambed."[31] The "seeds" of the first, involving prosecutions at international criminal tribunals, began with the establishment of the post-World War II courts in Nuremberg and Tokyo and then, after a long hiatus, gathered strength with the establishment of the International Criminal Tribunals for the former Yugoslavia (ICTY/1993) and Rwanda (ICTR/1994) and more recently the International Criminal Court (ICC/2002).

This first stream of "international prosecutions" was supplemented by a second stream of "domestic and foreign prosecutions," often pushed by "norm entrepreneurs," starting with trials in Greece (1975) and Portugal (1976) and then Argentina (1985) followed by Pinochet's arrest (1998). Meanwhile, a "hard law streambed" of international human rights and humanitarian law gradually emerged, beginning with the Genocide and Geneva Conventions in the late 1940s and continuing with laws such as the 1987 Convention against Torture and 1998 Rome Statutes.

At the turn of the twenty-first century, this "streambed" and these "streams" converged as the norm of international criminal accountability passed a tipping point and spread throughout the world in a "justice cascade," which Sikkink defines as "a rapid and dramatic shift in the legitimacy of the norms of individual accountability for human rights violations and an increase in actions (such as trials) on behalf of those norms."[32] Sikkink notes that this justice cascade was part of the larger transitional justice norm cascade promoting "accountability for past human rights violations."[33]

Sikkink places the ECCC directly within this justice cascade, noting, "The momentum from the work of these international courts contributed to the establishment in 2009 [sic] of a hybrid court in Cambodia to prosecute members of the

---

[29] "Progress," *Concise OED* 2011.
[30] Sikkink 2011; Sikkink and Kim 2013. See also Lutz and Sikkink 2001.
[31] Sikkink and Kim 2013.   [32] Ibid., 270.   [33] Ibid, 270.

Khmer Rouge."[34] Indeed, the ECCC is one of a number of "hybrid" tribunals established in the 2000s to offset problems that emerged with the ad hoc tribunals (the ICTY and ICTR) of the 1990s in terms of issues like cost, duration, and engagement with the affected populations.

Like other hybrid courts, the ECCC includes both international and domestic law and is composed of a mixture of international and Cambodian officials in all major offices, including co-lawyers, co-prosecutors, and co-judges.[35] "Uncle San, Aunty Yan, and the KRT" notes the hybridity of the ECCC and provides basic background, such as the court's date of establishment (2003) and mandate to try the "senior leaders" and those "most responsible" for the Democratic Kampuchea (DK) atrocities.

If cascade-like narratives provide a way of making sense of complicated histories and connections, they may also, in so doing, direct our gaze in certain ways by asserting discourses of progression while obfuscating dynamics ranging from politics to on-the-ground understandings and practices. Lived-experience, in other words, diverges, often in quite different ways, from this bird's-eye perspective, which suggests a relatively straightforward riverine flow. I return to this point below. More immediately, I note that Sikkink, like others, clearly places the Cambodia court within a progressivist narrative of global justice. The ECCC therefore provides an in-depth test case, allowing us to assess the claims of such models.

One of the arguments of this book is that, like other progressivist narratives about "global justice," the "justice cascade" is more a justice facade, an exteriorization of the transitional justice imaginary that masks as much as—or more than—it reveals. This point is important given that, despite critique,[36] the "justice cascade" idea circulates widely and is often invoked in a taken-for-granted and idealistic manner.

Universalism

This justice cascade metaphor also points toward another key aspect of the transitional justice imaginary, universalism. The 2004 UN Secretary-General report on "The Rule of Law and Transitional Justice," for example, states that transitional justice and the rule of law are part of a "common language of justice" meant to "enhance human rights, protect persons from fear and want, address property disputes, encourage economic development, promote accountable governance and peacefully resolve conflict."[37] Transitional justice and the rule of law, in turn, are based on "international norms and standards" outlined in the UN Charter and manifest in the "four pillars of the modern international legal system: international human rights law; international humanitarian law; international criminal law; and international refugee law," all of which are "universally applicable standards" and serve "as the normative basis" for UN work in this area.[38]

---

[34] Sikkink 2011, 114. Sikkink misidentifies the date of the establishment of the court (2003).

[35] On the structure and functioning of the ECCC, see Ciorciari and Heindel 2014; Meisenberg and Stegmiller 2016.

[36] See, for example, Clark 2012; Meierhenrich and Pendas 2017; Savelsberg 2015.

[37] UN Secretary-General 2004, paragraph 5.   [38] Ibid, paragraph 9.

These international norms and standards also figure prominently in Sikkink's cascade model, constituting one of the key "streams" feeding the justice cascade that characterizes the teleological transformation from authoritarian impunity (which she states was the norm prior to the 1970s) to democratic individual accountability (beginning with human rights prosecutions in Greece and Portugal and later Latin American countries).[39] Her model highlights the larger cascade-like linear underpinnings of the transitional justice imaginary, which assume a teleological movement (the "transition") from point A (authoritarianism with related attributes such as impunity, repression, lack of human rights, backwardness and underdevelopment, superstition and religion, tradition, and lack of political subjectivity) to point B (liberal democracy with the contrasting qualities of accountability, freedom, human rights, development, secularism, modernity, and neoliberal political subjectivity).

This transitional justice imaginary passage is usually predicated on universalist assumptions. If universals are characterized by commonality, they are also bound up with typology and conversion, asserting a quality of similarity across cases. Universalism involves, as the etymology suggests, a "turning" (*versus*) of the many into "one" (*uni-*). This productive impulse ("turning") of universalism is critical to note, since a universal does not just begin with what exists ("nature") but defines and produces it.[40] Different cases of transitional justice did not pre-exist: they only came into being through a categorical universal—"transitional justice"—that parsed reality in a particular way.[41]

If "transitional justice" is a universalizing category, its universalism is also contingent, linked to a primary Universal, Justice, and an umbrella of related Enlightenment Universals (Truth, Reason, Rights, Individual) bound with an aspiration, progress, and its emancipatory and liberating end, liberal democracy. The path to this end, in turn, lies in the application of science and reason, which yield proper design and technique, sometimes expressed in transitional justice and related discourses such as peacebuilding and development through the metaphor of the "toolkit." In this conception, the universal's opposite, the particular, stands in an uneasy place, both defined by the productive, transformative gaze of the universal and creating a messiness that the universal seeks to erase.

Essentialism

This universalizing, productive impulse of the transitional justice imaginary often leads to essentialism, modest shrinkage at best, something closer to Orientalism at worst, and binary reductionism in between. Such essentialism is closely tied to the imaginary's underlying premise of teleological transformation, which is predicated on a binary: a distinction between a pre-state (authoritarian and violence) and a post-state (liberal democracy and peace) with the transitional justice mechanism catalyzing change in between.

---

[39] Sikkink 2011; Sikkink and Kim 2013. See also Clark 2012 and Meierhenrich and Pendas 2017 on the narrowness of this framing.

[40] See Tsing 2005 on this point.

[41] See, for example, lists of cases folded under this conceptual umbrella in early canon-making works, such as Kritz 1995; Hayner 1994; O'Donnell and Schmitter 1986.

Related associations are implied and naturalized in this binary, which shrinks complexity and essentializes "peoples and places." Given the loose structure of the transitional justice imaginary, this essentialization varies in its manifestations even as it is often naturalized in characterizations of transitional societies and "individuals" living in them. The diagram below provides some examples.

Binary Essentialism in the Transitional Justice Imaginary

Transitioning society

Before	➔	Transitional Justice	➔	After
Authoritarian				*Democratic*
Violent				Peaceful
Barbaric / Savage				Civilized
Impunity				Rule of Law
Authoritarian				Democratic
Backward				Forward
Stagnant				Active
Past				Future
Exclusive				Inclusive
Monologue				Dialogue
Unequal				Equality
Divided				Reconciled
Regressive / Stagnant				Progressive
Underdeveloped				Developed
Tradition / Premodernity				Modernity
Child-like				Mature
Chaotic				Ordered
Oppression				Freedom
Poverty				Wealth
Impunity				Accountability
Local				Global

Transitioning individual

Before	➔	Transitional Justice	➔	After
Violent				Peaceful
Passive				Active / Engaged
Recipient				Agent
Invisible				Visible
Ignorance				Knowledge
Silent				Audible
Voiceless				Voice
Subject				Citizen
Oppressed				Rights-bearing
Traumatized				Healed

Many of these binaries, for example, circulate in the KID booklet, which presents Uncle San and Cambodia in an essentialized manner.[42]

In the extreme, such an imaginary takes on Orientalist overtones. And indeed, the transitional justice imaginary, like Said's notion of "Orientalism,"[43] is linked to a fantasy that essentializes, stereotypes, and says more about the person or group that projects this imaginary than the object of their facadist gaze. Related language circulates widely in transitional contexts. Cambodia, for example, is frequently depicted or described in Orientalist-like discourses and images—such as a "culture of violence," despotism, "culture of impunity," savagery, and exoticization (including the sexualized Apsaras)—that are counterposed to their binary "Western" (Occident, Civilization, Global) opposites characterized by the "rule of law," "good governance," "peace," and "democracy."[44] Such imagery not just stereotypes (transitional "peoples and places") and legitimates (projects of democratization and neoliberalism), but masks other dynamics and processes, including those related to structural violence, environmental degradation, and inequality.

Globalism

In keeping with this tendency toward binary essentialism, the transitional justice imaginary is often bound up with discourses of globalization and "the global," which are implicitly or explicitly counterposed to "localization" and "the local" (in keeping with its universalist conversion impulse). Indeed, international tribunals are often spoken about as instances of "global justice" and depicted as flowing across time and space in a linear and even evolutionary manner in keeping with the universalism, progressivism, and teleology of the transitional justice imaginary.

Linearity and Evolutionism: This globalizing linearity—and evolutionism in its stronger forms—is widespread and recently perhaps most famously suggested by the metaphor of the justice cascade, an influential transitional justice model that sets in relief key assumptions of transitional justice imaginary. If a cascade refers to a type of waterfall, it more broadly connotes the idea of movement in a specific direction, as in "a mass of something that falls, hangs, or occurs in copious quantities."[45] The connotation of trajectory is linked to the term's Latin root, "to fall" (*cascare*). A cascade is a rushed outpouring from a point A to a point B (or a series of points in succession), one that, in the justice cascade model, involves a teleology and transformation.

This stage conception is illustrated in a model Sikkink and a co-author elsewhere use to illustrate the "evolution and influence of norms," which they define as "a standard of appropriate behavior for actors" that have a "quality of 'oughtness.' "[46] They argue that the "life cycle" of a universalizing norm involves progression through

---

[42] Hinton 2013.   [43] Said 1989.
[44] See An-Na'im 2013; Springer 2015; Edwards 2007; Mutua 2001, 2015.
[45] "Cascade," *Concise OED* 2011.   [46] Finnemore and Sikkink 1998, 891, 894.

three stages. "Stage 1" of "Norm emergence" is driven by norm entrepreneurs who "call attention to" the norm in question.[47]

Propelled by their efforts (ie, the convergence of Sikkink's "streams"), things reach a tipping point resulting in a "norm cascade" driven by "states, international organizations, [and] networks."[48] This cascade propels the norm to its Stage 3 end of "Internalization" in which it becomes "habit," sometimes becoming "so widely accepted that they are internalized by actors and achieve a 'taken-for-granted' quality that makes conformance with the norm almost automatic."[49] This model was meant to critique static conceptions of norms by providing for change. While useful in this regard, this model nevertheless fails to address the issue of variation, agency, and lived experience in a significant manner. In this respect, among others, cascade-like models and the transitional justice imaginary more broadly are globalizing and awkwardly situated in relationship to the global's opposite and object, "the local."

This tension is evident in transitional justice discourses, acknowledged even if ultimately erased or glossed over by their universalist assumptions, as illustrated by the UN Secretary-General's 2004 Report.[50] "Uncle San, Aunty Yan, and the KRT" highlights this tension as it is, on the one hand, set in a distinctly "local" setting (Cambodian villages, clothing, habits, historical experience, and Buddhism) even as the primacy of the universal is asserted in Uncle San's transformation into an active, democratic, participatory, human rights-invested, neoliberal subject who, a symbol of Cambodia more broadly, undergoes a teleological transformation through the mechanism of the court and the Justice it represents.

The Local: Anthropology has something of importance to say about the place of "the local" in such models. "The local" is slippery and has a complicated history. It is often used instead of "culture," a term that was heavily critiqued for its potentially reductive and stereotypic portrayals of "others," the "savages" invoked to assert the primacy of "the civilized." While this reductive "stage theory" perspective is usually not directly stated, it lurks in the background, naturalized in assumptions about the binary of "the global" and "the local."

Much is masked by the transitional justice imaginary and related stage theories of progress. Universal teleological transformation binds people and spaces, fixing them into typologies in which the particular is produced by the universal. Such typologies transform complicated histories, identities, and politics into more simplified essences. These essences, in turn, facilitate the construction and use of grand transformative designs (the "plan" and the "toolkit") to catalyze transformation.

From this perspective, particular types of people are depicted as living in a "culture" or "locality" that is demarcated by given characteristics—a "type" of person living there—that are the imagined opposite of those ("Western," "global," "civilized," "developed") types associated with progress and the teleological transformation to which it aspires. In the transitional justice imaginary, the progressive modern and global (democratic) "peoples and cultures" are constituted by the construction of

---

[47] Ibid, 897.   [48] Ibid, 898.   [49] Ibid, 898, 904.
[50] U.N. Secretary-General 2004.

their opposite, the backward traditional and local (authoritarian) "peoples and cultures."[51] A similar move undergirds the development, modernization, socialist, human rights, humanitarian, and peacebuilding imaginaries.[52]

Cascade-like models are illustrative here, depicting a plethora of spaces transformed into one. These models, often found in broader descriptions of "globalization," frequently portray this process of transformation as relatively straightforward. These "uniformity models" assert a universalizing homogeneity. With little variation, a McDonald's is a McDonald's wherever you go in the "global village." Similarly, the justice cascade model suggests the spread of the norm of accountability, as part of the transitional justice and human rights movements more broadly, that, with insignificant aberrations and exceptions here and there, is "internalized" and eventually "taken-for-granted" in a statistically significant number of sites across the globe.[53]

Localization: Such uniformity models of globalization remain in tension with on-the-ground complexity and lived experience, which exceeds the limitations of the global-local binary as we shall see below. The 2004 UN Report was published at an interesting moment in this regard, as discourses about "globalization" were ascendant even as there was growing awareness of the need to attend to "the local."

Throughout the text, the 2004 UN Report alternates between making declarations that "international norms and standards" related to transitional justice and the rule of law are "universally applicable" while stressing the importance of local consultation, ownership, leadership, and meaningful public participation.[54] It warns of the dangers of "pre-packed" solutions and designs while insisting that transitional justice efforts remain "faithful" to universal norms and values.[55]

Such concerns in the 2004 UN Report reflected changes taking place within transitional justice and peacebuilding, where there was growing awareness of need to attend to the local, even as "the local" was predicated on the global-local binary and remained in tension with "global" (transitional) justice. If the ad hoc tribunals (ICTR and ICTY) and passage of the Rome Statutes (establishing the ICC) asserted the primacy of international law in the 1990s, the first hybrid tribunals were being established to deal with atrocity crimes in East Timor (2000), Sierra Leone (2002), and Bosnia-Herzegovina (2002).[56]

At the same time, the Truth and Reconciliation Commission (TRC/1995–2002) was established to grapple with crimes committed during apartheid South Africa. Besides helping to inspire TRCs in places like Guatemala, Sierra Leone, and Liberia,

---

[51] See, e.g. Gupta and Ferguson 1997.
[52] Hinton 2016; Ferguson 1994; Scott 1998; see also Edelman and Haugerud 2005, *passim*.
[53] On problems with such statistical human rights models, see Merry 2016.
[54] U.N. Secretary-General 2004, 6–7.
[55] Ibid, 7.
[56] See Fichtelberg 2015. More recently, courts have been established to deal with crimes in Lebanon (2009), Chad (2013), and Kosovo (2015).

the South African TRC, which garnered enormous international attention, was also described by Bishop Desmond Tutu and others as enacting a particular local "African" form of justice, *ubuntu*, characterized by "reciprocity, respect for human dignity, community cohesion and solidarity."[57]

The TRC was also important for introducing a strong emphasis on "healing" into transitional justice discourses, just as "truth" had emerged as a key issue in Latin American transitional justice efforts. Now, when people speak of transitional justice, they often almost seamlessly invoke the benefits of "truth," "healing," and "reconciliation" in addition to discourses about "justice," "peace," and "security"—even if "justice" remains the dominant discourse in the transitional justice imaginary. This was also evident at the ECCC.

Similarly, around the time of the 2004 UN Report, Rwanda was beginning to draw on the "local justice" tradition of *gacaca* to help deal with over 100,000 Rwandans—far more than could be tried by the ICTR or even a supplemental domestic court—who had been accused of involvement in the country's 1994 genocide.[58] Discussions of such "local justice" traditions began to increase with some, such as the "drinking the bitter root" (*mato oput*) ritual in Uganda,[59] sparking interest and research in the transitional justice community.

While there is a small but growing literature on "the local" in transitional justice studies,[60] then, "the local" is often invoked in transitional justice discourses by waves to notions of "local ownership" and "local traditions" of justice and reconciliation, a framing highlighted in the 2004 UN Report. As noted above, one solution to the tension in the "global-local" binary is to pay lip-service to the local while effacing it through linear and evolutionary uniformity models that erase the messiness of particularity.

In contrast, two "localization" approaches emerged that reflect broader discussions about the relationship of globalization to the local. These localization models acknowledge change and transformation though they often do so by asserting that a family resemblance remains or by implicitly assuming a static view of "the local" as "tradition." From this perspective, a McDonald's in Texas is not exactly the same as one in Japan, as there are tweaks to adapt it to local tastes, even if one still recognizes the McDonald's in Japan.[61]

There are different degrees of openness in such localization models, ranging from models in which the degree of modification is relatively thin ("thin" models of localization) to ones in which the change is deep ("thick" models of localization).[62] Those relatively few transitional justice studies that seriously consider locality often do so by using thin models of localization because of the universalist aspirations

---

[57] Wilson 2001, 9. For a list of TRCs dating to the 1970s, see Hayner 2002.

[58] On *gacaca*, see Clark 2011.

[59] On the "drinking the bitter root" ceremony, see Allen 2006; Clarke 2009.

[60] See, e.g., Hinton 2010a; Kelsall 2013; McEvoy and McGregor 2008; Shaw and Waldorf 2010; Sharp 2014; Ullrich 2016.

[61] See Watson 1997.

[62] The "thick" and "thin" contrast draws inspiration from Geertz 1973. For a transitional justice approach using this contrast, see McEvoy 2007.

and assumptions of the transitional justice imaginary and its related homogenizing impulse. There are a small but increasing number of studies that look at thick localization.[63] The "thicker" the localization, however, the more this universalism is undermined, even to the extent that a highly "local" transitional justice mechanism may be better characterized as restorative justice or an attempt at reconciliation.

The Justice Facade

If the transitional justice imaginary refers to a progressive aspiration (the teleological transformation from authoritarianism to democracy) and its imagined realization in particular localities, the justice facade is a metaphor highlighting this exteriorization and the imagined fulfillment—an image, or *imago* to use the Latin root, which connotes simulation—of the imaginary's universalist dream, imperative, and desire.[64]

By suggesting that the transitional justice imaginary is facadist, I mean to highlight that, while offering a limited set of benefits and possibilities, transitional justice may not necessarily penetrate far below the surface in places like Cambodia—even if the transitional justice imaginary asserts that it does. Instead of taking for granted arguments about some sort of global "justice cascade," then, we would do well to examine the "justice facade."

A facade is the "face" of a structure as seen from the outside. The term also carries the connotation of deceptive appearance, an exterior masking something different that lies behind it. I use the term "justice facade" in both of these senses. On the one hand, the justice facade refers to a surface-level exteriorization of the transitional justice imaginary (facade as exterior structure). On the other, this justice facade has a masking effect, obscuring what lies behind the surface (facade as deceptive appearance).

Drawing loosely on the idea of facadist architecture, we might consider the justice facade as an "exterior" surface aligning with the transitional justice imaginary's aspiration of teleological transformation. Facadist architecture foregrounds this interior/exterior relation, a "front"—often one preserving the semblance of "tradition" or "heritage" even as it is completely modernized within—that is seen from the outside. Accordingly, facadism asserts a relation between the visible and the masked, surface and depth, modernity and "tradition."

The cover of the KID booklet (Figure 2; see also the cover of this book) is interesting in this respect, as Uncle San and Aunty Yan stride toward the courtroom building, an exterior behind which rise the spires of a "traditional" Cambodian building (it is also surrounded by a "traditional" rural Cambodian landscape), which seems to blend with this ECCC edifice. Like Uncle San's concluding "modernity dream bubble," this initial facadist graphic juxtaposes past and future, tradition and modernity, and the local and the global.

---

[63] See Sharp 2014 for a review.   [64] See also Tsing 2005, 1, 6f on universal desire.

Figure 2 Cover page of "Uncle San, Aunty Yan, and the KRT." *Reprinted by permission of the Khmer Institute of Democracy.*

Within the field of transitional justice, a growing number of critiques of the obfuscations of "classic" transitional justice have emerged and are destabilizing the transitional justice imaginary. These critiques have proceeded in a number of directions, four of which I will briefly discuss here. First, there have been a number of critiques of the legalism of international justice, which has increasingly become the favored method of transitional justice. These critiques have noted that international tribunals tend to operate with an "experience-distant" perspective and degree of abstraction that facilitates legalistic, technocratic, and depoliticized enactments of transitional justice even as they claim to catalyze a teleological transformation to liberal democracy.[65]

Second, to begin to address this issue, a number of scholars have begun to argue for a more open definition of transitional justice, one that diminishes the "classic" end of democratization while asserting the importance of "redress," "social repair," and "reparation."[66] This shift is reflected by the working definition of (and work done at) the International Center for Transitional Justice (ICTJ), which used to foreground democratic transition and now emphasizes more diffuse terms such as "redress" and recently even "mosaics."[67]

Third, this opening of the purview of transitional justice has been accompanied by a call for attention to issues of structure and power. In some cases, these

[65] McEvoy 2007; Nagy 2008.   [66] Fletcher and Weinstein 2002; Mani 2002.
[67] "What is Transitional Justice," ICTJ website (https://www.ictj.org); Duthie and Seils 2017.

efforts are informed by related literatures on peacebuilding, including the notion of structural violence. Indeed, there is growing recognition of overlaps of transitional justice and peacebuilding,[68] just as there are many overlaps with the fields of democratization studies and human rights. Accordingly, some of these critical contemporary transitional justice scholars, working in the vein of "critical transitional justice studies,"[69] have called for greater attention to issues such as social justice, gender, economic inequality, and other forms of structural violence.[70] Still others have highlighted the masking of power in terms of issues like post-colonial legacies, geopolitical domination, and political machinations related to transitional justice initiatives.[71]

Finally, a growing number of scholars have called for attention to "the local." As noted earlier, in transitional justice this interest was catalyzed by a number of factors, ranging from the failures of the ICTY and ICTR to engage local populations to claims about "African justice" at the South African TRC. If the term "local" did not appear once in the 1992 "An Agenda for Peace," it was highlighted in the 2004 UN Report on transitional justice.

Soon terms like "transitional justice from below," "hybridity," "pluralism," "grassroots," and "local justice" began to appear, a trend that has continued into the present.[72] Similar language emerged in fields like international relations, development, human rights, and peacebuilding, including recent references to "the everyday" and "the local turn."[73]

What many of these critiques share is an uneasiness with the universalist assumptions of progressivist narratives leading to liberal democracy and recognition of the need to better take account of complexity in sites of transitional justice, development, humanitarian intervention, human rights, and peacebuilding. My book builds upon this critical scholarship as well as work in anthropology by offering a discursively-informed phenomenological approach to transitional justice that reorients attention to what is masked by the justice facade.

A Phenomenological Approach to Transitional Justice

Dynamic versus flat models of transitional justice

If thin models of localization share much in common with uniformity models, thick models of localization move closer to an alternative approach that emphasizes dynamism even as it moves beyond the global-local binary. The term "dynamic," etymologically

---

[68] Sharp 2015.   [69] Hinton 2010b.

[70] See, for example, Evans 2016; Mani 2002; Miller 2008; Nagy 2008; Sharp 2013.

[71] For example, An-Na'im 2013; Clarke 2009; Clark, Knotterus, and de Volder 2016; Drumbl 2007; Mutua 2015; Subotic 2009.

[72] See An-Na'im 2013; Drumbl 2007; Duthie and Seils 2017; Hinton 2010a; McEvoy and McGregor 2008; Sharp 2014; Shaw and Waldorf 2010.

[73] For example, Autesserre 2015; Fetcher and Hindman 2011; Hughes, Öjendal, and Schierenbeck 2015; Mac Ginty and Richmond 2013.

related to the Greek word *dunamis* ("force, power"), suggests "force producing motion," the study of these forces, and more generally that which is "active, potent, energetic, forceful." This movement is contrasted to its opposite, "stasis," or that which "stands" in place, "stagnant" and "inactive."[74]

Uniformity and localization models of transitional justice are dynamic in the sense that they involve linear motion brought about by the force of transitional justice. However, this dynamism is relatively flat and uniform and constitutes "the local" as a static, stagnant space that is acted upon, creating a singular movement characteristic of universalist and cascade-like renderings of transitional justice. Dynamic models of transitional justice, in contrast, have a much broader purview, focusing both on the multiplicity of interactions that generate "motion" without a singular, predetermined end and on the self-reflexive study of dynamics, including the relatively flat dynamics of the transitional justice imaginary.

To return to the cascade metaphor, a dynamic approach explores what is masked by a surface-level, flat view of "flow." This "justice cascade" of scalar uniformity is superimposed on—to return to the riverine imagery the cascade metaphor draws upon—dynamic "ecosystems" filled with eddies, whirlpools, turbulence, counter-current, still spots, and vortices. In contrast to the reductionism of the transitional justice imaginary, this suggestion of ecosystem is holistic and takes account of fluidity and a multitude of generative interactions masked by a surface-level, experience-distant, facadist perspective of "global justice." Moreover, from this perspective, the scalar and teleological global-local binary breaks down amidst the fluidity, interstitiality, heterogeneity, and multiplicity of this active riverine ecosystem. Such a dynamic approach recognizes that the global is itself local and the local global, thereby rendering the global-local binary obsolete.

Accordingly, dynamic approaches fit well with "critical transitional justice studies,"[75] which uses a critical lens to unmask the assumptions of transitional justice while seeking alternative ways to conceptualize the field. This book, like *Man or Monster?*, examines the "banality of everyday thought,"[76] or how articulations like the transitional justice imaginary simultaneously assert a way of knowing while backgrounding and redacting as they do so, editing out complicated realities such as those circulating in dynamic transitional justice "ecosystems."

Phenomenological transitional justice

This book uses one such dynamic approach, what might be called phenomenological transitional justice. This discursively-informed phenomenological approach to transitional justice can help reveal the taken-for-granted assumptions (and erasures) of the transitional justice imaginary and its justice facade enactments in places like Cambodia. It draws in part on the anthropology of phenomenology and its emphasis on lived experience.[77]

---

[74] "Dynamic" and "stasis," *Shorter OED* 2007.   [75] See Hinton 2010b.
[76] See Hinton 2016.   [77] Desjarlais and Throop 2011.

While there are many strands of phenomenology, much of it follows philosophers like Heiddeger and Husserl, who explored the way in which being is temporally mediated by a past, including the broader "lifeworld" (*lebenswelt*), to use Husserl's phrase, which informs experience in the present and movement into the future. This backdrop of the lifeworld includes much that is naturalized and taken-for-granted, even as there is an openness linked in part to critical reflection and acts of imagination amidst the new affordances and ways of seeing the future. A phenomenological approach, then, attends to these different aspects of lived experience in all their multiplicity including, in the context of phenomenological anthropology, issues like embodiment, morality, temporality, violence, and suffering.[78]

If the experiential focus of phenomenology has been critiqued for overly focusing on subjectivity and thereby diverting attention from structure and power, this potential shortcoming is linked more to the topical concerns of those working in the phenomenological tradition and is not an inevitable consequence of the approach.[79] The key is for the analyst to stay attuned to how lived experience and the contextual backdrop in which it is embedded are mediated by issues such as discourse, structure, and power—which is why I refer to a "phenomenological transitional justice" that is "discursively-informed."

The phenomenological transitional justice approach I am proposing draws selectively from this vast tradition, adapting it to enable an exploration of the power-dynamics and lived experience masked by the justice facade. If phenomenological approaches are concerned with destabilizing the commonsensical, naturalized, and taken-for-granted, a phenomenological transitional justice seeks to unpack transitional justice assumptions, including the "classic" assumptions of the transitional justice imaginary and its facadist renderings.

In doing so, a phenomenological transitional justice shifts the focus from totalizing universals to lived experience embedded in historical, social, and political contexts. Instead of assuming an imaginary with a specific liberal democratic end, a phenomenological approach also allows for consideration of the other possibilities and imaginative acts the transitional justice measure may enable on the ground in particular settings.

Discourse: As opposed to asserting taken-for-granted discourses, a phenomenological transitional justice seeks to unpack the discourses of transitional justice. This discursive focus, drawing inspiration in part from post-structuralism and post-colonial studies, considers how given phenomena are constituted through, to use Foucault's triangulation, claims about knowledge, truth, and power,[80] ones often informed by essentializing binary logics. Said's arguments about "Orientalism" provide one illustration of this line of thinking, as do post-colonial notions of subalterns, hybridity, and mimicry.[81] So, too, do anthropological critiques of locality, which focus attention on "place-making," or how "localities" are produced and naturalized and thereby mask power, history, and subjectification—arguments that

---

[78] Ibid.   [79] See Ibid.; Hinton and Willemsen 2018; Zigon 2009.
[80] Foucault 1990, 1995.   [81] Bhaba 2004; Spivak 1994.

have been made in relation to discourses of development, human rights, liberal peacebuilding, and modernization.[82]

Transitional Justice Assemblage and the Rhizomic: In considering power and this larger discursive backdrop of the lived experience of transitional justice, it is important not to slip into the universalist and globalist assumptions that undergird the transitional justice imaginary. One way to do so is to conceptualize transitional justice as a loose "assemblage" instead of a totalizing system of "global justice." While yet to be significantly applied to transitional justice, scholars in other fields have sometimes drawn on the notion of "assemblage" to escape the global/local binary. This scholarship often draws on the work of Deleuze and Guattari, including their notion of the (grass-like) rhizome, a heterogeneous mosaic that is organized in a loose, fluid, non-linear, ever-changing, and multidirectional manner, including interstitial sideways and bottom-up exchanges.[83]

Some scholars have explored "global assemblages," which focus on topics like organs trade, biomedicine, and the drug war that have parallels to transitional justice.[84] If discursive theorists might argue that assemblage approaches, like an overly individual-focused phenomenological approach, may lose sight of power dynamics, the latter nevertheless provides a way to think about transitional justice in a fluid and non-totalizing manner and to redirect attention to the spaces of lived experience and meaning-making within the transitional justice assemblage. From this perspective, for example, the Uncle San booklet itself is not simply a straightforward simulation of the transitional justice imaginary but part of a much looser assemblage that has sideways and bottom-up dimensions that together constitute the phenomenological backdrop through which transitional justice is experienced and understood.

Interstitiality: This focus on the rhizomic and on transitional justice as assemblage, in turn, redirects attention away from the totalizing binaries that undergird homogenizing discourses and toward the gaps and "middle" spaces "in between."[85] In doing so, it does not seek to refigure the global-local binary in terms of "levels," but to subvert its scalar verticality with attention toward the moments and spaces in which transitional justice is produced and experienced. For phenomenological transitional justice, a concern with interstitiality highlights the importance of mediation and networks, including the intermediaries who "vernacularize" human rights and transitional justice discourses,[86] translating, modifying, reframing, selectively using (and ignoring), and "dubbing" them given the affordances of the moment.[87] From a phenomenological transitional justice perspective, this process of "justice in translation," discussed throughout this book, can never proceed in a literal manner but must always be attuned to "lifeworld" backdrops, including structural power, competing interests, and discourse, that mediate lived experience.

---

[82] See Edelman and Haugerud 2005, *passim*; Escobar 1995; Ferguson 1990; Gupta and Ferguson 1997.
[83] Deleuze and Guattari 1987.   [84] Collier and Ong 2005.
[85] Merry 2006b. See also Clarke and Goodale 2010; Goodale 2007; Riles 2001.
[86] On "vernacularization," see Levitt and Merry 2009; Merry 2006b.
[87] Boellstorff 2003; Levitt and Merry 2009; Merry 2006b; Theidon 2014.

Interstitial approaches highlight the fact there is not merely a top/global and bottom/local level, but multiple points of contact that "combust" in different and often unpredictable ways. As opposed to international justice "norms and standards" being transmitted to the "local level" and "localized," for example, they land at multiple points within a transitional justice assemblage where other (often obscured) interests, conceptions, and discourses circulate. It is at such points that transitional justice may become meaningful—although in ways that diverge from the transitional justice imaginary—as it is enacted and experienced on the ground, including spaces far removed from the courtroom.

In contrast to the teleological claims of the transitional justice imaginary, transitional justice is mediated and appropriated in multiple ways that do not necessarily dovetail with this end. For example, transitional justice may be "hijacked" by state actors or selectively appropriated by intermediary organizations and actors to achieve different and even contrary goals.[88] By focusing on interstitiality, a phenomenological transitional justice highlights the importance of networks and nodal points that are loosened from the scalar logics and verticality of transitional justice imaginary's teleology and related global-local discourses. This book draws on this tradition by focusing a significant amount of attention on the NGOs involved in KRT outreach.

Practice and the Experience-near: Phenomenological approaches that focus on practice and the experience-near, especially those related to practice theory, shift attention from abstract categories like "the global" and "the local" to lived experience and the everyday. Bourdieu's theorizations of practice theory provide one example, linking experience to a given "lifeworld" (in his terminology the "habitus" and "fields" mediating lived experience).[89] Geertz's notions of the "experience-near" and "thick description" likewise shift attention to lived, on-the-ground experience that is mediated by his conceptual versions of the phenomenological "life-world," including culture, commonsense, and local knowledge.[90]

If less attention has been paid to such dimensions of lived experience and "the everyday" in transitional justice,[91] there is a growing literature on these topics in related fields like development studies, human rights, and now peacebuilding.[92] One key move of such phenomenologically-oriented approaches is to shift focus onto on-the-ground engagements that collapse categorical abstractions.

The use of the term "global justice," for example, suggests that there is a homogenous group of "internationals" (and "locals") who have the same interests and goals. These categories break down when analytical attention is focused on the everyday experience

---

[88] On "hijacked justice," see Subotic 2009. See also Clark 2011; Clarke 2009; Levitt and Merry 2009.

[89] Bourdieu 1977, 1987. On using practice theory to move beyond the global-local binary in human rights and law, see Goodale and Merry 2007.

[90] Geertz 1973, 1985.

[91] But see, for example, Alcalá and Baines 2012 as well as the work of others, especially anthropologists (e.g., Allen 2006; Burnet 2012; Doughty 2016; Drexler 2013; Dwyer 2015; Eltringham 2008, 2009; Fassin 2008; Hinton 2010a, 2016; Kelsall 2013; Rojas-Perez 2017; Ross 2003; Sanford 2003; Shaw and Waldorf 2010; Theidon 2014; Wagner 2008; Wilson 2001).

[92] See, for example, Autesserre 2015; Fetcher and Hindman 2011; Goodale and Merry 2007; Malkki 2015; Mosse 2013; Richmond and Mitchell 2012.

of "internationals" who, if often invoking the progressive aspirations of the transitional justice imaginary, do so to different extents and in various ways, have other goals such as the related desire "to help," and may be reflective and critical about their practice.[93] My study builds upon this phenomenological tradition by focusing throughout on lived experience and practice of particular individuals, including court officials, NGO workers, and Cambodians who participated at the ECCC as civil parties.

Combustion and the Imagination: This focus on lived experience and meaning-making also directs attention toward "combustion" (in contrast to uniformity or flat models of localization) or what is "ignited" through moments of contact in and around the transitional justice assemblage. Just as combustion results when two ingredients interact, so too is there a combustion when the transitional justice travels and lands in different moments and spaces, potentially enabling new ways of knowing and imagining the world—albeit not in the more or less straightforward manner that follows from "flat" uniformity or localization models predicated on a global-local binary. Such acts of imagination thereby have the possibility of opening up "lifeworlds" and enabling new possibilities. The possibilities created, however, do not follow from the assumptions of the transitional justice imaginary but instead the mediating backdrops of lived experience ("lifeworlds") as they potentially do (or do not) "combust" at point of contact in and around the transitional justice assemblage.

Anna Tsing's notion "friction" presents one illustration of such a combustion model (and indeed her metaphor is an inspiration for my metaphor), as does Arjun Appadurai's model of the "disjunctures" that emerge as groups and actors (re)imagine and act amidst flows of people, capital, ideas, media, and technology.[94] Sometimes the "combustion" is strong; in other situations it may smolder, fizzle, or fail to ignite. These encounters involve aspiration and desire—including the driving "heat" of structure and power—as well as acts of imagination on the part of a multitude of actors who are directly involved with or whose lives are touched by transitional justice initiatives.

As we shall see, a focus on "combustion," combined with a dynamic approach more broadly, enables us to reapproach the question posed at the beginning of this chapter about the point of holding international tribunals. If the transitional justice imaginary asserts an answer (teleological transformation to liberal democracy), the notion of combustion loosens and decenters it, allowing for a wide range of engagements (or disengagements) with courts like the ECCC, ones informed by other imaginaries and acts of imagination. From this perspective, someone like Uncle San may experience the court in ways that diverge markedly from the transitional justice imaginary that informs the KID booklet.

Book Structure

This book argues that finding an answer to the question I initially posed—what is the point of international tribunals like the ECCC?—requires identifying the

---

[93] Acharya 2004; Autesserre 2014; Baylis 2008; Eltringham 2008, 2015; Malkki 2015; Mosse 2011.
[94] Appadurai 1996; Tsing 2005. See also Inda and Rosaldo 2007; Ong and Collier 2005.

assumptions and manifestations of the transitional justice imaginary and looking behind its facadist exteriorizations. Doing so requires a dynamic approach, such as the discursively-informed phenomenological transitional justice discussed above, which denaturalizes the transitional justice imaginary and, once it has been decentered, reconsiders it from new directions that escape its universalizing and globalizing assumptions. To this end, the chapters are structured in two ways.

First, the chapters move inside and outside of the ECCC, examining the moments and spaces where transitional justice lands and the lived experience of those who engage with it. I focus on a key interstitial space (NGOs conducting KRT outreach), the experience of particular individuals (ranging from civil parties to cosmopolitan intermediaries), and the flow of knowledge and power within the transitional justice assemblage, with a particular focus on the transitional justice imaginary and ECCC outreach. I have also divided the book into Parts that play upon the riverine metaphor of the "justice cascade," noting how this sort of dynamic approach reveals "vortices," "turbulence," and "eddies" beneath the surface of the complicated assemblage-like "ecosystem" of transitional justice, including the interstices where transitional justice is produced, enacted, and may or may not combust.

Second, each chapter loosely focuses on different aspects of the transitional justice imaginary and its facadist manifestations at the ECCC, many of which are manifest in the KID booklet. Among other things, the dimensions of the transitional justice imaginary and its exteriorizations include: *temporality* (involving particular conceptions of time, teleology, and transition), *spatiality* (asserting place-making claims and having interstitial and rhizomic dimensions), *disciplinarity* (being mediated by given technologies of power and knowledge), *normativity* (making truth claims and moral assumptions), *performativity* (seeking to constitute, through enactment, the imaginary it desires), *subjectivity* (producing certain subject positions and types of being), *aesthetics* (asserting a "look" through visual, auditory, and verbal images, practices, and material artifacts), and *affectivity* (being predicated on dispositions and categories and linked to constellations of person, self, and emotion).

The chapters both explore the exteriorization of these aspects at the ECCC and look behind this justice facade to consider the dynamic processes of meaning-making and lived experience that have been masked. Each thematic section is preceded by an introductory preamble focused on a textual or performative manifestation of the transitional justice imaginary and includes a detailed description of the chapters that follow.

In Part I, "Vortices," I examine the genealogy of justice and human rights in Cambodia and its influence on ECCC outreach, which was initially done primarily by local NGOs. After a Preamble that discusses an outreach guide and discourses related to time and space, Chapter 1, "Progression," considers two earlier transitions obscured by the discourses of the transitional justice imaginary. The first comprised a series of initiatives, including a tribunal, undertaken by the People's Republic of Kampuchea (PRK) immediately after DK. Cambodia's second post-DK transition involved the transitional democratization and human rights efforts undertaken during the United Nations Transitional Authority in Cambodia (UNTAC). Focusing on two in-depth case studies (KID and the Center for Social Development

[CSD]), the next two chapters unpack the genealogies of these intermediary out-reach NGOs and the institutional practices that laid a basis for their specific KRT outreach activities. This history, as well as the background and vision of the NGO leaders, is critical to understanding how, in the interstices of the transitional justice assemblage, these NGOs "translated" global justice in complicated, uneven, and creative ways often by using simplification and vernacularization, including the use of Buddhist concepts.

Part II, "Turbulence," centers on the transitional justice encounter of three survi-vors involved in victim participation at the ECCC. Chapter 4, "Aesthetics," begins by discussing Theary Seng, a Cambodian-American who led CSD and became the court's first civil party. She later renounced this status, claiming the court was a "sham" and that she was being used as "décor" in a superficial performance of jus-tice. The chapter then turns to explore the differing aesthetics of the justice facade and local Cambodian understandings by focusing on the art and testimony of S-21 prison survivor and painter Vann Nath.

Chapter 5 considers the issue of "Performance," looking in part at the work of the head of the ECCC's Public Affairs Section, Reach Sambath. The chapter highlights the "justice troubles" the court faced in seeking to depict the court as smoothly enacting a Justice that was unstable and contested. The next chapter, "Discipline," discusses a second S-21 survivor, Bou Meng, whose civil party testimony is sugges-tive about the discourses and subjectivities transitional justice produces through its disciplines, including its modalities of translation.

In Part III, "Eddies," I focus on the outreach activities of the Documentation Center of Cambodia (DC-Cam) and civil party participation at the court. Chapter 7, "Subjectivity," is centered around a DC-Cam outreach initiative that brought vil-lagers to Phnom Penh to attend an ECCC hearing, visit a genocide museum, and discuss the court during discussion forums and productions of a play, "Breaking the Silence."

The second chapter in this Part, "Normativity," discusses the civil party testimony the outreach participants heard at court, which was mediated both by normative dimensions of the transitional justice imaginary that circulated and local Buddhist subjectivities and understandings. Drawing on interviews with Youk Chhang, the head of DC-Cam, Chapter 9, "Disposition," discusses the work of his NGO and the ways in which "the global and the local" were intertwined in "Breaking the Silence," which rural Cambodians and international actors often understood in very different ways.

The book's conclusion, "Justice in Translation," argues for a dynamic, discursively-informed phenomenological justice approach to transitional justice, one in keeping with the spirit of critical transitional justice studies and that foregrounds ethno-graphic attunement to lived experience, discourse, interstices, and the combustive encounters masked by the justice facade. To this end, the chapter reconsiders the meaning of justice in Cambodia through the lens of translation and the acts of imagination transitional justice may catalyze. Refocusing on "justice in translation" in this manner, the conclusion contends, enables us to rethink the ends of transi-tional justice and the paths forward after genocide and mass violence.

PART I
VORTICES

Preamble I

Discourse, Time, and Space

"Transitional justice processes ultimately aim to catalyze a shift of norms and values according to a culture of democracy and respect for human rights."[1]

This statement, a manifestation of the transitional justice imaginary, appears in the opening paragraph of "Making an Impact: Guidelines on Designing and Implementing Outreach Programs for Transitional Justice," a 2011 manual published by the International Center for Transitional Justice (ICTJ), perhaps the leading international non-governmental organization (NGO) working on transitional justice. To realize these "democratic aspirations [that are] in the background of the TJ [transitional justice] measure," the text continues, transitional justice mechanisms need to engage the public by disseminating information, explaining and advertising the process, and giving them "a voice" and "sense of ownership [in] the process" of "building the desired social changes."[2]

Such "public engagement," "Making an Impact" notes, is not easy. This is particularly true of international justice, as became clear in the initial failures of the International Criminal Tribunal for the former Yugoslavia and International Criminal Tribunal for Rwanda to directly engage the affected populations.[3] If hybrid tribunals help address this issue, outreach directly focuses on engaging the public—even if it is usually underfunded, understaffed, and implicitly viewed as secondary to the "primary" functions of a transitional justice mechanism.

More broadly, outreach is poorly understood and the "lessons learned" not yet systematized. "Not only is there still neither a common definition of the term 'outreach' nor a clear picture of the sorts of activities it entails," the guide continues, "but also, more worrisomely, there is a lack of official support and recognition of its unique role in the adequate functioning of TJ measures."[4]

To address this situation, "Making an Impact" notes, the ICTJ's Research Unit established a project on outreach in late 2009. The project focused on outreach in a number of transitional justice settings, including Bosnia, Timor-Leste, Peru, Morocco, Sierra Leone, the International Criminal Court, and Cambodia.[5] While a report on an outreach workshop in Cambodia was published,[6] "Making an Impact" was the major outcome of this ICTJ outreach project, one aimed "to provide practitioners with tools and usable knowledge to craft outreach programs that

---

[1] Ramírez-Barat 2011, 5.   [2] Ibid.   [3] Ibid. See also Stover and Weinstein 2004.
[4] Ramírez-Barat 2011, 6.   [5] Ibid.; see also "Outreach," ICTJ website.
[6] Ramírez-Barat and Karwande 2010; Balthazard 2010.

The Justice Facade: Trials of Transition in Cambodia. Alexander Laban Hinton. © Alexander Laban Hinton, 2018. Published 2018 by Oxford University Press.

are more sophisticated and sensitive to the challenges of current transitional justice processes."[7] While noting the difficulty of translating "outreach," the guide defines outreach in a technical manner as "a set of tools—the combination of materials and activities—that a TJ measure puts in place to build direct channels of communication with affected communities, in order to raise awareness of the justice process and promote understanding of the measure."[8]

Such tools, "Making an Impact" states, encompass outreach materials, information dissemination, and activities meant to "facilitate a participatory dialogue with the general public."[9] These materials and activities need to be "culturally appropriate and written as simply as possible" and made to appeal to different audiences ranging from victims and displaced people to community leaders and members of the international community.[10] Outreach also varies in terms of its level of depth, ranging from the basic dissemination of information to more dialogic, consultative, and participatory initiatives.[11]

Among other things, "Making an Impact" states, the outreach "set of tools" includes the following: *dissemination of information and distribution of materials* (for example, printed and written materials, information, information technologies like social media and websites, radio, and TV); *interactive activities* (for example, social media, town hall meetings, rural forums, training sessions, workshops, community programs, film screenings, public presentations, and visits to the transitional justice institution as well as related memorials and museums); *cultural activities* (for example, visual materials, art, music, and theater); *education activities* (pedagogic exercises, development of educational tools and materials, facilitating academic research, and training workshops); and *consultation mechanisms* (for example, workshops and meetings with stakeholders).[12]

In terms of implementation, the guide suggests, outreach and media relations should primarily be coordinated through the transitional justice institution. However, depending on the situation, it is useful to coordinate with intermediary domestic and international partners, such as government ministries, schools, theaters, community groups, foundations, scholars, and the United Nations (U.N.).[13]

NGOs are particularly promising in this regard.[14] If it is necessary for a transitional justice institution to be careful in vetting local NGOs given that they have their own mandates, goals, and capacities, NGOs have strengths that may supplement a transitional justice measure's outreach activities. Of particular importance are the local NGO's experience, networks, grassroots relationships, and ability to communicate more easily with local communities. Indeed, because of these strengths, "many transitional justice initiatives in the past have ... relied on NGOs to conduct outreach activities."[15]

This was the case with the Extraordinary Chambers in the Courts of Cambodia (ECCC). Little early investment in outreach was made, a failure heightened by the

---

[7] Ramírez-Barat 2011, 6.   [8] Ibid, 7.   [9] Ibid, 15.   [10] Ibid, 15, 23–27.
[11] Ibid, 7–8.
[12] The above lists of outreach materials and activities are taken directly from ibid, 15–23, italics mine.
[13] Ibid, 28.   [14] Ibid, 28–30.   [15] Ibid, 29.

prominent role of victims participation in the proceedings. Initial ECCC efforts were primarily conducted by the court's Public Affairs Section and only later augmented by the Victims Unit (later reorganized as the Victims Support Section). Instead, local NGOs like Khmer Institute of Democracy (KID) took the lead in undertaking ECCC outreach.

NGOs have often been viewed as a key intermediary between "the global" and "the local" in post-conflict and "development" settings.[16] In these framings, civil society more broadly is seen as a space that may bypass suspect and even authoritarian government institutions to more effectively implement development projects, humanitarian aid efforts, peacebuilding and democratization projects, and human rights and transitional justice initiatives.[17] In this regard, NGOs and other civil society initiatives are often depicted as microcosms of incipient liberal democracy, a space in which rights-bearing individuals associate, participate, and are empowered.

As this discussion suggests, the transitional justice imaginary is manifest in the ICTJ outreach guide in a number of ways, including such assertions of the global/local binary. The manual echoes the KID booklet in its aspiration for teleological transformation to a new stage of liberal democracy, a "democratic culture" governed by human rights, dialogue, agency, political participation, and the rule of law. And it highlights the imaginary's techno-legalistic framings, which suggests that practitioners can use specific "tools" to catalyze liberal democratic change.

"Making an Impact" also reflects the imaginary's temporal and spatial dimensions, the focus of this book section. If the transitional justice imaginary aspires for a teleological transition to liberal democracy, this end state is opposed to a specific beginning of violence and authoritarianism that is depicted as "inhering" in transitional spaces like Cambodia. As noted in the introduction, such discourses are often essentializing and sometimes even Orientalist, constructing this space as chaotic, violent, savage, authoritarian, and lacking basic elements of "civilization," such as "the rule of law."[18]

In the transitional justice imaginary, this "lack" extends broadly to include its subjects, who are depicted as not having basic rights, agency, and well-being. Relatedly, Cambodia and its inhabitants are often framed in terms of discourses of dysfunction, ranging from characterizations of the country as a "failed state" and "broken society" to depictions of its inhabitants, like Uncle San suffering from nightmares in his hammock, as traumatized and not yet healed. The transitional justice imaginary aspires to fill the lack, delivering the "gift" of civilization.

Such discourses fix time and space in a scalar model with a type of beginning and teleological end. In doing so, they may occlude hierarchy and power, erase history, depoliticize, and create "peoples and places." The court's temporal jurisdiction provides one illustration of this point, as it directs its temporal gaze on Democratic Kampuchea (DK), excluding related events before and after. By asserting a static present (remaining stuck in the authoritarian DK past) and progressive future (the civilized liberal democracy global justice will deliver), the transitional justice

---

[16] Merry 2006a. See also Goodale and Merry 2007; Levitt and Merry 2009; Ullrich 2016.
[17] See Christie 2013; Richmond and Mitchell 2012.
[18] Springer 2015. On rule of law, see Seidel 2015.

imaginary erases other historical trajectories that led to the present moment—even as the imaginary asserts what this moment is.

The chapters in this section seek to move behind the facade of such transitional justice imaginary discourses asserting a "Cambodian" time and space and to reintroduce obscured histories, politics, and power dynamics that inform the everyday lived experience at points of contact with the transitional justice assemblage. It does so by focusing on interstitial space, Cambodian NGOs, and related sets of practices—outreach programs inflected by longer histories obscured by the justice facade, ones that were also enmeshed with backgrounds, visions, and experiences of NGO leaders and their staff.

Drawing on the experience of Thun Saray and Kassie Neou, two leading Cambodian human rights advocates, the next chapter, "Progression," explores how these discourses involve temporal erasures, masking other important historical post-DK "currents" that inform the contemporary transitional justice moment. These include a first post-DK "transition" undertaken by the People's Republic of Kampuchea (PRK) regime in the 1980s and a second transition: UN democratization and peacebuilding efforts during the early 1990s, which helped catalyze a proliferation of Cambodian human rights NGOs.

The current "transition," in other words, follows two other important transitional moments that are largely obscured even as they mediate the current moment in different ways. In making this point, the chapter also discusses ECCC defense arguments highlighting such temporal erasures, including the pre- and post-DK events that, they contended, undermined a standardized "Manichean" historical narrative about DK—one that, if taken-for-granted, was highly politicized and thereby raised questions about the impartiality and credibility of the court.

The following chapter, "Time," picks up this line discussion by looking at the history of KID and how the Uncle San booklet was linked to the NGO's earlier aims and practices. By exploring the creation and use of this booklet, the chapter also explores different "vortices," or whirlpools of movement that, if affected by the force of the "global justice," are also informed by other contextual factors and are combustive in the sense of generating acts of imagination. By focusing on an NGO and particular individuals who played a direct or indirect role in the creation of the booklet, this chapter foregrounds lived experience and interstitiality, thus seeking to go beyond the global-local binary in different ways.

The last chapter, "Space," continues to focus on interstitiality, lived experience, and the combustive acts of creativity and imagination that take place behind the justice facade. It examines another NGO "vortex," the Center for Social Development, which was led by two Cambodian-Americans, Chea Vannath and Theary Seng and known for high-profile Khmer Rouge Tribunal outreach "Public Forums." The chapter traces the origins of the NGO and the public forum project, noting how the forums changed in accordance with the historical moment and the vision of these leaders, including Chea Vannath's deep Buddhist belief and Theary Seng's Christianity even as both were also influenced by time spent in the United States. The chapter concludes with a return to the ICTJ outreach project and a discussion of the public forums as imagined "public spheres," alleged "spaces" of liberal democratic being asserted by transitional justice imaginary discourses.

1

Progression (Cambodia's Three Transitions)

"I was put in jail two times."

I sit in the office of economist Thun Saray, the head of the Cambodian Human Rights and Development Association (ADHOC), the first Cambodian human rights non-governmental organization (NGO) in Cambodia. ADHOC is well known for its educational efforts, monitoring, and advocacy, including speaking out on behalf of those under threat or arrest. Indeed, when I interviewed Thun Saray in his busy Phnom Penh office in March 2016, ADHOC was just becoming embroiled in a conflict between the government and an opposition leader that would lead to accusations against and the arrest of several ADHOC staffers who were jailed for over a year. Saray himself would subsequently flee from the country.[1]

Saray was not new to political intimidation as his remark about being jailed twice suggested. Indeed, for Saray this statement was provided as a succinct way to begin to answer my questions about the origins of ADHOC and the NGO's Khmer Rouge Tribunal (KRT) outreach.[2] With rounded spectacles and piercing eyes, Saray told me the story of his first imprisonment, at the start of Democratic Kampuchea (DK), with a slow sad tone.

A student and civil servant, Saray was sent to a re-education camp for ten months. "They considered us petite bourgeoisie," Saray said as he explained how he and other former civil servants and intellectuals lived in miserable conditions as they were forced to do hard labor under the watch of armed guards. Saray was eventually released and survived DK, which served as the origin point of his story about the organization's path to KRT outreach.

DK also constitutes a key temporal marker at the Extraordinary Chambers in the Courts of Cambodia (ECCC), constituting the "before" to which present transitional justice moment and the liberal democratic future to which its classic imaginary aspires are counterposed. This transitional justice imaginary discourse of a (authoritarian, violent) "before" transformed by the current transitional moment into a (peaceful, liberal democratic) "after" is omnipresent and also frames the narrative of "Uncle San, Aunty Yan, and the KRT."

The first line of the booklet delimits the temporal boundaries of the past, as the introductory note explains, "The Khmer Rouge Regime is generally recognized

---

[1] Khy 2016; *The Cambodia Daily* Staff 2017.
[2] Author interview with Thun Saray, Phnom Penh, March 11, 2016.

The Justice Facade: Trials of Transition in Cambodia. Alexander Laban Hinton. © Alexander Laban Hinton, 2018. Published 2018 by Oxford University Press.

as the time between April 17, 1975 and January 6, 1979. This was a time in Cambodian history where the Communist Party of Kampuchea held control over the entire country and committed many crimes against the Cambodian people." Here, at the very start of the booklet, time is immediately constructed in four interlinked ways. First, in terms of periodicity, time is placed within a delimited span, the DK era.

This interval is then inflected in two ways. On the one hand, it constitutes a juridical frame, what is called the temporal jurisdiction of the court. On the other hand, this interval is marked as one of criminality as a criminal act ("many crimes") has been committed by a perpetrator (the Communist Party of Kampuchea) against a victim ("the Cambodian people"). In this temporal frame, there are perpetrators and victims and nothing in between.

This temporal marker also lays the ground for the linear, progressive transitional justice imaginary time of the Khmer Institute of Democracy (KID) booklet. If the first few pages of the booklet are concerned with DK, it then leaps from this period to the ECCC present signified by the outreach session. In the booklet, the KID Citizen Advisor highlights a second key temporal marker, the 2003 Agreement establishing the tribunal.

$$1975–1979 \text{ (DK)} \quad \rightarrow \quad 2003 \text{ (ECCC)}$$

In other words, the booklet jumps from DK to the transitional justice present. The events that took place before and between these dates are erased.

If the transitional justice imaginary marks DK as the beginning of its desired teleological transition to liberal democracy, then, it dehistoricizes and localizes the process by pushing into the background the events prior to DK and the launch of the ECCC. These events range from French colonialism in Cambodia to the Vietnam War and Cold War geopolitics, which helped catalyze the Khmer Rouge rise to power and Cambodia's post-DK international isolation.[3] Through its techno-legalism, this imaginary depoliticizes history, a fact suggested by the long-term political intimidation Saray and his human rights co-workers faced, as well as numerous events, including human rights abuses, media and opposition party crackdowns, and land dispossession, which took place during the ECCC.

By dehistoricizing and depoliticizing, then, the transitional justice imaginary obscures key events and dynamics at odds with the transitional justice measure's goals and claims. This chapter focuses on this historical and political backdrop to the ECCC that is masked by its justice facade. I begin by discussing defense arguments criticizing the court's limited jurisdiction, including its erasure of pre-DK history. I then turn to look at two key post-DK transitional "currents," also obscured even as they are invoked at times by defense teams, which are critical to understanding the current ECCC "third transition" in Cambodia.

---

[3] Chandler 1991, 2007; Fawthrop and Jarvis 2004.

If one of these transitions, the early 1990s United Nations Transitional Authority in Cambodia (UNTAC), is occasionally acknowledged, the other, initiatives launched by the regime that followed DK, the People's Republic of Kampuchea (PRK), is seldom mentioned. Although these PRK efforts were highly politicized, they overlap in ways with contemporary conceptualizations of transitional justice as addressing "large-scale human rights violations" and involving accountability and redress for victims.[4] This chapter explores these obscured histories, in part by drawing on the experience of Thun Saray and a second Cambodian human rights pioneer, Kassie Neou.

Before the Transition

Victor's justice

"Justice is only for the winner," Thun Saray told me with a chuckle, recalling how a scholar once suggested to him that the ECCC is victor's justice. This charge has been levelled at international courts ranging from Nuremberg to Milosevic's trial at the International Criminal Tribunal for the former Yugoslavia (ICTY),[5] thereby raising questions about the meaning, politics, and legitimacy of transitional justice in places like Cambodia. Perhaps because Saray had been imprisoned twice and long fought for human rights, he argued that such courts, including the ECCC, nevertheless could be valuable.

Like Saray's friend, a number of critics, including former Khmer Rouge leaders and their defense teams, have dismissed the ECCC as victor's justice. In 2006, Chea Vannath, the head of the Center for Social Development (CSD), asked former DK Head of State Khieu Samphan about his thoughts on the tribunal. He replied that he was more focused on corruption and land-grabbing even as he critiqued the ECCC for its limited temporal jurisdiction, asking her, "What is Justice? [The court] is framed from 1975 to 1979 and it's called justice [while other implicated] people go free, the United States, Australia, Vietnam, King Norodom Sihanouk and so on! It's justice? What does justice mean?"[6]

He was arrested along with four other suspects the following year. One Duch (b. 1942), the former head of S-21 prison, was the first to be tried in 2009 (Case 001). He was convicted and sentenced to life imprisonment after pursuing a defense in which he apologized even as he claimed he was just a cog in the machine, partly cooperated with the court, and acknowledged the execution of over 12,000 people at the prison, many after torture.[7] S-21 operated directly under the control of the Communist Party of Kampuchea (CPK), whose DK policies and crimes were the direct focus of the second trial (Case 002).

---

[4] "What is Transitional Justice?" ICTJ (https://www.ictj.org).
[5] Bass 2001; Koskenniemi 2002.
[6] Author interviews with Chea Vannath, Phnom Penh, Cambodia, March 9 and March 11, 2016.
[7] Hinton 2016. See also Cruvellier 2014.

Case 002, which began on November 21, 2011, involved the other four suspects including Khieu Samphan (b. 1931) and "Brother Number Two" and Deputy Secretary of the CPK Nuon Chea (b. 1926). To facilitate the proceedings, in part due to the advanced age and poor health of the defendants, the Trial Chamber split Case 002 into two parts, the first of which (Case 002/01) focused on DK population movements and related crimes against humanity. The two other Case 002 defendants—Pol Pot's brother-in-law and DK Deputy Prime Minister for Foreign Affairs Ieng Sary (1925–2013) and his wife, DK Minister of Social Affairs Ieng Thirith (1932–2015; released in 2012 due to dementia)—died during the proceedings.

The Trial Chamber convicted Nuon Chea and Khieu Samphan of Crimes against Humanity, including extermination and other inhumane acts, on August 7, 2014, though the Supreme Court Chamber reversed the extermination conviction in a November 23, 2016, appeals ruling. A life sentence was upheld. Closing arguments in the second part of their case (Case 002/02), which includes the charge of genocide, concluded on June 23, 2017, with a verdict expected in 2018.

Rupture

While the strategies of the Case 002 defense teams varied, they often sought to undercut prosecution arguments that power during DK was highly centralized and that the accused played an active role in the crimes that took place. Defense lawyers sometimes did this by arguing that DK leader Pol Pot, who died in 1998, held power while their clients just followed orders. From start to finish, however, defense lawyers questioned the court's legitimacy, accusing it of political bias and victor's justice. Their critiques focused, in part, on events before and after DK that were erased by the court's temporal jurisdiction.

These attacks were perhaps most famously and initially launched by Khieu Samphan's French lawyer, "the devil's advocate" Jacques Vergès, who had defended notorious clients like Klaus Barbie and Carlos the Jackal. Vergès was known for his defense strategy of "rupture" that involved using the juridical platform to attack the court itself, disrupting the proceedings by playing to public opinion, and asking questions that undermined a court's legitimacy.[8]

Vergès, who had met Pol Pot and Khieu Samphan while they were students in France, deployed these tactics at the ECCC. At the same time he argued that his client was a powerless figurehead, Vergès sought to undermine the legitimacy of the ECCC, raising questions about corruption and political interference at the court, juridical failures such as the lack of translation, and the role of foreign powers in the conflict, including massive US bombing during the civil war that facilitated the Khmer Rouge rise to power.[9]

---

[8] Christodoulidis 2009; Giry 2009; Koskenniemi 2002.   [9] Giry 2009; Kersten 2013.

The head of the crocodile

Although Vergès died in 2013, others would continue the critiques, including Nuon Chea and his lawyers. Nuon Chea did so using the metaphor of the body of a crocodile, an animal often viewed as deceitful in Cambodian oral tradition and associated with Vietnam. His use of this metaphor went straight to the issue of temporal jurisdiction.

When given the floor during opening arguments in 2011, for example, Nuon Chea opened by paying his respects to "our ancestors who sacrificed their flesh, blood, bones, and life to defend our motherland ... from the policy of incursion, annexation, land grabbing, racial extermination from [Vietnam] and other neighboring countries."[10] A key focus of his defense, Vietnam, was here immediately revealed. While he wanted to "serve justice," ascertain "the truth," and reveal "proper history" in the court, Nuon Chea continued, the tribunal was "unfair" since it focused on DK. "Only the body of the crocodile is to be discussed" at the court, Nuon Chea complained, not the "head and tail" of the crocodile, or the events that transpired "pre-1975 and post-1979."[11]

By the "head" of the crocodile, Nuon Chea was referring to the "root causes" of DK, particularly the long history of Vietnamese meddling in Cambodia, a long-time focus of Khmer Rouge propaganda. Indeed, much of Nuon Chea's crocodile defense mirrored DK tracts like the 1978 publication *Black Paper: Facts and Evidences of the Acts of Aggression and Annexation of Vietnam against Kampuchea.* The introduction to *Black Paper* argues that Vietnam "has always had the ambition to annex and swallow Kampuchea, and to exterminate the nation of Kampuchea through its sinister strategy of 'Indochina Federation.'"[12] Indeed, the first chapter of the tract, entitled "The Annexationist Nature of Vietnam," chronicles the long history of alleged Vietnamese expansionism and land-grabs, including its co-option of Kampuchea Krom, or what is now Southern Vietnam.

This trope of Vietnam's "southward march" has long circulated in Cambodia and was also invoked by Nuon Chea's defense, though it foregrounded a more recent manifestation, Vietnam's desire to create and dominate an Indochina Federation that included Cambodia. For a variety of reasons, including the emergence of a new intellectual elite and the first Khmer newspapers in the late 1930s, a growing sense of nationalism began to take hold in Cambodia, a sentiment that helped fuel an anti-French movement leading to independence in 1953.

As the movement grew and became more radicalized, so, too, did ties to the Indochinese Communist Party (ICP), which Ho Chi Minh had established in 1930 on the basis of the Soviet model of a transnational federation of communist states.[13] This notion of Vietnamese-dominated federation proved to be a key source of tension between the Cambodian revolutionaries and their Vietnamese counterparts.

---

[10] Transcript of Trial Proceedings, Case 002/01 Trial Day 2, November 22, 2011, 77—hereafter formatted as "Day 2 (Case 002/01), 77." See also Nuon Chea Defense Team 2013, 2017.
[11] Day 2 (Case 002/01), 77.   [12] DK 1978, 1–2.   [13] Morris 1999, 27.

Nuon Chea's defense blamed Vietnamese ambitions for much of what went wrong during DK. If the Vietnamese and Cambodian communists worked together to foment revolutionary struggle prior to 1975, the relationship was characterized by increasing mistrust.[14] According to Nuon Chea's defense, Vietnam sought to sabotage the Khmer Rouge revolution by developing networks within the country and seeking to overthrow the DK regime. In response, the leadership of the DK regime had to use force to put down or prevent plots and rebellions, which lead to deaths.

Ultimately, Vietnam and DK went to war in 1978 after a series of skirmishes. Vietnam achieved its ambition of dominating Cambodia, the defense argued, when it overthrew the DK regime in January 1979 and placed in power its "puppet" PRK government, led in part by Khmer Rouge defectors who remain key figures in the current Cambodian government.[15] These events, Nuon Chea, argued, deeply influenced the "tail" of the crocodile, or the post-DK history that influenced the ECCC.

If the Nuon Chea defense focused on Vietnamese, the "head of the crocodile" included a number of other important pre-DK events that had been "arbitrarily and unfairly" excised from the purview of the court. "For decades," one of their closing briefs states, "Prince Sihanouk, Lon Nol, the United States and Vietnam, committed atrocities on Cambodian territory. In many cases, those crimes were similar in character to the allegations against Nuon Chea," including those committed by the United States (U.S.), which "murdered an estimated 150,000 Cambodians in the course of their futile and unprovoked eight-year campaign of terror in [and mass bombing of] the Cambodian countryside."[16]

The ECCC, the Nuon Chea closing brief went on, now "chose to condemn Nuon Chea for the unintended consequences of his effort to liberate Cambodia while blindly ignoring the conduct which motivated Nuon Chea to act in the first place." Instead, the defense argued, Nuon Chea was a patriot. Thus Nuon Chea concluded his Case 002/01 opening remarks by stating that "injustice ... compelled me to devote myself to fight for my country. I had to leave my family behind to liberate my motherland from colonialism and aggression and oppression by the forces, by the thieves who wished to steal our land and wipe Cambodia off the face of the world."[17]

The prosecution, of course, strongly contested the crocodile defense. In their closing arguments in Case 002/02, the international co-prosecutor stated that the Khmer Rouge had long sought to assert this "alternative history," which was based on distortion and lacked evidential support. More broadly, the crocodile defense directed attention away from the many specific crimes committed during DK, ones in which the accused were implicated.

The Office of the Co-Prosecutor (OCP)'s own closing brief in Case 002/02 ranged far and wide, arguing that power was centralized and hierarchical during DK and crimes against humanity and genocide had taken place throughout. The OCP brief laid out this case in detail, linking particular crimes (genocide, crimes against humanity, and grave breaches of the Geneva conventions) to specific "facts" regarding relocations, work camps, prisons, enslavement, forced marriage, rape, torture,

---

[14] See Chandler 1991, 2007; Morris 1999.   [15] Nuon Chea Defense Team 2013, 7.
[16] Ibid.   [17] Day 2 (Case 002/01), 111.

purges, executions, and so forth.[18] This evidence had been presented during 274 trial days that included documentary evidence as well as testimony from witnesses and civil parties.[19]

Even as they critiqued the defense and laid out their case, however, the prosecution said almost nothing about "the head" of the crocodile, the pre-1975 root causes of the conflict. If the arguments of Vergès and the Nuon Chea defense team had many shortcomings and at times veered toward denialism, their critique of the court's limited jurisdiction highlighted a key potential flaw in such tribunals, which, even as they claim to reveal the truth, are only able to do so within certain parameters and therefore in a partial manner.

Due to its narrow focus on DK, the ECCC justice facade masks critical background dynamics and root causes of the violence, as the defense teams noted. These temporal erasures included: French colonialism, the Vietnam War, Vietnamese, Thai, and Asian regional interests, Soviet, US, and Chinese geopolitical interests, class antagonisms, poverty and landlessness, Cold War politics, and the US interference in and carpet-bombing of Cambodia during the civil war.[20] The Nuon Chea defense arguments about the "tail of the crocodile" (the post-1979 consequences of DK), if similarly flawed, point towards other temporal maskings of the court, including the "first transition" and politics of memory during the PRK regime, which brings us to ADHOC President Thun Saray's second imprisonment.

The First Transition (PRK Justice and Memorialization)

"Phnom Penh looked like a dead city," Saray recalled as he described his post-DK return to Phnom Penh in early 1979. "No shopping. No markets. No schools."[21] Besides a small number of PRK civil servants and Vietnamese advisors, there were "no people, nothing ... no taxis or cars." There was "a lot of rubbish" but, besides books and property that had been removed from some houses, Phnom Penh looked almost exactly as it had in April 1975 when Saray and his family had joined hundreds of thousands of other urbanites who were expelled from the city.

After DK, Saray considered fleeing to Thailand, but decided not to after he heard stories about bandits and feared for his family. Instead, he took a job in a district office "in order to feed my family. But we lived in a poor condition. The salary was only some rice.... But we survived. My life has involved a lot of suffering: prison, war, poverty."[22] While working there, Saray met Vandy Kaonn, a French-trained sociologist.[23] Like many Cambodians, both intellectuals were somewhat skeptical of the new PRK regime, which had taken power with the support of overwhelming Vietnamese military support and wielded influence over the new government.

---

[18] OCP 2017.   [19] Public Affairs Section, "Case 002/02 Factsheet," undated.
[20] Chandler 1991, 2007; Hinton 2005, 2016; Kiernan 2004, 2008.
[21] Author interview with Thun Saray, Phnom Penh, June 28, 2009.   [22] Ibid.
[23] Gottesman 2003, 6.

Legitimacy and the PRK atrocity narrative

Indeed, the PRK regime found itself in a difficult situation. On the one hand, the country's infrastructure and institutional capacity was devastated. Entire government departments and ministries had to be rebuilt in a situation in which the number of professional and educated Cambodians had decreased significantly due to the Khmer Rouge targeting of former elites and urbanites and the flight of others to the Thai border and abroad. The new regime nevertheless made significant progress in areas like education.

On the other hand, the PRK regime confronted a crisis of legitimacy. Due to Cold War politics, the regime faced sanctions and hostility from the U.S. and its allies, including Thailand, and China, which had long supported the Khmer Rouge. The PRK regime aligned with Vietnam and Soviet bloc countries. Geopolitics resulted in the PRK regime being denied Cambodia's seat at the United Nations in 1979; instead it was given to the Khmer Rouge.

Domestically, most Cambodians were relieved to be liberated from the violence of DK—even if many remained concerned that the PRK was also socialist and that a number of its top officials were former Khmer Rouge, many of whom had fled DK purges. Among them was Hun Sen, the young PRK Foreign Minister who would in 1985 become Prime Minister, a position he has held ever since. Many Cambodians were also wary of the PRK regime's subordination to Vietnam. The resurgent Khmer Rouge immediately began to warn that Vietnam was committing genocide against Cambodians and wanted to "swallow" the country.

Cambodia's first transition took place amidst this volatile and politicized situation, as the PRK regime sought to help people deal with the past, but in a manner that would inflame hatred. To enhance its domestic and international legitimacy, the PRK regime asserted an atrocity narrative that focused on genocide while personalizing the violence, depicting it as the result of a maniacal plot hatched by Pol Pot and his cronies who, the PRK regime contended, had diverted Cambodia from the true path to socialist revolution—one the PRK would now undertake.[24] In this way, the PRK regime staked its claim to legitimacy as the true bearers of the revolutionary mantle and, crucially, as the ones who, with the help of their Vietnamese "brothers," had liberated the people from this "hell on earth."

In the PRK narrative, the regime remained the people's protector, a "back" (*khnang*) upon which they could rely to ensure that the horrors of the DK past were not repeated. With the growing Khmer Rouge insurgency on the border, this role was of enormous importance to the populace. To assert this narrative, the PRK regime almost immediately began to build Tuol Sleng on the site of S-21, structuring the genocide memorial in accordance with the PRK's atrocity frame.[25]

People's Revolutionary Tribunal (August 1979)

The PRK regime's second major initiative in this regard was the establishment of the People's Revolutionary Tribunal (PRT)—despite the fact that only a small number

---

[24] Gottesman 2003; Hinton 2016; Ledgerwood 1997.
[25] Hinton 2016; Ledgerwood 1997; Schlund-Vials 2012.

of legal personnel had survived DK, a legacy that, combined with the PRK regime's politicization of the judiciary and the international isolation of Cambodia during the 1980s, contributed to Cambodia's contemporary judicial problem. Nevertheless, these two efforts at memorialization and accountability served as a first local attempt at something resembling what is now called transitional justice, even if both initiatives were heavily politicized and not aimed at liberal democracy.

Held before a packed crowd at the Chaktomuk Theater in Phnom Penh, the PRT lasted five days. The bulk of the proceedings consisted of witness statements and the reading of investigative reports supplemented by occasional films, the presentation of material evidence, and a preliminary site visit to Tuol Sleng prison.[26] Testimony was given by a broad array of people, including monks, Muslim Cham, ethnic Vietnamese, child victims, doctors, legal experts, and foreign lawyers. Just part of one afternoon was set aside for the defense, which in any event did almost no cross-examination. Closing arguments were made on the last morning; the verdict was delivered in the afternoon.

Virtually everything in the proceedings, even the defense statements, was in some way geared to rewrite the past and advance the new PRK political line. Everywhere the Khmer Rouge became the "Pol Pot-Ieng Sary clique" or "traitors," who were "savage," "barbarous," "fascist," "genocidal," and "Maoist" and ultimately manipulated by the "Peking hegemonists" or "expansionists." In the end, the court convicted Pol Pot and Ieng Sary of genocide and sentenced them to death and the confiscation of their property. Since the proceedings lasted one week and were run through the Ministry of Information, Press and Culture with the assistance of Vietnamese advisors, the PRT was widely dismissed as a show trial.[27]

Thun Saray was directly involved in this initiative. In May 1979, PRK officials invited Vandy Kaonn to undertake research in preparation for the PRT. Kaonn, in turn, asked Saray to help with an investigative report, an effort that involved interviewing victims and gathering documents.[28] Saray also testified. He noted that the reports and testimony had to accord with the PRK's larger atrocity narrative. The PRK regime and its Vietnamese advisors sometimes "dictated" parts of the victim testimony, such as the attacks on China. The President of the Court "was not a judge and [defense lawyer] Dith Munty didn't defend at all. This trial was a product of socialist times. Everyone knew it was political."[29]

Despite his awareness that the PRT was a show trial, one involving Vietnamese and even Soviet advisors, Saray decided to participate in the PRT since his interests aligned with those of the government in terms of believing there was a critical need "to tell the stories of the suffering" and expose the Khmer Rouge atrocities to the world.[30] He stressed that, if the stories had to accord with PRK rhetoric, they were nevertheless for the most part true. "Nobody told [us] to say this or that," Saray said. "They allowed everybody to tell their own stories according to the truth."[31]

---

[26] De Nike, Quigley, and Robinson 2000, 67–69.   [27] Gottesman 2003, 4, 63.
[28] Ibid, 6.
[29] Thun Saray, quoted in McDermid 2007, 8–9. See also *Phnom Penh Post* Staff 2007, 9.
[30] Author interview with Thun Saray, Phnom Penh, June 28, 2009.   [31] Ibid.

Moreover, the proceedings, which were broadcast by radio throughout the country, were also emotionally powerful: "There were horrible, horrible stories. A lot of people cried when they heard the terrible things that happened to other people."[32] Regardless of its politicization, then, the PRT seems to have struck an emotional chord with many Cambodians and offered a meaningful state narrative that, even as it advanced the PRK atrocity narrative, may have helped people make sense of the nightmare through which they had just lived.[33]

The politics of transition

Indeed, a number of post-conflict PRK initiatives—not just the PRT and the creation of the Tuol Sleng Museum of Genocidal Crimes but later efforts such as a petition campaign and the establishment of memorials throughout the country[34]—helped Cambodians deal with the past in a manner that, if not transitional justice in the classic sense, nevertheless resonated with some of its aims. These efforts have largely been erased by the temporal horizon of the court, which creates a justice facade suggesting that Cambodians have been frozen in (backward, ahistorical, static) time awaiting the transformation claimed to be effected by transitional justice.

More broadly, transitional justice imaginary discourses "localize" such domestic initiatives, often framing them as a lesser form lacking "international standards." There have been, for example, domestic courts held in places like Argentina and Bangladesh that have accomplished a great deal. Too often, however, national courts are viewed as political and as delivering a lesser form of justice even though they are potentially much more effective in terms of being attuned to the local context. This situation creates a hierarchy of justice in which "global" international courts are valorized and domestic courts largely ignored and diminished. Interestingly, there are horizontal (rhizomic) exchanges between such countries that bypass the transitional justice industry paralleled by a rise in scholarly interest in such different "architectures" of transitional justice,[35] a notion captured by the idea of transitional justice as assemblage.

Finally, Cambodia's first post-DK transition is also important because it is revealing about the current Cambodian government's position regarding the KRT. Indeed, as noted earlier, this government is dominated by the Cambodian People's Party (CPP), which includes many former PRK officials, some of whom were Khmer Rouge. For many years, the PRK regime called for a Khmer Rouge tribunal, a request that was ignored due to Cold War politics.[36] During the mid-1990s, the government effectively offered amnesty to Khmer Rouge soldiers and officers to entice them to defect, a policy that facilitated the collapse of the revolutionary movement. The government has argued that, to preserve a peace that was decades

---

[32] Thun Saray, quoted in McDermid 2007, 8–9.   [33] See Ledgerwood 1997.
[34] See Ly 2014; Gottesman 2003.   [35] Hazan 2017.
[36] Fawthrop and Jarvis 2004.

in-the-making, it was necessary to limit the number of trials—a key point of contestation with the international side of the court.

At the same time, the work of the ECCC also dovetails with the PRK and CPP legitimacy claims to have liberated Cambodia from DK horrors, rebuilt the country, and brought it peace, stability, and now justice—language echoed in the goals stated in the Uncle San booklet. This point has not been lost on the defense teams.

Indeed, this politicization of the court is central to the Nuon Chea defense team's arguments about "the tail of the crocodile," or the post-1979 backdrop to the ECCC. In their Case 002/02 closing brief, for example, the Nuon Chea defense team argues that the PRK atrocity narrative, later inflected by academic, media, and refugee accounts, has produced a dominant "Manichean" view of DK in which the period is viewed in monolithic good and evil terms with "monsters" like Pol Pot and Nuon Chea playing a central role. The "crocodile defense," which echoes the arguments of scholar Michael Vickery about a dominant "Standard Total View" of DK that ignores variation and complexity,[37] argues for an alternative history that largely exonerates Nuon Chea—even as the defense narrative effectively gives its own totalizing "Standard Total View" that, in the end, largely reduces everything to Vietnamese malfeasance.

Their closing brief argues that, unfortunately, the ECCC judges and prosecution more or less took this politicized Manichean narrative for granted.[38] This was, the defense team argued, in no small part due to Cambodian government interference and control over the Cambodian side of the court,[39] which sought to affirm the PRK's Manichean atrocity narrative that enhanced the CPP's legitimacy.[40] The international side of the court was complicit, though Nuon Chea's defense lawyers acknowledged that the 2016 Supreme Court Chamber Case 002/01 appeals ruling had addressed some shortcomings.

If these "tail of the crocodile" arguments are overstated, they nevertheless again highlight the way in which the justice facade erases politics and history as it asserts discourses related to teleological transformation. This obfuscation is critical, since it diverts from a key part of "the truth" the court is supposed to reveal. As the Nuon Chea defense team highlighted, this masking included the PRK atrocity narrative and ways in which such PRK and CPP narratives had influenced the juridical process and findings.

Similarly, the globalism of the transitional justice imaginary diverts attention from the multiple levels and interstices of transitional justice, including how state-level actors like the CPP may co-opt transitional justice for their own purposes.[41] The "global-local" binary obscures such dynamics, including the interests and uses of transitional justice for a variety of domestic, regional, and international actors, including state governments and NGOs.

Finally and as we have seen, transitional justice discourses also shift attention from other transitional efforts, including the "first transition" during the PRK. If the

---

[37] Vickery 2000. See also Nuon Chea Defense Team 2013, 2016. See Ledgerwood 1997 for a contrasting view.
[38] Nuon Chea Defense Team 2017.   [39] Ibid.   [40] Ibid.   [41] Subotic 2009.

PRK atrocity narrative was Manichean in many ways, it also provided a way to help Cambodians begin to come to terms with the past.[42] Cambodians were not simply passive actors who followed the dictates of the state. As is the case with transitional justice, they acted creatively within the constraints and affordances of the moment, including those of state discourse and power. Accordingly, Cambodians attended PRK memorialization events, including days of remembrance and local memorials.

Many Cambodians fused state-level PRK initiatives, including commemorations and the construction of local memorials, with everyday understandings and practices as they began to transact with the spirits of the dead—even if Buddhism remained somewhat muted due to PRK socialist policy.[43] As we shall see, such lived experience, obscured by the justice facade, continued even as Cambodians adapted to new affordances, including those during Cambodia's second transition, the international peace-building and democratization efforts undertaken by UNTAC in the early 1990s.

The Second Transition (UNTAC and Human Rights)

Kassie Neou and human rights

"Democracy in Cambodia is just a one-and-a-half-year-old baby," Kassie Neou, founder and Executive Director of the Cambodian Institute of Human Rights (CIHR), told me as we sat in his office in 1995. He was referring to democratization efforts during UNTAC, which culminated in 1993 elections. This "second transition" in Cambodia had helped create the seeds of a "new generation" to catalyze Cambodia's "transition from autocracy to democracy."[44] According to Neou, however, the success of this transition remained tenuous and "unclear" due to Cambodian tradition.

"To understand human rights in Cambodia," Neou stated, invoking place-making discourses characterizing Cambodia as authoritarian and violent, "you need to know the history of Cambodia, which comes from authoritarian rule," the most recent manifestations of which were "Pol Pot's dictatorship" and the "PRK socialist set-up." He continued, "For thousands of years, Cambodian officials have thought that when … they have the law in their hands, they are the law. When they are the law, they can do anything." He referred to the people who thought like this as "the lost generation."[45]

Like Saray, Neou had been imprisoned during DK. An English teacher, Neou was arrested after being overheard speaking this foreign language. He survived by telling his young captors Aesop's Fables. He chuckled to himself as he recalled that in so doing he was indirectly teaching them about human rights.[46]

While Saray decided to remain in Cambodia after DK, Neou fled to Thailand. He volunteered to work as a US interpreter the day he arrived at a border camp and

[42] Ledgerwood 1997.   [43] Guillou 2012; Harris 2005; Ledgerwood 2012.
[44] Author interview with Kassie Neou, Phnom Penh, June 6, 1995.   [45] Ibid.
[46] Author interview with Kassie Neou, Phnom Penh, March 18, 2016. See also Mydans 1997.

was granted entry to the US two years later in 1981. He would teach English, drive a taxi, and even run a gas station. In 1983, Neou's path crossed with David Hawk, the executive director of Amnesty International USA. Hawk interviewed Neou about his experiences and invited him to tell his story in public. "I didn't plan to become a human rights advocate," Neou told me. "It just grew within me."[47]

As part of his work with Hawk, who would go on to direct the Cambodian Documentation Center in the mid-1980s, Neou began translating human rights documents. This experience served him well when, in 1992, he joined an elite UNTAC team that did translation for top UNTAC officials. Neou's efforts focused in particular on texts related to law and human rights, though he engaged in other activities such as human rights training.[48]

United Nations Transitional Authority in Cambodia

For nearly a decade following DK, the PRK regime, supported by Vietnam and the Soviet bloc, continued to battle the revitalized Khmer Rouge, who renamed themselves the Party of Democratic Kampuchea (PDK) and two other resistance factions, the Khmer People's National Liberation Front (KPNLF) and the royalist National United Front for an Independent, Neutral, Peaceful, and Cooperative Cambodia (FUNCINPEC).[49]

This triad was allowed to jointly represent Cambodia at the UN after 1982. Besides making the PRK regime a pariah state, the decision meant that Cambodia would not have access to key UN and Western non-emergency economic aid, which was sorely needed in the aftermath of DK. During PRK, Cambodia endured international isolation, continued civil war, and the loss of over a quarter million Cambodian refugees living on the Thai border.

This geopolitical stalemate broke with the end of the Cold War in the late 1980s. Following the reductions in Soviet aid and a new geopolitical landscape, in 1989 Vietnam withdrew tens of thousands of its troops, which had been helping the PRK regime battle the Khmer Rouge and other resistance groups for a decade. That year, the PRK renamed itself the State of Cambodia (SOC) and initiated a number of reforms, ranging from expanding property rights to loosening restrictions on Buddhism, to increase the popularity of the government and begin a process intended to transform Cambodia "from a battlefield to a market place."[50]

Such developments laid the groundwork for new peace talks that were launched in Paris in 1989 and culminated in the October 23, 1991 Paris Peace Agreement (PPA), which authorized the UNTAC to hold "free and fair elections" in order to "restore and maintain peace," "promote national reconciliation," repatriate 350,000 refugees, and allow for the "right of self-determination" in Cambodia.[51]

These events took place amidst the post-Cold War "new world order" that seemed to offer new possibilities for global liberal emancipation and peacebuilding. The UN

---

[47] Author interview with Kassie Neou, Phnom Penh, March 18, 2016.   [48] Ibid.
[49] Fawthrop and Jarvis 2004.   [50] See Chandler 2007; Gottesman 2003.
[51] ECCC 2003. See also Heder and Ledgerwood 1996, 244.

"Agenda for Peace" provided a mandate for "preventive diplomacy, peacemaking and peace-keeping" that would enable the UN, after the long Cold War hiatus, to realize its original goals "of maintaining international peace and security [. . . and] securing justice and human rights."[52] Cambodia, a prominent site of geopolitical conflict and stalemate, would be one of its first testing grounds.

At the heart of the PPA was a radical idea: while nominally under the control of a newly created Supreme National Council (SNC) of Cambodia, comprising the representatives of the four warring factions, including the Khmer Rouge, UNTAC personnel would take over key government offices while each Cambodian faction laid down its arms.

UNTAC, which cost over $1.5 billion and involved 16,000 UN soldiers,[53] ran into trouble from its start, beginning with deployment delays. Besides diminishing UNTAC's reputation, the delayed start made it difficult to meet the goals for disarmament and taking control of government offices. Perhaps partly because of this failure, which was crucial to creating a "neutral political environment," the Khmer Rouge, claiming that Vietnamese remained in Cambodia, refused to disarm and eventually pulled out of the election.[54] SOC, in turn, claimed that it could not disarm its army since it was being attacked by the Khmer Rouge. SOC retained far more control of the government than planned and at times used violence to intimidate FUNCINPEC and KPNLF, which continued to participate in the elections.

Despite such setbacks, UNTAC did succeed in some areas.[55] The rehabilitation unit helped rebuild parts of Cambodia's infrastructure, including its roads. Hundreds of thousands of refugees were repatriated. UNTAC's Information/Education section also operated an effective radio station and outreach effort, educating Cambodians about the electoral process. And, in the end, the elections themselves were a success. Over 90 percent of registered voters went to the polls and, after some political in-fighting, a new coalition government was formed even if fighting with the Khmer Rouge would continue.

These events connect to the ECCC in several ways. Since Cambodia was now ruled by an internationally recognized government, countries that had for so long only referred to DK using phrases like "the policies and practices of the past" now began to use the word "genocide" in relationship to DK and to call for the creation of an international tribunal.

The creation of UNTAC also exemplified a key premise of the "new world order," the assumption that more "backward" countries like Cambodia would make the "transition" to liberal democracy after the Cold War. This conception was forcefully laid out in Francis Fukuyama's assertion that the world had reached "the end of history," with the cessation of the Cold War marking "the end point of mankind's ideological evolution and the universalization of Western liberal democracy as the final form of human government."[56]

[52] Boutros Boutros-Ghali 2012.   [53] Heder and Ledgerwood 1996, 27.
[54] On UNTAC, see Roberts 2001; Heder and Ledgerwood 1996.
[55] See Ledgerwood 1994.   [56] Fukuyama 1989, 3.

Drawing on a Hegelian conception of stage theory, or the belief that "mankind has progressed through a series of primitive stages of consciousness on his path to the present," Fukuyama argued that liberalism constituted the "final rational form of society and state," one that is democratic, capitalist, and egalitarian, is governed by the rule of law, and protects human rights and freedoms.[57] "Third World" countries like Cambodia might remain "mired in history" and a "terrain of conflict" for a time, but eventually they would advance to this higher state of "economic and political liberalism."[58] If the idea of transitional justice was still emerging, Fukuyama's ideas directly paralleled its classic imaginary's aspiration for progress and teleological transformation.

In this line of thinking, prevalent after the Cold War, a country like Cambodia could be labeled a "failed state," one that had "descended into violence and anarchy," was characterized by "massive abuses of human rights," and was ultimately "unable to function as independent entities."[59] Such place-making discourses deemphasize or gloss over the complex geopolitical entanglements that fueled conflict in places like Cambodia, instead implicitly depicting them as residing in a primitive state of backwardness and savagery. Such states needed to be "saved," a notion that dovetails with Boutros-Ghali's "agenda for peace" and call for a much greater UN role in post-conflict peacemaking, including facilitating transitions to liberal democracy.

While admirable in sentiment, such teleological conceptions of democratic "transition" oversimplify the realities on the ground and provide a legitimation not just for establishing a liberal democracy, but also opening up new markets. The second transition in Cambodia, despite the successful elections, was anything but smooth, with local power elites, patronage networks, patterns of resource allocation, and political influence undercutting the aspired-for liberal democratic end.[60]

UNTAC and human rights

Another key link between the ECCC and the 1993 elections was UNTAC's attempt to institutionalize human rights and democracy. Human rights discourses had circulated in Cambodia for decades, linked in part to the legacy of French colonialism, study abroad, Khmer nationalism, the independence movement, anti-colonial struggle, and even earlier democratization movements. Neou recalled first hearing about human rights while in primary school around 1953 or 1954, shortly after independence, though the concept was unfamiliar and "didn't capture much attention from the public or the teachers."[61] Human rights discourses were invoked by the Khmer Rouge and discussed by the PRK regime.[62]

The proliferation of human rights, however, was directly linked to the peace negotiations. The KPNLF resistance faction, for example, was a leader in arguing for

---

[57] Ibid, 4, 5.   [58] Ibid, 15.

[59] Helman and Ratner 1993, 3.   [60] See C. Hughes 2003; Roberts 2001; Springer 2015.

[61] Author interview with Kassie Neou, Phnom Penh, March 18, 2016. See also Mydans 1997.

[62] Gottesman 2003.

the insertion of human rights language into the 1991 PPA.[63] Article 15 of the PPA stated that "All persons in Cambodia and all Cambodian refugees and displaced persons shall enjoy the rights and freedoms embodied in the Universal Declaration of Human Rights and other relevant international human rights instruments," which obligated the country to "ensure respect for and observance of human rights and fundamental freedoms" and to "adhere to relevant international human rights instruments."[64] During Cambodia's "transitional period," UNTAC would be tasked with "fostering an environment" in which such human rights would be upheld.[65]

These PPA provisions provide an institutional grounding that gained momentum during the UNTAC period. Cambodia's SNC, the local caretaking governance body, proceeded to sign or accede to a number of international human rights treaties.[66] And, in accordance with the PPA, human rights language and provisions were added to the Cambodian constitution promulgated after the 1993 elections.

Thun Saray and the establishment of ADHOC

The PPA provided Saray with the opportunity to establish ADHOC, the first human rights NGO in Cambodia. Doing so had not been easy. Saray and Vandy Kaonn had gained a degree of independence during the 1980s while running the Institute of Sociology.[67] In 1989, Kaonn, who had become increasingly critical of the government, fled the country, leaving Saray in charge.[68] Saray's second arrest soon followed.

Kaonn's departure took place just as the political situation in Cambodia was beginning to change. In late 1989, a group of Saray's friends decided to form a new political party, the Free Social Democratic Party (FSDP).[69] The following May, the government arrested the group, including Saray who had been given a copy of the group's platform. "I was just curious," Saray explained. "I only got a few papers, like this," he added, holding up a tiny stack of papers. "Then they put me in a dark cell . . . with shackles. It was hot and there was not enough air to breath."[70]

It was because of this experience that Saray established ADHOC. He explained, "It is not acceptable for people in power to [treat Cambodians] like animals or slaves, killing, torturing, and putting them in jail" without cause. "We had the Khmer Rouge already, why again?" Saray continued, "So after I was released I set up [ADHOC]. . . . We cannot accept this anymore and have to change society, doing education on human rights, monitoring human rights. That is our main task from 1992 until now,"[71] an aim reflected by ADHOC's mission (creating "a society that respects human rights and law").[72]

[63] Author interview with Lao Mong Hay, Phnom Penh, February 7, 2012.
[64] United Nations, "Agreements on a Comprehensive Political Settlement of the Cambodia Conflict", Paris, October 23, 1991, Article 15.
[65] Ibid, Article 16.
[66] United Nations Human Rights Office of the High Commissioner, "Reporting Status for Cambodia," undated.
[67] Gottesman 2003, 219.   [68] Ibid, 305.   [69] Ibid, 339.
[70] Author interview with Thun Saray, Phnom Penh, March 11, 2016.
[71] Ibid.
[72] "Vision, Mission and Goals," ADHOC website (http://www.adhoc-cambodia.org).

After seventeen months in jail, Saray and the leaders of the FSDP were released just prior to the signing of the October 23, 1991 PPA and as PRK changed its name to the State of Cambodia and announced liberalization reforms.[73] By December, Saray was working with fellow former prisoners to draft bylaws to establish ADHOC.[74] When the SNC first met in mid-January 1992, it announced that, in keeping with the PPA, it would allow the formation of political parties, NGOs, and trade unions. The next day Saray and his colleagues submitted their application to establish their NGO. They received a letter of approval from Hun Sen in mid-March.[75]

From the start, Saray and his colleagues faced political intimidation. Even as he worked on the bylaws, Saray was being tracked by police. "They followed me, watched me—even around my house. And they sent threats through my relatives and friends."[76] This is the reason he held a press conference immediately after submitting his application to the SNC. The intimidation continued. On the day Saray received the letter of approval to establish ADHOC, one of his colleagues died under suspicious circumstances.[77] As illustrated by Saray's 2016 flight from Cambodia and the 2017 media and opposition party crackdown, the intimidation has continued into the present.

ADHOC quickly commenced operation. In mid-1992, ADHOC held the first of 650 UNTAC-era training courses.[78] By the end of the year, the NGO had over 10,000 members and had opened ten offices, some on the grounds of pagodas.[79] Eventually, ADHOC would establish a network of human rights offices, staffers, and volunteers that encompassed 171 districts throughout Cambodia.[80] If ADHOC's initial efforts focused on human rights training, monitoring, advocacy, and assistance, it also worked on related issues such as land rights, women's and children's rights, dispute resolution, and, eventually, the ECCC.[81] During this early phase, ADHOC, like a small but growing number of other new human rights NGOs, received support from UNTAC's Human Rights Component.

The UNTAC Human Rights Component

UNTAC's Human Rights Component (HRC) sought to further promote the institutionalization of human rights through a number of initiatives, including monitoring, investigation, training, and education.[82] The HRC, however, faced a number of problems, including being understaffed and underfunded.

In its final report, the HRC stated that, upon "UNTAC's arrival, Cambodian society was singularly lacking in the basic institutions and structures upon which the safeguarding of fundamental human rights depends," including an "independent judiciary, an effective and non-political bureaucracy, a professional police force, a

---

[73] Author interview with Thun Saray, Phnom Penh, March 11, 2016; Gottesman 2003, 344–45.
[74] Author interview with Thun Saray, Phnom Penh, March 11, 2016; Gottesman 2003, 346.
[75] Author interview with Thun Saray, Phnom Penh, June 28, 2009.
[76] Author interview with Thun Saray, Phnom Penh, March 11, 2016; see also Gottesman 2003, 347.
[77] Author interview with Thun Saray, Phnom Penh, March 11, 2016; Gottesman 2003, 344–45.
[78] Palan 1994.   [79] Munthit 1992.   [80] Raab and Polunda 2010, 8.
[81] "ADHOC's Background," ADHOC website (http://www.adhoc-cambodia.org).
[82] UNTAC Human Rights Component (HRC) 1993; C. Hughes 1996; Ledgerwood and Un 2003.

free press, and human rights and other non-governmental organizations representing popular interests." Human rights were a critical part of a "peacebuilding package" that would restore "a capacity for good governance" and facilitate "a genuine transition to democracy."[83]

The unit perhaps had its most success in the area of education, which a UN report had identified as "the cornerstone" of efforts to "foster" a human rights environment.[84] To this end, the HRC undertook a range of formal to non-formal educational initiatives.[85] If 90,000 students attended human rights courses during the UNTAC period, many more learned about human rights through the extensive mass media campaign that included the use of radio, television, leaflets, slogans, posters, videos, and stickers. The HRC sought to make its educational content "culturally relevant" by ensuring its human rights messages "would be consonant with concepts and principle of Cambodian society."[86]

These efforts included simplification and the use of Cambodian traditions and idioms, including Cambodian music, songs, and storytelling. They also introduced a comic and created programming featuring dialogues between Cambodian characters referred to as "Uncle," "Auntie," "Niece," and "Nephew."[87] If such fusions of international human rights norms and everyday Cambodian understandings had begun in the Thai border camps, UNTAC initiatives in this regard were undertaken on a vast scale and with more resources.

While the HRC held training sessions for key target groups such as judges, defenders, educators, and police, it also sought to "train the trainers" who could continue human rights work after UNTAC.[88] Human rights NGOs were of particular importance since the HRC recognized that its work was "only the beginning of a long term process tied in part to a successful transition to democratic government" that would be carried on by such groups.[89]

Besides training, the HRC provided direct grants to NGOs.[90] This pattern—in which international actors would provide funding to democracy and human rights NGOs in Cambodia to undertake work linked to the donor's democratic transition objectives—was also evident during the KRT.[91]

Cambodian human rights NGOs

It was in this context that ADHOC and a number of NGOs focusing on human rights, democratization, and the rule of law were established. KID, established in 1992, was among the first. Others that would play a prominent role in ECCC outreach included: the Cambodian Defenders Project (1994) and a group that would splinter from it, Legal Aid of Cambodia (1995); the Center for Social Development

---

[83] UNTAC HRC 1993, 1.   [84] Boutros Boutros-Ghali, "Report," 3.
[85] UNTAC HRC 1993, 48.   [86] UNTAC HRC 1993, 58. See also Marston 1997.
[87] UNTAC HRC 1993, 61; Ledgerwood and Un 2003, 535.
[88] UNTAC HRC 1993, 54f.   [89] Ibid, 9.   [90] Ibid, 55.
[91] Christie 2013; C. Hughes 2003, 2009; Sperfeldt 2012a, 2013.

(1995); and the Documentation Center of Cambodia (1997).[92] ADHOC would also take a lead in this regard.

In 1992, three other important human rights or human rights-related NGOs also opened, the Khmer Buddhist Society in Cambodia (linked to Cambodian refugees in Seattle), the Cambodian League for the Promotion and Defense of Human Rights (LICADHO) headed by a Franco-Khmer doctor (1992), and Neou's Cambodian Institute of Human Rights (CIHR) (1992). By 1995, fueled in part by donor funding, the number of NGOs had risen sharply, including at least ten focused on human rights. The numbers would continue to rise.[93]

Like Neou, many of these leaders had lived abroad for many years, where they obtained degrees while being exposed to liberal democratic norms and practices that informed their human rights work and enabled them to serve as intermediaries between the international human rights regime and on-the-ground realities in Cambodia. This knowledge often also helped them procure significant donor support.

These civil society actors and their organizations confronted the issue of how to translate liberal democratic concepts and practices in the Cambodian context. As we shall see in later chapters, their work was informed by a variety of factors, such as the NGO's mission, staff composition, donor aid, international and domestic networks, sociopolitical constraints, and leadership experience and vision. UNTAC facilitated these efforts by building the human rights infrastructure in Cambodia through training, the ratification of human rights instruments, the creation of a local UN Centre for Human Rights, constitutional safeguards, and so forth.

From these different streams, the NGOs began to develop practices that sometimes echoed the work of the UNTAC HRC. Some undertook monitoring efforts looking for human rights abuses during elections, at courts, and in everyday life. They also launched training and educational efforts, including the use of mass media. In terms of messaging, the human rights NGOs also often used simplification, story-like dialogue, and comics, which were more accessible given low levels of literacy in Cambodia. The KID booklet followed from this tradition.

The UNTAC HRC, viewing monks as "a particularly effective vehicle for reaching the public at large, especially in remote areas,"[94] targeted monks for training and used pagodas as a venue for human rights education. At this time Buddhism was in the midst of a resurgence and provided a key basis of moral authority in Cambodia. Building on work done in the camps and by UNTAC, a number of NGOs sought to graft human rights ideas in the Cambodian context through Buddhism.[95]

Kassie Neou, translation, and CIHR

Neou was one of the strongest proponents of using Buddhist concepts and other vernaculars to teach human rights. His view in this regard dated back to the 1980s when

---

[92] C. Hughes 1998, 375f. [93] C. Hughes 2003, 142; see also Yonekura 1999.
[94] UNTAC HRC 1993, 56. [95] Dobbs 1992.

David Hawk asked Neou to translate the Universal Declaration of Human Rights (UDHR) into Khmer. When Hawk gave Neou a formal, complicated version of the Declaration, Neou said, "I can translate it, but who is going to understand it? If you do a word to word translation it is not understandable."[96] So they changed course and produced "a simple version of the UDHR in Khmer, vernacular Khmer – not academic Khmer. In very simple spoken words." Later they would distribute 50,000 copies in border areas.[97]

This experience influenced Neou's subsequent work. "This is my style of translation until today," he told me. "Many of my friends translate word for word. When it comes to concepts of human rights [and] international law, you cannot transfer word for word. You have to say something else that has the meaning of that concept. That's what I did."

To illustrate, Neou turned to Buddhism. "The right to life," he began, "is linked to the first of the five Buddhist precepts. No killing. Simple. The right to life is no killing. And [it's easy] when you know how to link [such human rights concepts] to existing pieces of culture. They see it right away."[98]

In a 1997 essay, "Teaching Human Rights in Cambodia," Neou stated that the life of the Buddha provided evidence that democracy had "historical roots" in Cambodia, including notions of "democratic systems and good governance."[99] After recounting a Buddhist story to support this idea, Neou added that, in Cambodian villages, decisions were often made "democratically" by village elders.

CIHR drew on such ideas in its human rights training program, including the creation of a "Human Rights Teaching Methodology" used to train thousands of Cambodian teachers. CIHR also created copious instructional materials, including comics. The NGO's human rights initiatives were supported by a wide range of donors, including "Western governments and international organizations."[100]

Neou stressed that, in the end, the intermediaries CIHR trained were best suited to teach their communities about human rights. To illustrate, Neou recalled how teacher trainees had elaborated on ideas like the right to life, extending it to "animal life. Some people went on to nature, the trees because we depend on them too. We thought we were the experts, but when we go to their community, they are!"[101]

Monks, Neou asserted, were particularly effective. "They were trained to preach. They know [the] Buddha stories and they read them over and over. All we need to do is to give them another tool from our side, the human rights message [to use] where they see fit."[102] Human rights and Buddhism, Neou stated, dovetailed in terms of their ultimate goal: human harmony. "To live together we need to respect each other's rights ... And these rights are all in the Buddha stories. The message is there."

---

[96] Author interview with Kassie Neou, Phnom Penh, March 18, 2016.   [97] Ibid.
[98] Ibid. See also Neou and Gallup 1997.
[99] Neou and Gallup 1997, 160. On human rights NGOs drawing on Buddhism, see also C. Hughes 1998, 2001; Ledgerwood and Un 2003; Marks 2005; and Marston 1991.
[100] Neou and Gallup 1997, 157–58, 159.
[101] Author interview with Kassie Neou, Phnom Penh, March 18, 2016.   [102] Ibid.

This synergy, Neou contended, meant that monks could teach about human rights "much better than us. You'd go sit and listen to them and think, 'Oh my God, this man is a genius!'" The monks would "convey the message within the story without any interruption ... So smooth! They were trained in that particular skill. We just gave them an additional tool."[103] Buddhism would likewise play a role in the translation of transitional justice during Cambodia's third transition.

The Third Transition (ECCC)

Behind the justice facade (the uneven path to the ECCC)

While periodically discussed, the possibility of a trial of former DK leaders became more realistic after UNTAC. The 1996 defection of Ieng Sary and his supporters, which splintered the Khmer Rouge movement, marked a pivotal moment in the building of momentum for a trial. It was in this context that, in April 1997, the UN Commission on Human Rights passed a resolution offering to consider any requests "for assistance in responding to past serious violations of Cambodian and international law."[104] Two months later the Cambodian co-Prime Ministers, Norodom Ranariddh and Hun Sen, responded by formally requesting UN assistance in "bringing to justice" those responsible for the Khmer Rouge genocide.[105]

Kofi Annan then appointed a "Group of Experts" to assess the feasibility of holding a tribunal. Their February 19, 1999 report recommended the establishment of an international ad hoc tribunal modeled after the ICTY and ICTR (the International Criminal Tribunals for the former Yugoslavia and Rwanda). The new court, they suggested, should be held in a nearby country and try former Khmer Rouge leaders for crimes committed during DK, a temporal frame mandated by the UN Secretary-General.[106]

The progressivist aspirations of the transitional justice imaginary are also evident in the Group of Experts report, which highlighted some of the many transitional justice benefits a Khmer Rouge tribunal would deliver, including: "a sense of justice," "promoting internal peace and national reconciliation," increasing understanding, prevention, healing, repair, "closure," and "strengthening democracy" and "the rule of law."[107] Many of these goals would be incorporated into ECCC law and appear in related transitional justice imaginary discourses, including those manifest in the KID booklet.

By 1999, however, the political situation in Cambodia had changed. In July 1997, Hun Sen's CPP launched a coup that ousted First Prime Minister Norodom

---

[103] Ibid.
[104] UNHCR 1997. On the negotiations, see Ciorciari and Heindel 2014; Fawthrop and Jarvis 2004; Meisenberg and Stegmiller 2016; Scheffer 2011.
[105] Lallah, Stephen, and Ratner 1999, paragraph 5.   [106] Ibid, paragraphs 10, 6.
[107] Ibid, *passim*.

Ranariddh and his FUNCINPEC party, which had received the most votes in the 1993 UNTAC elections.

A catalyst for the violence was the incipient implosion of the Khmer Rouge. When Ieng Sary's faction defected in 1996, Hun Sen and Ranariddh competed to forge alliances with the defectors. Pol Pot was toppled by his former revolutionaries on June 10, 1997 after ordering the execution of his former DK Minister of Defense, Son Sen. Ironically, Pol Pot was tried by a Khmer Rouge kangaroo court and placed under house arrest until his death on April 15, 1998, even as the U.S. and its allies were close to taking custody of him in advance of a trial.[108] Nuon Chea and Khieu Samphan defected later that year, effectively ending the revolutionary movement.

Shortly afterward, Nuon Chea and Khieu Samphan were given baskets of flowers and feted at a luxury hotel. During a press conference, Khieu Samphan said that people should "let bygones be bygones" and "forget the past," a sentiment echoed by Nuon Chea.[109] Hun Sen stated, "We should dig a hole and bury the past and look ahead to the 21st century with a clean slate."[110]

Hun Sen was widely criticized for these statements. While he no doubt had genuine concerns that a trial of the leaders of the defecting Khmer Rouge factions might undermine a newly emerging peace after roughly thirty years of war, he and his PRK and later CPP colleagues had, since the 1979 PRT trial, been seeking to hold "the Pol Pot clique" accountable for their crimes. Indeed, they had staked their legitimacy on liberating Cambodians from the DK regime. This was part of the impetus that had led the government to start discussions about creating a tribunal in 1997.

Accordingly, at the same time Hun Sen made the above statements, he reassured a UN official involved in the negotiations that he agreed "completely that there must be justice ... I promise you that no one will be spared."[111] Hun Sen was partly playing to two audiences, advocating for peace and forgiveness in domestic public appearances aimed at Khmer Rouge defectors and internal constituencies opposed to an international court while continuing to seek a tribunal in discussions with the UN and Western counterparts.

The tension between the protection of a long-awaited peace and the desire to finally try the senior DK leaders would continue to inform negotiations for a tribunal, centering largely around the issue of how many suspects should be tried. On the second day of Case 001, for example, Hun Sen, echoing comments he had made as far back as 1999,[112] warned against indicting more suspects beyond the five detainees currently in custody, stating "I would prefer to see this tribunal fail instead of seeing war return to my country."[113] Sometimes he invoked a Cambodian proverb, "If a wound does not hurt, you should not poke at it with a stick to make it bleed."[114] Hun Sen's position would be supported by Cambodian court personnel at the ECCC on a number of occasions, one of many signs of political interference highlighted by defense lawyers.

---

[108] Scheffer 2011.   [109] Mydans 1998a.   [110] Mydans 1998b.   [111] Ibid.
[112] Giry 2012.   [113] Madra 2009.   [114] Mydans 1998b.

For the most part, the international side pushed for additional trials, arguing that this was critical for the legitimacy of the court. Others suggested that Hun Sen's statements about restricting the number of trials was also linked to his desire to avoid opening investigations that might implicate him or other members of the CPP who had Khmer Rouge pasts.[115]

Defense lawyers were quick to jump on these suggestions of political interference and bias. During a 2009 Pre-Trial Chamber (PTC) hearing, for example, Vergès, deploying his strategy of rupture, raised the issue of corruption at the court. When stopped by the PTC judge, Vergès replied that he would not continue because he wanted to give the court the "presumption of innocence" sometimes denied to the accused. "And I shall also remain silent," he continued, "because the head of ... this state [Hun Sen], has publically said that he wants this Chamber to be brought to a conclusion. In a sense, you are mere squatters."[116] He added, "It's not good to [shoot] on ambulances and victims and the wounded.... [or] dying people or institutions."

Defense lawyers would press this point. The Nuon Chea defense team's Case 002/02 closing brief highlighted the fact that their attempts to call high-ranking witnesses, including Hun Sen, had been denied without justification. This was part of a larger pattern of failure to look at exculpatory evidence, the brief stated, including key witnesses and transcripts related to a documentary about Nuon Chea, "Enemies of the People."[117]

Such refusals, the brief argued, demonstrated the politicization of a court that was controlled by the CPP, adhered to its Manichean atrocity narrative, and avoided evidence and testimony that could implicate CPP officials. Indeed, defense lawyers had repeatedly requested that both Cambodian and international judges be removed due to bias. They cited critiques of the Case 002/01 judgment as further evidence of bias and incompetence that, instead of revealing the truth, had instead led to "a complete farce" and exercise in "victor's justice."[118]

Already then, even before the 2003 Agreement was signed, there were many signs of international and domestic tensions that would haunt the court. As the deliberations continued, both sides showed ambivalence. To secure peace, the Cambodian government back-tracked, alternatively suggesting that the country hold a truth and reconciliation commission, a domestic trial of just Ta Mok, or a predominantly national tribunal.[119] The UN side, in turn, remained wary of the weakness and politicization of Cambodia's judiciary, political influence more broadly, and the possible taint of a UN-sanctioned court that failed to meet international standards.[120]

The negotiations that ensued between the UN and the Cambodian government were characterized by stops and starts, miscommunications, and compromise, as the two parties worked to create a new type of transitional justice mechanism, a "mixed" or "hybrid" tribunal, a model that would be used elsewhere even before the ECCC finally began operation on July 3, 2006.

---

[115] Giry 2012.   [116] Khieu Samphan Pre-Trial Appeal Hearing, April 3, 2009, 47.
[117] Nuon Chea Defense Team 2017.   [118] Ibid, 3, 8.
[119] See Etcheson 2006, 8–9; "Report of the Group of Experts," 3.
[120] Scheffer 2011.

Ultimately, the 2003 Agreement established a hybrid tribunal that would be a special chamber within the Cambodian court system and use a combination of domestic and international law and rely on a complicated judicial voting system established as a check on domestic political influence.[121] A "supermajority" of judges is required for conviction and to prevent a case from moving forward, thereby ensuring that at least one foreign judge must join any decision made by the PTC (four out of five judges), Trial Chamber (four out of five judges), or Supreme Court Chamber (five out of seven judges), each of which has a majority of Cambodian jurists. Similar checks were placed on the Office of the Co-investigating Judges to prevent one judge from stymieing a case. Even after the agreement was signed and the court commenced operation, the international and domestic sides continued to disagree over given issues, including the internal rules, the scope of civil party participation, and the number of trials.

Like other tribunals, the early ECCC deliberations failed to specify how victim participation would be administered. Local NGOs, many of which traced their origins to the second transitional and related human rights initiatives, initially stepped in to fill this void, serving as key intermediaries between the court and the Cambodian population. If the transitional justice imaginary masks complicated histories, such as Cambodia's two earlier transitions, and depicts time in a simplified, progressive manner, this facade, as we shall see, also obscures complicated processes, practices, and acts of imagination that take place within these NGO outreach "eddies."

ADHOC and KRT Outreach

Like other NGOs, ADHOC's KRT outreach activities drew on their existing strengths that were repurposed for the current moment. ADHOC's interest in the ECCC extended back to the late 1990s. Saray pointed to the late December 1998 moment when, after Nuon Chea and Khieu Samphan defected, Hun Sen stated that Cambodian's should "forget the past."[122]

"We could not accept this," Saray said. "We need to have justice and peace, not peace and forget the past … We didn't agree with the position of the government. This is the reason why from that time on we did a lot of advocacy campaigns to have the Khmer Rouge tribunal."[123] The NGO's first response was to lead a pro-tribunal petition effort resulting in the collection of roughly 80,000 signatures and thumbprints.[124]

At this time, a number of events related to transitional justice were underway, such as the 1998 passage of the Rome Statutes establishing the International Criminal Court. ADHOC worked with the French-based international human rights organization FIDH (International Federation for Human Rights) and other groups to push for Cambodia's ratification, which took place in early 2002. Building on these efforts, ADHOC received a major grant of over one million Euros to launch a project largely focused on ECCC outreach.

---

[121] ECCC 2003.   [122] Mydans 1998a.
[123] Author interview with Thun Saray, Phnom Penh, March 11, 2016.
[124] Ibid; Raab and Polunda 2010, 7.

This first phase of ADHOC's KRT project was launched in December 2006. ADHOC initially engaged in more monologic outreach efforts meant to provide people with basic information about the tribunal. These efforts involved roughly 103,000 "ordinary" Cambodians from across the country, "including 'multipliers' such as local officials, teachers and monks," who attended "participatory outreach workshops."[125] ADHOC later began including more detailed information about victim participation and assisting civil parties, who eventually became its primary focus.

In contrast to some of the other NGOs who had difficulty finding funding after the ECCC's Victims Support Section began operation, ADHOC was able to procure support from Oxfam Novib for a second phase of its KRT project once its European Union funding ended on March 31, 2010. The second phase centered almost exclusively on civil party participation as Case 002 got underway, with ADHOC assisting almost half (1,791) of the 3,866 civil party applicants.[126]

During this second phase, ADHOC efforts were two-pronged, focusing on keeping the civil parties informed and facilitating their legal representation. Given the large number of Case 002 civil party applicants, ADHOC developed a Civil Party Representative (CPR) scheme in which 122 of the civil parties served as "focal point" liaisons between ADHOC, the lawyers, the court, and civil parties who lived in their areas.[127]

As was the case with the first phase of its KRT project, ADHOC grafted its phase two outreach onto its existing strengths and structures—in this case its country-wide network of local human rights offices and staff. While there were variations and multiple flows of information and interactions, the ADHOC headquarters often provided information and training to its ADHOC regional staff, who—along with civil party lawyers—did the same for the ADHOC CPRs who, in turn, interfaced with local civil parties at periodic meetings.[128]

If, like other NGOs, ADHOC sometimes used simplification to help villagers understand unfamiliar legal concepts and processes, they appear to have done so less than some of the others. From the start, Saray noted, ADHOC had used the PPA and key human rights documents as part of their training, though they would sometimes draw on local literature or Buddhism.[129] More broadly, Saray argued, the concept of human rights was not a foreign imposition but a long-standing idea in Cambodian history and culture. ADHOC had made this argument in the 1990s to counter "Asian values" claims by then co-Prime Minister Norodom Ranariddh.

To illustrate, Saray recalled the famous Buddhist story of Prince Vessandara, who was so generous he was willing to give away all of his possessions, including his children. At one point, after Vessandara gave away a magic elephant that had helped his country prosper, he was sent into exile. The story, Saray said, shows that, "even if you are king, you cannot decide on your own. You have to respect the interests of the

---

[125] "Khmer Rouge Tribunal Project," ADHOC website (http://www.adhoc-cambodia.org). See also Raab and Polunda 2010, 8.

[126] "Khmer Rouge Tribunal Project," ADHOC website. "Statistics: Civil Party applicants per Case File," ECCC website (https://www.eccc.gov). See also Balthazard 2013.

[127] "Khmer Rouge Tribunal Project," ADHOC website. Kirchenbauer et al. 2013.

[128] Balthazard 2013, 16. See also "Khmer Rouge Tribunal Project," ADHOC website.

[129] Author interview with Thun Saray, Phnom Penh, March 11, 2016.

people. That is democracy and it existed already a long time ago in Buddhist theory. The right to life. That democratic principle is also there ... [as well as] the right to protest against the decision of the leader."[130] Everybody in Cambodia, Saray added, was familiar with this story.

If generally supportive of the ECCC itself, Saray also had ambivalence and acknowledged the tribunal's shortcomings. In response to the accusation that the court was mere "victor's justice," Saray replied that "there is no perfect justice" and that injustices were infrequently addressed due to real-world politics. "Progress is step by step," he stated, adding that all tribunals offered an "imperfect justice" in the end.[131] But this "limited justice for the victims" and "the dissuasive effect of the trials" were nevertheless worthwhile. Acknowledging the Cambodian government's concerns, Saray also noted that the trials needed to strike a "balance between justice and peace."

At the same time, he was well aware of the limitations of Cambodia's judiciary and a host of other problems that Cambodia faced, including structural violence and political intimidation. Indeed, from its inception, ADHOC had been directly involved in these other issues that were pushed out of sight by the dehistoricizing and depoliticizing discourses of the transitional justice imaginary at the ECCC.

As illustrated by Saray's 2016 flight from the country, and the 2017 media and opposition crackdown, throughout the ECCC trial proceedings there were numerous incidents and reports about political intimidation and the politicization of the Cambodian judiciary—including controversies about the Cambodian judicial officials serving at the ECCC. Meanwhile, the long-term poverty and structural disempowerment of the poor remained unacknowledged. As noted in my introduction, the transitional justice literature has increasingly recognized this gap in classic, techno-legalistic conceptions of the transitional justice imaginary, arguing for the need to attend to such economic factors. Others have contended that transitional justice is closely bound up with neoliberalism, which, as opposed to liberating Cambodians, has contributed to structural violence, landlessness, disempowerment, and poverty.[132]

From Saray's perspective within one of the "eddies" that intersected with the transitional justice apparatus, the tribunal would not lead to a utopian state of liberal democracy. It was one small step in a process, one that had the possibility to help the human rights situation in Cambodia by offering a different vision for what might be possible. "If we cannot have justice in society," he would say, "how can we reduce poverty?" The KRT could be beneficial in this regard by presenting an alternative that might spark the imagination, as Cambodian judges learned from the "international process" and people "watch a fair trial and compare it with trials they have seen in the past, and in the future."[133]

If many people discuss such a transitional justice "legacy" in places like Cambodia, the "legacy" is often defined in very different ways, ranging from the utopian

---

[130] Ibid.   [131] Saray 2006.   [132] Springer 2015.
[133] Saray 2006, 111. On the possible legacies of the ECCC, see also Hinton 2017.

progressive aspirations of the transitional justice imaginary to the more pragmatic and limited possibilities imagined by Saray. As this chapter has shown, the idea of "progress" manifest in the transitional justice imaginary—in the sense of a singular movement from a time and place (Point A) to "a better" time and space (Point B)—is highly problematic as it depoliticizes and dehistoricizes.

Instead of a singular, cascade-like current suggested by the transitional justice imaginary, mechanisms like the ECCC must take account of and be understood in terms of much longer histories and political dynamics. To explain away Cambodia's past in terms of temporal and place-making discourses (as "backward," "authoritarian," "violent" and so forth) is to obscure politics and history behind the justice facade. Instead, we need to explore what lies below this surface-level view. The next two chapters build upon this one by examining more NGO "eddies" within which transitional justice unfolds and in which the global-local binary of the transitional justice imaginary breaks down. This will become evident in the next chapter, which focuses on KID, including the creation of the Uncle San booklet.

2

Time (The Khmer Institute of Democracy)

"He finds what he wants."

Nou Va, a former Khmer Institute of Democracy (KID) Khmer Rouge Tribunal (KRT) project leader in his mid-thirties, is pointing at the modernity dream bubble on the last page of the Uncle San booklet. "He wants justice. Now he has filed a complaint. He gets justice. He gets what he wants. Then everything is finished. He lives peacefully."[1]

We sit at a table in a large, second floor room at the non-governmental organization (NGO) Youth for Peace, where Nou Va moved in 2009 after working at KID for four years. On the walls around us are photographs and watercolor paintings related to Youth for Peace's work with youth, survivors, and monks.

When I first met with Nou Va in 2011, he told me about some of his new KRT outreach duties at Youth for Peace. I was interested, but I had come to try to solve a puzzle: How and why had the Uncle San booklet been created? And how was it related to the NGO's broader goals and practices as well as the court and transitional justice more broadly? When I inquired at KID, I was told that Nou Va had been a key part of KID's KRT outreach project and involved in the creation of the booklet, an effort led by his associate "Suon," who now worked for an international organization.

Our discussion had quickly turned to the KID booklet, including a page-by-page discussion of its content. When Nou Va arrived at the last page, he suddenly flipped back to the graphic in which Uncle San is afflicted by the trauma of the past. "On this earlier page," Nou Va began, pointing at Uncle San, "he lives in a bad [state], nightmares." Uncle San's memories of the Khmer Rouge past, he continued, were on "his mind every day, every night." Flipping back to the modernity dream bubble page, Nou Va stated, "Then at the end, after he gets information about the ECCC [Extraordinary Chambers in the Courts of Cambodia], participates, files a complaint—after the KRT finishes … his dreams are better." The page illustrated, Nou Va would later tell me, "the hope" for and "imagination of development" in the peaceful future.[2]

By juxtaposing the two pages in the booklet (see Figures 2.1 and 2.2), Nou Va had inadvertently highlighted its transitional teleology as well as its related assumptions about time (particular conceptions of duration, including constructions of

---

[1] Author interview with Nou Va, Phnom Penh, June 30, 2011.
[2] Nou Va, e-mail communication, May 23, 2017.

Figure 2.1 Uncle San dozing with no more bad dreams. "Uncle San, Aunty Yan, and the KRT," p. 33. *Reprinted by permission of the Khmer Institute of Democracy.*

Figure 2.2 Uncle San's Nightmares. "Uncle San, Aunty Yan, and the KRT," p. 5. *Reprinted by permission of the Khmer Institute of Democracy.*

"the past") and temporality (the lived experience of time). In keeping with the teleology and progressivist aspirations of the transitional justice imaginary, the booklet depicts time as linear and scalar (having vertical directionality and magnitude, or a graded weighting as illustrated by stage theory).

Thus, Uncle San is depicted as living in a static, backward, ineffective state characterized by frequent nightmares. Then he enters the timescape of the transitional justice imaginary and everything speeds up as he files a complaint and achieves "what he wants" and enters a new space of justice, peace, and healing. Here the discursivity of the transitional justice imaginary in terms of time is revealed as it defines a before, during, and after that involves a lack (the inability to "move forward"), asserted desire ("justice" and modernity), and related subjectivity (the trauma victim who needs empowerment). As a discourse, the transitional justice imaginary is also bound up with power, as the reality it asserts involves specific claims, including about what time is as well as who passes through it—and when, how, and why this happens.

If the last chapter highlighted some of the complicated historical currents shaping Cambodia's current transitional justice moment, this chapter illustrates how they are manifest in one "vortex" in the ECCC assemblage, KID, the vision of the NGO's leaders and staff, and one key artifact related to these efforts, the creation of the Uncle San booklet. In doing so, the chapter seeks a dynamic approach that moves beyond the reductive "global/local" binary to see how transitional justice is understood, practiced, and experienced on the ground and through time: precisely the sort of lived experience amidst the interstices of the transitional justice assemblage that is masked by the justice facade.

Khmer Institute of Democracy

Lao Mong Hay and the origins of KID

"No law means barbarity. Law is the expression of reason. And when law ends, that's it: dictatorship."

For Lao Mong Hay, who headed KID from 1995 to 2002, the purpose of human rights and democratization efforts in Cambodia was clear. While taking a long-term perspective and well aware of the geopolitical machinations in Cambodia, Lao viewed the United Nations Transitional Authority in Cambodia (UNTAC) and the establishment of human rights NGOs like KID as a way to combat the "feudal system, authoritarianism, [and] dictatorial rule" that had long plagued Cambodia.

These efforts to promote the rule of law in Cambodia, Lao told me, were a "civilizing mission," an effort launched by foreign countries and donors that Lao viewed positively and as successful. "UNTAC had a civilizing mission," he told me during an interview. "Our people changed from being subjects to being citizens."[3] His own efforts in running KID, including his establishment of the NGO's Citizen Advisor program, were devoted to such rule of law advocacy.[4]

KID was one of the first Cambodian human rights and democratization NGOs, launched on October 6, 1992 at the beginning of Cambodia's second transition. Its establishment by a group of Cambodian-Americans and Ambassador Julio Jeldres[5] reflected the NGO's attempt to mainstream democracy and human rights norms in Cambodia.

In part because of the donor-driven movement to localize Cambodian NGOs, Lao was appointed Executive Director of KID in early 1995. Like Kassie Neou, Lao, who was in England when the Democratic Kampuchea (DK) regime took power, came to his position after living abroad for many years. He returned to Site

---

[3] Author interview with Lao Mong Hay, Phnom Penh, March 7, 2016.

[4] Author interview with Lao Mong Hay, Phnom Penh, February 7, 2012; see also C. Hughes 1998, 219.

[5] "The Khmer Institute of Democracy," KID homepage, http://www3.online.com.kh.

2 on the Thai-Cambodian border in 1988 to work as an official for the Khmer People's National Liberation Front (KPNLF) resistance faction.[6]

In these capacities, Lao was directly involved in efforts to promote human rights and democracy in the border camps. At KPNLF leader Son Sann's behest, the Human Rights unit translated the Universal Declaration of Human Rights and began training a new generation of civil servants. Lao taught some of the courses.[7] "We brought to the Cambodian communities on the border—and later, inside the country—the concepts of human rights, the rule of law, and democracy," Lao recalled in an interview. "Later on when people were repatriated ... the seeds of human rights and democracy were [there]."[8]

Lao was invited to take the helm of KID in early 1995. His background and interests fit with the KID's mission "to foster democratic values" and "promote a liberal democratic order as determined by the Paris Peace Agreement of 1991, based on a multi-party liberal democracy system [and] human rights."[9]

Already, the human rights and democracy NGOs were creating distinct ways of approaching these issues. The traditions that each developed, while shifting over time in accordance with the given historical moment, were influenced by factors including funding, size, mission, and the vision of the leaders.[10]

Thus if KID previously had a more confrontational approach, Lao, while one of the more critical civil society leaders, emphasized dialogue.[11] He saw the UNTAC-era arrival of human rights in Cambodia as part of a long process. Like Neou, Lao noted that there were strong resonances between notions of democratization and human rights and long-standing Cambodian Buddhist principles, village-level practices, and literature and folk tales.[12]

At the same time, he pointed to alternative traditions of strong centralized power and patronage that had dominated Cambodian politics through the French colonial era. Toward the end of the colonial rule, Lao stated, "Western ideas" began to circulate more freely due to improved communications, the introduction of print media, the growing presence of French and other foreigners, and the emergence of new educated elites.[13] Nationalism also increased at this time, particularly after World War II, brief Japanese occupation, and the subsequent collapse of French Indochina.

In an attempt to stave off Cambodian independence, the French granted Cambodians the right to establish political parties, an assembly, and a constitution. The new Consultative Assembly, elected in 1946, was dominated by the progressive Democratic party, led by Prince Yuthevong who had been educated in France and sought to bring its democratic practices to Cambodia.[14] Accordingly, the new constitution that was developed over the next year was inspired by France and empowered the Assembly. "Democracy was born in Cambodia in 1947 when the

---

[6] "Lao Mong Hay," Conciliation Resources, undated (http://www.c-r.org). Author interview with Lao Mong Hay, Phnom Penh, February 7, 2012.

[7] Author interview with Lao Mong Hay, Phnom Penh, February 7, 2012.

[8] Neth and Strangio 2009.   [9] KID website, undated (http://kidcambodia.org).

[10] C. Hughes 1998, Chapter 7; Yonekura 1999.   [11] Yonekura 1999, 146.

[12] Author interview with Lao Mong Hay, Phnom Penh, February 7, 2012. See also Lao 1999a, 1999b.

[13] Chandler 2007, 184f. See also Edwards 2007, 210f.   [14] Chandler 2007, 213.

country adopted its first constitution," Lao has stated, since this event "transformed the age-old absolute monarchy into a constitutional monarchy with multiparty democracy."[15]

This momentum toward the establishment of democracy in Cambodia, Lao notes, was lost after Independence as Prince Sihanouk abdicated the throne and led the country "under the cloak of 'guided democracy.' This guided democracy soon turned into authoritarianism."[16] In Lao's view, democratic ideas made a small resurgence under General Lon Nol, who led a coup against Sihanouk in March 1970. These ideas completely disappeared during DK and remained muted throughout the People's Republic of Kampuchea (PRK).

"Democracy began to revive in 1991," Lao argues, "when the Paris Peace Accords gave it a new lease on life," one leading to the 1993 elections and "the adoption of a new constitution that enshrined liberalism, pluralism, human rights, and the rule of law."[17] It was at this time that NGOs flourished as part of the emerging post-UNTAC civil society in Cambodia. However, part of this democratic momentum, Lao said, was soon lost due to political machinations and strategic mistakes.

During this early period, KID remained modest in size, holding training workshops and hosting a television debate program.[18] The NGO received technical support from the UN Centre for Human Rights as well as funding from international donors.[19] In contrast to other NGOs, KID put greater emphasis on potential human rights violators.

"Our target was government officials first and foremost," he recalled. "We trained them in democracy, rule of law, and human rights."[20] He added, "Personally, I am critical of UNTAC for targeting the masses in their human rights training. I say yes, it's good for stats—the same as for the Khmer Rouge Tribunal now. Numbers." Instead, Lao said, it was necessary to target "the potential violators. When they understand, then we can train the masses . . . That was our strategy. Women's rights, the same . . . target men first, not women" since men were the ones committing human rights violations.

Perhaps the greatest mistake, Lao stressed, was the failure to focus enough attention on the judiciary.[21] The Paris Peace Agreement (PPA) had specifically "provided for the rule of law by spelling out the principles of a new constitution in an annex, principles that included respect for human rights and the obligation in Cambodia to create an independent judiciary to protect these rights."

This issue was all the more critical because of the judicial "legacy from the communist days." During colonial rule, France had introduced a more formal civil law legal system in Cambodia that continued under Sihanouk and then Lon Nol even if the judiciary lacked full independence.[22] This system was dismantled by the Khmer Rouge, who burned law books, shut down the law school and the courts, and targeted legal professionals for execution. Few survived.[23]

---

[15] Lao 1998, 169.   [16] Lao 1999b.   [17] Lao 1998, 170.
[18] Yonekura 1999, Appendix 5, p. 12.   [19] Yonekura 1999.
[20] Author interview with Lao Mong Hay, Phnom Penh, February 7, 2012.   [21] Ibid.
[22] Donovan 1993, 69.   [23] Ibid, 69.

As a result, the PRK regime had to completely rebuild the legal sector. It did so in a politicized manner that accorded with socialist ideology and drew on Vietnamese and Soviet models.[24] Even as the legal system was rebuilt, it remained subordinated to the Party.

In this situation, PRK police and other government officials were able to operate with a degree of impunity. A 1985 PRK Council of Ministers report complained that officials "abuse their power" and that Cambodian citizens were "arrested, detained, and imprisoned in political cases" and even for "ordinary criminal offenses ... commonly hit with sticks and tortured by interrogating organizations until they confess."[25]

From the start, Cambodian human rights NGOs became involved in monitoring and investigating such human rights violations, which included political threats and arrests, extra-judicial violence, and assassinations. Some, including Lao, received threats or faced intimidation.[26] While the human rights situation was much better by the time of the ECCC, violations continued, in part because of the weakness of the Cambodian judiciary.

Cambodia's judicial sector weakness stems not just from the judiciary's lack of authority and enforcement powers, but also from shortages of resources and training, corruption, and politicization.[27] With regard to political influence, Lao noted that despite constitutional safeguards for the separation of powers, "The courts are biased already because almost all the judges and prosecutors and officers are members of the ruling party."[28] It was for such reasons that KID pursued the larger strategy of "targeting government officials first."

To do so, according to Lao, KID decided to undertake grassroots work that would "bypass the provincial and district level" and directly reach out "to our partners on the grassroots: teachers, party and government officials" who would then "organize themselves."[29] This idea was the "kernel" from which the Citizen Advisor program would grow.

KID Citizen Advisor Program

While living in England, Lao had observed British Citizen Advisors who have "small offices on the city corners ... [If] you have trouble with the law or anything, you go there and seek their advice."[30] If the British Citizen Advisors emerged in the context of World War II, Lao noted that the idea dated back to Swedish Kings who created ombudsmen to serve as a governance check on civil servants. Today, ombudsmen have proliferated throughout the world and often serve as a local level mechanism to ensure human rights, accountability, and good governance.[31]

---

[24] Ibid, 69–70, 81–82; Gottesman 2003, 238f; Un 2009, 74.
[25] Gottesman 2003, 239.
[26] Author interview with Lao Mong Hay, Phnom Penh, February 7, 2012.
[27] Un 2009, 75f.
[28] Author interview with Lao Mong Hay, Phnom Penh, February 7, 2012.   [29] Ibid.
[30] Ibid.   [31] Ayeni 2014; Frank 1970.

Lao had discovered a number of ideas about human rights, democracy, and the rule of law that he wanted to introduce in Cambodia.[32] Indeed, while speaking, he sometimes would invoke theorists such as Locke and de Tocqueville on democratic ideas. Nevertheless, such ideas, even if "known and understood" by many Cambodians, had "yet to be fully internalized as cultural values. There is a need to cement democratic values to Cambodia's traditional cultural and moral values of Buddhist origin."[33]

KID sought to "cement" the Citizen Advisor concept on the grassroots level using local traditions of third party mediation, often by respected and knowledgeable community members.[34] Along these lines, KID targeted "teachers and other educated people" to serve as Citizen Advisors since such groups "are more capable [and] have an understanding of human rights concepts and the basic structures of rule of law." Such individuals were better-placed to help KID's "Proto-Ombudsman Program (Citizen Advisors project)" fulfill its objective of assisting "local people in remote areas, where there is a poor knowledge of democracy and limited respect for human rights."[35]

KID explicitly framed its Citizen Advisor's program as an "alternative dispute resolution (ADR) technique" aimed at providing legal services, including education and advisement, which would serve as a "bridge between the community and citizens."[36] This program, a KID webpage states, has "vast potential, as the formal system of justice (the court system) is usually not accessible for the rural poor. Most people rely instead on [ADR] mechanisms, such as conciliation and mediation to help them solve their personal and/or legal problems or disputes." The program explicitly targeted "largely poor and illiterate" communities that had "failed to grasp their role in the recently formed democratic system."[37]

As is the case with most NGOs, the longevity and use of such programs varied and changed over time. In part because of tensions with Julio Jeldres, the co-founder of KID who had continued to serve as Chairman of its board, Lao resigned in early 2002.[38]

KID and KRT Outreach

Early outreach efforts

Following the 2003 Agreement to establish the ECCC, attention and donor funds began to focus on the court. Like other NGOs, KID repurposed its existing

---

[32] Author interview with Lao Mong Hay, Phnom Penh, February 7, 2012; see also C. Hughes 1998, 221.

[33] Lao 1999b.

[34] "Citizen Advisors as Mediators: A Network for Rural Cambodia Human Rights Defense," KID website, undated (http://kidcambodia.org).

[35] "Proto-Ombudsman Program (Citizen Advisor Project)," KID website, undated (http://www3.online.com.kh).

[36] "Citizen Advisors as Mediators," KID website.   [37] Ibid.

[38] Myers and Reed 2002.

structures, programs, and areas of expertise to take up the related human rights and democratization issues that were being foregrounded. Citizen Advisors were involved in much of this new work.

Already, by 2004, as the Cambodian government was finalizing ECCC law, KID had launched a preliminary study to familiarize staff with "the survivors' hopes and expectations for the upcoming Khmer Rouge trial in order to prepare an outreach project ... aiming at building up peoples' awareness of the trial and strengthening the rule of law."[39] Relatedly, the survey was meant to prepare "six young Program Officers," five of whom had studied law, to work on the project. Like half the Cambodian population, the survey stated, all six had been "born after 1979 and know little of their country's recent history."

While this statement overstated the situation, a growing number of Cambodian youths were unfamiliar or unconcerned about the Khmer Rouge past, particularly those who received their schooling after UNTAC, when discussion of DK began to be removed from the curriculum in the name of peace and reconciliation.[40]

While not a random sample, the survey, which focused on older Cambodians (30–83 with an average age of 49) who had lived through DK, found that the majority of its respondents still thought about the past and wanted a trial, though a quarter were unaware that a trial was being established.[41] As the sample was skewed toward a more urban and educated audience, the numbers were likely much lower in the countryside.

Such results highlighted the importance of effective outreach. In the case of KID, the Citizen Advisors would eventually play a central role. However, the first iteration of KID's outreach project, which ran from 2005 to 2007, involved KID project staff, including youths involved in the survey and was carried out with the goal of "eliminating Cambodia's culture of impunity, ensuring respect for the rule of law, and facilitating people's participation in the tribunal process."[42]

During the initial phase (August to November 2005), KID staff focused on providing historical background and information about the structure of the court to 12,208 people, including 6,429 women, from seven provinces.[43] The next phase, which ran from February to April 2006, shifted the focus to witness and victim protection as well as fair trial principles. Almost 10,000 people participated.

Suon, the KID Project Coordinator who oversaw the creation of the Uncle San booklet, explained that the objective of this first KID outreach initiative was to "get the grassroots to know clearly what the ECCC was: its objective, why it was established, its functioning ... The last objective was to encourage grassroots people to contribute to the tribunal."[44] They used the ECCC slogan, "We monitor the KRT process." This could entail "passive monitoring," or following at home on radio or TV or more "active monitoring," which involved "going to the court to see directly or lodging a complaint with NGO assistance." Project staff sought to reframe the

---

[39] KID 2004, 1.   [40] Hinton 2008; Dy 2013; Münyas 2008.   [41] KID 2004, 2–7.
[42] "Outreach Activities," Khmer Institute of Democracy, http://www.khmerrough.com.
[43] Ibid.   [44] Author interview with Suon, Phnom Penh, February 6, 2012.

court in terms that would make sense to a predominantly rural population with little formal education or experience with courts.

KID, OSJI, and monologic and dialogic outreach

During this early period, as KID and other NGOs began developing methods of KRT outreach, the Open Society Justice Initiative (OSJI) sponsored a study to examine how to enhance outreach in Cambodia.[45] This study was linked to the OSJI's broader concern with international justice and legal capacity-building in post-conflict societies. Their early efforts included the facilitation of a "Working Group on the Extraordinary Chambers" that included international and national NGOs.[46]

OSJI publications around this time, for example, noted that while limited due to the quite recent recognition of the importance of outreach, a number of outreach techniques existed that could be adapted for the ECCC. The Special Court for Sierra Leone (SCSL) stood out in this respect. Despite funding limitations, the SCSL had undertaken a number of initiatives featured in the International Center for Transitional Justice outreach guide, ranging from media programming to rural town hall meetings.[47]

Such initiatives provided a model for the ECCC and also reflected a concern with shifting from what might be called "monologic" to "dialogic" outreach.[48] Monologic outreach efforts involve one-way communication concerned primarily with transmission: conveying knowledge to target populations whose participation is critical to the transitional justice process. Dialogic outreach is aimed at the same target populations but is more interactive and seeks to engage with them through two-way communication.

These categories are ideal types involving many gradations. Dialogic outreach, for example, usually involves "call-and-response" activities consisting of a "call" (about specific transitional justice issues) that allows for a greater or lesser degree freedom in the "response." The response may be a formulaic and predictable echo of the call. On occasion, dialogic approaches might have more openness, allowing for a creative engagement on the part of target populations.

In the mid-2000s, as the ECCC was getting underway, there was growing awareness of the importance of involving domestic and international NGOs in outreach efforts to facilitate such engagement.[49] OSJI's "Working Group on the Extraordinary Chambers," for example, issued a "list of standards that reflect the most recent thinking" on outreach that included the use of NGOs since they were already trusted and had "established communication mechanisms with the

---

[45] Urs 2006; see also Urs 2007.

[46] Working Group on the Extraordinary Chambers and Open Society Justice Initiative, "Standards for the Treatment of Victims and Witnesses in Cambodia's Extraordinary Chambers," May 1, 2004.

[47] Open Society Justice Initiative, "Priority Issues for Interested States Concerning the Extraordinary Chambers," New York: OSJI, April 2006, 6. See also Gurd 2006, 127; Urs 2006, 27; Pentelovitch 2009.

[48] Peskin 2005; Gurd 2006, 121; Urs 2006, 27.

[49] UN Secretary-General 2004, 5; OSJI, "Priority Issues for Interested States," 5–6.

people."[50] Local NGOs provided a means to make transitional justice more "local," even as potential tensions and fissures between on-the-ground understandings and the "universally applicable standards" remained.

OSJI outreach study and simplification

This tension emerged in the OSJI outreach study, which was directly influenced by these trends in the early-to-mid 2000s. The needs assessment study was launched in May 2005, shortly after the completion of the KID survey and as KID was undertaking their first phase of outreach, which was more monologic, involving the one-way transmission of information about the court and victim participation.

From June to December, the team, headed by an international lawyer (Taras Urs) working with a Cambodian law student and a local anthropologist, interviewed 117 people living in rural parts of five provinces in order to "gauge local perceptions of the trial, community structures, interest in outreach, and access to information, among other things."[51] The findings were then to be used to design an outreach program with a local NGO (KID).[52] The researchers sought to interview "community stakeholders," including local government officials.[53]

The report was not optimistic.[54] The study found that most Cambodians were not familiar with formal justice and that the court might conflict with Cambodian forms of social organization, such as patronage, as well as Buddhism. While there were broader mechanisms that could be used to convey information about the court, including television, radio, and print media, it was also important to engage in grassroots outreach and to avoid a one-way flow of information—of the sort characteristic of monologic outreach approaches. And, critically, the report stressed the importance of framing content so it would be accessible to all Cambodians, including the majority of the population living in the countryside.

Simplification was critical. So, too, was using colloquial language and clear and accessible graphics with culturally appropriate colors, large print, and visual images. Given the low levels of familiarity with legal discourse, the report recommended the use of analogy and the creation of materials such as "posters for one simple message," flipcharts, videos, "instructional pictures booklets," and "drama performances and films ... theater and puppetry, songs, discussions, and questions-and-answer games."[55]

The author of the study, Taras Urs, had a close relationship to KID, where she had an office and where the survey results "were put into practice."[56] To do so, she worked with local KID staffers including Nou Va. Nou Va, who had a Bachelors of Law, had written his thesis on human rights and had a passion for the freedom of civil and political rights.[57] On the basis of this background, Nou Va had been accepted into a KID short-course on "Critical Legal Thinking" taught by two German lawyers, one

[50] Working Group, "Standards for the Treatment of Victims and Witnesses," 1.
[51] Urs 2006, 3; Urs 2007, 62.   [52] Gurd 2006, 122.
[53] Urs 2006, 4; Urs 2007, 90.   [54] Urs 2006, 2007.   [55] Urs 2006, 13.
[56] Urs, 2007, 62.   [57] Author interview with Nou Va, Phnom Penh, March 10, 2016.

of whom worked for the German Development Service, which would be active in funding KRT outreach. From 2002 to 2004, these jurists had provided legal advice to KID and training for KID staffers and Citizen Advisors "on human rights, rule of law, separation of power and democracy."[58]

Nou Va told me that the course made an impact on him, one that continued "until today."[59] It had also helped create a cohort of young Cambodian jurists trained in Western notions of law, human rights, and critical thinking. Many of the students, Nou Va said, had gone on to become human rights activists, some studying abroad and others joining international and domestic NGOs. This experience provides yet another example of the multiple flows that converge—and the combustion that may be sparked—as justice and human rights norms are translated in interstitial spaces like an NGO.

KID's KRT outreach projects illustrate this point. To implement the OSJI report's recommendations, Urs and KID staffers first undertook the creation of new outreach materials, including a banner, a flipchart, and a film, which also could be used by other NGOs. From the start, they confronted the problem of translation. "In Cambodia," Nou Va said, "outreach is very difficult. Because, as we know, Cambodian people are mostly illiterate and they don't understand a lot about law. They don't know what justice and law are, for example, especially legal procedure. So we asked how can we do outreach to make the people understand . . . So my team and I, we tried to translate the legal terms into very simple terms."[60]

KID flipchart

This process of simplification was painstaking, as illustrated by the process of creating a large KRT outreach flipchart, which foreshadowed the later creation of the Uncle San booklet. The intent of the flipchart, however, was to provide a broad introduction to the tribunal and legal procedure, while the Uncle San booklet would be more focused on victim participation. The flipchart team included Tara Urs and an assistant along with two KID staffers, Nou Va and Chantara Chou. Urs provided advice about legal procedure and law while the Cambodian team members worked to make the text and images suitable for a rural Cambodian audience.

One of the initial difficulties the team confronted was how to convey the idea of jurisdiction. "The people did not know a lot about the ECCC," Nou Va recalled. "They thought the ECCC would sentence many people . . . We wondered how to fix this sort of problem so . . . we made the flipchart." To address this particular problem, they included an image of a pyramid with four echelons at the top of which was a small number of Khmer Rouge signified by their Mao caps and red scarves. Accompanying text noted that just five to ten of these "big boss leaders from the highest level" (the translation of "senior leaders") would be tried.

[58] "Workshop on 'Critical Legal Thinking,'" Khmer Institute of Democracy Legal Unit, undated (http://www.bigpond.com.kh).

[59] Author interview with Nou Va, Phnom Penh, March 10, 2016.

[60] Author interview with Nou Va, Phnom Penh, June 30, 2011.

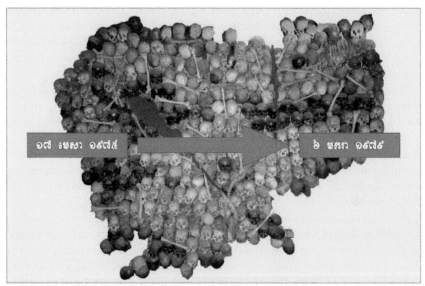

រូបភាពនេះ៖ បង្ហាញអំពីអំឡុងពេលនៃបទល្មើសធ្ងន់ធ្ងរ ដែលតុលាការមានអំណាចយកមកកាត់ទោស។

Figure 2.3 "Map of Skulls," KID Flipchart. *Reprinted by permission of the Khmer Institute of Democracy.*

Another page conveyed the ECCC's temporal jurisdiction by superimposing the beginning and ending dates, connected by an arrow, across a map of skulls in the shape of Cambodia (see Figure 2.3).

Nou Va explained, "If you just put the date at the beginning and at the end [connected by an arrow], they easily understand: this time to that time."[61] Other images, ranging from photographs to cartoon graphics, discussed the crimes to be tried, the creation and functioning of the court, and the ECCC's hybrid structure and personnel.

The team spent a great deal of time discussing the content of each page. There was a constant tension between the need to simplify and to retain fidelity to law. Nou Va explained, "We tried to make it very simple: The court is the place where they can find who committed rights and wrongs and is responsible for their acts. So we don't use the word for judge or judgment. They don't know what these [legal] terms mean."[62] The notion of "discerning right and wrong" also resonated with Buddhist understandings of sin (bad deeds), ignorance (a source of bad actions), and morality (the discernment of right and wrong that leads to good/bad deeds).

Word choice could also be politically fraught. Nou Va noted that the production team avoided the use of inflammatory words that might antagonize former Khmer

---

[61] Author interview with Nou Va, Phnom Penh, March 10, 2016.   [62] Ibid.

Rouge, who were also a target population. He explained, "We only showed the suffering [during DK]. We didn't describe it with words like 'cruel' or 'savage' … We had to have balance and think about the Khmer Rouge living along the border of Cambodia. Or it could make some [of them] feel afraid and reluctant to support [the court]."[63]

When the content was finally agreed upon, the team hired an artist to paint many of the images, which Nou Va, who could draw, had sketched out. They then tested the draft booklet in the countryside. Nou Va recalled that he went over each page of the booklet, "one by one to see whether they understand or not."[64] They found that the villagers still didn't understand certain words, legal concepts, and images, including the text in the cartoon thought bubbles. Based on this feedback, the team revised the flipchart. Instead of text, for example, the team placed images in the thought bubbles.

After this last revision process and completion of final text, hundreds of flipcharts were printed so there would be enough for other NGOs. This broader dissemination of the flipchart had been planned, as had the creation of a booklet version of the flipchart, which was subsequently printed for mass distribution. If villagers came to an outreach event and "learned by seeing the flipchart," Nou Va explained, it would be difficult for them to remember the information. By giving people a booklet version, villagers would not just "bring it back home," but also "spread it to other people" like their families and neighbors.[65] This was the first of several KID booklets, many of which, including the Uncle San booklet, would draw upon the content and style of the flipchart.

From start to finish, the creation of the flipchart involved both local and international actors (ranging from donors to advisers) and an effort to translate "global justice" in the Cambodian context. In addition to KID, the partners included the ECCC, the German Development Service (DED), the Open Society Institute, and OSJI. The influences are linked to events near and far (for example, the outreach experiences of other tribunals, UNTAC and the emergence of human rights NGOs, and the promulgation of UN strategic reports) and mediated by the understandings of domestic and international actors. Within this outreach context, justice is ultimately translated, with greater or lesser success and fidelity to "international norms and standards," in terms of locally meaningful concepts and realities, such as low literacy rates, the importance of Buddhism, social organization, and understandings of power and law.

This process of translation continued as the flipchart was used in the field. In one sense, this use was informed by the structure of the flipchart, which consisted of a frontal image the audience would see and, on the backside, accompanying text read by an outreach staffer that included rhetorical questions and the informational answers. As Nou Va illustrated how the flipchart was used, he told me, "We stood behind and showed [the images]. And we read the text and explained. So it's easy. It's like watching TV. They don't see the text … [only the images]."[66]

---

[63] Ibid.   [64] Ibid.   [65] Ibid.
[66] Author interview with Nou Va, Phnom Penh, June 30, 2011.

The flipchart booklet was structured similarly so that it could be folded to display the frontal images to an audience while a presenter read the text on the page, which had been folded back. Subsequent booklets, including "Uncle San, Aunty Yan, and the KRT," followed this model. After the flipchart was produced, KID held a training session for outreach personnel from other NGOs in which they introduced the flipchart and demonstrated how to use it.

Citizen Advisors and KID outreach

In the case of KID, Citizen Advisors (CA) were quickly trained to use the flipchart. By this time, KID's outreach efforts were well underway. The KID outreach team had selected around 200 of its best CAs to participate. Most were teachers or school directors living in target areas. According to Nou Va, they sought CAs who were respected and active in their communities. They also wanted CAs who were "clever and full of understanding about the law background we had taught them before," which was "related to human rights, law, land conflict law, and how to deal with conflict in the community." He explained, "In the [KRT] outreach program we have, for example, court procedure. So if [the CA] doesn't know about the court system and criminal law, how can they explain to people?"[67]

By selecting respected community figures, Nou Va said, the Citizen Advisor program directly played upon Cambodian understandings of conflict resolution and was therefore a "mix of modern or Western culture" and local understandings and social practices. "For me," he explained, "it is a new idea we can receive or copy from Europe [where they] have proto-ombudsmen. But it is a mix. In Cambodia, if we have a problem we have to go to the elderly person, an *achar* [religious lay expert], or a respected monk to ask their advice."[68] These respected figures would then instruct people about "how to deal with the conflict without violence or how to [get along] with each other."

If these respected elders, who often drew on Buddhist ideas, were frequently effective in resolving low-level conflict, they had difficulty dealing with more contentious issues. Disputants might next turn to local officials, such as a village or commune chief, to serve as third party mediators. However, these officials, who sometimes worked together (for example, a commune chief working with a police chief), often charged a small fee or might accept bribes to settle a dispute.

At this stage, the stakes rise in terms of cost, prestige, and a final verdict that will result in a winner and a loser. Ultimately a case might end up in court, though even the courthouse has an office that works on reconciliation.[69] Many Cambodians, especially in the countryside, are fearful of the courts, which are expensive for poor farmers and viewed as corrupt, the path to becoming the "winner" of a case being paved with payoffs and political connections.[70] In fact, judges often give priority to "good cases" that involve bribes.[71]

---

[67] Author interview with Nou Va, Phnom Penh, March 10, 2016.   [68] Ibid.
[69] Luco 2002, 145, 167.   [70] See, for example, Un 2004; Hinton 2005; Luco 2002.
[71] Un 2004, 198.

Nou Va noted a common saying in Cambodia, "I harm you and then pay money [to "win" again in court]" (*vay ban luoy*). "Hit someone, pay a bribe," Nou Va repeated. "Everyone knows this saying, especially in the countryside. It means you hit, then pay [a bribe] and the case is finished."[72] These local practices led some observers to regard the ECCC with skepticism, an attitude amplified by allegations of corruption at the court.[73]

The CAs, who KID paid a small fee for each case they resolved, provided an alternative to this system, especially in cases where the local authorities were involved. In more minor conflicts, such as land disputes, CAs sought to solve the issue without filing a complaint. But, Nou Va added, when serious crimes like rape had taken place, CAs would assist the victim as the criminal case proceeded. In some places, CAs worked in partnership with local authorities, who might refer people to the CA. Elsewhere, there might be tension between the CAs and the local authorities, partly because the CAs didn't charge fees and led to lost income for the local officials. If the situation was tense or complicated, CAs could seek help from KID. Nou Va noted that the villagers weren't familiar with the more formal term "Citizen Advisor" (*ti pruksar borat*) but "mostly know the name of the [CA] focal point."[74]

CAs received periodic training at the KID office in Phnom Penh. As Nou Va noted, this background knowledge provided a basis of human rights and legal understanding upon which KID's KRT outreach program could build as it commenced in 2005. Nevertheless, CAs often found the intricacies of legal procedure tricky. Some CAs had difficulty answering questions during outreach sessions; others had trouble with basic explanation.

To address this problem, KID trained CAs, group by group, as materials were developed. The flipchart, in particular, served as a sort of quality control. "We wanted to make sure all of the trainers remembered and read [the text] carefully. We didn't want to allow them to talk outside of the topic," Nou Va explained. "One sentence to another is critically important. So the trainer has to read all [of the text on the backside] and the audience listened to the trainer and saw the pictures [on the front]."[75] The flipchart, Nou Va said, improved the situation considerably.

The second phase of KID outreach

If the first phase of KID outreach was largely monologic and informational, the second phase, in which the Uncle San booklet was produced, had a somewhat more dialogic emphasis, focusing both on information transmission and on victim participation. The exact content of the program varied as donors funded particular modules on topics like victim participation and witness protection. Graphic booklets were created to provide content on these topics. Several featured a character named "Uncle Soy," who closely resembled Uncle San. The booklets borrowed content from earlier texts as well as the flipchart.

[72] Author interview with Nou Va, Phnom Penh, March 10, 2016.
[73] Giry 2012; Gillison 2011.
[74] Author interview with Nou Va, Phnom Penh, March 10, 2016.   [75] Ibid.

It was in this context that the Uncle San booklet was produced as part of KID's second major outreach initiative, which relied heavily on KID's Citizen Advisor network. In 2007, KID launched its "Citizen Advisor Training and Outreach Program," a "training the trainers" initiative in which groups of CAs received four days of training.

Afterward, each CA was tasked with conducting outreach half-day workshops in 16 villages. KID's project webpage notes the hoped-for multiplier effect: "If 30 villagers attend each session, then information is being exchanged with over 57,000 rural Cambodians."[76] In the provinces, the trainers, using the booklets at times, would provide a basic explanation of what the tribunal was, how it operated, and how victims might participate. Indeed, the CAs also helped potential civil parties fill out applications.

KID's outreach activities shifted as events unfolded. The DED remained a donor, whose support was augmented by the Konrad-Adenauer-Stiftung (KAS) and the European Union (EU). This funding enabled KID to hire Suon as KRT Outreach Program Coordinator in 2007. Like Nou Va, Suon had a background in law. Urs and the German Advisor had left by this time. Johanna Macdonald, a lawyer from Canada, became the Program Manager. Nou Va remained as Program Officer, while Dina Nay served as KID's Executive Director before stepping down in 2008. She was replaced by an Australian-Cambodian, Chhaya Hang. KID would ultimately implode under Hang's leadership, as KID lost its donor support. The NGO now exists largely only in name.

"Uncle San, Aunty Yan, and the KRT"

The Uncle San booklet was created by this new team, led by Suon. In many respects, the process of creation resembled that of the flipchart. Over the course of two months, the project team met periodically to discuss the booklet, which was to focus on victim participation. Most Cambodians, Nou Va explained, "don't know what a civil party means. They don't know their right to participate in the ECCC or the law procedures."[77] The booklet was meant to help familiarize people with the court and teach them about participatory rights, ranging from filing a complaint to formally becoming a civil party, actions with which KID could assist.

Suon, who led the booklet development efforts, noted the importance of simplification: "We tried our best to mainstream the ideas to the grassroots people ... [using] this tool, simple language."[78] The first step was internal "brainstorming," as the team members "sat down together to try to develop this simple story."[79] Each team member took responsibility for creating a given section of the booklet, perhaps three pages or so. The team then met again to discuss the content, selecting materials that were "understandable [and] appropriate for the grassroots."[80]

---

[76] "Citizen Advisor Training and Outreach," Khmer Institute of Democracy, http://www.khmer-rough.com.

[77] Author interview with Nou Va, Phnom Penh, June 30, 2011.

[78] Author interview with Suon, Phnom Penh, February 6, 2012. [79] Ibid.

[80] Ibid.

The foreign law expert, Johanna Macdonald worked with the team to ensure fidelity to the law. "We'd dialogue constantly, nit-pick over words," including victim-witness terminology itself, Macdonald explained. "I'd communicate my legal opinion about what Western legal terms meant, dialogue with Suon about what Khmer words meant, come to a common understanding, then filter [it] down to pictorial understandings."[81] The discussions were often intense and necessitated breaks.

Once the booklet was drafted, the team began consultations. First they showed it to the ECCC's Public Affairs Section, which offered suggestions about wording and the sequence of narrative frames. Each time they received feedback they would revise the booklet. Toward the end of the process they conducted a pilot study. "We asked our Citizen Advisors to read the whole story," Suon recalled. The CAs then selected villagers including "illiterate people to see if they understood."

Suon gathered together the comments, which focused on language and image, and revised the booklet again. The staff met one last time and reached agreement about the final form of the booklet. Afterward, Suon worked with a Cambodian student from the School of Fine Arts to complete the booklet. He would explain the meaning of a given page to the artist, who would sketch a pencil draft. "He'd hand it over to me and say, 'Do you like this [drawing] or do you want to add more [color],'"[82] Suon recalled. The process took almost a month.

KID sent the booklet to the donors, who had no comments and approved the use of their logos on the back page of the booklet. This is not to say they hadn't influenced the process since donors impacted outreach projects through their funding priorities and promotion of transitional justice.

KAS, for example, is a German political foundation that seeks to promote "trans-Atlantic community values" such as "freedom, justice, and solidarity" as well as "Democracy, the Rule of Law, Human Rights, and Social Market Economy."[83] The ECCC intersected with this work in different ways, especially in terms of "rule of law" efforts, which led KAS to co-fund, with the EU, KID's outreach proposals on CA training and efforts on "Victim and Witness Protection."

Such NGO proposals and the projects they enable must broadly correspond with the donor interests; compliance is monitored by reports, evaluations, and audits. In some situations, a foundation may serve as more of a partner, funding direct costs such as salary and participating in some NGO's activities. This appears to have been the case with KAS, which directly funded KID staff costs, including staff salary, and whose country representative was present at various CA training workshops.[84]

A KAS summary of the project, to which KAS contributed 500,000 Euros, describes its goals as contributing to "a transparent and effective functioning" of

---

[81] Author phone interview with Johanna Macdonald, December 6, 2011.
[82] Author interview with Suon, Phnom Penh, February 6, 2012.
[83] Konrad-Adenauer-Stiftung Cambodia Office website, undated (http://www.kas.de).
[84] Author interview with Suon, Phnom Penh, February 6, 2012; "Citizen Advisors' Training on Victim and Witness Protection," Konrad-Adenauer Stiftung Cambodia Office, undated (http://www.kas.de).

the ECCC and educating "the general public of Cambodia about the procedural guarantees to which they are entitled through national and international instruments."[85] The phrase "international standards" recurs throughout the project summary as does the implicit goal of helping to "bring" Cambodia and the ECCC "into compliance" with them through this KID outreach project.

The Uncle San booklet was published in early 2008 after KID's 2007–2009 outreach initiative had commenced and groups of around thirty Citizen Advisors at a time were being brought to Phnom Penh for training. "Uncle San" appears to have been quickly introduced. His name appears on the agendas of the second round of workshops, which were centered on victim and witness protection.

Each workshop devoted a significant amount of time to victim participation, including two days focused on "psychosocial interview skills," a visit to the ECCC, and brief discussion of Uncle San as well as "Mr. Soy" and "Aunty Kolap" from earlier KID booklets. The five-day workshops began with the "distribution of learning materials," including, presumably, the outreach booklets. Suon, Nou Va, and Johanna Macdonald were all involved in the sessions, which included talks by ECCC representatives, the presentation of lesson plans and outreach materials, discussion of law and "international standards," role play, and case studies focused on the booklet characters.[86]

In one session, CAs made two-minute presentations related to "Uncle Soy" that answered questions such as "What is the purpose of the ECCC," "Is Uncle Soy a Victim within the jurisdiction of the ECCC?" "How does Uncle Soy participate in the ECCC," and "How does Uncle Soy submit a complaint form?"[87] By April 2008, the workshops included a session on "legal education" led by Suon and focused on a booklet, presumably "Uncle San." The workshops included modules on the Victim Information Forms. There was also discussion of logistics, CA obligations, and the outreach contracts CAs signed at the end of the workshop. Meanwhile, the CAs were in the field at work, conducting outreach sessions and recruiting civil parties.

Due to a lack of resources, a slow start, and the advantages of using local intermediary organizations that had networks and practices in place, the ECCC Victims Unit had been relying heavily on NGOs like KID not just to help raise awareness and understanding about the court but to assist with victim participation, including the completion of civil party applications. NGOs helped file about 84 percent of the applicants in Case 001 (94) and Case 002 (3,866).[88] During the early phases of the court, NGO representatives continued to assist civil parties by helping them find representation, setting up meetings with their lawyers, bringing them to court, responding to questions, and keeping them informed throughout the legal process.[89]

[85] "Victim and Witness Protection (VWP) Standards for the Khmer Rouge Tribunal (ECCC) and Beyond," Konrad-Adenauer-Stiftung, undated (http://www.kas.de).

[86] "Citizen Advisors' Training on Victim and Witness Protection," March 3–7, 2008, Konrad-Adenauer-Stiftung Cambodia Office, undated (http://www.kas.de).

[87] "Citizen Advisors' Training on Victim and Witness Protection," March 17–21, 2008, Konrad-Adenauer-Stiftung Cambodia Office, undated (http://www.kas.de).

[88] Sperfeldt 2012a, 151.   [89] Ibid; Thomas and Chy 2009.

KID was active in this regard, which was a key reason for the increased use of the Uncle San booklet. Chhaya Hang, who directed KID's outreach work during this period, said that the booklet was meant to give the message: "you can participate."[90] Once the villagers "understand what's involved, then 'bang.' We ask them if they want to file a victim complaint form." The KID representatives would explain that, by participating, "You can have a say. You can get justice [for yourself and your] loved ones," though ultimately it was an opportunity they had to willingly choose. So KID staffers would emphasize, "You need to make the decision." Here, in his remarks, we find another manifestation of the transitional justice imaginary and its idealized subjectivity of rights, free choice, and agency.

Thus, in the context of the KID's attempt to create a booklet that would convey legal ideas in a form that was simple, engaging, and locally appealing, the outreach team worked hard to ensure the fidelity of the content. This attempt to remain true to "international standards" was reinforced during the CA training sessions, which provided legal education and detailed explanations about the meaning and use of outreach materials.

This meant that the format, content, and quality of outreach could vary depending on how the CA retranslated the outreach ideas they had learned during training sessions. If the flipchart and booklets provided carefully worded text to accompany the images, the CAs still varied in their degree of understanding, motivation, teaching skills, and ability to engage their local communities. Macdonald recalled that the quality of CA outreach sessions depended on the "capacity and personality of each [CA] and how they might run things a bit differently ... And certainly some [CAs] were more proficient ... or involved in their community. And each community was different."[91]

There was also local variation in the degree of interest in and understanding of the outreach materials presented by the CAs. If the flipchart and Uncle San booklet helped convey legal ideas to less educated and sometimes illiterate villagers, the participants still struggled with the often complicated and unfamiliar content. Some CAs had trouble understanding the nuances.

The process of helping villagers fill out the Victim Information Forms was also often difficult, especially since many villagers were unfamiliar with bureaucratic forms and recounting their stories in a manner that emphasized legality and criminality rather than Buddhist notions of suffering and karma that accorded with local oral traditions and understandings. Sometimes outreach staff would need to directly work with and sometimes even fill out the forms for potential civil parties.

In addition, villagers had different degrees of interest in the court. If the transitional justice imaginary assumes that victims will naturally want legal accountability, this was not always the case in Cambodia. In addition to the lack of familiarity and even distrust of courts, some people thought it was better not to raise a matter that had happened long ago and instead preserve a peace that had taken years to achieve. Other Cambodians might invoke Buddhist understandings holding that it

[90] Interview with Chhaya Hang, Phnom Penh, June 23, 2011.
[91] Author phone interview with Johanna Macdonald, December 6, 2011.

is better to release one's anger and have compassion even for one's enemies, who had been blinded by ignorance and would suffer the consequences of their crimes when reincarnated.

Suon recalled that, when first called to outreach sessions, participants would often question the need for a tribunal. As he and I looked at the third page of the booklet, when Uncle San is introduced as a 64-year-old villager who had suffered under the Khmer Rouge, Suon explained that this image did not just introduce a criminal act (forced relocations) and site (a prison in Siem Reap) but signified that Uncle San was "a real victim." But sometimes, he noted, "this kind of elderly person just stays in the pagoda and does not care about the legal process or the tribunal."[92]

When beginning an initial outreach session, the majority of villagers often had reservations about the court. "Let's say there were 20 participants," Suon said, "18 of them might have a negative point of view." They might ask, "Why have you come here to disseminate information about the KRT? We are living in peace. Why do you want me to revisit my past related to the crimes, make me unhappy by encouraging me to talk about the killing and what I witnessed?"[93] Sometimes they emphasized this point by invoking the saying, "If a wound doesn't hurt, don't jab it with a stick."

In response, Suon continued, the CA or KID outreach team member would acknowledge that talking about the past could be upsetting but would stress that it was important in order to educate Cambodian youth, some of whom didn't believe the stories about DK, and the foreign judges who weren't familiar with their stories. Participating would also provide justice through the judgment, he would tell them, "If you would like to find justice for yourself or your missing family members."[94] After the third or fourth session, Suon went on, the villagers "would begin to understand the importance of the court" and eventually half or more participants would express interest in filing a complaint. Most of those who didn't indicated they would still participate passively, monitoring the proceedings.

All of the half dozen KID staff members I interviewed who were involved in the production of the Uncle San booklet or its use in KRT outreach viewed it as a success. The booklet was able to convey a basic understanding of the court to rural villagers, even those who were illiterate. It did so by translating international norms in a simplified form that made sense in the Cambodian context.

The staffers acknowledged problems. But, as Suon noted, the CA outreach system was able to convey information to large numbers of Cambodians, many of whom knew little or nothing about the court. The NGO was also able to encourage a degree of dialogic participation through monitoring or direct participation. Chhaya Hang noted that the booklet was "something they can have in their hands and they can [take] back and share."[95]

The booklet was aimed at a particular target group: older villagers who had survived DK. Uncle San, who lived and looked like them, provided a point of identification. His journey to the ECCC and interest in victim participation served as an

---

[92] Author interview with Suon, Phnom Penh, February 6, 2012.   [93] Ibid.
[94] Ibid.   [95] Interview with Chhaya Hang, Phnom Penh, June 23, 2011.

imaginary map of their future. Uncle San's journey was an invitation for them to step into the timescape of the transitional justice imaginary.

The Hidden Fourth Transition of Everyday Life

In the KID booklet, this invitation is perhaps most dramatically depicted in the speech bubble juxtaposed to the image of Uncle San lighting incense and praying to the spirits of his ancestors, as an "interested" and "curious" Uncle San is hailed, like the reader of the booklet, to participate in a KID outreach session (see Figure 2.4).

Standing in front of EU and ECCC posters affixed to a wooden beam, a KID Citizen Advisor is shown reading from one of the KID outreach booklets to twenty villagers (several also hold booklets) as he informs the villagers about the tribunal and its objectives.

An accompanying graphic shows Cambodian and UN officials in suits signing the agreement. No one in this frame looks like Uncle San. Here the temporality of the transitional justice imaginary is manifest in the jump from the Khmer Rouge period (1975–79) to the origin of the transitional justice mechanism in 2003. Uncle San, the Cambodian everyman who is figuratively locked in a static, traumatized, primitive, and savage time of the past, steps into the progressive, healing, developed, and civilized time of the present transitional justice moment and the future

Figure 2.4 Aunty Yan hailing the praying Uncle San to attend a KID Outreach meeting. "Uncle San, Aunty Yan, and the KRT," p. 9. *Reprinted by permission of the Khmer Institute of Democracy.*

it promises to bring. What happened prior to 1975 and between 1979 and 2003, is flattened and obscured—a temporal erasure that is one of the hallmarks of scalar and dichotomous time in the transitional justice imaginary.

In other words, the temporal discourses of the transitional justice imaginary dehistoricize and depoliticize in contrast to the truth claims with which it is often associated. We learn nothing about the origin or the immediate aftermaths of the conflict and Cambodia's first and second transitions. Time is reduced to the third transition and in a truncated manner as the transitional justice imaginary is a reductive exteriorization, a facade behind which temporal complexity is obscured.

Uncle San, in turn, is depicted as having lived in a backwater, both in the sense of a stagnant space unreached by the currents of modernity or even time more broadly and in terms of existing in a space in which "no development or progress is taking place."[96] Uncle San's experiences could be those of any Cambodian village survivor. Indeed, Chhaya Hang, the former KID Director, told me that the names "Uncle San" and "Aunty Yan" were selected because they were "common names among [the] rural population ... very poor, grassroots type of names."[97] Individual difference is thereby elided as Uncle San's experiences could be those of any rural Cambodian survivor. He stands as an emblem of the Cambodian survivor-victim and, through metonymy, of Cambodia itself, which is thereby depicted as a stagnant backwater.

This backwater is a time and space of lack, the necessary corollary of the transitional justice imaginary, which aspires to catalyze a teleological transformation that will bring the "gift" of progress, as illustrated by Uncle San's modernity dream bubble. Uncle San's contrasting "trauma nightmare bubble" (see Figure 2.2) depicts his stagnation as extending to psychological well-being, which persists, unchanged, manifesting in a set of trauma symptoms, including re-experiences (flashbacks, bad dreams, and nightmares), avoidance behaviors (trying "not to think about the past"), and, as the frowning photo of him in the hammock suggests, hyper-arousal (difficulty sleeping and feeling tense).

These sorts of biomedical trauma discourses, which circulate widely in transitional justice contexts and are directly linked to transitional justice imaginary discourses, erase the everyday Cambodian understandings hinted at by Uncle San's praying. Little is said about the strategies Cambodians may engage in when their balance is upset and they are "uneasy" (*min sruol khluon*)—a situation often reflected by disrupted bodily humoral flow and distinct somatic symptoms and idioms.[98]

These strategies include: "coining," "cupping," moxibustion, taking medication, using tiger balm and other "heating" and "cooling" ointments, getting a massage, pinching and pulling stress points in the body. Cambodians may also visit a monk, nun, or religious lay practitioner, meditate or pray, enlist the services of a traditional healer or spirit possession medium, consult a fortune teller or astrologer, or simply speak to a friend, relative, loved one, or respected figure such as a village

---

[96] "Backwater," Concise OED.
[97] Interview with Chhaya Hang, Phnom Penh, June 23, 2011.
[98] Hinton and Hinton 2014; Marcucci 1994.

chief.[99] The biomedical discourses of the transitional justice imaginary erase such everyday understandings and practices through which Cambodians interpret psychological experience. Instead, like Uncle San, the "local" is depicted as ineffective and backward.

The court is the vehicle of deliverance from this stagnation. It also signifies Cambodia's lack, the modernity it has not achieved. Uncle San notes the technology at the court even as the graphic images, including the sleek bus that transports Uncle San and Aunty Yan to the ECCC, suggest its modernity.

At the conclusion of the transitional justice process, Cambodia will attain what it lacks. Thus, after their visit to the court, Uncle San, Aunty Yan, and their neighbors discuss not just the court but the future of their country. The accompanying graphics contain a picture of the court as part of a series of interlinked images that suggest this better future: criminals (who lived freely because of a "culture of impunity" and a lack of "the rule of law") are taken to jail as justice is upheld; the scales of justice balanced; a stupa symbolizing peace for the dead and reparations for the living; and a well signifying reparation, development, social justice, and repair.

Once again, at the end, Uncle San himself embodies this new state of transformation and progress as he, like Cambodia, is democratized, becoming a liberal, rights-bearing subject who is healed through the process. Indeed, he now lives in a new world of modernity. The last graphic shows Uncle San sleeping in his hammock near a thatched house, where he dreams of a new Cambodia, like him remade, one with electricity, fancy wooden houses, and the factory in the distance (see Figure 2.1).

In contrast to the initial hammock frame in which a frowning Uncle San is plagued by the nightmares of the past, the last graphic shows him sleeping comfortably in his hammock, a slight smile on his face as he dreams of this new Cambodia. The accompanying caption reads, "Then ... I slept the whole night with no bad dreams" (34). Uncle San, like Cambodia, is imagined as purified, renewed, and remade through the mechanism of the court as he passes through the timescape of the transitional justice imaginary.

Suon was explicit about the message of this last frame, "Here, Uncle San, after his participation, a long walk and journey, comes [back] to his own house. He can now close his eyes peacefully. He [dreams of] a peaceful situation and happiness."[100] Flipping back and forth between the initial graphic of Uncle San's "bad dreams" and the modernity dream bubble on the last page, Suon explained, "This one [the first page] is tragedy, bad things, the [last page has] good things ... birds and trees ... kids who go to school in peace. The villagers have jobs [and] there is no mistreatment of monks ... And you can see [that the village] now has electricity ... Normally only the rich have money to buy wood tile [houses]. So [this page] means that there is prosperity ... no famine ... [and] where we have factories, [we have] development."

Suon explained that the meaning of the booklet was that people would live "peacefully after participating in the court process. This is the real output we would like to explain to the grassroots ... That is your benefit." Uncle San, he continued, is a

---

[99] Witzel 2007, 139.   [100] Author interview with Suon, Phnom Penh, February 6, 2012.

changed man, who no longer has psychological syndromes or bad dreams. "We let the reader conclude that the court changed him because of his participation."

The factory, in turn, symbolized economic development in a rural landscape that normally lacks such industry. The people imagined in Uncle San's modernity dream bubble "go to the factory to produce the final product [that is sold on the] market. That is the development process." Here Suon, just as Nou Va had done when looking at the booklet, explicitly describes the end point of time in the transitional justice imaginary: a liberal democratic order occupied by functional, rights-bearing individuals, capitalism, and the qualities that supposedly come with it—peace, happiness, and progress.

Through such discursive exteriorizations, the transitional justice imaginary erases the agency and lived experience of Uncle San and the Cambodian population he symbolizes. Cambodians had been dealing with the past for roughly three decades before the ECCC commenced, what might be called, for contrast, a hidden fourth transition, the "everyday transitions" masked by the justice facade and often informed by different aspirations and conceptions of time.

This everyday lived experience of dealing with the past has intersected with the three transitions in important ways, sometimes through the mediation of NGOs. Thus, as we saw, during the second transition, some NGOs sought to promote human rights by emphasizing Buddhist resonances. Similar sorts of efforts continued with the KRT outreach. These encounters are not ones of passivity, as "stagnant" people from a "failed state" are suddenly transformed. Cambodians have selectively and creatively engaged with human rights and transitional justice, blending, adapting, or sometimes more or less ignoring them.

The same was true of the first transition, when Cambodians participated in PRK state-level initiatives.[101] At the same time, many villagers engaged in ritual transactions with the spirits of the dead, which were thought to have trouble being reborn after suffering violent deaths—in addition to related beliefs about tutelary deities, ghosts, and witches.[102] Buddhist conceptions of life and death, however, are often informed by a circular conception of time, one of birth and rebirth, karma and samsara, the wheel of life, and the impermanence of being. The relatively slow pace of such "hidden transitions" may also be very different than that of transitional justice, which moves fast in accordance with the speed and efficiency demands of transition and its teleological end, liberal democracy, modernization, and neoliberal market exchange.[103] This temporally (fast) pace also creates expectations for victims and societies, who are expected to "heal" quickly during the transition—which stands in contrast to the often much longer (and slower) and uneven pace of coping with the past, including addressing socioeconomic issues and structural violence masked by the justice facade.[104]

---

[101] R. Hughes 2006; Ly 2014.   [102] Ang 1987; Davis 2015; Guillou 2012.
[103] Muller-Hirth 2017; Ross 2003. On multiple temporalities operative in transitional justice, see also Igreja 2012.
[104] Muller-Hirth 2017.

Such temporal understandings contrast with the linear, teleological timescape of the transitional justice imaginary that, through its discursive force, masks them as well as the many "vortices" of lived experience and practice in which they are embedded. In the next chapter, we shall turn to look at the outreach efforts of another NGO, the Center for Social Development, which reveals other vortices obscured by this justice facade.

3

Space (Center for Social Development and the Public Sphere)

"I was the very first one."

I am meeting with Theary Seng, the Director of a Cambodian non-governmental organization (NGO), the Center for Social Development (CSD), at Café Living Room, a Phnom Penh restaurant committed to hiring Cambodians from at risk groups and frequented by NGO staffers, court staff, and expats, many of whom are quietly chatting or working on computers. We sit on a wicker couch and chairs on the spacious second-floor porch of the large villa-café, which overlooks a lush garden, as she tells me her story of becoming the first Extraordinary Chambers in the Courts of Cambodia (ECCC) civil party, participating in Case 002 pre-trial hearings, and undertaking Khmer Rouge Tribunal (KRT) outreach work at CSD.

It is June 29, 2009, near the mid-point of Case 001, the trial of Duch, the former head of S-21 Security Center. At the ECCC, S-21 survivor Vann Nath is giving testimony. As I talk with Seng, a fan swirls, breaking the heat until the electricity suddenly goes out. The fan slows, the blades still.

She adds, "They called me the poster child for the civil parties."

Two years later, on November 15, 2011, Seng would withdraw her civil party application while calling the court a "political farce."[1] The story of how this happened is suggestive about the transitional justice imaginary and its facadist maskings, including related conceptions of space and creative meaning-making within the "vortices" of the transitional justice assemblage that are illustrated both by CSD's KRT outreach and Seng's experience at court.

Daughter of the Killing Fields

In many ways, Theary Seng was an ideal civil party, someone whose suffering and loss correspond closely to conceptions of victimhood the transitional justice imaginary asserts. Uncle San and Aunty Yan exemplify the prototypic victim, individuals who have endured enormous loss and suffering. Their experiences are an extreme

[1] Khmer Rouge Victims in Cambodia Press Release 2011.

The Justice Facade: Trials of Transition in Cambodia. Alexander Laban Hinton. © Alexander Laban Hinton, 2018. Published 2018 by Oxford University Press.

manifestation of the attributes required of an ECCC victim, which the court defines as "Any person or legal entity who has suffered from physical, psychological, or material harm as a direct consequence of the crimes committed in Cambodia by the Democratic Kampuchea regime between 17 April 1975 and 6 January 1979 that are under the jurisdiction of the ECCC."[2]

Like Uncle San and Aunty Yan, Seng suffered greatly during Democratic Kampuchea (DK), an experience she recounts in a 2005 memoir, *Daughter of the Killing Fields*.[3] Just four-years-old when the Khmer Rouge took power, she and her family were, like other residents of Phnom Penh, forced to evacuate. Days later, her father, a former teacher, heeded an announcement calling on former Lon Nol civil servants and soldiers to return to Phnom Penh to help rebuild the country. He never returned.

Eventually, Seng, her mother, and her four brothers ended up at the home of her paternal grandfather, Ta Duch, in Chensa village, Svay Rieng province. The family had a degree of protection since Ta Duch was an "old person" who had lived in a Khmer Rouge zone during the war and had many relatives in the village. In the revolutionary society, such "old" or "base people" had greater rights and were more likely to survive than the "new people" who, like Seng's family, had lived in the cities during the civil war and were therefore suspect.

Eventually, in 1978, Seng's family lost their protection when Ta Duch fell into disfavor after unintentionally insulting soldiers. Seng's family was arrested and ended up at Bung Rei prison, where 20,000 to 30,000 people were killed, including her mother.[4] Afterward, Seng and her brothers, who had witnessed brutalities at the prison, were released and, now parentless, allowed to return to Chensa. Seng's book begins, "I am an orphan of the killing fields."[5]

After DK, Seng and her siblings fled to a refugee camp on the Thai-Cambodian border. With the assistance of a Christian church group, the family emigrated to Michigan in 1980. Seng dates her conversion to Christianity to this time.[6] The family was supported by Christian organizations and lived in a Michigan Christian community. Seng went to a Christian elementary school and recalled her teacher speaking about the Resurrection: "I was so drawn to it. It resonated with my personal experience."[7]

Seng's family later moved to Southern California. While she excelled in high school, Seng described her experience as "awful" as she was depressed, gained weight, and had low self-esteem.[8] She states that many Cambodians experienced post-traumatic stress disorder (PTSD), leading one brother to pursue psychiatry.

---

[2] "Victims Participation" Victims Support Section (http://www.eccc.gov.kh/). See also Rule 23 in the ECCC Internal Rules.

[3] Seng 2005.

[4] Ibid, 27; see Phong-Rasy, "DK Prison" and "Burial" (http://www.d.dccam.org/Projects/Maps/Mapping.htm).

[5] Seng 2005, 3.   [6] *The War Cry* Staff 2005, 4–5; Seng 2005, 208f.

[7] *The War Cry* Staff 2005, 5.   [8] Ibid, 4; Seng 2005, 229, 236.

She found solace by meditating on the *Book of Psalms*, which she transcribed in calligraphy. "I still relate to the Psalms because of all the emotions you find in them," she explained. "[I]n a psalm you can have someone cursing God, but at the same time concluding that he is the God of perfect justice and perfect love."[9]

Seng's Christianity was one manifestation of a bicultural identity and upbringing that informs her life and work. At home, she spoke "Cambodianglish" and recalls having to bend her head before elders and address them with honorifics. Meanwhile, at school, she learned about human rights, equality, and individuality that clashed with this "suffocating social hierarchy" and Buddhist emphasis on karma and fate.[10] Over time, she learned to effectively draw on both heritages, tempering "American individualism with Asian communalism, American assertiveness with demure passivity."[11]

Seng went on to attend Georgetown University and the University of Michigan Law School, from which she graduated in 2000,[12] and began returning to Cambodia, where she taught English, volunteered at a legal aid organization, and even gave the news in English on national television. In 2004, Seng moved permanently to Cambodia, where she worked for two years as a commercial lawyer before becoming, in March 2006, Executive Director of CSD.[13]

Seng's experiences directly influenced her KRT outreach work at CSD, including high-profile public forums. But, as was the case with the Khmer Institute of Democracy (KID) and Lao Mong Hay, these forums were also informed by historical currents and the efforts of her predecessors, especially Vannath Chea.

Vannath Chea and the Center for Social Development

Vannath Chea's path to CSD

Like KID, CSD was established in June 1995 in the wake of Cambodia's second transition. The NGO was established "to promote democratic values and improve the quality of life of the Cambodian people through practical research, training, advocacy, awareness-raising and public debate." CSD's objectives included building citizen "participation in the democratic process," advocating "for good governance through the institutionalization of democratic values" and strengthening "the implementation of human rights."[14]

Prior to Seng's arrival, CSD had been led by Vannath Chea, one of the group's founders. Like Seng, Chea suffered greatly during DK and eventually fled to Thailand and the United States (U.S.), though Chea was older. She grew up in relative wealth, learning to speak French and English on her way to getting a degree in public finance and becoming a civil servant.[15] She married a doctor and had one son.

---

[9] *The War Cry* Staff 2005, 4.   [10] Seng 2005, 226–27, 237–38.   [11] Ibid, 239.
[12] Ibid, 240.   [13] Ibid, 240f; Theary C. Seng, "Biography" (http://www.thearyseng.com).
[14] Center for Social Development (CSD) 2006, 31.   [15] *World People's Blog* Staff 2007.

Chea and her family were also forced to the countryside, where they were suspect as urban elite "new people." "I worked in the fields, planting and harvesting rice," she recalled. "Daily work was from 4am to 10pm. Sometimes, the Khmer Rouge called for meetings that lasted up till 1am . . . People had to confess any unfaithful thoughts, negative feelings or mistakes committed. Whoever complained . . . disappeared."[16]

Her deep Buddhist belief helped her cope with DK. She recalls how once she had an "enlightenment" experience when she was ill and on the brink of death. "I silently prayed for mercy from my parents and the Buddha . . . Little by little, my mind and body became serene and calm," as she learned the importance of maintaining "mental balance" and "equilibrium" in the face of adversity.[17]

Chea's DK experiences led her to become an activist. She believed that passivity, including her own, had facilitated the Khmer Rouge rise to power.[18] She fled to a Thai refugee camp, where she began advocating for the vulnerable. Her engaged citizenship continued in Oregon where she did refugee assistance work during the 1980s while obtaining a MA degree.[19] Chea returned to Cambodia during the United Nations Transitional Authority in Cambodia (UNTAC), when she was a translator. She subsequently worked for the Asia Foundation before becoming Vice-President of CSD in 1996 and then President in 1998.[20]

Structural violence and transition

While CSD launched various programs, many focused on democratic transition, as Chea noted in a 2003 talk.[21] Cambodia, she stated at the time, "is in a transition period from an emergency stage to a developing and nation building stage. The opening of the country in the early 1990s brought . . . the good, the bad, and the ugly."[22] If the country had achieved macroeconomic stability and sustained growth, "36 percent of the Cambodian populace lives below the poverty line" and poor Cambodian families were caught in a "cycle of poverty, ill health, and high health care costs." As illustrated by deforestation and natural resource depletion, Chea contended, "money and material wealth" were replacing "traditional Buddhist morals."

Cambodia's transition had involved "a radical transformation from a communist and control market economy to an open, free for all, market economy," fueled in large part by roughly "$500 million of foreign aid annually, representing half of the Cambodian budget." This aid, she noted, came from donors with varying agendas and expectations. While significant assistance had been given to "promote democracy . . . and the rule of law," the outcomes were unclear.

There remained significant governance problems, such as widespread corruption, in part due to patronage, which was "strongly rooted in [Cambodian] society." Chea's remarks echoed critiques of classic transitional justice as well as specific criticisms of both UNTAC and the ECCC for masking inequality, legitimating

---

[16] Korah 2010.   [17] Ibid.   [18] *World People's Blog* Staff 2007.
[19] Ibid; Korah 2010.   [20] Ibid.   [21] Chea 2003, 9.
[22] The quotations and paraphrasing in the next two paragraphs are from Chea 2003, 1–3.

Cambodian People's Party (CPP) rule and neoliberal policy, and failing to deliver democratic and human rights change.[23]

Chea concluded by stressing Buddhist ethics. In Cambodia, Buddhist scripture and the Middle Path provided a basis for good governance, moral leadership, and a way of life based on loving kindness and equanimity as opposed to "the greed of the few that underlies the poverty of so many."[24]

In many ways, Chea's paper provided an overview of CSD's work. Corruption and transparency, for example, were two foci of CSD initiatives on global governance. During 1998, CSD undertook a major study of public attitudes about corruption, which revealed that 84 percent of Cambodians viewed corruption as normal and 98 percent disliked it.[25] In response, CSD launched a Transparency Task Force project.[26]

Soon after its establishment, CSD also began holding public forums on sensitive issues. CSD's website explains that its "Public Forum Unit" was established in 1996 to provide "an outlet for public sentiments" and as a means to build "Cambodia's foundation as a democratic society."[27]

CSD public forums

In 2016, I met with Chea at her home, a large villa with a patio garden located just fifty meters from the Tuol Sleng Genocide Museum. I thought of how prisoners were interrogated, tortured, and executed on the larger S-21 prison compound, which extended far beyond the grounds of Tuol Sleng.

I mentioned the proximity to Tuol Sleng to Chea, who remarked, "Oh, we found bones here."[28] She explained that construction workers found the skeletal remains of two adult bodies in 2000. The bones were still tied by black and white cords, along with the clothing of a baby. In tears, Chea wrapped the remains in white cloth and placed them in a small box. "I invited five monks to perform a ceremony under a mango tree" at her house. Late in the day, as it grew dark, "the burning bones produce a whistling sound with a bright green phosphoric flame."[29] The next day, Chea placed the ashes in a marble urn and sent them to a rural pagoda.

The idea of the cremation ceremony, she explained, "is to liberate the souls so that they can be reborn." Otherwise, their souls may become trapped and "become bad spirits that cause a lot of problems. If we go through the ritual with monks, it can help calm down the souls, release the soul of the person so they can be reborn."

While Chea had never been disturbed by ghosts, visitors were sometimes afraid to stay at her home. Some neighbors found even more remains on their property.

---

[23] C. Hughes 2003; Springer 2015.   [24] Chea 2003, 9.
[25] CSD 1998; Nissen 2005. See also Hinton 2005.   [26] Chea 1999.
[27] "Public Forum Program," Center for Social Development, undated (http://www.csdcambodia.org).
[28] What follows about the remains is based on: author interview with Vannath Chea, Phnom Penh, March 11, 2016 and Chea 2016.
[29] Chea 2016, 116.

Others told her that they had "seen many ghosts wandering around on the street. So believe it or not, I don't know." Chea added that she sometimes heard dogs howling, usually at dawn, when some Cambodians believe dogs can see ghosts. At such moments, "I burn incense and pray for the victims' lost souls to be liberated, and to be reborn in a better world."[30]

Later I asked Chea where the idea for the public forums had originated. She replied, "It's from me." Chea explained that, while living in the U.S. she had watched town hall meetings on TV. "The city hall would invite the people having concern about a specific issue to come and discuss."[31] She was also inspired by League of Women's Voters debates: "I felt like I'd like to be a moderator or facilitator among different and diverse interests, providing a platform for them without having [a vested interest]."

Just as Lao Mong Hay had been influenced by a long-standing institution in England, so too was Chea inspired by a U.S. town-hall model dating back to the governance of the New England colonies. Chea likewise adapted the practice in the Cambodian context, taking account of local political organization and sensitivities as well as Buddhism.

Indeed, Chea's orientation as the leader of CSD was informed both by cosmopolitan ideas about democracy and human rights, many learned in the U.S., and Buddhism. Equanimity was at the center of her approach. Equanimity, she explained, arose from maintaining balance and not reacting to sensation. Otherwise, "the reactive sensation would accumulate and [the cycle would go] on and on. . . . That's what you call karma. Equanimity means to remain mindful with no reaction."[32]

This perspective, she went on, informed Buddhist injunctions against vindictiveness. "Revenge won't stop by revenge," Chea explained. "That's what the Buddha said. . . . Don't look at a bad thing as bad. Look at the bad thing as just a normal, natural phenomenon. And don't try to react to those natural phenomena. Let us go with equanimity, just observe it."[33] Thus Chea could forgive even Pol Pot. She traveled to his grave, where she lit incense and prayed for his soul. "Why should I hate him?" she said. "What he did is an act of nature. . . . In Buddhism, we try to maintain the balance of equilibrium, equanimity, no hate, not to enjoy, no sadness, no happiness. Maintain your equanimity. Whatever happens, just accept it."[34]

This Buddhist perspective, she noted, mediated the way many Cambodians understood human rights and justice, for which there was "no exact foundation" and "little understanding." "The concept of human rights is so confusing for people, even now," Chea contended. "Why? Because we just took the concept from the Westerners while we did not have any foundation [as a basis upon which] to apply the concept of the rule, the procedures, the enforcement of the law."[35]

---

[30] Ibid.

[31] What follows on the origin of public forums is from: author interview with Chea Vannath, Phnom Penh, March 9, 2016.

[32] Author interview with Chea Vannath, Phnom Penh, March 11, 2016.   [33] Ibid.

[34] Ibid. See also Chea 2016, 117.

[35] Author interview with Chea Vannath, Phnom Penh, March 9, 2016.

Such a situation didn't "mean that there are not human rights in Buddhism. It's just much, much more subtle." The moral precepts were a point of similarity. But, Chea noted, Buddhist stories often revolved around the notion of karma, suggesting that "people are different based on their good or bad karma. That's why you have the rich and the poor, the beautiful and the ugly, the powerful and the powerless.... It's nature. But somehow you say on the one hand do not harm any being. But on the other, people are born different."

In practice, she observed, these beliefs could lead to situations where people might explain misfortune or violence fatalistically, saying that bad karma was the reason a robber was beaten or a person rendered destitute. Noting the first precept and Buddhist compassion, she added, "That's not what the Buddha said, it's just the custom."[36]

These beliefs mediated everyday understandings of justice. Chea had trouble finding a Cambodian gloss for "justice." Instead, it might be better translated "by compassion, by cause and effect, by loving kindness, by equanimity. [It's] not European justice or American justice, 'black and white.' No, [Cambodian justice] is not black and white. It's very blurred."[37] Along these lines, Chea added, there were "many layers of justice," including "justice by man" (legal justice), justice in the next life (karmic justice), and "individual justice" (revenge or personal justice).

This Buddhist perspective informed the public forums. Because of the long-standing conflict in Cambodia, Chea told me, "very few people are able to stay above [the conflict] and maintain objectivity. And I like to do that. So we took a lot of new initiatives." The CSD Public Forums unit addressed a variety of issues, ranging from elections to sanitation and hygiene. The debates, broadcast on TV and radio, involved "candid debate and caught a lot of people's attention." Chea said she was "amazed because I assumed that the Cambodian people were shy and didn't want to speak up. But in reality, during the forums, you had a hard time [stopping] them."

2000 public forums on "The Khmer Rouge and National Reconciliation"

In 1999, shortly after the implosion of the Khmer Rouge movement, negotiations to hold a tribunal were intensifying. "They started talking almost every day about the Khmer Rouge Tribunal," Chea told me. "But not here, not with the Cambodian people, but in New York, in France, in Indonesia, in the United Nations.... So when the media started asking me [about the KRT], I said 'I don't know.' I was the head of an organization, and I knew nothing."

Chea and her team decided to hold three forums to make the debate public and help Cambodians "find the truth and voice their opinions."[38] The structure of their program necessitated "that we have representatives from all sides of the debate," including former Khmer Rouge.[39] CSD's decision was controversial since the Khmer Rouge had only recently laid down their arms. "I have been much criticized

---

[36] Author interview with Chea Vannath, Phnom Penh, March 11, 2016.
[37] Author interview with Chea Vannath, Phnom Penh, March 9, 2016.
[38] CSD 2006, 1.   [39] Chea 2002, 304.

for inviting" them to participate, Chea recalls, sometimes "for even speaking to them."[40]

To prepare, Chea and her staff traveled to two former Khmer Rouge strongholds. There, her team "discovered a very mercurial situation ... There seemed to be no confidence that peace would hold."[41] Initially CSD planned to focus on the KRT. After seeing the situation, however, her team "realized that the crucial issues were those of long-standing peace and national reconciliation, of which a tribunal would be a component."[42] The theme was broadened to "The Khmer Rouge and National Reconciliation."

The 2000 forums were held in Battambang, Phnom Penh, and Sihanoukville, which had different demographics. Each forum had a similar structure as one to two hundred participants gathered for three hours to voice their opinions during proceedings covered by the media. The first forum, held in Battambang city involved 124 participants, including "ordinary people," local officials, Buddhist monks and nuns, teachers and students, members of civil society, and even a U.S. diplomat.[43]

The proceedings revealed that there were significant differences of opinion about the necessity of trials. Former Khmer Rouge warned a tribunal could threaten peace since "national reconciliation [is still] in its infancy." Moreover, it was unfair to only try the Khmer Rouge since the conflict involved a number of parties, domestic and international.[44] Some echoed Hun Sen's call to "let bygones be bygones."[45]

Others argued in favor of a tribunal, stating a trial was necessary for lasting peace and to uphold the rule of law, particularly given Cambodia's politicized judiciary. Chea recalled, "Attendees said that a fair trial would be an important component of national reconciliation. It would provide peace of mind and closure."[46]

Public Opinion

A CSD survey of forum participants suggested commonalities about popular attitudes toward a possible tribunal. A majority of the participants (68%) agreed that "former Khmer Rouge leaders must be tried," while even more (82%) agreed that a trial would contribute to national reconciliation.[47] This preference for a tribunal has been found in almost every subsequent poll.[48]

If such findings are sometimes taken as proof of support for transitional justice in Cambodia, these "highlights" obscure nuance and variation. While there was broad support for the trials, for example, the extent of support was not constant. In Battambang, for example, the support dropped significantly, with only 40.5 percent of the respondents agreeing former Khmer Rouge should be tried.[49] This statistic

---

[40] CSD 2006, 1.   [41] Chea 2002, 304–05.   [42] Ibid, 305.
[43] CSD 2006, 7.   [44] Ibid. See also *Phnom Penh Post* Staff 2000, 12.
[45] CSD 2006, 7–8.   [46] Chea 2002, 305.   [47] CSD 2006, 23.
[48] KID 2004; Pham, Vinck, Balthazard, Hean, and Stover 2009; Sonis, Gibson, de Jong, Field, Hean, and Komproe 2009; Chy 2009; Pham, Vinck, Balthazard, and Hean 2011; Kirchenbauer, Balthazard, Ky, Vinck, and Pham 2013.
[49] CSD 2006, 11.

suggested, not surprisingly, that former Khmer Rouge favored "letting bygones be bygones." Similarly, 26 percent of the Battambang participants agreed that "the past should be forgotten." In the compiled results, just 9 percent of the respondents held this view.

Buddhism was invoked to support and oppose trials. Several monks who were interviewed around this time, for example, emphasized the importance of ending cycles of vindictiveness, compassion, and the karmic principle that one's actions condition one's future. However, monks also emphasized the importance of discernment, truth, and understanding and suggested that a tribunal, if fair, could contribute to such insight and the process of peace and reconciliation.[50]

There were also significant differences among the large number of survey participants who expressed support for a trial. Some respondents maintained the tribunal should be international, others domestic. Disagreements also emerged about whether foreign countries should be held accountable for their role in the conflict.

Broader public opinion in Cambodia also diverged on such issues. A February 2009 DC-Cam survey found that the vast majority of its 1,100 respondents (92.7%) wanted former Khmer Rouge leaders put on trial.[51] But only a slight majority (56.8%) thought that five to ten former senior leaders should be tried as opposed to those (41.4%) who favored restricting the number to the five senior leaders already arrested—the position of Hun Sen's government. A generational difference emerged as well, with 67.5 percent of younger Cambodians born after DK favoring additional prosecutions.

Youk Chhang, the Director of DC-Cam, noted some of the demographic nuances in Cambodian attitudes toward the tribunal. A sizeable number of survivors more or less supported the position of Hun Sen, he noted, and were somewhat skeptical of and preferred a more limited role for the international community.[52] Another group, including many Cambodian refugees who had been repatriated, was more suspicious of the government and favored greater international involvement. Similar divisions were characteristic of Cambodian expatriates and the young.

Relatedly, the DC-Cam study also revealed another undercurrent beneath the "highlight" statistic of high levels of support. If 92.7 percent of the respondents expressed support, the majority knew little about (44.2%) or have never even heard about (17.3%) the tribunal.[53] Only 11.6 percent of the respondents had "heard a lot" about the ECCC—and the survey was taken in February 2009. This lack of knowledge was not addressed by the 2000 CSD study, which consisted of more informed participants. If many Cambodians were aware a tribunal was taking place, most had a limited understanding of it.

They also often feared courts, which were noted for corruption. These perceptions were evident in CSD's 2004 follow-up to their 1998 survey. Only 1 percent of the respondents reported having "had contact with the judiciary during the past year," even as many viewed the judiciary as "highly corrupt and favoring the rich and

---

[50] See also Chea 1996 and *The Phnom Penh Post* Staff 2000, 13, 15.   [51] Chy 2009.
[52] Chhang 2007.   [53] Chy 2009, 13.

powerful because they can pay bribes." As a result and as discussed in the last chapter, Cambodians frequently turned to alternative dispute resolution mechanisms to settle a conflict.[54] Indeed, participants ranked judges and court officials as the most dishonest groups (by 53% of the respondents).[55] More broadly, the study found that corruption pervaded almost every sector of Cambodian society.

Theary Seng, Public Forums, and CSD Outreach

CSD KRT outreach forums

Seng joined CSD after Vannath stepped down in 2006,[56] just as the ECCC was commencing. Like KID, CSD was in the process of adapting its public forum project to fit the moment, beginning with three 2006 "Justice and National Reconciliation" public forums on the ECCC. The first took place in March 2006 while Chea was still in charge. The forum retained much of the earlier half-day structure and format, with experts and official speakers delivering short lectures and participants expressing their views.

Seng ran the next two 2006 forums, in Kampot and Kratie provinces, before procuring funding from the German Development Service (DED) and Diakonia/Sida to undertake an expanded series of forums from 2006 to 2009. From the start, Seng introduced changes reflecting her background and leadership style.

Prior to holding a forum, for example, CSD staff would "conduct ground preparation activities with target people in the concerned provinces and municipalities for two to three weeks," including small group meetings with local leaders that focused on "the topics, venues, jurisdictions and [possible] participants."[57] In addition, CSD brought fifty local stakeholders to Phnom Penh to visit the Tuol Sleng, Choeung Ek, and the ECCC.[58]

If the forums focused on "peace and national reconciliation," their goal was: "(i) to disseminate information regarding the KR years, the ECCC, [and] processes of just peace, healing, reconciliation, (ii) to help manage the expectations of the participants ... and ultimately (iii) to create a multiplier effect in these participants as ambassadors to their families and neighbors."[59]

Dialogue and the court of public opinion

As a court of law, Seng noted, the ECCC had limitations. However, it could nevertheless serve as a "catalyst" for the more important "court of public opinion." In this regard, the ECCC provided Cambodians with the opportunity "to discuss other

---

[54] Nissen 2005, 30.   [55] Ibid, 59.   [56] Chandara 2006.   [57] CSD 2007, 3.
[58] Ibid, 13. On the politicization of a 2008 CSD Forum, see Manning 2011. See also Lesley-Rozen 2014.
[59] CSD 2007, 13.

issues of greater importance: a just peace, healing, reconciliation, rule of law, history, human rights."[60]

During our meeting at The Living Room, Seng elaborated on this distinction between the "court of law" and the "court of public opinion."[61] The former, encompassing the domain of legal procedure and process, was limited in its possibilities, particularly given the amount of time that had passed since DK and the political controversies surrounding the court. As a "court of public opinion," however, the ECCC held transformative promise. "In the court of law, you have to talk about legal and factual issues," Seng explained: "In the court of public opinion, it's impressions, sentiments, history, allowing people to cry, allowing people to rant, to talk about things that don't need to be verified but that is a catharsis of releasing emotions ... processes that can't be had in the very narrow confines of limited judicial process."[62] The two processes were complementary. "One is sharp, one is blunt and," she said after a pause, "open."

Because it was open, the court of public opinion could be molded in different ways. As an example, Seng noted the "rupture" defense tactics of Vergès, who "understands this, uses it. He is functioning in the court of public opinion more than he is functioning in the court of public law." CSD's forums, she continued, were another manifestation of the court of public opinion, one "we can shape." The human rights and democracy building efforts begun during the UNTAC period were "preparatory grounds" since Cambodians were still "unprepared for the actual day of exercising dialogue." The ECCC allowed for the realization of the process, the building of a "culture of dialogue. I see this topic of the [KRT] and Khmer Rouge history as the first time Cambodians can be speaking freely."

She contrasted such dialogue with traditional Cambodian society, which "is a society of directives, the parent to the child, the husband to the wife, the leader to the governed. [T]his process has changed the equation."[63] Nevertheless, the dialogic space of engagement remained "very anti-Cambodian, an anti-Cambodian thinking. The fatalism of always constantly waiting to be impacted on. This is Cambodian. You see this all of the time [with people saying] 'Oh, it's karma, it's fate, this is my destiny ... I can't do anything about it so what's the point of acting because this is my fate.'" By participating in outreach activities like the public forums, Seng contended, Cambodians were starting to do "the opposite ... saying 'I want to impact this process. I want impact.' It's empowering. And it is."[64]

Translation and turbulence

The 2007 forums lasted from 7am until late afternoon and were divided into two parts, the first focusing on the ECCC. A Svay Rieng forum, "History, Justice (Looking at the Past, the Present ...)," was moderated by Seng and a colleague.[65]

---

[60] Ibid, 13.
[61] What follows on the "court of law" versus the "court of public opinion" is from: author interview, Theary Seng, Phnom Penh, June 29, 2009.
[62] Ibid.   [63] Ibid.   [64] Ibid.
[65] The description of the forum is based on an agenda from CSD 2007, 18.

After an introductory session, which included donor remarks, participants were shown a film about DK before listening to short presentations by four speakers, including an ECCC Press Officer and a court monitor. These remarks were followed by two longer "Open Discussion and Dialogue" sessions.

As with KID outreach, many participants in the CSD public forums had trouble understanding the court's complicated history, structure, and legal process. Seng noted the difficulty of explaining "law to individuals who are afraid of [Cambodia's] legal system and judiciary" and viewed it as corrupt.[66]

Seng contrasted the situation to the U.S.: "We learn about law through *Chips, LA Law*, through *Ally McBeal*. That's how we learn our rights, right? And already we're conditioned to know the term 'prosecutor.' But here we can't take that for granted [as people ask] 'a prosecutor—what's that? Is it a thing?' Some participants couldn't tell the ECCC speakers apart. Others thought the court was a NGO." Seng added, "At one point, the term for victim, civil party, witness, and complainant were all being lumped together and used interchangeably" not just by the forum participants but speakers from civil society and even forum facilitators. "[Only] now," she noted, "is it being slowly, slowly clarified."

The solution was "constantly to simplify." During forums, she would sometimes draw a diagram of the court with circles, boxes, and arrows naming the key personnel and units, such as the Office of the Co-Investigating Judges (OCIJ) and Trial Chamber. She would use the same methods to describe the roles of the prosecution, defense, civil parties, and witnesses. Nevertheless, the participants were often confused, even if her team used vernacular language. "At the end of the day," Seng added, "we have to use the word prosecutor, judge, or investigating judge."

In the afternoon the focus of the forums shifted from the court to healing and trauma. The afternoon of the Svay Rieng forum, for example, included a half hour of breathing exercises followed by short presentations and then discussion on "Just Peace & Reconciliation" and "Trauma & Healing." Counselors offered psychological support.

For Seng, the introduction of this new segment on trauma and healing illustrated how the court could serve as a catalyst to shape the court of public opinion. If it were not possible, beyond limited moments such as "the very rare expert opinion," to talk about trauma in the court of law, the KRT provided the opportunity to "shape the topic of trauma ... in the court of public opinion. We can introduce the concept, we can shape it. And now, we have shaped it because more and more people ... are talking about their emotions and trauma."[67]

These efforts were undergirded by a trauma booklet distributed at the forums and used as a focus for discussions.[68] One of Seng's first initiatives, the booklet was partly a collaboration with the DED, which provided a consulting psychologist, Matthias Witzel.[69] Witzel authored the handbook while leading breathing exercises and offering counseling at forums.

---

[66] What follows on simplification is from: author interview, Theary Seng, Phnom Penh, June 29, 2009.

[67] Ibid.   [68] Witzel 2007.   [69] Theary Seng's preface to Witzel 2007.

Seng's attempt to create the booklet was turbulent. When she first "pushed for this my staff was very angry with me. And the word on the street was that Seng thinks every Cambodian is crazy.... It was very hurtful and painful."[70] In response, Seng realized she needed to acknowledge her own psychological struggles, which included "30 years of angst, disorder, of suicidal thoughts, of trauma more generally."[71] And so, Seng recounted, "I told them how traumatized I was, how I had suicidal thoughts in my healing process. And then they realized, 'Okay, Theary is not just being critical.' And now my staff and more and more people are very comfortable with this." As Seng's remarks suggest, part of the "turbulence" she encountered was the result of trying to graft Western psychobiological concepts into the context of Cambodia and the KRT.

Leadership and vision

The addition of the afternoon sessions thus marked a departure from earlier iterations of the forums. As with KID, the focus and structure of the CSD forums shifted over time in accordance with the concerns and donor funding priorities of the moment as well as with the leadership, staffing, and capacity of the NGO. Despite the fact that both Chea and Seng had spent time in the U.S. that influenced their leadership vision, they differed considerably in their approaches. Perhaps this was partly due to their different ages when they left Cambodia (Chea was roughly thirty years older than Seng) and their upbringing (for much of her childhood, Seng was raised without her birth parents and in a Christian community while Chea spent her youth in Cambodia).

Religion was one key difference. If Chea and Seng both viewed the public forums as a space to promote reconciliation and social development, they viewed their roles somewhat differently. Chea preferred to stay in the background, whereas Seng was front and center as an agent of change. From Chea's Buddhist perspective, the forums were a space in which differing opinions should be expressed and heard in a balanced manner that accorded with the principle of equanimity.

Seng, in contrast, viewed this space as a place where, if people voiced their opinions, they did so in a manner "shaped" in a particular direction. The "court of opinion" provided an opportunity for people to be healed by coming to terms with trauma; accordingly, she modified the forums to take up this topic. Likewise, she viewed the forums as a place where Cambodians could become active agents empowered by rights exercised in the context of the affordances offered by the court. This notion of social transformation accorded with her Christian belief. Seng's Christianity also informed her view of forgiveness, which she saw as a "part of the healing process,"[72] something that could take place alongside justice.

She directly linked this point to her own story, which informed her conviction there was a larger need to discuss trauma in Cambodia. Ultimately, depending on

---

[70] Author interview, Theary Seng, Phnom Penh, June 29, 2009.
[71] Ibid. See also Seng 2005, 228, 236, 259.   [72] *The War Cry* Staff 2005, 5.

the person, she told me, the process of forgiveness "can take a year. It can take a lifetime. But I can say without qualification it's a better position to be in. Because the alternative is to be angry and that is really destructive."

If Chea was also influenced by human rights discourses, Buddhism informed her approach to dialogue, reconciliation, and healing. She stressed balance and equanimity more than forgiveness, viewing them as a path to mental health and healing.[73]

Likewise, she recognized the importance of Buddhist rituals in healing, including the role of monks in transmitting merit to the dead. One of the most important ceremonies where this is done is *pchum ben*, when Cambodians make offerings to the spirits of the dead. Chea recalled the post-DK return of this ceremony in 1979, when people flocked to "a pagoda in suburban Phnom Penh, bringing food to offer to the monks. The beliefs are that the offerings convey blessings and food to the dead people, for the liberation of their souls to a better world."[74] She directly links this Buddhist holiday to healing, recalling how after DK, "The opening of the pagoda, the reappearance of the monks, the religious prayer and ritual provided magic medicine to relieve mental depression and anxiety from millions of traumatized victims."

Yet, the role of such Buddhist ceremonies in healing is largely left out of biomedical trauma discourses, yet another example of how the justice facade elides critical spaces, histories, and practices related to well-being that are a key part of the lived experience of many Cambodians and their relationship to the DK past. Indeed, such Buddhist beliefs directly impacted upon the way many Cambodians understood the court and CSD outreach activities—and also the way in which the next rung of intermediaries working on outreach, program officers and staff, conveyed information about the court.

Sophea Im and the "Dark" and "Light Worlds"

For example, Sophea Im, a member of CSD's public forum staff, told me that he frequently used Buddhism when conducting outreach. Im, who had been a reporter for *The Cambodia Daily*, began working with CSD in 2006, shortly after Seng became director. He served as her Executive Assistant and also a co-facilitator of the public forums, running the afternoon sessions.

Im noted that, when explaining the court to forum participants it was necessary to adhere to legal language and concepts, his team would "simplify it in an understandable way, in Cambodian everyday talk." To explain the idea of jurisdiction, for example, he would use the appropriate legal term but make an analogy to the everyday life of the villagers, telling them, "You own a piece of land and have a fence. You can only plant plants or vegetables within this boundary even if you want to do more . . . So the court is like you" and can't exceed the "boundaries" of its jurisdiction.[75]

---

[73] Chea 2016; Korah 2010; Author interview with Chea Vannath, Phnom Penh, March 11, 2016; Chea 1996.

[74] Chea 2010, 46; see also Davis 2015; Ledgerwood 2012.

[75] Author interview with Sophea Im, Phnom Penh, September 15, 2010.

One of the most difficult things to explain was the personal jurisdiction of the court to try "senior leaders and those most responsible." To clarify, Im might liken the limitations of the court to the offerings to the dead that Cambodians make during festivals and ceremonies. "When you make offerings," he would say, "you make a lot [of food] but you only offer a small portion to the dead, placing it under a tree or some other place and lighting incense."[76] To offer more would be a "waste of resources" and mean nothing since the offerings were symbolic.

If Cambodians make such offerings to the dead and local spirits, the ECCC was symbolically "offering" the trial of a small number of former Khmer Rouge leaders to the DK dead. By framing his explanations in this manner, Im directly linked the ECCC to the everyday understandings of justice, which diverged in critical ways from the legalism of the justice facade.

Im acknowledged this point even as he stressed that he sought to educate villagers about the goals of transitional justice. Perhaps in part due to Seng's international networks and the high profile of CSD's Public Forums, Im and other CSD staffers were invited to participate in related training sessions in Cambodia and abroad. Im himself had attended human rights and democratization workshops abroad as well as International Center for Transitional Justice (ICTJ) courses in Japan.

He sought to incorporate transitional justice into his outreach work, discussing the broad idea of transitional justice and how it related to ECCC. As he did so, he simplified, explaining things in ways that resonated with the everyday life of the villagers. But, in the end, he would return to the spirits of the dead since this was "the driving force that made them feel the obligation to seek justice" at the ECCC.[77]

Ultimately, there were at least two key circuits of meaning mediating understandings of and discourses about the court. To illustrate, Im invoked a distinction Cambodians sometimes make between the "light world" and the "dark world." The former, he explained, was "something you can see with your eyes ... light is something you see, you can touch."[78] Law and legal procedure operated in this domain. The "dark world" was more obscure, involving those things that could not be directly seen and encompassing magic, spirit beliefs, and religion.

For many Cambodians, then, the primary function of the court was not abstract Justice but a transaction with the souls of the dead, something occluded by the justice facade. Another way to think of this is to consider the justice facade as a "light world" veneer masking the "dark world" of magic and spirit beliefs that are much more familiar and central to everyday life. Thus, for many Cambodian villagers, the court was almost like a *bangsokol* ceremony in which merit was transmitted to the dead to placate the spirits and enhance their prospects for rebirth. It was for this reason that the civil parties held an actual *bangsokol* ceremony at the time of the verdict in which justice, as manifest in the judgment, was transmitted to the dead.

To "move forward," one's relationship to the souls of the dead must be transformed by making the offerings that placate them and facilitate their rebirth—as opposed to the turbulent state in which those who suffer violent deaths are often

---

[76] Ibid.   [77] Ibid.   [78] Ibid.

thought to be suspended. Indeed, like *neak ta* and other entities in the "dark world," the souls of the dead may afflict the living, leading them to become sick, have misfortune, or suffer psychosomatic woes. In this "dark world" sense, the judicial process may contribute to healing—not by "accountability" but by enabling a transaction with the souls of the dead that stops them from afflicting the living.

As had been the case with the forums Chea held, the CSD KRT outreach forums involved monks. On the one hand, the presence of the monks helped create a more peaceful environment for the proceedings. On the other side, the monks might offer insights into justice, reconciliation, and healing.[79]

Nevertheless, the role of Buddhism in the CSD forums under Seng was relatively limited, likely because of Seng's more secular and Christian orientation. Seng did not encourage the use of Buddhist concepts. "I'm not Buddhist. I'm a Christian," she explained. "I'm anti-fate … [and] opposed to the deep, deep, deep passivity" Buddhism could foster while inhibiting discussion and action.[80]

Similarly, she noted that Buddhist ideas about extinction of desire were at odds with Christian love. Seng was also uneasy with the notion of karma, which suggested victims were to blame for their misfortune. Here again we see how the ideas of NGO leaders shaped outreach initiatives and constrained the action of their staff members, even if the staffers had some latitude to vernacularize.

Theary Seng and victim participation

As Im's comments suggested, civil party participation became an increasingly important part of the forums as Case 001 drew near. From the start, human rights NGOs had advocated for a prominent role for victims in the court, something enabled by Cambodian civil law tradition.

During deliberations about the internal rules, the French International Co-Investigating Judge (OCIJ) had pushed for expansive civil party participation modeled after French practices. His position, with the support of civil society, was incorporated into the first version of the Internal Rules on June 12, 2007 despite the fact that victim participation had not been envisioned in the 2003 Agreement to create the court.[81]

Internal Rule 23 granted civil parties significant participatory rights, both in terms of "supporting the prosecution" and in seeking "collective and moral reparations."[82] These rights were extended to those who had suffered "physical, material, or psychological" injury. Rule 23 further stipulated that, to qualify as a civil party, a victim needed to submit an application that would be evaluated by the OCIJ or Trial Chamber. If approved, a civil party would be granted the right to legal representation. A new Victims Unit (VU), which was established by Rule 12, would assist civil parties in this process. Ultimately, victims had three possible ways to participate

[79] CSD 2007, 9.   [80] Author interview, Theary Seng, Phnom Penh, June 29, 2009.
[81] Ciorciari and Heindel 2014, 207, 373; Jarvis 2014; ECCC Internal Rules, version 1, June 12, 2007.
[82] ECCC, Internal Rules, version 1, June 12, 2007.

in the legal process: as witnesses, complainants, or most directly and extensively, as civil parties.

While granting victims an unprecedented degree of involvement in an international trial, problems quickly emerged due to the fact that this participatory role had not been initially foreseen. Difficulties ranged from the bureaucratic (how to administer the VU and interface with victims) to the financial (how to pay for the VU and civil party participation, including their lawyers and reparations).

Meanwhile, the legal process was in motion. The prosecution, which had started its investigation almost immediately after the court began operation in mid-2006, submitted its Introductory Submission on July 18, 2007, just a month after the Internal Rules were finalized.[83] The OCIJ almost immediately detained Duch (July 30, 2007) and soon thereafter the four other suspects named in the Introductory Submission: Nuon Chea (September 19), Ieng Sary and his wife Ieng Thirith (November 12), and Khieu Samphan (November 19). On the same day Nuon Chea was arrested, the OCIJ separated Duch's trial (Case 001) from that of the other defendants.

In the midst of this activity, even as NGOs continued their outreach, the victim participation process needed to be quickly sorted out. Seng recalled her dissatisfaction with the pace of the deliberations, which involved a lot of talk but were always "stuck at step two. And then we'd meet again and start over at step one," returning to theoretical discussions of the internal rules and civil party rights. Nothing was "moving forward."[84] Seng herself, who was trained in common law, was initially uncertain how best to proceed. Then, she said, everything suddenly "clicked" as she understood that it would be possible to engage people "at a different level at the forums" since they would now have a "personal interest" with the ability to file complaints and be directly involved.[85]

She decided to jumpstart the process by applying for civil party status. "It was still early. I'm not sure there was a head [of the victims unit] yet. It was September 2007 ... [just] days after Nuon Chea was arrested. No one was thinking about this. There was no victims unit, no financing" and the court officials and civil society workers were "overwhelmed" with work.[86] Since there was not yet an official application form, Seng had to compose her own, a two-page document she submitted to the OCIJ on September 25, 2007. She told reporters, "I wanted to test the process."[87]

Thus, Theary became the first Cambodian civil party and helped catalyze victim participation. In early October, in consultation with civil society representatives including Seng, the court issued a directive on victim participation.[88] The directive included a five-page Victim Information Form (VIF) initially modeled on the form used at the International Criminal Court before, Seng said, being modified to be less

---

[83] Trial Chamber 2010.
[84] Author interview, Theary Seng, Phnom Penh, June 29, 2009.   [85] Ibid.
[86] Ibid.   [87] *The Cambodia Daily* Staff 2007, 3.
[88] ECCC 2008. See Thomas and Chy 2009, 235.

"intimidating."[89] In addition, the Practice Direction detailed the process involved in becoming a civil party.

The VU was placed at the center of the process, serving as "the sole contact for victims and their representatives."[90] After processing VIF applications, the VU was supposed to send them to the appropriate office, with complaints going to the Office of the Co-Prosecutors and civil party applications to the OCIJ or Trial Chamber. The VU would also assist civil parties in procuring legal representation.

Yet the VU existed largely only in name. The directive included an address for the VU, but the VU lacked staff, funding, and leadership. Regardless, others began to submit civil party applications almost immediately. In November, the ECCC appointed an international deputy head of the VU. It was only in February 2008 that Keat Bophal, a former human rights worker, was hired as the Cambodian head of the office.

Indeed, one of the graphics in the KID booklet depicts Uncle San sitting at the desk of the "Head of the Victims Unit," a Cambodian woman who KID staffers loosely modeled on Keat Bophal.[91] In the graphic, she is portrayed as carrying out the idealized function of the VU, seamlessly facilitating victim participation. The reality, however, was quite different. Due to severe resource and staffing constraints and lack of planning, the VU was initially unable to engage with victims in a significant manner. Intermediary organizations filled this void, refocusing their efforts on victim participation.

The creation of the Uncle San booklet highlighted this shift at KID. Additional NGOs heavily involved in outreach and then victim participation included DC-Cam and ADHOC.[92] Others provided more specific services, ranging from psychological support (Transcultural Psychosocial Organization) to legal services (Legal Aid of Cambodia and the Cambodian Defender's Project), as they adapted their existing structures and practices to the exigencies of the moment.

CSD outreach and civil party participation

Seng viewed victim participation as a significant opportunity to catalyze change in Cambodia and instructed her staff to begin looking for possible civil parties when doing ground preparations for the forums. The forums were expanded to include a half-day session with perhaps twenty victims on the morning following the main public forum.

Seng explained that it was necessary to "piggyback" in this manner due to logical and financial constraints since CSD was primarily supported by DED funding at this point. Given the state of the VU, however, donors began to prioritize NGOs like KID and CSD who were working on outreach and civil

[89] Author interview, Theary Seng, Phnom Penh, June 29, 2009.
[90] ECCC 2008, 1. See also Thomas and Chy 2009, 235.
[91] Author interview with Suon, Phnom Penh, February 6, 2012.
[92] On civil society involvement in ECCC outreach and victim participation, see Balthazard 2010, 2013; Latt, Kirchenbauer, and Wünsche 2014; Lambourne 2012; Sperfeldt 2012a, 2012b, 2013.

party participation. As a result, CSD was able to procure more substantial funding over the next year and a half and to begin to expand its civil party target base to include widows, prisoners, and child soldiers in addition to orphans. Her idea was to create groups that would have a larger voice and function like US class action suits.

Seng was galvanized by the transformative possibilities of civil party participation. Just as the "court of public opinion" allowed for Cambodian subjectivities to be reshaped in terms of trauma and psychological well-being, so too might it enable the creation of new political subjectivities and a "culture of dialogue."

Previously, the public forums had served as conduits of information, education, and dialogue. But, Seng noted, the role of participants was still akin to that of a "listener." Victim participation gave them a direct interest in the process, one of "empowerment, engagement" that greatly "deepen[ed] the process of outreach work." The difference was "night and day. The interest of an invitee to a public forum is 'well, I want to know information.' The interest of someone ... becoming a civil party [is that] now they are putting their heart and soul into the process. They *want* to know." If they now heard the term "prosecutor," for example, "they would think 'oh, this is a term I need to know for my application.' It is a deeper level of education."[93]

Victim participation made the court and ideas like rights "very real because they are actually exercising their rights," not just legal rights but "sociopolitical rights, civil and political rights, the right to be given accountability as a citizen. And more than that. At the end of the day, the benefit of this process is not just the civil party but the forums ... and the building of a culture of dialogue" as opposed to one of directives and passivity. "This process has changed the equation. Because the dialogue is more equal. Dialogue implicitly recognizes the value of diversity and diverging opinions. So this is real democracy building."[94]

But, if civil parties might be more invested, it was still difficult for many to understand the legal process. Even the term for civil party was unfamiliar. Im recalled that it was impossible to simply use this term, "I had to start from the beginning and explain the role of the lawyer, investigating judge, prosecutor, trial judge, even the clerk and judicial police—[describing] each key player and what they do."[95] Then he would turn to the process for filing a complaint and the possibility of compensation. Like Seng, Im would stress personal interest. But, in contrast to her emphasis on neoliberal subjectivity, he framed this interest in terms of seeking justice for the dead, mixing notions of transitional justice and international law with Buddhist ideas.

As Im's comments suggest, the new sessions were time-consuming and difficult. "It's really intensive," Seng told me. "One full day of engagement and then [on the second morning] 4–5 hours at five times the intensity. In the forums, other voices are being expressed. But here it's just me trying to explain basic law" to people

---

[93] Author interview, Theary Seng, Phnom Penh, June 29, 2009. [94] Ibid.
[95] Author interview with Sophea Im, Phnom Penh, September 15, 2010.

who had "never had the judiciary and legal system demystified for them" and who thought of the courts as a corrupt "market place" to be feared. "And the legal terms," she exclaimed. "It's like a whole new language!"[96]

The VIF presented another challenge. Indeed, it was the ultimate focus of the civil party segment. The twenty or so potential applicants gathered in a quiet area, where they would ask questions before eventually trying to fill out the complaint form. An emotional support team was present if participants became upset.[97]

Many found the legalistic language and structure confusing, including the requirement that victims tell their complicated stories in a succinct form focused on criminality. If some NGOs directly assisted the civil parties with applications, CSD took a more hands off approach. While providing guidelines, CSD viewed it as unrealistic to expect a villager to finish an application in just a few hours. Moreover, they wanted the process to be "thoughtful" and "deep" and have "meaning beyond the law." Seng explained, "We have a short term and a long term view. The short term view is [helping] them pass the threshold from victim to civil party. The long term view is that they need to be thoughtful and write it themselves."[98] CSD would wait several weeks before picking up civil party applications.

Even as, through 2008 and into 2009, CSD was undertaking these activities and gaining significant attention and donor support, it became embroiled in an internal struggle. The tensions may also have been partly over vision as Seng had changed the orientation of CSD and the forums, turning them in a less Buddhist and more secular, liberal democratic direction. Issues of status might also have been involved, as Seng gained an increasingly prominent profile as a human rights activist and the "poster child" of the genocide and victim participation.[99]

The struggle, which included various legal and political maneuverings, continued through July 2009, when Seng was finally forced out. CSD lost most of its funding even as it continued to operate in diminished form. Seng argued that her removal, which involved the Cambodian courts, was an attempt to "silence an outspoken civil society voice" and illustrated that Cambodia was still operating under an authoritarian regime that "uses the semblance of democracy to combat democracy."[100]

Despite the controversy, public forums related to ECCC outreach continued. Most immediately, Seng and a number of former CSD staffers, including Sophea Im, created a new NGO, the Center for Justice and Reconciliation (CJR). CJR soon launched a series of public forums that included former CSD KRT outreach staffers like Im.

---

[96] Author interview, Theary Seng, Phnom Penh, June 29, 2009.
[97] Author interview, Sok Leang, Phnom Penh, July 30, 2010. On the complexity of the VIF, see Thomas and Chy 2009, 235.
[98] Author interview, Theary Seng, Phnom Penh, June 29, 2009.   [99] Kinetz 2008.
[100] Theary Seng website, http://ki-media.blogspot.com.

Im and VSS outreach

In August 2010, Im took a post with the VU, which in February had been renamed the Victims Support Section (VSS) as civil party participation was streamlined in a fifth revised version of the Internal Rules.[101] Prior to this name change, NGOs, backed by donor funding, took the lead in interfacing with victims. All of the more than ninety civil party applicants in Case 001 had filed with the assistance of NGOs. The same was true of the 3,866 applicants, including Seng, who filed for civil party status in Case 002. Overall, NGOs helped file roughly 84 percent of the 8,200 VIFs submitted in Case 002, the majority of which were facilitated by KID (2,486), ADHOC (1,848), and DC-Cam (1,744).[102]

The VU had remained dramatically understaffed and underfunded until the end of 2008, when the German Technical Cooperation Agency (GTZ) earmarked 1.5 million Euros to support the unit. This was in addition to smaller amounts of funding and advisors that the German government provided to NGOs.[103] This funding enabled the VU to begin to expand though the number of staff remained relatively small and the German funding underutilized.[104]

With the 2010 changes in the Internal Rules, the VSS took on a more significant role in assisting civil parties with legal representation and in seeking reparations and non-judicial measures, sometimes working in collaboration with other court units including a newly created Civil Party Co-Lead Lawyers section.[105] The VSS, which received an additional 1.2 million Euros from the German government in late 2010, also continued to work with intermediary organizations, though the role of and donor support for NGOs diminished with this growth of the VU/VSS.[106]

Im took over as VSS Outreach Coordinator amidst this expansion. In doing so, he sought to introduce a number of outreach practices that CSD and other NGOs had been using. These innovations included a new VSS newsletter, website, and radio programming.[107] But perhaps his most significant initiative was to repurpose the CSD public forum model, which the VSS focused on civil party participation.

The first "Regional Public Forum on Civil Party Applicants in Case 002" took place in Battambang on August 30–31 and was attended by 250 civil parties and civil party applicants. Like the CSD forums, the VSS forums included talks by court officials and civil society leaders about the court and its progress. Transcultural Psychosocial Organization (TPO) staffers also spoke about mental health issues, but this was not a central focus.

Instead, the proceedings were meant, as Rong Chhorng, the head of the VSS said during welcoming remarks, "to detail recent developments at the court ... [and] to assess the needs of Civil Party applicants in Case 002 and provide an opportunity for them to meet their lawyers."[108] In addition, Case 001 civil parties spoke about

---

[101] ECCC, "Internal Rules (Rev. 5)," February 9, 2010.
[102] Victims Support Section n.d.; Sperfeldt 2012b, 468, n52, 2013, 351.
[103] Jarvis 2014, 26 n26.   [104] Ciorciari and Heindel 2014, 207.
[105] On ECCC reparations, see Sperfeldt 2012b.
[106] ECCC Public Affairs 2010; Sperfeldt 2012a.
[107] Sophea Im, personal communication, November 7, 2016.
[108] Victims Support Section, 2010a.

their experience testifying. On the second day, the civil party participants met with their lawyers to discuss reparations, "expectations, legal representation, and general questions."

Im was able to incorporate Buddhism to a greater degree. A report from the second VSS forum, held in Kratie province, highlights that, just after registration, the proceedings were launched with "a Bangsokol, a Buddhist Commemorative Ceremony, for victims who [died] under the Khmer Rouge [regime]. Five Buddhist monks dedicated the forum to the deceased victims of the regime through prayers."[109]

For Im, this innovation, which brought together the "dark" and "light" worlds, was critical. "We want to speak in two ways," he told me, so that the villagers would see the parallel between legal justice and offerings to the dead. When talking to older Cambodians, Im continued, "we say 'you have prayed for the dead for many years with the monks giving a bridge [to the dead] during ceremonies, so you can make an offering and feel release . . . But, in the light world we talk about law!' "[110]

In this manner, Im was making a direct link between making offerings to the dead (the dark world) and legal justice (the light world), with monks and judges serving as the conduits (the "bridge") to a justice that was linked to karma (dark world) and law (light world). For some Cambodians, then, the ECCC trials were understood as a sort of legal *bangsokol* that yielded an offering to the dead and facilitated healing of the sort that a *bangsokol* might deliver. The trial, Im stated, "is just like a *bangsokol*."[111]

The *bangsokol* also served as a sort of reparation. In Cambodia, a person who is injured is often directly compensated. In ECCC law, however, civil parties are only allowed "collective and moral reparations." The *bangsokol* again provided a way to overcome this dissonance between abstract law and local practice. "It's not about money. It's symbolic," Im would say to the civil parties. "Why do you need money? Because you want release. When you get money, you may arrange a ceremony and pray to [the spirits of the dead]. But now the ceremony is already arranged. It's a short cut way for the dead to get what they deserve. Then we can calm [their spirits],"[112] which provides "release"—both for the souls of the dead to stop haunting the living and be reborn and for the living who were afflicted by these unsettled spirits who would thereby be placated and stop disturbing their lives.

For Im, the public forums involved a necessary "mixture" of elements, some of which were from international law and transitional justice, other parts from Cambodian understandings like Buddhism. This reflected his own background as a Cambodian civil society practitioner and then court official who was Buddhist but had also received extensive training in human rights, law, and transitional justice. But the "mixture" was also difficult to make. "We don't have a Cambodian way of life," Im explained, "where people sit down and discuss what happened to an individual. They only go to pray quietly to Buddha."[113] Many Cambodians, he

---

[109] Victims Support Section 2010b.
[110] Author interview with Sophea Im, Phnom Penh, September 15, 2010.   [111] Ibid.
[112] Ibid.   [113] Ibid.

continued, "don't have the courage to speak publically. We feel ashamed if we talk in front of others, it's part of the way we were brought up."

This hesitation was amplified in public situations like the CSD forums—which again stand at odds with the transitional justice imaginary suggesting people "naturally" want to engage in dialogue—and could make outreach difficult. "You cannot force people to swallow this type of understanding," he said. "It requires time and different methodologies [aimed at groups with] different levels of understanding."[114] It also involved trust-building. This is part of the reason why outreach teams were sent to a forum locale three times prior to the event itself: first to build trust (initially the team would say little about the court) and then prepare them for the forum format. If people might be hesitant to speak, Im noted, many ended up asking questions during the forums.

In part because of this trust issue, several NGOs undertook outreach work on a smaller scale and longer-term basis with rural communities.[115] Youth for Peace, for example, sought to promote intergenerational dialogue about DK, one of a number of projects related to its goal of promoting peacebuilding and social change through youth empowerment. Another, Kdei Karuna, used dialogic and participatory methods in their KRT-related "Justice and History Outreach" program and "Promoting Gender Equality" projects.[116] Indeed, Gender and Gender-based violence projects became increasingly salient foci of outreach, with the Cambodia Defender's Project also taking a leading role in this area beginning in 2009.[117] The same was true of the issue of mental health, with TPO, which partnered with CSD at the forums, taking the lead in terms of KRT outreach. In each case, the NGOs created their own "mixtures," blending international justice, their institutional practices, and everyday understandings in varying ways and to different extents.

Dialogue, the Public Sphere, and the Transitional Justice Imaginary

As illustrated by the prominence of the forums, which were widely covered in the media, dialogue remained a primary issue throughout the trial process. Outreach on dialogue-related issues also remained relatively well-funded, even as NGO KRT outreach funding began to diminish.

One reason is that dialogue suggested engagement and interest. Shortly before Im took over as head of VSS outreach, UN Secretary-General Ban Ki-moon had given remarks during a pledging conference at the ECCC noting the importance of the trial to "bring justice to the people of Cambodia, and to prevent impunity for the most heinous of crimes" as well as to "secure Cambodia's long-term well-being" through international justice. "Most importantly," he went on, Case 001,

---

[114] Ibid.

[115] For a description of NGO ECCC outreach, see Latt, Kirchenbauer, and Wünsche 2014; Sperfeldt 2012a, 2013.

[116] Latt, Kirchenbauer, and Wünsche 2014; Kdei Karuna n.d.

[117] Cambodia Defender's Project, "Gender-Based Violence under the Khmer Rouge."

which had just recently concluded, "demonstrated the deep interest of the people of Cambodia" as reflected by the fact that "more than 31,000 people visited the Chambers during the hearings, most … from Cambodia's provinces. This is a truly astounding figure."[118]

On the other hand, dialogue and engagement suggested the success of one of the primary goals of the tribunal, transforming Cambodia through the creation of a public sphere, an idealized transitional justice imaginary space. The idea of the dialogic public sphere pervades place-making transitional justice imaginary discourses, which assert that mechanisms like international courts create a space of democratic communicative interaction in which citizens exercise political agency and rights— in contrast to the space to which it is opposed, the repressive, silenced sphere of authoritarian regimes. The public forums suggested this liberal democratic public sphere was being created.

Not surprisingly, the public sphere is the framing concept of the introduction to the first comparative volume on transitional justice and outreach, *Transitional Justice, Culture, and Society: Beyond Outreach*, edited by Clara Ramírez-Barat, as a follow-up to the ICTJ's outreach project and her "Making an Impact" guide.[119]

Transitional Justice, Culture, and Society reflects this broad purview, with contributions from people working on outreach in a variety of contexts and modalities. Several discuss outreach at tribunals, including the first chapter on the Special Court for Sierra Leone (SCSL).[120] The knowledge and practices from such courts circulated in Cambodia as the ECCC was commencing.

In each case, however, these flows traveled differently, as the knowledge and practices were selected, adapted, and modified based on local conditions, individual preferences, and on-the-ground understandings. This dynamic is illustrated by the creation of the KID booklet and the conceptualization of CSD public forums— which, if drawing on models that flowed from various sources, ranging from SCSL town halls to the South African Truth and Reconciliation Commission forums, was repurposed to fit the Cambodian context and involved the grafting of practices such as the *bangsokol* ceremony.

Indeed, this sort of dialogic public space was front-and-center in discussions of transitional justice in general and outreach in particular, as illustrated by the introduction of *Transitional Justice, Culture, and Society*, "Transitional Justice and the Public Sphere."[121] The introduction begins with a discussion informed by the transitional justice imaginary. "Justice interventions," Ramírez-Barat states, invoking a temporal frame, are "backward looking" (in the sense of dealing with the past) "future-oriented projects" meant to "break with the past" through the "construction of a democratic and peaceful future." Such transitional justice measures "ultimately

---

[118] Ban Ki-moon 2010.

[119] Ramírez-Barat 2014a, 2014b. See also, International Center for Transitional Justice, "Outreach," n.d.; Ramírez-Barat and Karwande 2010.

[120] Peskin 2005; Stover and Weinstein 2004; Karwande 2014; Lambourne 2012.

[121] Ramírez-Barat 2014b.

aim to catalyze a transformation of a previous culture of impunity and conflict into one of respect for the democratic rule of law and human rights."[122]

Within this project, she continues, "outreach programs" offer "a set of tools and strategies" intended to "build direct channels of communication" in transitional societies, by disseminating information, promoting dialogue, establishing "consultation channels with different stakeholders," and creating "avenues for local participation."[123] By "raising awareness and promoting understanding," these "outreach programs ultimately aim to contribute to the legitimacy of transitional justice initiatives and engage the social body according to the values of the normative democratic shift they seek to promote."[124] Here again we find a manifestation of the transitional justice imaginary with its teleological, normative, temporal, spatial, aesthetic, and subjective assumptions.

All of these coalesce in the spatial domain that is at the center of Ramírez-Barat's introduction: the public sphere. Adapting this concept, originally formulated by Habermas, to the transitional justice context, Ramírez-Barat focuses on the public sphere as a space of non-state "communicative interactions" characterized by the "political agency" (as opposed to passive "recipients") of "individuals" exercising their "citizenship" and "rights-based claims."[125]

From this perspective, outreach programs like the public forums are imagined as local spaces reflecting the larger public sphere that the transitional justice imaginary aspires to create. In Ramírez-Barat's introduction, as is the case with discourses related to the transitional justice imaginary, individual participants—like the society as a whole—are depicted as undergoing transformation as they enter into and become part of the "(re)generated" democratic space of the public sphere. These place-making qualities are almost exactly the same as those manifest in the KID booklet, with Uncle San serving as a graphic representation of the transformation as he moves through the participatory space of a KID outreach session and then the public sphere of the ECCC.

Outreach forums were also often described in terms informed by the transitional justice imaginary, though the enactment and understanding of the space of the forum varied, as illustrated by the contrast between Chea's, Seng's, and Im's visions for the forums. Seng explicitly viewed the forums as a transitional justice space for catalyzing change, describing the pre- and post-states with binaries (voiceless/voice, mystified/demystified, ignorance/knowledge, passive/active, monologue/dialogue, impacted/proactive, trauma/healing, subject/citizen, and so forth).[126]

While Im also described the forums as a dialogic transitional justice space, he emphasized the idea of "transformation" to a much lesser extent and viewed the process as a necessary "mixture" of the "light" and "dark" worlds. Im's distinction illustrates a key problem with the spatiotemporality of the transitional justice imaginary, which asserts a straightforward current of transformation within a particular type of

---

[122] Ibid, 27.   [123] Ibid, 29.   [124] Ibid, 29.

[125] Ibid, 33. Ramírez-Barat cites Habermas 1991, while noting she is adapting his work to the transitional justice context.

[126] Author interview, Theary Seng, Phnom Penh, June 29, 2009; see also Seng 2010.

place. Transitional justice may lead to significant and needed change and create new possibilities, but it may also engender a facade that masks critical on-the-ground knowledge and practices.

These understandings are not simply local glosses. As illustrated by Buddhist beliefs and the *bangsokol* ritual, everyday knowledge, which mediates the experience of those participating in spaces like the forums, may diverge dramatically from the seemingly smooth "light world" flow of the transitional justice imaginary. In other words, many Cambodians, especially the older rural survivors upon whom Uncle San is modeled, understand the court in terms of Buddhism first and foremost—just as had been the case with the translation of human rights in Cambodia before—not "global justice."

The transitional justice imaginary elides such complexity, assuming that people crave justice in a straightforward manner, as illustrated by Ban Ki-moon's remarks. While many Cambodians are happy to see the former Khmer Rouge leaders tried and may imaginatively engage with the court, their investment varies. Public forums and other outreach initiatives may also mask tepid interest—sometimes even a complete lack of interest—on the part of Cambodians more focused on earning a living in often difficult circumstances that may be linked to structural violence and social justice issues obscured by the justice facade.

Moreover, as illustrated by the depiction of Uncle San in the KID booklet, the transitional justice imaginary depicts victims as living in stasis, unable to "move forward" until justice arrives. But, as suggested by the frame in which Uncle San prays to the dead before being hailed to the KID outreach meeting, Cambodians began coping with the past long before the ECCC arrived, in part through the use of Buddhist (and Muslim Cham) religious beliefs and practices.[127]

From this perspective, the court, as opposed to being a sudden, transformative change, may be viewed as a "combustive" new opportunity for Cambodian villagers to continue what they have for many years been doing—such as transacting with the dead—within the affordances of the current moment. Indeed, some Cambodian villagers reading the Uncle San booklet may very well have read the frame in which he is hailed to attend the KID outreach session not as a transformative departure from past practices, but as a continuity with them, with the court offering a new opportunity to make offerings to the spirits of the dead.

The transitional justice imaginary masks such histories and local understandings and practices, asserting a facade focused on "light world" transactions within the dialogic space of the outreach forums and the court itself. Seng occupied an interesting position in this regard. If she was a civil society leader who sought to help catalyze change in the "court of public opinion," she also chose to become a civil party and thereby entered into the public sphere in a different capacity. In doing so, she tested the limits of this performative space, revealing more cracks in the ECCC justice facade.

---

[127] Guillou 2012; Ledgerwood 2012; So 2011.

PART II

TURBULENCE

Preamble II

Re/enactment

Silent and pitch black, the film begins. Then, suddenly, the frame is full of color and light.

Duch, the former commandant of S-21 prison where over 12,000 people perished, many after being interrogated and tortured, stands in the covered terrace of Building E at Tuol Sleng, the memorial site built at his former prison. Duch's face is silhouetted by the darkness within and the outside light. His defense lawyers stand at his side along with a dozen security officers and court officials. In partial sunlight, their shadows are cast toward the inner room, where prisoners were once processed.

It is February 27, 2008, and Duch has returned to Tuol Sleng for the first time as part of an "on-site investigation," alternatively referred to in court documents as a "reconstruction" or "reenactment." The Internal Rules empower the Office of the Co-Investigating Judges (OCIJ) to initiate such site visits in the interest of "ascertaining the truth."[1] Two documentary filmmakers were authorized to record the proceedings.[2]

At the start of the five-hour recording, the two Co-Investigating Judges stand in the terrace near Duch and his lawyers, explaining how the proceedings would unfold.[3] The participants would traverse the Tuol Sleng compound, pausing at key evidentiary locations to provide explanation and, if necessary, discuss divergent accounts in what was sometimes referred to as a "confrontation."

The previous day, a reconstruction had taken place at the Choueng Ek "killing field." Duch and several former subordinates had traversed the grounds identifying key locations and describing how S-21 prisoners were executed there. According to reports, Duch wept and prayed before a tree against which babies are said to have been smashed and at the large memorial stupa where exhumed skulls and bones of the dead were interred during the People's Republic of Kampuchea (PRK).[4]

The Tuol Sleng reconstruction had a key difference: Duch would revisit the site not just with his former men but with three survivors, Vann Nath, Chum Mey, and Bou Meng. The three men stood on the opposite side of the terrace with a small group that included the Co-Prosecutors, civil party lawyers, and several former cadre designated as witnesses. The reenactment resembled a performance in which key actors in Duch's case assembled to play their juridical roles in a preview of his Case 001 trial.

---

[1] ECCC Internal Rule 55.5.   [2] OCIJ 2008a.
[3] The following description is based on the footage recorded at the reenactment and related ECCC reports (OCIJ 2008b, 2008c).
[4] Munthit 2008b.

The Justice Facade: Trials of Transition in Cambodia. Alexander Laban Hinton. © Alexander Laban Hinton, 2018. Published 2018 by Oxford University Press.

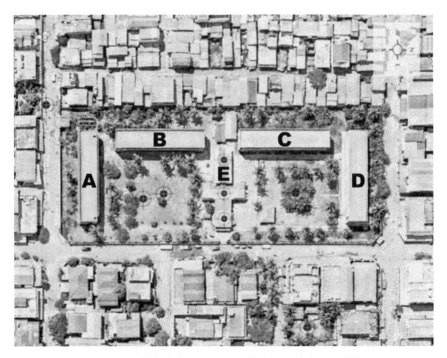

Figure 1 Aerial view of Tuol Sleng Genocide Museum. *Image courtesy of the ECCC.*

After the participants had been formally identified, the group of former S-21 cadre and prisoners remained in the terrace to discuss how prisoners were arrested and registered, including being given ID numbers and photographed, before being sent to their cells. And so the reenactment proceeded, as the cameras rolled and a photographer took snapshots.

The group next moved from the terrace into the Building E room that had served as an artist workshop before moving to Building A, which had been a special prison in the latter stages of DK.

In Building D, the group looked at different objects and photographs, including one of Koy Thuon, a high-ranking cadre who Duch personally interrogated. At a display of torture instruments in Building D, Prak Khan, a former interrogator who would testify, commented: "The knife and the hatchet were only used for intimidation." He explained. "You could practice minimal torture, but you were not allowed to cause injury."[5]

The group then moved on to the front of Building C where they talked about how the blood of some prisoners was drained from their bodies and other forms of execution. At Building C, the parties discussed whether a list of

[5] OCIJ 2008b, 7–8.

prison regulations displayed at Tuol Sleng was authentic, with Duch maintaining they were a fabrication.

To conclude, the group returned to the terrace of Building E, where Duch read a statement from a single sheet of paper. With his international defense co-lawyer, François Roux, standing by his side, Duch put on his glasses and, head bowed slightly, began reading. "Your Honors," he started. "I was frozen with terror when I stepped into this place as I recalled the dreadful, appalling calamity which befell my country, my people and myself."[6] Pausing for the translation and glancing at his former prisoners, seated on chairs a few feet away, Duch continued, "[First,] I recall the wretched victims and their families who were subjected to suffering, torture, disgrace and countless inhuman acts before they lost their life. I am filled with indescribable remorse; therefore I bow myself . . . [and promise to help them] receive justice."

Looking increasingly upset as he spoke, Duch also expressed his "deep remorse" to his former subordinates who, like him, were "forced to perform their tasks," which they hated. Duch said he was "caught in a spiral" at the time, and was now pained and "angry with myself for . . . blindly respecting their criminal orders."

"Please allow me, Your Honors," Duch said, "to offer my apology to all the victims who suffered . . ."

Duch stopped suddenly and gasped. On the verge of tears, he handed his statement to Savuth Kar, his Cambodian defense co-lawyer.

"He cannot read it anymore,"[7] Kar told the participants.

"If so," International Co-Investigating Judge Lemonde replied, "let's end it now."

Roux handed Duch a tissue and, motioning in the air, encouraged Duch to continue. Duch suddenly reached out and took the text back from Kar.

After taking a breath, he repeated, "Please allow me to offer my apology to all the victims who were subjected to the utmost suffering at this place . . ." He went on to apologize to the victims and their "families who have been living in pain for the past 33 years without their beloved family members and who have not yet obtained justice." He urged them to "leave a door open to me" before briefly raising his hands in respect (*sampeah*) toward his former captives who, so many years ago in this same place, had not dared to meet his gaze.

"May I make a brief comment?"

As Duch was concluding, S-21 survivor Chum Mey had listened intently, nodding his head slightly at times. Now he wanted to speak. Chum Mey's civil party lawyer leaned forward and placed his hands on Chum Mey's shoulders, comforting him. Rising from his chair and addressing the Co-Investigating Judges, Chum Mey stated, "This is what I want." Previously at S-21, he said, glancing at Duch, anyone who contested a matter would be killed "with a hoe, a bamboo club, or a cart axle." In contrast, Chum Mey was now "free to speak out."

---

[6] The quotations from Duch's apology during the reconstruction are taken from ECCC 2012, 13–15.
[7] ECCC 2012, 14.

Chum Mey then raised his hands in respect and said, "I would really like to thank Mr. Duch for speaking before the court. He has admitted his mistakes and I hold no grudge against him." In response, Duch raised his hands though, in a reflection of their new statuses in the court and at S-21, he raised his hands higher than Chum Mey had, acknowledging a position of subordination. Chum Mey concluded, "What I want is justice and peace for a million or so Cambodian people who lost their lives. I am very grateful. My only concern was that he [might] not speak truthfully before the court."

During this interchange between Chum Mey and Duch, Roux had placed his hand across his heart, touched by the moment. Indeed, the exchange seemed to fulfill the oft-mentioned promise that the Extraordinary Chambers in the Courts of Cambodia (ECCC) would bring peace and reconciliation to Cambodia, the realization of the aspirations of the transitional justice imaginary. The reconstruction had itself symbolized a new return to S-21, one mediated by juridical frames. Duch, the Chairman, was now a defendant, his former cadre had become witnesses, and some of his former prisoners were civil parties. Together, they had traversed S-21 again, seeking legal evidence for use in a court of law in the rooms and corridors where Duch had once sought hidden plots and suspected enemies were interrogated and tortured.

S-21 had produced confessions. The ECCC would yield a verdict and more. Justice and the sort of reconciliation and healing the transitional justice imaginary aspires to deliver seemed to have taken place between Chum Mey and Duch at the very site at which the former prisoner's victimization had occurred. Transitional justice appeared to be revealed in this justice facade moment.

At several points during Duch's trial, Roux would return to this event. At the very first hearing, Roux linked his defense to transitional justice, arguing for mitigation in accordance with the transitional justice goal of repairing ruptured human relations. In doing so, he quoted the work of transitional justice scholar Pierre Hazan, who argued that reconciliation requires perpetrators and victims to "accept the past" and recognize one another's humanity as part of the "one key formula" of transitional justice: "truth, justice, forgiveness, and reconciliation."[8] As we have seen, such terms—a cluster of ideas naturalized by the transitional justice imaginary—circulated in and around the ECCC dating back to the court's origins.

The chapters in this book section shift the discussion from the vortices of nongovernmental organization outreach to the turbulence of the lived experience of Cambodians who participated in the ECCC with a particular focus on victim participation. While the chapters all involve multiple dimensions of the transitional justice imaginary, each chapter emphasizes a particular aspect.

Chapter 4, for example, is loosely structured around the idea of aesthetics and the experience of two victims who participated in the proceedings, Theary Seng and former S-21 prisoner Vann Nath. If the 2008 reenactment highlighted the performative dimensions of the transitional justice imaginary, it also suggested an implicit

---

[8] Duch Trial, Initial hearing, Day 1, February 17, 2009, pp. 112–13; Hazan 2010.

aesthetics as a former prison that had been converted into a genocide museum was, in this moment, envisioned as a crime site now inhabited by court personnel, victims and witnesses, a defendant, and evidence. The ECCC has a similar aesthetics of justice, ranging from court regalia and symbols to courtroom demeanor, technologies, styles of speech and movement, and public participation.

The first part of the chapter centers on the experience of the first civil party, Theary Seng. Originally skeptical of the ECCC, Seng came to believe the court had transformative possibilities in terms of promoting democracy in Cambodia. To this end, in a series of pre-trial hearings, she sought to speak directly in court. Initially successful, Seng was eventually silenced as the Pre-Trial Chamber ruled that civil parties could only speak through their lawyers. Seng, for her part, became increasingly critical of the court, stating that she refused to be a piece of "décor" in a "sham." Eventually, she would renounce her civil party status and become an outspoken critic of the ECCC, which was increasingly beset by controversy.

The remainder of the chapter focuses on Vann Nath's Case 001 testimony. On the day of his testimony, the 500-seat courtroom was packed, as it would be during many subsequent trial sessions. Vann Nath's art, much of which he had produced during PRK for display at Tuol Sleng, was reintroduced as juridical evidence and shown in court. The chapter explores some of these aesthetic dimensions of the transitional justice imaginary even as it considers the lived experience and practices that informed Vann Nath's art, including Buddhist aesthetics and beliefs.

The next chapter shifts from aesthetics to performativity, even as the two are intertwined. Just as the parties came together at Tuol Sleng in a performance of transitional justice and law, one that seemed to realize the transitional justice imaginary's aspiration for transformation, so too did the civil parties enter into legal proceedings that had clear performative dimensions, including an ethnodramatic structure that led some to refer to it as "the show."[9]

Indeed, justice itself is a momentary enactment of law, structured by power including legal codes and the force of law, which is plagued by the impossibility of realizing the universal in the particular—a dilemma Jacques Derrida has discussed in terms of justice always being something that is "to come."[10] Other scholarship, ranging from Judith Butler's ideas about the performativity of gender to Jacques Lacan's theorization of the self,[11] similarly discusses how idealizations break down even as they are performatively asserted within the momentary manifestation of the particular never able to fully accord with idealized aspirations—including those of the transitional justice imaginary and its facadist externalizations.

The chapter begins with a discussion of the ways in which Vann Nath's testimony illustrates how the court seeks to performatively assert justice through courtroom rituals, roles, and discourses. Chapter 5 then turns to examine the related work of the court's "public face," the Public Affairs Section (PAS), which promoted its success in busing in tens of thousands of Cambodians as evidence of public engagement

---

[9] Hinton 2016. On transitional justice and performance, see Payne 2008.
[10] Derrida 1992. See also Bourdieu 1987.   [11] Butler 2006; Lacan 2007.

with the court. The chapter discusses some of the ways in which the head of the PAS, Reach Sambath, who was sometimes referred to as "Spokesperson for the Ghosts," translated justice when interacting with such Cambodians with many of whom he shared a deep Buddhist belief. I then explore the issues of "Justice Trouble," or some of the ways in which the instability of the juridical performance at the ECCC broke down, including Theary Seng's later condemnation of the court.

The last chapter in this book section explores how the performance of justice, with its associated aesthetics and normative codes, involves disciplines that seek to "translate" discourse, bodily movement, and subjectivity into a juridical form—one that asserts the liberal democratic, right-bearing subjectivity the transitional justice imaginary aspires to produce. Drawing in part on translation theory, this chapter notes that such translation involves power, discourse, control, and a sort of exile as speech and actions are shaped into a form according with juridical order. These attempts to realize the transitional justice imaginary, however, are unable to contain an excess—a surplus of meanings creating cracks in the justice facade—that emerges from the lived experience and understandings of particular actors.

These juridical disciplines were manifest at the reenactment, as the victims and defendants were invested with rights and agency that enabled (and constrained) their actions within this juridical performance. They were also evident in the testimony given by another S-21 artist and survivor, Bou Meng, who participated as a civil party in Duch's trial and is the focus of Chapter 6. In particular, the chapter explores how the court disciplined Bou Meng, "translating" what he said, how he felt, and even how he moved his body into a legalistic form. Despite this juridical canalization, an excess of meaning was evident throughout Bou Meng's testimony, as illustrated by his invocation of Buddhist understandings and spirit beliefs, including his primary concern with the spirit of his wife. This "bushy undergrowth" of meaning is largely occluded by the justice facade even as it remains central to lived experience and practice.

4

Aesthetics (Theary Seng, Vann Nath, and Victim Participation)

Theary Seng, Voice, and the "Décor" of Civil Party Participation

Nuon Chea pre-trial hearing (February 7, 2008)

"I could not have imagined this day—that I/victims would be in a court of law face-to-face with the highest ranking surviving Khmer Rouge leader."[1]

With these words, at the start of her statement during Nuon Chea's pre-trial detention hearing on February 7, 2008, Theary Seng became the first civil party to address the court. She had filed her application only a few months before. "We victims of Mr. Nuon Chea," she stated as she concluded her remarks, "have been waiting for 30 years for justice."

Seng's remarks before the Pre-Trial Chamber (PTC) captured headlines around the world. The Extraordinary Chambers in the Courts of Cambodia (ECCC) Victims Unit, still barely operational, issued a statement calling the event "a historic day in international criminal law," which had never before so fully "involved victims and civil parties, giving them full procedural rights."[2] In mid-January, the statement noted, the Office of the Co-Investigating Judges (OCIJ) had accepted the applications of four civil parties, including Seng, who appeared in court.

Seng appeared unlikely to be in this position. At the end of her 2005 memoir, Seng opined that the court would, "inevitably lead to a parody of justice that would curdle even the blood of the dead."[3] She warned that the Cambodian courts were widely regarded as "lacking independence" and were often "used as a political tool" by the Cambodian government. As a result, the court would fall "short of universal legal standards of justice" and reflected the "condescension and arrogance of some Westerners" who were giving Cambodia "second-class justice."

Despite her concerns, Seng had changed her mind after coming to understand the potentialities of civil party participation. With proper outreach, she believed,

---

[1] Seng 2008.
[2] Victims Unit 2008. On Seng's testimony, see Theary Seng's webpage (http://www.thearyseng.com).
[3] Seng 2005, 257–58.

The Justice Facade: Trials of Transition in Cambodia. Alexander Laban Hinton. © Alexander Laban Hinton, 2018. Published 2018 by Oxford University Press.

the tribunal could empower Cambodians and lead to "real democracy building,"[4] a process that had been launched by the 1993 elections and human rights movement but was incomplete. It was for this reason that she filed to be a civil party, which would give her unique status, moral authority, and voice that she could exercise in the "public sphere [of the court]."[5]

At this early stage, the court remained uncertain about how to manage civil party participation. The civil parties forced the issue. When their lawyers notified the court they would appear at Nuon Chea's hearing, a discussion immediately broke out about whether they had the right to participate. This issue was debated at the start of the hearing, with defense lawyers arguing for a restrictive interpretation of civil party rights and the co-prosecutors and civil parties advocating for a much broader scope. The PTC judges ruled that the proceedings could go forward while reserving judgment.[6] This ruling allowed Seng to take the floor during Nuon Chea's pre-trial detention hearing.

Nuon Chea is widely viewed as the second most powerful member of the Khmer Rouge after Pol Pot.[7] He had worked in the revolutionary movement almost from the start and was deeply involved in crafting Khmer Rouge ideology and policy.

He showed little remorse. When he defected with Khieu Samphan in late 1998, Nuon Chea had offered a seemingly half-hearted apology, stating, "Naturally, we are sorry not only for the lives of the people of Cambodia, but even for the lives of all the animals that suffered because of the war."[8] Even as he would offer some limited expressions of remorse during his trial,[9] Nuon Chea remained adamant about the patriotism and legitimacy of the Khmer Rouge struggle to prevent the Vietnamese "crocodile" from "swallowing" Cambodia. "It was Vietnam who killed Cambodians," he claimed.[10]

At this early stage, the hearings were held in a small room. "There was only one entry way," she recalled, so "we would walk past each other."[11] She paused and repeated, "He would walk past me."

Participating gave Seng a sense of moral authority. She explained, "To think that here is this [young] child 30 years ago now having the right to talk to the person who controlled the whole thing ... [and] was responsible for the loss of childhood. It's amazing. It's an amazing injection of power."[12] This sense of empowerment was further heightened by the "pomp and circumstance" and the media.

For the first time in Cambodian history, a survivor was allowed to speak in front of a senior Democratic Kampuchea (DK) leader on trial. Even as she struggled with tears, Seng realized that she was "setting a precedent so [couldn't] be a basket case ... There's always potential for messiness. So I was very aware I needed to be composed ... [and] act within the decorum of the court. I knew [this] was the opening, the introduction of civil party participation."[13]

[4] Author interview, Theary Seng, Phnom Penh, June 29, 2009.   [5] Ibid.
[6] PTC 2008b.   [7] OCIJ 2010.   [8] Mydans 2007.
[9] Nuon Chea Defense Team 2017.   [10] Trial Day 4 [Case 002], 52.
[11] Author interview, Theary Seng, Phnom Penh, June 29, 2009.   [12] Ibid.
[13] Ibid.

Palms pressed on the top of a small wooden table, Seng made a twenty-minute statement. If officially "my words were addressed to the court, to the bench," she said, "I was physically addressing Nuon Chea in terms of being directly turned face-to-face with him."[14]

In her remarks, she noted the irony that Nuon Chea was being "afforded all of the protection of the best legal principles and ideals" while, at the age of seven, she and her four-year-old brother were "put in prison where there was no due process–arbitrary arrest, no charges made or given, arbitrary detention, inhuman conditions, shackles; the graves were my playground."[15] Still, she added, his rights and legal protections were proper.

And justice was, in part, about legal standing. Thus, Seng stood in the court-room both as an individual victim and civil party who was orphaned by the Khmer Rouge and as a representative of Cambodian victims in general "who do not have a voice … Despite our different backgrounds, skin tones, accents," she added, "we share in the fellowship of suffering, tied together in our loss and our demand for justice…. For victims, this is your court. Participate."[16] She concluded by offering Nuon Chea a Center for Social Development (CSD) trauma handbook.

About two weeks later, she spoke again at Khieu Samphan's detention hearing. Throughout the process, she recalled, her goal was to "create a space, an exception for victims to address the court. Because there is great value [in this] that can't be matched by a lawyer."[17]

Civil party rights

Meanwhile, the PTC had solicited submissions and expert commentaries on the issue of civil party participation in such hearings. While much of the discussion revolved around the extent to which civil parties were empowered in Cambodian courts and by the Internal Rules, a more fundamental dispute revolved around the issue of how to "preserve a balance between the rights of the parties" as stipulated by Internal Rule 21. To what extent, for example, might the civil party right to partici-pate in the proceedings clash with the defendant's fundamental right to a fair trial?[18]

On the one hand, defense lawyers argued that the fact they would have to deal with two parties (prosecution and civil parties) instead of one violated the "equal-ity of arms" principle. Indeed, defense lawyers contended, the presence of the civil parties, who physically sat inside the courtroom with their lawyers and would make powerful statements, potentially introduced an element of bias into the proceedings, suggesting the guilt of the accused. On the other hand, the participation of poten-tially huge numbers of civil parties threatened to dramatically slow things down, contravening the right to an expeditious trial.

In its March 20, 2008 decision, the PTC found that the Internal Rules were "clear in its wording that Civil Parties can participate in all criminal proceedings … [and]

---

[14] Ibid. [15] Seng 2008. [16] Ibid.
[17] Author interview, Theary Seng, Phnom Penh, June 29, 2009. [18] PTC 2008a, 9.

have active rights to participate starting from the investigative phase of the procedure." Such participation, the PTC stated, was both consistent with international standards and served the pursuit of national reconciliation, as stipulated in the preamble of the Internal Rules.[19] To ensure fair trial rights, civil parties would be required to make written submissions to which the defense could respond.

Victim rights groups hailed the decision, with one group calling it "a landmark decision in international criminal justice and a major achievement for victims of gross human rights violations, whose voices have long gone unheard."[20]

The euphoria would diminish after Seng next appeared in court.

Ieng Sary pre-trial detention hearing, June 30–July 2, 2008

On June 30, 2008, the PTC convened for the pre-trial detention of another senior leader, Ieng Sary. It was the first ECCC hearing I attended. Two key issues at stake concerned Ieng Sary's past conviction by the 1979 People's Revolutionary Tribunal and the royal pardon and amnesty deal he received after defecting in 1996.

Ieng Sary did not resemble the monster media accounts suggested. At 82, his face marked by sun spots, his hair speckled with grey, Ieng Sary could have been anyone's parent or grandparent. And indeed, at times during the trial, he exchanged glances with his middle-aged daughters sitting at the front of the gallery.

When he entered the courtroom, Ieng Sary walked slowly using a cane. Flanked by a guard, he unsteadily sat down, alone, at a desk inside the court's dock, a water bottle and microphone before him. Ieng Sary looked defiant, his chin lifted.

After living for many years in a large villa in Phnom Penh, Ieng Sary was arrested on November 12, 2007.[21] While disputing the charges against him at his adversarial hearing, Ieng Sary stated that he was "very happy that this Court has been established because it will be an opportunity for me to discover the truth and also to share what I know."[22]

One of the highest-ranking DK leaders, Ieng Sary was tied to key policy decisions made by the regime, including purges within his Ministry of Foreign Affairs.[23] A Provisional Detention Order accused Ieng Sary of "directing, encouraging, enforcing, or otherwise rendering support for CPK [Communist Party of Kampuchea] policy and practice" and having "instigated, ordered, failed to prevent and punish, or otherwise aided and abetted in the commission of the aforementioned crimes."[24]

On the first morning of Ieng Sary's pre-trial detention hearing, the PTC did not respond favorably when Seng's lawyer asked if she could make a brief statement. When Seng stood to speak, several judges raised their hands, palms facing her, signaling her to stop. Mouth agape, Seng paused then slowly sat down. As the judges

[19] PTC 2008b.
[20] International Federation for Human Rights, 2008, "Cambodia Tribunal Allows Victims of the Khmer Rouge to Participate in Proceedings," March 28 (http://www.fidh.org).
[21] OCIJ 2007, 1.   [22] Ibid, 2–3.
[23] Ibid, 2010; see also Heder and Tittemore 2004, 75–92; Picq 1989.
[24] OCIJ 2007, 2.

listened to arguments about whether she should be allowed to address the court, Seng sat in her chair, fists pressed.

The next afternoon, international civil party co-lawyer Silke Studzinsky informed the court that Seng had dismissed her lawyer and wished to address the court for about ten minutes on double jeopardy. When Seng stood to speak, however, she was again informed she could only speak through her lawyers. A bit later in the proceedings, Seng informed the court, "It's no benefit ... to the proceedings for me to take up this space, since I have no voice." After a pause, she added, "I would like to wait until I have a voice ... to be in this court." She exited the courtroom and sat in the auditorium, dabbing her eyes with a tissue. She did not return after the break.

Seng told me, "I was really, really upset ... [and] in tears afterward." She continued, "So I walked out. Can you imagine? ... I'm a party to the proceedings and as a party you have rights. They are fundamental ... So basically there I am, recognized by the court as a party, and then I had no mode of means to express my interest."[25]

Anyone who was a party to a trial should, she argued, have a choice about whether to be represented by a lawyer or to self-represent. From Seng's perspective, she had been stripped of this fundamental right. "So I thought what's the point of being in the courtroom," she explained. "I can't communicate my interests. I'm no longer a party ... I'm not going to be a potted flower. I'm not going to be part of the décor, a decoration."

Her dismissal illustrated that, despite the hype regarding civil party participation, "in terms of substance it means nothing." And she wasn't "going to be used. A voice is an interest ... I thought why am I ... feeding into this sham of civil party participation. And it was a sham. I mean the process ... [and the promises] not being translated into reality."

As she related her experience at the hearing, Seng repeatedly emphasized how upset she had been. Beyond the implications for civil party participation, the significance of the moment was amplified by the highly public setting and international media attention. Finally, with a short, ironic laugh, she said, "Yeah, so that was the Ieng Sary hearing ... in Cambodia drama is the norm."

Civil party voice

The court's decision, effectively reversing the precedents that had been set at the Nuon Chea and Khieu Samphan pre-trial hearings, had been presaged by an earlier directive of the court stating that to ensure fair trial rights, particularly given the growing number of civil party applicants, civil parties would be required to make observations through their lawyers.[26]

In its decision at the Ieng Sary hearing, the PTC judges invoked Internal Rule 77(10), which interpreted a line stating that only "Co-Prosecutors and the lawyers for the parties may present brief observations" during pre-trial hearings to mean that "only lawyers for civil parties" had this right.[27] Noting a contradiction between

[25] Author interview, Theary Seng, Phnom Penh, June 29, 2009.
[26] PTC 2008c.   [27] PTC 2008d.

Internal Rule 77(10) and Internal Rule 23, which guarantees the participatory rights of civil parties, Australian Judge Rowan Downing dissented, stating that the decision to prevent Seng from speaking could result in "the extinguishment of her right to bring a claim against the Charged Person." Seng viewed Judge Downing's dissent as important, since it acknowledged her rights and laid the groundwork for appeal.

If Downing's dissent was remarkable in the Cambodian judicial context, where dissent is rare, the majority decision was perceived by many as marking a diminishment of civil party rights at the ECCC. Two months later, the ECCC Rules Committee, noting that the number of civil party applications had grown dramatically, revised the rules to impose filing deadlines and require civil parties to form groups.[28] During its next meeting, the judicial officers formally changed the rules to require civil parties to speak through their lawyers.[29]

In addition, just days before the March 29, 2009 opening of Case 001, the Trial Chamber ruled that the civil parties, unlike the prosecution and the defense, were not entitled to make opening statements in accordance with the principle of "balancing the rights of the various parties in view of [their] differing roles."[30] When the defense was given the floor to make their opening arguments, the defendant, Duch, was allowed to speak. His right to do so highlighted the perceived diminishment of civil party voice. The tension would persist.

Eventually the victims would be given the chance to speak, beginning with S-21 survivor Vann Nath.

Vann Nath, Aesthetics, and Justice

June 29, 2009, ECCC courtroom

"Uncle, Uncle!" Non Nil, the President of the Trial Chamber instructs. "Look at this drawing, Uncle, Uncle Nath."[31]

On the court monitor, in black-and-white, the half-naked man crouches. His left arm is hooked over the edge of a basin that dwarfs his emaciated frame as he scoops water to bathe. The man gazes at a small object in his right palm. Two guards stand just yards away. One sits, hands cupping a cigarette he is lighting. The other narrows his eyes at the prisoner.

"What does it mean, Uncle?"

Vann Nath, the first survivor to testify during Duch's trial, sits in the testimony stand and glances across the empty center "well" of the courtroom at President Non Nil and the four other judges of the Trial Chamber. Behind Vann Nath, a latticed floor-to-ceiling plate glass wall separates the courtroom from the 500-seat public gallery, packed with international observers as well as Cambodian villagers,

---

[28] "Joint Press Statement by Judicial Officers," ECCC, September 5, 2008.
[29] "5th Plenary Session of Judicial Officers—Closing Press Statement," ECCC, March 2009.
[30] Trial Chamber 2008, 5.   [31] Day 35, 40; Khmer, 33.

students, and civil society personnel. In the first row, a Buddhist monk in saffron robes watches.

"Your Honor, Mr. President," Vann Nath begins, his voice flat and eyes downcast, almost closed. "This image is a sketch of me, myself, on the very first day I was allowed to come down from my cell. The sketch is a recollection that I drew as a souvenir of that time, a remembrance of when I began to have hope that I might live a little longer, perhaps even survive."[32]

Vann Nath and a small number of prisoners who had skills needed at S-21—ranging from fixing generators to creating revolutionary art—had managed to escape the fate of almost every one of the more than 12,000 prisoners who were executed at S-21. Vann Nath was the first to speak.

The trial of Duch (Case 001)

From the start, Duch had more-or-less dominated the proceedings. Sometimes, echoing his background as a mathematics teacher, Duch seemed to lecture the court about Khmer Rouge policy and S-21.

Out of remorse or the realization the evidence against him was overwhelming, Duch said he wanted to co-operate and frequently took the stand to answer questions or make observations. He admitted that horrible acts had taken place at S-21, a place where prisoners were regarded as if they were "already dead" and treated like "animals" before being executed, often by being struck in the back of the neck and having their throats cut. Duch also acknowledged that he had trained the interrogators, who used torture—beatings, electrocution, suffocation by plastic bag, waterboarding, stress positions, and eating fecal matter—to extract confessions.

Even as he made these admissions, Duch apologized on the second day of his trial. Stating that he was "racked with remorse" for the S-21 crimes, ones for which he accepted "legal responsibility," Duch said that he "wished to apologize" and pleaded with the victims to "leave the door open for me to seek forgiveness."[33] It was an apology that he would offer again and again.

Many of the civil parties doubted his sincerity. As the proceedings progressed, they increasingly felt he was admitting only those acts that were clearly documented. Meanwhile, Duch's defense argued he was a "cog in the machine" who would have been killed if he didn't follow orders.

Sometimes, Duch's defense team depicted him as a tragic hero, someone who had joined the revolution to help liberate the poor and oppressed only to find himself "caught in the gears of the revolutionary machine."[34] He likened himself to the wolf in a nineteenth-century French Romantic poem, a noble creature hunted down as it tries to protect its family.

At such times, Duch sought to use art to suggest a refinement that clashed with the image of a ruthless zealot. Duch claimed he avoided the main prison compound

[32] Day 35, 40; Khmer, 33. For a longer discussion of Vann Nath's testimony, see Hinton 2018.
[33] Day 2, 68; Khmer, 52; ECCC 2012.   [34] Day 66, 85; Khmer, 63.

as he became disillusioned. Instead, he stayed in his office annotating the confessions his interrogators extracted and relaying the orders he received from his superiors to his subordinates. He did take trips to the prison's artisan workshop where, Duch said, he sought solace amidst the art.

These events formed the immediate backdrop to Vann Nath's testimony, which took place following a week focused on the functioning of S-21, including the detention conditions and the process of interrogation, torture, and execution. Vann Nath and other survivors were called to tell their side of the story.

"Self-portrait with a mirror"

Later, as Vann Nath provided testimony about his path to S-21 and suffering at the prison, Vann Nath was asked about his art, including his paintings of the atrocities that hang at the Tuol Sleng Museum of Genocidal Crimes. Eventually, the discussion returned to Vann Nath's sketch of himself sitting by the water basin at S-21 (see Figure 4.1).

"Uncle, Uncle–Uncle Nath!" Non Nil began. "In this sketch there are two men, who appear to be guards. And a man sits by a water basin and is putting his left hand into the water. What does it mean, Uncle? Who does the sketch depict? Did you see this happen to another prisoner? Or is it a sketch of you, yourself?"[35]

Vann Nath had stated that his drawings and paintings were based on three sources. "First," he stated, "there are the images based on what I saw myself with my own eyes. Second, others are based on what I heard but didn't see, what I imagined given the situation at that time. And third are the ones based on what other prisoners whispered and told me about."[36]

The man in the water basin sketch, Vann Nath explained, was an image of himself shortly after meeting Duch and being given three days to clean up and rest. "They brought me there to shave my beard and cut my hair," Vann Nath recounted as the sketch was displayed on the court monitor. "And they let me bathe, as you can see there. More than a month had passed since the time I was first arrested until that moment when I was allowed to bathe by the water basin."

"But what was most important about that moment," Vann Nath continued, his voice flat, "was that by the basin there was piece of mirror, a little bigger than the size of a toe. I found it right there by the water basin." Vann Nath had picked up the piece of mirror and "looked at my reflection in the piece of mirror...[and] saw that my face was so exhausted and withered." The two guards, Vann Nath noted, were "watching me in case there was a problem. So I drew this sketch to depict myself at that time. That's what I'd like to tell Your Honor."

Non Nil then interjected, "So this sketch, it shows the deeds of Angkar and its Khmer Rouge staff, the things they did to you, Uncle, from the time you were arrested in Battambang until the time you came to paint in the artisan workshop at Office S-21? Is that right?" Vann Nath simply replied, "Yes, Your Honor, Mr. President."

---

[35] Day 35, 40; Khmer, 33.   [36] Day 35, 39; Khmer, 32.

Figure 4.1 Self-portrait with a mirror. Painting by Vann Nath. *Image courtesy of the ECCC.*

The mirror and the gap

A mirror. And a reflection. I consider Vann Nath's self-portrait.[37] The sketch depicts the moment when Vann Nath was able to look at himself again. It also combines a number of elements suggestive about aesthetics, performance, and the transitional justice imaginary.

When we look in a mirror, we gaze at it with an idealized image of ourselves, one never to be matched by what is seen, leaving a disjuncture. Thus Vann Nath compares how he looks to how he thinks he should look and instantly sees the gap, as he has become almost unrecognizable due to the prison conditions.

Even when a mirror offers a "look" that seems to accord with an idealized image, the lack persists due to factors like perspective. The simple act of inversion that mirrors enact, seamlessly and without a hint of what takes place, highlights the gap between that imagined sense of self and wholeness and the reality that is observed. The reflection seen in the mirror, in other words, always contains a lack more or less perceived.

The mirror is an evocative metaphor about which much has been written to describe self and society. Lacan's mirror stage provides an illustration, as the dependent infant begins to fashion a sense of self from a mirror image to which the infant's gaze is

---

[37] This sketch may have first been made in the early-to-mid 1990s. In 1995, Vann Nath completed a color portrait based on the sketch entitled "Self-portrait with a mirror." See Phay-Vakalis 2010a.

directed by affect-laden others, parents, relatives, and caretakers.[38] The mirror is also found in Buddhism, where it may symbolize clarity of thought, but it is a clarity recognizing the illusion of self reflected in the mirror—an existential reality of fleeting, momentary coherence mistakenly assumed to endure, which unceasingly fragments amidst the samsaric cycle of impermanence and change. For both Lacan and Buddhist philosophy, then, the imagined self is always illusory and entailing a subjective lack.

Lacan highlights the importance of the gaze, since the infant's nascent sense of self, imagined in its reflection in the mirror, is both a subjective gaze (of the infant) and an intersubjective one (conditioned by others). This gaze is also one that is affect-laden, infused with the infant's negative affect, terrifying lack of control, and bodily distress as well as the directing look of powerful others with whom the infant's early emotional life is deeply intertwined. For Lacan, this mirror stage establishes a psychosocial situation that persists through life, as people imagine a self, like a reflection in the mirror, which is always idealized and illusory and conditioned by directives from others.

The gaze is likewise central in Vann Nath's sketch, as he looks at his reflection in the piece of broken mirror. He contemplates the image of the self that he observes, an act of seeing conditioned by the context, his guards, his predicament, and life at S-21 and in DK. And he notices a gap, created by the devastating prison conditions that transformed his appearance.

Vann Nath has depicted this moment through an aesthetic act, a black and white sketch. Drawing on the metaphor of the mirror, we might define aesthetics as a set of sensuous (visual, auditory, and oral) practices and material artifacts helping to give rise to an affect-laden sense of something transcendent. As opposed to asserting that something like "transcendent beauty" (in the sense of the Platonic forms) exists, this notion of aesthetics exists "on-the-ground" in a set of interwoven sensuous practices, objects, and semiotic codes that aim toward a "transcendent-like" imaginary that, due to the inevitable gap between this visual culture and what has been imagined, is never fully attained, something, as Vann Nath would note about justice, which is in the making, always still to come.

Aesthetics of justice

The transitional justice imaginary is likewise characterized by an aesthetics undergirding its aspiration for an idealized state of justice and transformation into liberal democratic order. This aesthetics is linked to a set of visual practices, codes, and objects that circulate at places like the ECCC as the transitional justice imaginary is enacted.

Vann Nath's mirror sketch is illustrative in this regard. If, on one level, the sketch reflects DK revolutionary aesthetics and the directive gaze of the DK regime, it is reframed at the ECCC in terms of a juridical aesthetics and authoritative gaze. This "reframing" is literally asserted through a border of the Vann Nath sketch, which is

---

[38] Lacan 2007.

stenciled with an identifying court document number as well as the Khmer Rouge Tribunal's official name and address. The sketch is dated and numbered by hand and, on the side, marked by a thumbprint, ostensibly Vann Nath's. The sketch has been certified by a case file officer, who recorded the original date and time of receipt of the sketch (9:40am on February 18, 2008) on a stamp that states, in block letters at the top: "ORIGINAL DOCUMENT." In court, as Vann Nath's sketches were about to be displayed, they were also framed by the computer screen border tabs and the Zylab database screenshot.

In all these ways, the mirror sketch, like Vann Nath's other drawings and paintings displayed in court, are reframed in terms of a juridical aesthetics suggesting the modernity, regulatory and bureaucratic functioning, and authority of justice. Under the juridical gaze of the court, Vann Nath's art also becomes part of legal practice as what is depicted is recast as legal evidence—as had been the case with Tuol Sleng during the reenactment. Thus, after Vann Nath described why he had drawn the sketch and what it meant to him—a return to a humanity of a sort and the possibility of surviving—Non Nil recast Vann Nath's testimony in juridical terms, stating that it reflected the inhumane treatment and criminal acts at S-21.

This moment is suggestive about the broader aesthetics of justice circulating at the ECCC. If the DK regime, like all states, asserted its legitimacy through key aesthetic practices and signs including revolutionary art, so too do juridical institutions. This aesthetic of justice is manifest in the everyday life of the court in a variety of ways: the color of the robes of the lawyers and judges, the ritual entrance and exit of the judges, the honorifics used, the spatial architecture of the court with the Trial Chamber sitting higher than everyone else—and even the stylized bureaucratic procedures asserting the regulative authority and functioning of the court and, by implication, the ECCC and justice more broadly.

The ECCC emblem is a key aesthetic image that is found everywhere from the large flag on the wall above the judges to the seats in the public gallery. The blue-and-white ECCC emblem consists of two key images. The first is a regal-looking figure sitting cross-legged on a platform with a sword in his hands. The official court booklet explains that this figure, dressed in formal traditional attire, "is seated on a dais and is holding a sword to symbolize the authority of the court." The booklet continues, "This is the central figure of the mural in the former Appeals Court in the Ministry of Justice in Phnom Penh, where he is flanked by two assistants."[39] This figure is surrounded by a wreath composed of the branches of an olive tree, the second key image in the ECCC emblem. For many observers, the wreath is instantly recognizable as the one that surrounds a flattened map of the world on the United Nations (U.N.) flag.

The ECCC emblem connotes the hybridity of the court, as the official ECCC booklet highlights, "by combining a depiction of the administration of Cambodia justice during the ancient period of Angkor with the United Nations' wreath of olive branches symbolizing peace."[40] Like the emblem, the hybridity of the court is

[39] ECCC Staff undated, 5.   [40] Ibid.

everywhere on display both in ways obvious (such as the court personnel and languages) and less obvious (the menu at the court canteen). All of these images, including the spatial layout of the court, help generate an idealized image of the seemingly transcendent Justice being enacted at the court.

"International Standards" and the Performance of Justice

Like the reflection in the mirror in Vann Nath's sketch, this idealized image of the ECCC, a justice facade of imagined harmonious dispensing of international justice in a domestic hybrid court that paves the way for a liberal democratic transformation, is found lacking. As we saw in earlier chapters, problems arose from the very start of the negotiations to establish the ECCC, as UN and Cambodian officials clashed over the composition and functioning of the court.

And even after an agreement was reached, preexisting tensions haunted the court. Cambodian court personnel, echoing the comments of Hun Sen, also argued that only five living people fell under the court's jurisdiction, while international prosecutors and investigating judges pushed to expand the number of cases, an effort that was hindered. Other controversies, such as allegations of corruption, political interference, and a failure to uphold "international standards" similarly arose.[41]

International standards

From the start, a number of international groups voiced concerns about "international standards." In 1997, for example, the UN Commission on Human Rights passed a resolution noting its concern about the "rule of law" and "system of justice in Cambodia," as well as "numerous instances of violations of human rights, including extrajudicial executions, torture … illegal arrest and detention." These problems, the Resolution stated, highlighted the importance of "due process of the law and international standards."[42] Groups like Amnesty International and Human Rights Watch similarly issued concerns about the tribunal.[43]

From such reports, court proceedings, and other statements about the ECCC it is possible to get a sense for the sorts of things associated with international standards of justice. More broadly, a jurist from the ECCC told me, international standards refer to human rights documents and international jurisprudence as well as Cambodian procedural law that is "basically copying from French law."[44]

In the context of the courtroom, however, the meaning was often directly linked to ECCC law, in particular Article 12 of the 2003 UN-Cambodian agreement to establish the court.[45] This frequently invoked Article stipulates that ECCC

---

[41] See Fawthrop and Jarvis 2004; Giry 2012; Hammer 2015.
[42] United Nations Commission on Human Rights 1997.
[43] Amnesty International Press Release 2002, 2003; Human Rights Watch 2002.
[44] Author interview with ECCC jurist, Phnom Penh, March 4, 2013.   [45] ECCC 2003.

"procedure shall be in accordance with Cambodian law." In those situations "where there is uncertainty ... regarding the consistency ... with international standards, guidance may also be sought in procedural rules established at the international level."[46]

The second part of Article 12 clarifies things, noting that the ECCC has to operate "in accordance with international standards of justice, fairness and due process of law, as set out in Articles 14 and 15 of the 1966 International Covenant on Civil and Political Rights [ICCPR]."[47] Article 13 of the Agreement on the "Rights of the Accused," invokes the ICCPR clauses ensuring that a defendant always has the right "to a fair and public hearing; to be presumed innocent until proven guilty; to engage a counsel of his or her choice; to have adequate time and facilities for the preparation of his or her defense." An accused also must "have counsel provided if he or she does not have sufficient means to pay for it" and should have the right "to examine or have examined the witnesses."[48]

"International standards," like the "rule of law" (as opposed to a "culture of impunity"), are closely associated with justice and linked to a set of aesthetic images. On one level, such justice is associated with "the international" and by implication the universal. "The international" is signified by the UN in manifestations such as the UN flag (and the grafting of the olive branch onto the ECCC emblem), the foreigners working at the court, key moments such as the widely circulated photograph of the signing of the 2003 UN-Cambodia Agreement (an image that is included in the Uncle San booklet), legitimating statements by Kofi Annan and later Ban Ki-moon in places like the official ECCC booklet, and accoutrements of modernity including the court's technology, equipment, bureaucracy, computer infrastructure, the professional demeanor of the court's personnel, procedural rituals, and juridical spaces such as the court buildings, offices, and courtroom.

Perhaps the most famous icon of Western justice, is "Lady Justice." While "Lady Justice" has a complicated genealogy and multivalent and sometimes ambiguous symbolism,[49] she is now commonly depicted as standing blindfolded and dressed in white robes while holding a sword in her right hand and scales in her left. Each of these objects connotes idealized qualities of Justice.[50] The white gown, for example, suggests purity and nobility even as her gendered body has long been associated with "natural order" as well as virtues and vices, exemplified in the court by justice (virtue) and crimes (vice).

Lady Justice's blindfold implies impartiality and reason, qualities sometimes associated with the phrase "blind justice." The blindfold serves as a barrier that separates justice from the vagaries of the senses, emotion, and influence. Instead, Justice stands apart with its rational gaze fixed on the law. Scales are also linked to law through their association with objective standards, measurement, balance (of rights), and the impartial "weighing" of evidence and arguments. Finally, the bared sword connotes

---

[46] Ibid, Article 12.1.   [47] Ibid, Article 12.2.   [48] Ibid, Article 13.1.
[49] Curtis and Resnik 1987.
[50] The discussion of the symbolism that follows draws from Curtis and Resnik 1987.

the independence, power, and authority of law as well as decisiveness and the execution of justice and punishment.

This aesthetics of justice is also manifest in the court's everyday routines, including its language. The judges, for example, sit apart from the other parties in the courtroom and work in their "chambers," which are located both by the courtroom as well as their offices on the top floor—marking their esteemed position—of the court administrative building. The impartiality and exalted position of the judges is suggested by the fact that they are frequently more abstractly referred to as "The Chamber," "Your Honors," or even the "Guardians of Justice." Reference is also made to the scale metaphor through the use of language of "balance," "weight," and "equality of arms." And, of course, the everyday regulative actions, ranging from convening each session to determining who is given the floor, are all performative and aesthetic acts of justice.

Even as this idealized image of justice is asserted, it is constantly undermined by lack as the realities on the ground diverge from the ideal imagined. The notion of "international standards" is frequently contested both inside the court (by the parties) and outside (by observers, monitors, civil society, diplomats, politicians, and human rights groups), as different parties argue about what these standards are and whether they are being properly upheld.

During Ieng Sary's pre-trial detention hearing, for example, International Co-Defense Lawyer Michael Karnavas directly attacked the notion of a universal standard of international justice. Motioning toward the large ECCC flag, Karnavas noted, "When I first stepped in here yesterday for the very first time, I couldn't help but notice what is behind your Honors: Kingdom of Cambodia, Nation, Religion, King. I think that says it all. That tells us that this is indeed a Cambodian courtroom, a Cambodian judicial system, within the existing Cambodian judicial system, being helped by the international community."[51] To support this point, Karnavas read Article 12 of the 2003 Agreement.

International standards, Karnavas continued, were not the same as international law and varied. "Having practiced in various jurisdictions," Karnavas stated, "international standards are rather malleable. It depends on where you are. It depends on who you have on the bench. It depends on who's defending and who's prosecuting. It depends on the resources available."

This variation could be seen in a range of cases, Karnavas contended. Even at the International Criminal Tribunal for the former Yugoslavia (ICTY), where Karnavas had practiced, "six trials are being held, one in the morning and one in the afternoon [and] in all [three] courts, you'll see six different procedures. If you take that tribunal and compare it say with Rwanda, you'll see the difference in resources. If you then compare the Hague with Sierra Leone, it's beyond night and day. What are international standards?"

The prosecution and civil parties, Karnavas argued, could not simply go "law shopping" for international legal precedents. "It's as if there is a sort of

---

[51] Ieng Sary Pre-Trial Detention Hearing, July 1, 2008.

smorgasbord approach" suggesting that "if you don't like Cambodian law, [you should] go someplace else. Justice à la carte." The way in which the prosecution and civil parties were "applying and interpreting the jurisprudence and the rules," he suggested, made the proceedings seem "like being in Alice in Wonderland."

Vernaculars of justice

If Karnavas's comments highlighted the potential for varying interpretations of international standards, such interpretations could further break down in a context like Cambodia that has a large rural, predominantly Buddhist tradition—as opposed to the Judeo-Christian tradition to which Lady Justice and much "global" jurisprudence is linked. As noted earlier, this formal legal system is far removed from the everyday lives of most Cambodians, who have relatively low rates of formal education and do not have an extensive "legal culture" in the sense of being mobilized toward, conscious of, familiar with, engaged in, and attuned to law.[52] Instead, many Cambodians, particularly in the countryside, prefer to resolve disputes through third party mediation.

When local mediation efforts fail or are bypassed, a dispute may be taken to higher authorities, who also sometimes attempt to solve a case through reconciliation.[53] However, as noted earlier, as opposed to being independent and impartial, then, Cambodian court officials are often influenced by bribes and political pressures linked to patronage networks. Such pressures emerged as a key issue at the ECCC when the kickback allegations emerged.[54]

Vann Nath, Buddhism, and aesthetics

When many Cambodians see the ECCC emblem, then, they may interpret this aesthetic image in very different ways. Instead of serving as an icon of "blind justice," like "Lady Justice," the seated Angkorean figure might just as well suggest a feared authority best avoided. Historically, Angkorean kings or surrogates did adjudicate disputes, but their word was final and the punishment could be severe.[55] As opposed to basing their decisions on formal law, such figures were oriented toward cosmological principles such as dharma (*thomm*). Indeed, I have spoken with Cambodian informants who say that the Angkorean figure is a Buddhist guardian deity (*tevoda*).

In Cambodian temples, it is also possible to find images of the Buddha that resemble the Angkorean figure in the ECCC emblem, again suggesting the close

---

[52] Merry 2010.   [53] See, for example, Un 2004; Luco 2002.
[54] Open Society Justice Initiative 2007; Goldston 2007; Gillison 2011.
[55] Jacobson 2006.

association of justice and Buddhism. Youk Chhang, the head of Documentation Center of Cambodia (DC-Cam), even has one behind his office desk and noted this direct connection between the court logo and Buddhist imagery.[56]

Further, the Khmer term that is usually translated as "justice," *yuttethoa*, also implies what is fair (*yutte*) or in accordance with proper action and moral law (*thoa*), but is derived from the Buddhist term, dharma (*thomm*), which suggests the ultimate reality or cosmic foundation of existence that the Buddha perceived.

One of the central tenets of this reality is law of karma (*kâmm*), which holds that one's current station is preconditioned by virtuous or bad actions in the past. Those who commit bad deeds in the present are believed to suffer from the consequences of their actions in the future. This conception is often mentioned in relationship to DK as Cambodians, sometimes invoking the popular maxim "act meritoriously, obtain merit; act sinfully, receive demerit" (*thvoe bon ban bon; thvoe bap ban bap*), assert that Khmer Rouge who did bad deeds will suffer in the Buddhist Hells or be reborn as a lowly, hideous sort of being, such as a malevolent spirit (*preta*).

Such Buddhist beliefs were a cornerstone of Vann Nath's understanding of the world, part of a set of beliefs and practices that had taken shape in his youth while studying at a pagoda.[57] Afterward he decided to become a painter, first training with an artist before opening a modest commercial business that painted "cinema placards, private portraits," and billboards.[58] This deep connection to Buddhism provided Vann Nath with a way to cope with his past suffering and to approach the future, including meetings with former perpetrators.

In a 1998 memoir, for example, Vann Nath recalled how, after Pol Pot died in 1998, he was "flooded with a jumble of confused thoughts and emotions."[59] Ultimately, however, Vann Nath viewed the death of Pol Pot and high-ranking DK officials through a Buddhist frame. His book concludes, "I believe there will be justice. A person harvests what he has sown. According to the Buddhist religion, good actions produce good results, bad actions produce bad results. The peasant harvests the rice, the fisherman catches the fish. Pol Pot and his henchmen will harvest the actions they committed. They will reap what they have sown."[60]

Here Vann Nath invoked a Buddhist vernacular conception of time mediating lived experience in Cambodia. From this Buddhist perspective, our being is constituted and reconstituted in a cyclical fashion. On a cosmic level, the universe is created and then degrades before being renewed. Ontologically, the doctrine of *samsara*, or the cosmological cycle of life, death, and rebirth, holds that being is fleeting, a momentary coalescence of constitutive elements. Each moment of coalescence is conditioned by what preceded it, a notion that is reflected in the doctrine of karma (*kamma*) that Vann Nath invoked in the passage above. Those who do good will receive good; those who do bad deeds will suffer the consequences. A form of cosmic justice is at work, as punishment for bad deeds is an inevitable part of being.

---

[56] Youk Chhang, personal communication, February 23, 2015.   [57] Panh 2011.
[58] Ibid, 1.   [59] Vann Nath 1998, 116.   [60] Ibid, 118; see also Panh 2011.

This Buddhist vernacular of time is at odds with the linearity and progressive teleology of juridical time and related conceptions linked to the transitional justice imaginary, which assert a binary of trauma/ill-health and health/closure. For if there are other ways of achieving "closure," such as Buddhist beliefs and practices centered around the notion of meritorious and demeritorious action, one of the key justifications of the ECCC would be undermined.

Such Buddhist beliefs also influenced Vann Nath's aesthetics, though his art was enmeshed in the politics of memory. Vann Nath's most famous art was produced at Tuol Sleng, where he began working in August 1979. It was a time of high politicization during the "first transition," as the People's Republic of Kampuchea (PRK) sought to gain domestic and international legitimacy through its atrocity frame demonizing the "Pol Pot–Ieng Sary clique."[61]

The Tuol Sleng exhibitions were meant to shock and provoke outrage, showing things "as they were" beginning with photos of the bloated and bloodied corpses of executed prisoners. Vann Nath's Tuol Sleng paintings, which include graphic depictions of torture and execution, fit with this PRK aesthetic. Vann Nath's early Tuol Sleng paintings are thus informed by multiple aesthetic influences: his experience painting movie billboards prior to DK, a common Cambodian painting style depicting everyday life or ancient Angkorean myth in a pictorial fashion, perhaps socialist realism, the PRK atrocity narrative, and his desire to authentically depict the violence of S-21 and suffering of the prisoners.[62]

Indeed, Vann Nath was constantly aware of the spirits of the dead while working at Tuol Sleng, since they were believed to haunt the site.[63] Vann Nath said that his artistic work helping to establish the Tuol Sleng museum "was the most meaningful thing I had ever done"[64] and, he hoped, assisted the spirits of the dead in finding peace.

Over time, even as many Cambodians continue to associate Tuol Sleng with the spirits of the dead and the atrocity frame endures, Vann Nath's art has been read in new ways. With the arrival of the United Nations Transitional Authority in Cambodia (UNTAC), Vann Nath's paintings, like Tuol Sleng as a whole, has been increasingly construed, especially by foreigners, in terms of a human rights frame, including aspects of humanitarianism, global citizenship, human rights crimes, evil, and the prevention and pedagogic imperative of "never again."[65]

If Vann Nath frequently spoke about his experiences during PRK, he increasingly framed his remarks—as well as his art—in such human rights terms. Vann Nath also began to be described as a "human rights activist" and in 2007 received an award from Human Rights Watch. As we have seen, his ECCC testimony—as well as his art that was introduced and classified as legal evidence—was framed by these global

---

[61] See Hinton 2016, 23f; see also Caswell 2014; Ledgerwood 1997; Schlund-Vials 2012.
[62] On influences on Vann Nath's art, see Phay-Vakalis 2010b, 208.
[63] Author interview with Reach Sambath, Phnom Penh, July 2, 2009.
[64] Vann Nath 1998, 108.
[65] Hinton 2016, 26f. On Tuol Sleng tourism, see also R. Hughes 2008.

human rights discourses and aesthetics linked to the aspirations of the transitional justice imaginary.

Vann Nath also became involved in institutionalized forms of remembrance. He starred in Franco-Khmer filmmaker Rithy Panh's documentary, "S-21: The Khmer Rouge Killing Machine," beginning a friendship and collaboration that would include "memory workshops" and continue until Vann Nath's death. And he continued to paint. If much of Vann Nath's post-UNTAC art focused on S-21 and was rendered in a more realist style, some of his later paintings were more abstract and in keeping with his growing association with high art as the "Goya of Cambodia."

For example, one of Vann Nath's memory workshop paintings, "The Two Lotuses" (2009), depicts a large lotus that has risen from a bleak, arid landscape. Beneath it, a smaller lotus begins to flower.[66] In Buddhism, the lotus is a key symbol of purity, protection, enlightenment, rebirth, and growth. "The Two Lotuses" highlights Vann Nath's Buddhist belief, illustrating how Buddhism helps people cope with suffering and find renewal even after the extremes of DK. So did art, which Vann Nath told a journalist, released "the pain that devours me."[67]

As "The Two Lotuses" suggests, Vann Nath's motivations for producing his art and participating in the trial often did not align with the justice facade. This was evident at several points during his testimony, such as when the issue of why he chose not to become a civil party arose. Vann Nath explained that he wanted to seek justice for the dead. Indeed, the spirits of the dead remained constantly on his mind. Vann Nath, for example, told Rithy Panh that he returned to S-21 because he was guided by "the souls of the dead." Rithy Panh later would say that Vann Nath was their "voice" and "spokesperson."[68] Each time Vann Nath went to Tuol Sleng, he was haunted by the dead: "I believe that those victims are still here, near me, and encourage me to paint" as well as to "show what happened."[69]

These spirits were also present in what may have been Vann Nath's final piece (see Figure 4.2), completed in 2010 after Duch had been convicted. The painting depicts Duch sitting between two columns of skulls and bones that recede into the distance. Vultures circle in the sky, perhaps a Buddhist symbol of the attachment and craving that drive people to sin. A copy of the verdict lies before Duch, who gazes into the distance.

This new painting may have been modeled on a self-portrait Vann Nath painted of himself in his S-21 cell. Both figures assume the same posture with the same dejected expression. The two walls of the S-21 cell have been replaced with the two columns of skulls and bones. Instead of the iron shackles, Duch is "bound" by the verdict.

But the new painting is also a Buddhist one, suggesting both that, like a shadow, the deeds of Duch's past trail behind him, conditioning his future and that Duch's judgment is an offering to the spirits of the dead. Here he mixes the "dark" and the "light worlds," Buddhist aesthetics and international law, fusions revealing a lack

---

[66] Phay-Vakalis 2010a, 73.   [67] Bopha 2008.   [68] Panh 2011.
[69] Bopha 2008.

Figure 4.2 Duch Verdict. Painting by Vann Nath. *Image courtesy of DC-Cam/SRI.*

and an excess, something important masked beneath the transformative rhetorics of the facadist enactments of the transitional justice imaginary.

Grafting

As we have seen, despite this underlying tension between this justice facade and the everyday understandings it often masks, different NGOs nevertheless sought to translate legal concepts by "grafting" them onto more familiar Buddhist idioms (or Islam in the case of the minority Cambodian Muslim Cham population), including Buddhist aesthetics.

DC-Cam, for example, would often hold its outreach forums, including sessions in which the Duch verdict was televised and discussed, in the countryside in Buddhist pagodas, sometimes close to Buddha statues. This environment was much more familiar to the villagers and also linked the juridical process to the Buddhist understandings, including the notions of karmic justice Vann Nath invoked. Youk Chhang, the Director of DC-Cam, explained that DC-Cam held outreach forums in pagodas and mosques because, traditionally, "Cambodians use these places for almost everything, including weddings, funerals, education, social gatherings [and so forth]" and these religious spaces were a "source of healing" and required "being honest."[70]

---

[70] Youk Chhang, personal communication, June 18, 2015.

Chhang noted that the architecture of the ECCC court has an aesthetics disso-
nant with local understandings and that villagers are more likely to associate, and
even tell, the truth in a Buddhist compound than in a courtroom setting. "Design
affects how people feel," he stated. "The glass [wall dividing the ECCC courtroom
from the public gallery] blocks the connection between people" and the adversarial
positioning of the parties in the court might make a Cambodian villager uncomfort-
able. "Face-to-face is a Western way–it's not our culture."[71] As Chhang's remarks
suggest, a "deep translation" that will decrease dissonance must tap into everyday
understandings, practices, and aesthetics.

If DC-Cam's use of pagodas and mosques provides one illustration of this
point, so too does the Khmer Institute of Democracy (KID) booklet. The cover
page itself highlights this point, as it grafts the image of the court onto a landscape
familiar to Cambodian villagers, including a rural landscape, a tutelary spirit, and
traditional architecture in the background. Uncle San and Aunty Yan stand in
the dirt and grass wearing traditional Cambodian scarves, sandals, and clothing.
Other pages also locate Uncle San in a familiar Cambodian context, such as when
he chats with a small group of villagers on one page and sleeps in a hammock in
the next.

Connections to Buddhism and spirit beliefs are made as well, particularly
in the graphic of Uncle San being hailed by Aunty Yan—as he stands in a traditional raised house holding incense and praying to the spirits of his relatives
and friends who perished during DK—who invites him to the KID outreach
session. Here the booklet both suggests the stasis of traditional religious practices (which have not healed Uncle San) and the promise of the court, which,
through juxtaposition, is simultaneously likened to a traditional healing practice and differentiated from it by offering a more effective alternative that can
help Uncle San, and Cambodia by extension, "move forward" from a static,
regressive state to one of true healing and progress associated with the "modern"
and the "international."

Suon, the KID Program Officer who oversaw the design of the booklet was
quite aware of the need to take account of local aesthetics. In the last frame, for
example, as Uncle San rests in his hammock, his dreams of DK horrors replaced
by a peaceful village landscape promising development. The frame includes
Buddhist images. A line of monks walks down a road and a pagoda is set in the
distance. And lotus rises from a pond. "Normally in Buddhism," Suon added,
"the Buddha sits on the lotus and normally we take lotus flowers to pray before
the Buddha. It's a calm and fresh flower" connoting peacefulness, happiness,
prosperity, and healing that would come through involvement with the court.
The lotus is an evocative Buddhist image of this "rising up" from the muck to a
higher state of enlightenment.

If Suon's comments highlight the attempt at grafting, they also illustrate a facadist
enactment of the transitional justice imaginary of a transformed political body as

---

[71] *The Phnom Penh Post* Staff 2014.

liberal democratic citizens actively participate in a newly established public sphere. As Seng's and Vann Nath's experiences illustrate, the realities on the ground often revealed a lack, as what was seen and enacted frequently diverged, often dramatically so, from what was imagined—a justice facade seen from afar that masks what lies behind it. As we shall see in the next chapter, one response to this situation is to assert this imaginary through performance and related discourses, even if ultimately a tribunal may still run into "Justice Trouble."

5

Performance (Reach Sambath, Public Affairs, and "Justice Trouble")

Performing Justice

The justice gap

"What I want … it's …"

Vann Nath paused as he considered his reply to French Trial Chamber judge Jean-Marc Lavernge's question about his expectations for Duch's trial. What he wanted, Vann Nath continued, motioning in the air, was "something that can't be seen. It's justice for those who died. For this justice, I am relying on this Chamber. But in my heart, I'm not certain what this justice is." He glanced up at the judges. "It is only when this court is over that we may know the answer to the question: justice, what is it? I'm not certain. What is justice? In my heart I hope that it is something that will be an outcome resulting from the actions of Your Honors, of this court."[1]

What is justice? Vann Nath's remarks highlighted a key issue in international justice as well as a crucial fissure in the justice facade: the meaning of justice itself. If the transitional justice imaginary asserts a universal Justice, it is one notoriously difficult to define and undercut by particularity. Karvanas's remarks about the variability of "international law" at the International Criminal Tribunal for the former Yugoslavia (ICTY) highlighted this point. So too did Seng's experience of being used as part of a facade ("décor" as she put it) and defense arguments challenging the court's legitimacy. This "justice gap" was suggested by Vann Nath's mirror sketch as it threw into relief the disjuncture between idealization and the complexity of our interpersonal worlds.

This gap is also manifest in the performative structure of justice. On the one hand, the performance of justice is premised on an underlying and taken-for-granted discursive order that structures the proceedings and asserts given identity positions and the reality of justice itself. On the other hand, the performance is unstable.

Judith Butler's arguments about performativity and gender highlight these points. If she plays on the instability of gender performativity with her book title *Gender*

[1] Day 35, 55–56; Khmer, 45.

The Justice Facade: Trials of Transition in Cambodia. Alexander Laban Hinton. © Alexander Laban Hinton, 2018. Published 2018 by Oxford University Press.

Trouble,[2] so too might justice performativity be described as "Justice Trouble." Although open to subversion and fragmentation, the juridical discursive order is linked to power and structurally asserted in a number of ways, including through aesthetic images discussed in the last chapter.

Performativity and courtroom ritual and symbolism

The performativity of justice is also related to courtroom ritual.[3] The courtroom is shaped like a theater, with a curtained plate glass wall separating the interior "actors" from the public gallery "audience." Each morning begins with a daily ritual, as the curtains are drawn, revealing the interior courtroom to those seated in the public gallery, moments before everyone is required to stand in respect through a call—"All Rise!"—as the Trial Chamber judges enter. They do so in a single file line, with the President heading the procession as they ascend the steps of the dais to their elevated seats. Once they are all standing in their places, the President, positioned in the middle, leads as they sit down in unison. "Please be seated," the President then instructs everyone in the courtroom and public gallery. "The Court is now in session."

This performative ritual, repeated at the beginning and end of every trial session, signals both the court's power and the enactment of justice. Three gigantic emblems unfurled on the wall above and behind the judges affirm the authority of the court: a Cambodian flag, the United Nations (U.N.) flag, and, between them, the official Extraordinary Chambers in the Courts of Cambodia (ECCC) emblem.

Each day then commences with bureaucratic matters symbolizing the court's regulatory control, the first of which is a statement about the focus of the day's proceedings and request for the court clerk to confirm the parties are present. The Trial Chamber may then call a witness or turn to pending administrative issues.

On the day of Vann Nath's testimony, Non Nil did the former, announcing that, in the interest of justice ("a fair and expeditious trial"), the court had decided to remove several people from the witness list. As Non Nil announced the decision, he referred to the judges in the third person as "The Chamber," a depersonalized title suggesting the impartiality of Justice. After such announcements are made and any other preliminary matters discussed, the Trial Chamber initiates the main part of the proceedings.

Through such ordering acts, the court asserts a given discursive order with particular identity positions (judge, defendant, prosecution, civil party, witness, "public," and so forth) and with their related "roles" (the authority of the Trial Chamber, the rights of each party, and the set of actions enabled by the juridical "scripts" of rules, norms, and regulations). With the identities, roles, expectations, and rules in place, the action then begins on the courtroom "stage," with the performance of Justice reinforced by aesthetics (architecture, positioning, dress, honorifics, demeanor, and symbols).

---

[2] Butler 2006.
[3] On the performative dimensions of the ECCC and Duch's trial, see also Hinton 2016.

The ECCC "stage" on which Vann Nath testified resembles the one depicted in the Khmer Institute of Democracy (KID) booklet (see Figure 5.1). The booklet correctly shows that the open witness stand is positioned in the back-middle part of the court next to the more enclosed "dock" where the accused sits. Both the testimony stand and the dock face the judges, who sit at the other end of the courtroom behind a row of clerks. To the left of the testimony stand sit the civil party lawyers (and behind them rows of seated civil parties) and the prosecution. They face the defense, which is seated at desks on the other side of the courtroom, separated by a large empty space sometimes referred to as "the well."

But there are key differences as well. For example, the booklet, written for the purpose of victims participation, visually accentuates the civil parties and their lawyers.

In the actual courtroom, the Trial Chamber judges are spatially foregrounded. When President Non Nil addressed Vann Nath, for example, he did so from the raised dais where the judges sit, higher than anyone else and dominating the center space along with the enormous flags and emblem hung high on the wall behind them. Here the justices occupy a panoptic position, observing and controlling the proceedings to ensure the smooth flow of "Justice." The performance and related discourses of Justice are further asserted by the "validating public"[4] within and outside the court, efforts that, at the ECCC, are largely orchestrated by the Public Affairs Section (PAS).

"The Face of Justice" (Reach Sambath and the Public Affairs Section)

Turbulence was a constant problem for the court. From a performative perspective, a successful court is one in which justice flows smoothly from the court to the people for whom it is rendered. To be "received," this justice must be understood and desired.

During my research, I made a number of trips to the countryside to get a sense for how villagers, who constitute the vast majority of the Cambodian population, felt about the tribunal. As suggested by outreach efforts and surveys, I found a range of views. Some people had never heard of the tribunal. Others didn't care or were only vaguely interested. A handful invoked the "don't poke an old wound" proverb or noted the government position on prioritizing peace and reconciliation. Others wondered why the tribunal was so slow or why so much money was being spent when the funds would better serve rural development. There were also a number of people who were closely paying attention to the proceedings. Most rural villagers with whom I spoke, regardless of their degree of interest, shared one thing in common: they had little familiarity with formal legal justice.

---

[4] Eltringham 2012.

Main courtroom of the ECCC

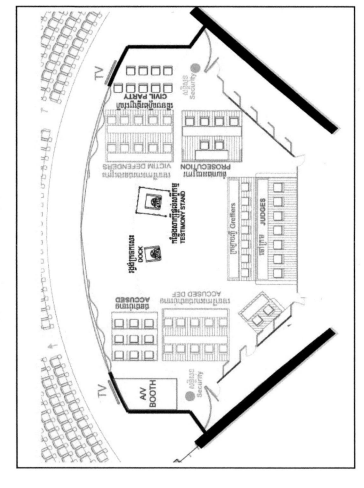

Figure 5.1 ECCC Courtroom.

Source: ECCC Court Report, August 2008. Image courtesy of the ECCC.

This situation posed a key problem for the tribunal since justice requires a legitimating public.[5] There is, for example, a legal need for a public since "international standards" require a fair and open trial. Article 14.1 of the International Covenant on Civil and Political Rights (ICCPR) states that "everyone shall be entitled to a fair and public hearing by a competent, independent and impartial tribunal established by law," a right referenced in the 2003 UN–Cambodian Agreement. Rule 84 of the ECCC Internal Rules stipulates that, unless there are extenuating circumstances, the hearings "shall be conducted in public" and broadcast publicly.[6] To facilitate this task, the Office of Administration established a Public Affairs Section (PAS) comprising, like other ECCC offices, international and domestic staff, and vested with the "duty of disseminating information to the public."[7]

While the PAS was formally created with the establishment of the Internal Rules in 2007, official efforts to disseminate information about the court begun soon after the signing of the Agreement—indeed, even earlier if one considers the efforts of the Cambodian government's Khmer Rouge Trials Task Force (KRTTF) and civil society actors. Along these lines, ECCC outreach may be divided into three key phases:[8] (a) the period from the 2003 Agreement to the 2007 Internal Rules that formally created the Victims Unit (VU) and PAS; (b) a second phase from the 2007 Internal Rules until the middle of 2009; and (c) a phase from this point, and especially after the 2010 establishment of the Victims Support Section (VSS), into the present. Vann Nath gave testimony just as the shift to the third phase—marking a significant increase in official ECCC involvement and corresponding diminishment of civil society participation—was getting underway.

If, as illustrated by the work of KID, the Center for Social Development (CSD), the Documentation Center of Cambodia (DC-Cam), and the Cambodian Human Rights and Development Association (ADHOC), civil society was more active in outreach than the ECCC during the first and second phases, the court took a number of early steps in this regard, particularly after the establishment of the PAS. Already, in 2004, the KRTTF had created the first edition of its booklet, *An Introduction to the Khmer Rouge Tribunal*.[9] Helen Jarvis, a Cambodian citizen and an advisor to the KRTTF, was appointed the head of the PAS, initially working with a former Cambodian journalist, Reach Sambath, and UN appointee, Peter Foster.[10]

The PAS webpage states that the Section is "the external face of the ECCC" and works with the different court organs to carry out the ECCC's "policy of reaching out to the community, the media, the diplomatic corps, donors, researchers and other interested parties" and providing "as much information as possible on the activity of the Court [and] working transparently to build public confidence in

---

[5] Ibid.
[6] ICCPR, Article 14.1; UN-Cambodia Agreement, Article 13; ECCC Internal Rules, Version 1, Rule 84.
[7] Internal Rules, version 1, Rule 9.
[8] See Balthazard 2010 for a four-phase model from which this three-phase model is adapted.
[9] Jarvis 2014.   [10] Pentelovitch 2008.

the judicial process."[11] To fulfill these tasks, the PAS engages in outreach and public information, media relations, and audiovisual recording. The decision to bring together public affairs and outreach in the PAS was inspired by the Sierra Leone and East Timor courts, partly to help focus the court's message.[12]

Outreach, listed first on the PAS list of activities, is perhaps its most important task. The webpage explains that the PAS Outreach Program "aims to inform Cambodians throughout the country about the work of the court generally, and the trial process in particular, to facilitate their understanding and involvement, and to foster support for this work, in the context of Cambodia's limited communications infrastructure and low levels of literacy."[13]

To this end, the PAS "reaches out to the people" using its informational materials, conducting outreach forums, and participating in media programs, seminars, and conferences. Moreover, the PAS "amplifies the message of the ECCC" by working with domestic and international non-governmental organizations (NGOs) as well as different Cambodian government offices.

Many of these NGO partners, including DC-Cam, CSD, and KID, periodically brought villagers and civil parties to the court to observe hearings, sometimes combining court visits with informational meetings and visits to Tuol Sleng or Choeung Ek. As a result, during the first part of Duch's trial, the courtroom was at times partly full and on other days relatively empty.

The month before Vann Nath testified, however, the structure of the PAS was shuffled. Jarvis left to head the VU, while Sambath, the Section's Cambodian Press Officer, became the new PAS Chief.[14] I met with Sambath a few days after Vann Nath's testimony. Like Seng, Sambath's family was from Svay Rieng and he was orphaned during Democratic Kampuchea (DK), losing his parents and three of his four brothers.

This loss was the reason he worked at the ECCC. During the People's Republic of Kampuchea, Sambath had returned to school and, among other things, supported himself as a bicycle taxi driver.[15] Eventually, he had received a scholarship to go to India before working as a journalist during and after the United Nations Transitional Authority in Cambodia, including working for *The New York Times*. In 2000, he won a scholarship to study journalism at Columbia University. He told me that, as he wrote about his DK experiences in a graduate school application letter, "I just couldn't stop crying. There were tears all over the keyboard. They just kept flowing."[16]

From the time he first started working for the court, Sambath had been afflicted by bad dreams, often arriving at the office sleepless, his eyes bloodshot. "I need [treatment from] TPO," he told me, referring to the Transcultural Psychosocial Organization that provided psychological support to the court. But, Sambath said, he also knew "how to treat myself," raising birds at his home, where he had a pond, flowers, chickens, dogs, and a water fountain that made a calming sound. "So this

---

[11] "Public Affairs Section," ECCC website, undated (http://www.eccc.gov).
[12] Balthazard 2010, 22; Lambourne 2012, 248.   [13] PAS website.
[14] "Press Release," PAS, ECCC, May 18, 2009.   [15] PAS Staff 2009b, 7.
[16] Author interview with Reach Sambath, Phnom Penh, July 2, 2009.

is how I cure myself," he continued, chuckling as he added, "And I think it's better to drink some alcohol to calm your tension. So I have to find a way to treat myself, though [my position] is not an easy job. Because when you talk about it, [the past] comes back. Everything."[17]

When I asked why he nevertheless wanted to work at the tribunal, Sambath replied, "I went through the Khmer Rouge time. I lost all my family. Some people call me the 'spokesperson for the ghosts' . . . It means I'm speaking not just on behalf of my parents. I'm speaking and doing the job on behalf of the entire court, and also on behalf of the victims who were killed under the Khmer Rouge regime . . . for those who have no representatives."[18]

After telling me of his suffering and loss during DK, Sambath stated, matter-of-factly, "I believe in spirits." When the spirit of his father had visited Sambath's wife in a dream, for example, Sambath traveled to the place where he thought his father had died and gathered soil, which he brought home and placed in a jar in a room dedicated to the spirits of his parents. Sometimes he would turn on the air conditioning for them or even sleep in the room to be with them. "I think they are there," Sambath said. "Sometimes they call to me."[19] On holy days, he lit incense and made offerings to their souls.

Even as he served as the (dark world) "spokesperson for the ghosts," Sambath recognized that he and his PAS staffers were the (light world) "external face of the court," which meant that the PAS took "the message from the court to the entire population of Cambodia through different means" including print, electronic, and social media.

Every trial day, the PAS distributed the court's information booklet, along with stickers and brochures, to everyone attending the proceedings. Sometimes attendees are even given ECCC T-shirts or hats, though these are produced in more limited numbers. Sambath showed me statistics stating that, in 2008 alone, PAS had distributed roughly 100,000 booklets, 15,000 posters, 50,000 stickers, 1,150 caps, and 1,701 T-shirts.[20]

The PAS, Sambath continued, also used new and old media. For instance, the PAS had to constantly update its website, which included announcements, a live stream of the proceedings, court-related documents, information about the court, and a video and photographic archive. This content had to be updated constantly, especially the photos and video that the news media needed. Eventually, the court's social media presence expanded on platforms like Flikr, Facebook, Twitter, and Instagram.

Sambath noted that the court worked closely with the "old" media. "We have to get the press what they want," Sambath said. So he and his staff sometimes took photos for the media to use.[21] The PAS also issued press releases and organized regular press conferences. As a former journalist, Sambath was familiar with the needs of the domestic and international press, which are critical to the court's goals.

---

[17] Ibid.   [18] Ibid.   [19] Ibid. See also Neuman 2006.
[20] Author interview with Reach Sambath, Phnom Penh, July 2, 2009.
[21] See "ECCC Publications" (https://www.eccc.gov).

In addition, PAS officers regularly appeared in the media, providing quotes for articles and speaking on domestic television and radio shows. These appearances were among several outreach activities in which Sambath was involved, including CSD public forums. Motioning to a PAS outreach map on his office wall, Sambath told me, "You see the provinces I have marked? I have myself been to all of them except one, even the remote areas."[22] While the PAS staff consisted of only five full-time staffers plus a few interns at the time, one person was focused on outreach and would make monthly trips to the field.[23]

Sambath distinguished such outreach work from the PAS's "inreach" efforts. "When we say outreach, we go to them," he explained. "But with inreach, we bring people here. It's essential."[24] Just the month before, shortly after becoming the head of the PAS, Sambath and his new press officer, Dim Sovannarom (who would take over as PAS chief after Sambath died in 2011), used radio appearances to invite Cambodians to the court. They gave out their cell phone numbers and offered bus transportation.[25]

The response was overwhelming. Villagers from all over the country began visiting the ECCC. Later, this PAS inreach program came to include a visit to Tuol Sleng or Choueng Ek. The week Vann Nath testified, the number of observers spiked dramatically. On the day of Vann Nath's testimony, the public gallery was packed and included hundreds of villagers from Kandal Province.[26] A few weeks later, the PAS announced that more than 12,000 people had attended hearings since Duch's trial began, figures that it would regularly update and advertise—20,000 by the end of August 2009, 31,000 in total for the Duch trial, and over 150,000 by the middle of 2014—to demonstrate "the continued public interest" in the court.[27]

Sambath interacted with villagers in various ways, ranging from radio programming to such inreach efforts, when he would often speak to groups of villagers inside the courtroom shortly before the hearings began. He used simplification and vernacularization when doing so. "I speak in a very simple Khmer way," he told me, "Not like a judge. Because if a real judge speaks, [the villagers] may not understand because [the judges] have their own language." Sambath's media background proved valuable. He explained, "I used to be a journalist and I wrote simple stories that people could read and understand. So [now] when I speak I use simple language villagers can easily understand."[28] Otherwise the audience would lose interest.

He provided several examples. The Khmer word for "mandate" or "jurisdiction" (*yuttatekar*) was quite hard for villagers "to understand because they have never heard this word in their village." So instead of using this term, Sambath used the word "power" (*amnach*), explaining, "It's the power of the court. Everybody knows what power means. The power of the court means this court has the power to try only Khmer Rouge senior leaders and those most responsible."[29]

---

[22] Author interview with Reach Sambath, Phnom Penh, July 2, 2009.
[23] Author interview with Hem Vichet, Phnom Penh, April 9, 2009.
[24] Author interview with Reach Sambath, Phnom Penh, July 2, 2009. On inreach, see Lambourne 2012.
[25] PAS 2009.   [26] ECCC Public Affairs Staff 2009a, 6.   [27] PAS 2010, 2014.
[28] Author interview with Reach Sambath, Phnom Penh, July 2, 2009.   [29] Ibid.

On other occasions, Sambath would draw on Buddhism and "dark world" analogies. When elderly participants once asked why only five people were being tried, for example, Sambath invoked a saying from a famous Buddhist monk whose sermons were well-known and frequently played on radio: "Greediness is a sin that nobody can repair."

Like Im, Sambath also used the analogy of offerings to the dead. Sambath explained, "I ask them, 'Do you offer food to your ancestors?' And they all say 'yes!'" When he asked the villagers how many chickens or bowls of soup or rice they offered to their many ancestors, they would respond, "two or three." Sambath would conclude, "'Do you think your offering will be delivered to your ancestors?' And they would say, 'yes!'" The trial of a limited number of suspects, he would suggest, served a similar purpose. Moreover, returning to the Buddhist sermon, Sambath would tell the villagers that greediness leads to suffering and that they should not be greedy about having too many trials.[30]

The PAS frequently highlighted the number of Cambodians visiting the court, featuring the figures on the ECCC website. PAS staff took pride in their accomplishments, particularly since the inreach activities were funded by the Cambodian government and undertaken without adequate personnel. The lack of time and resources was one reason PAS outreach and inreach efforts were predominantly monologic, despite the Cambodian staffers' skill in simplification and vernacularization.

On the other hand, the large number of visitors also gave the impression that a new public sphere—one of the fetishized manifestations of the transitional justice imaginary—was being created. In part, these efforts were aimed at the international community, including the donors who sought confirmation their funds were being effectively used to help establish a liberal democratic order in Cambodia.

To this end, the PAS also published the monthly English-language *The Court Report*. While *The Court Report* includes a regular section ("Judicial Updates") on the activities of the different ECCC offices, most of the content is devoted to outreach and public participation and includes photos of international visitors and Cambodians attending the proceedings or outreach sessions.

In the July 2009 edition published shortly after Vann Nath's testimony, the "Public Information & Outreach" section described how the PAS transported Cambodians to the court. The text included a photo of monks boarding a bus and of Mr. Pen Vuth, a commune chief from Kandal who had worked with the PAS to bring 450 villagers to the court on the day of Vann Nath's testimony. In the photo, he stands in front of the court building wearing a blue ECCC T-shirt adorned with the court emblem.

A column is devoted to his "Reaction" to Vann Nath's testimony. Mr. Pen Vuth states that the day was "very emotional for people, and also for me. My father, my younger sister and my younger brother were all killed under the Pol Pot regime. The people who came with me ... have similar situations."[31] He wanted to hear Vann Nath's testimony in order "to know if what has been said about the Khmer Rouge is true or not true.... Now I know that it is true." Upon returning home, Mr. Pen Vuth added, he planned to hold a meeting to "share with people who were not able to come, or who did not want to come, what we experienced and let them know the truth."[32]

---

[30] Ibid.   [31] ECCC Public Affairs Staff 2009a, 6.   [32] Ibid.

Even as they include a passing reference to those "who did not want to come," Mr. Pen Vuth's remarks, which implicitly stand for those of his group, accord with the transitional justice imaginary of an involved public: an emotional investment suggesting popular concern with the proceedings, a parallel between the hearings and the villagers' lives thereby highlighting the court's relevance, a "takeaway" about "the truth" showing the court is fulfilling one of its mandates, and an intention to hold a meeting that will further disseminate information about the court (the coveted "multiplier effect").

If a public is needed to demonstrate that fair trial rights are being upheld, then, a seemingly engaged public is also required to affirm the legitimacy and success of the tribunal—in the sense of both having a concerned public and having one that is enacting the transformation of Cambodia that the justice facade naturalizes. In the latter sense, public participation is imagined as another manifestation of a nascent "public sphere" (discussed in Chapter 3): a sign of the teleological transformation for which the transitional justice imaginary aspires—one in which a community that has suffered through authoritarianism and mass human rights violations "re(constructs)" itself on the basis of liberal democratic norms and political agency that leads to a new "democratic public sphere" and "culture of democratic citizenship."[33]

This imaginary space is asserted through performative and aesthetic practices, such as the extensive use of photographs in *The Court Report*. The issues are filled with large photographs of Cambodians participating in the transitional justice process, ranging from villagers attending court sessions to civil parties giving testimony. Ultimately, however, *The Court Report* is aimed at an educated, cosmopolitan English-speaking audience, especially donors.

The idealized image of a nascent public sphere is part of a justice facade asserting the existence of a newly engaged liberal democratic citizenry, an image that diverges greatly with realities on the ground. This posed an immediate problem for the PAS and NGOs working on outreach, since any flow of information "to facilitate understanding" and popular "involvement" and "support" confronted inevitable dissonance.

This issue of dissonance in "justice in translation" in Cambodia was handled in different ways by the PAS and NGOs, though the degree of dissonance also varied depending on audience (for example, a group of Cambodian law students versus a group of Cambodian villagers from a remote area). In some situations, the efforts at translation were weak and the difficulty in understanding high. Sometimes this was a result of logistical, staffing, or financial factors as well as a lack of "skill," as Sambath put it, in engaging villagers through simplification and reframing.

For example, while the PAS bused tens of thousands of Cambodian villagers to the court, they spent relatively little time educating the visitors about what transpired. Often the villagers boarded buses in the middle of the night. When they arrived at

---

[33] Ramírez-Barat 2014b.

the court in the morning, they sometimes went straight into the courtroom or sat in a courtyard where they might watch ECCC informational videos.

Once the villagers were seated in the public gallery, PAS staffers usually provided a brief overview of the trial and the different parties involved, but these talks out of necessity tended to be relatively short, sometimes twenty minutes or less. Some of the Cambodian PAS staffers, especially Sambath, were quite effective in framing their remarks in language the villagers could understand—some less so.

The villagers also received the official ECCC booklet, the pages of which they sometimes flipped, though often looking at the pictures rather than the text, which could be difficult to read depending on eyesight and literacy. Regardless, the limited amount of information the villagers received, and the way in which they received it, led to a monologic outreach process largely characterized by "thin translation," with the level of dissonance high.

During the many times I sat in the courtyard or next to villagers in the courtroom, I often asked questions to assess understanding. While a number of villagers expressed interest in the tribunal and were able to identify some of the parties in the court, others had little idea what was transpiring. Due to exhaustion, the technical court proceedings, and their lack of understanding, villagers sometimes fell asleep in their seats. The level of interest seemed higher when the tours included visits to Tuol Sleng and Choueng Ek.

The PAS staffers were aware of the limitations of their efforts, but did their best given their funding and staff shortages. Indeed, it is remarkable that they accomplished as much as they did, in part due to their dedication and hard work. Sambath, for example, said that some villagers referred to him as "Judge Sambath" because they heard his voice so often in the media: "They think I know all the legal issues. I try my best. I read day and night . . . because I'm working for the people of Cambodia."[34]

If Sambath served as both the "external face of the court" and the "spokesman for the ghosts," he noted that other people sometimes took on such an intermediary role. He pointed to civil party and S-21 survivor Chum Mey, who testified the day after Vann Nath, as an example of someone who monitored the court on behalf of all Cambodians even as "all the spirits of the dead from Tuol Sleng depend on him. Because ghosts cannot speak to judges."[35] This intermediary role was one of the key benefits of civil party participation, since the civil parties represented Cambodians as a whole, both living and dead.

Vann Nath also fulfilled this role. When Judge Lavergne asked Vann Nath what he sought from the court as he testified, Vann Nath, shortly after noting that he was "haunted" by the past, invoked a "dark world" and "light world" distinction, saying he sought "something that can't be seen, that is, justice for the dead." The court would be the medium of this justice, yielding a more tangible "result" through its actions even if this justice for the dead remained "unclear."[36]

[34] Author interview with Reach Sambath, Phnom Penh, July 2, 2009.   [35] Ibid.
[36] Duch Trial, Day 35, 55–56.

The verdict constituted one materialization of this justice, even as (and in contrast to symbolizing the Justice of the transitional justice imaginary) it could also signify an offering to the dead. Indeed, the day of the Duch verdict, civil parties held a *bangsokol* in which they made offerings, including the justice rendered, to the spirits of the dead.

Like Sambath, Vann Nath viewed the court in part through "light world" idioms related to law and transitional justice. Remarks he made about the importance of testifying for memory, truth, prevention, and the next generation illustrated this point. But, like Sambath and many other Cambodians, Vann Nath also interpreted the legal proceedings in terms of Buddhism and common sense understandings of the "dark world," including spirit beliefs as illustrated by his comments about hauntings and seeking justice for the dead.

Justice Trouble

The justice facade and performance

Even as the PAS sought to provide a positive face for the court, discursively asserting its legitimacy and public support, its efforts were undermined by controversies and a growing number of critics. Theary Seng was among them, as she would come full circle and denounce the ECCC as an "irredeemable political farce."

A November 15, 2011 press release announcing that Seng was withdrawing as a civil party explained, "She believed the ECCC to be necessary as a 'court of law' in catalyzing benefits in the 'court of public opinion' and viewed these benefits to outweigh the deep problems of political interference, UN apathy, corruption, incompetence, etc."[37] On her website, Seng labeled the ECCC the "Extraordinary SHAMbers" and included a modified version of the court emblem featuring a clown in Angkorean dress juggling balls. Her subsequent critiques of the court were unsparing.

Like Seng, many international human rights organizations and foreign governments had been concerned about political influence. The final agreement about the structure of the court involved compromise, but left the Cambodian government in a position of power. Many of the people appointed to the national side of the court had political connections, including the national co-prosecutor, Chea Leang, the niece of Deputy Prime Minister and head of the Cambodian government's KRT team, Sok An.

Several of the judges also had politicized backgrounds,[38] a fact not lost on defense lawyers who sometimes petitioned for their disqualification due to bias.[39] This weakness and politicization of the Cambodian judiciary is a key reason why the UN

---

[37] Khmer Rouge Victims in Cambodia Press Release 2011. On the "Extraordinary SHAMbers," see Theary Seng's website (http://www.thearyseng.com).

[38] "Cambodia: Opposition MP Jailed after Sham Trial," Human Rights Watch, August 9, 2005 (http://hrw.org).

[39] PTC 2008d. See also Pike 2002; Defense 2012.

initially sought an international tribunal. In 1997, as discussions were about to commence, the UN Commission on Human Rights expressed "serious concern" about the rule of law in Cambodia.[40] Besides citing the Cambodian legal system's lack of "independence," "impartiality," and proper "due process," the resolution cited the "continuing problem of impunity."

These concerns about international standards were echoed in the "Group of Experts" report, by diplomats, in subsequent UN statements, and in reports and press releases by Amnesty International, Human Rights Watch, and other international NGOs.[41]

Later, in early 2007, the Open Society Justice Initiative revealed that the United Nations Development Program (UNDP) was auditing the tribunal amidst kickback allegations involving Cambodian judges.[42] The UNDP report recommended a number of changes but referred the corruption allegations to the Cambodian government, which declined the UNDP's request to investigate.[43] A subsequent report found that the ECCC had adequately addressed human resource management issues raised in the UNDP report, though corruption allegations soon arose again and were likely behind the departure of the ECCC's Cambodian Chief of Personnel.[44]

Other controversies continued to plague the court. Already, in 2008, the long-standing disagreement about the number of former Khmer Rouge to be tried reemerged when the International Co-Prosecutor sought to launch investigations into Cases 003 and 004, an action opposed by his Cambodian counterpart, Chea Leang. Her reasoning echoed that of the Cambodian government, asserting that the 2003 Agreement only envisioned a few trials while invoking "Cambodia's past instability and the continued need for national reconciliation."[45]

Cambodian officials openly asserted that only a small number of trials would proceed. For example, during his 2010 visit to the ECCC, Ban Ki-moon had emphasized the independence of the court. Hun Sen, in turn, told the UN Secretary-General there would be no further trials. Cambodian officials explained that Hun Sen "clearly affirmed that Case 003 will not be allowed. We have to think about peace in Cambodia or the court will fail."[46]

Cambodian personnel at the ECCC repeatedly adhered to this open government position, leading critics, including defense lawyers, to argue that the court lacked independence and was being manipulated by the Cambodian government. These criticisms were amplified in 2011, when reports emerged that the Office of the Co-Investigating Judges (OCIJ) had prematurely shut down the investigation into Case 003.[47] A number of court staff resigned in protest before an inquiry supposedly uncovered "indications of the falsification of evidence, including witness tampering, and the back-dating of orders."[48] The International Co-Investigating Judge resigned

---

[40] United Nations Commission on Human Rights 1997. See also United Nations 1997.
[41] Amnesty International 2002, 2003; Human Rights Watch 2002. For a critique, see Stanton undated.
[42] Open Society Justice Initiative 2007.   [43] Veasna 2008.
[44] Human Resources Management 2008; Munthit 2008a; *Macau Daily Times* Staff 2008; see also Hall 2008.
[45] OCP 2009.   [46] Sokha and O'Toole 2010.   [47] OCP 2011a, 2011b.
[48] Gillison 2011.

in October. The UN, in turn, failed to launch an investigation, side-stepping an issue that could derail a court that was already controversial and in which they had invested millions of dollars.[49]

At the end of October, Nuon Chea's defense lawyers filed a criminal complaint at the Phnom Penh Municipal Court alleging that high-ranking government officials, including Hun Sen, had a "common criminal plan" to interfere with justice at the ECCC, a situation that threatened to undermine the court's legitimacy.[50] Defense lawyers also objected that their requests to call senior government officials to the stand were not upheld. By December 2012, several of Nuon Chea's lawyers left the court in frustration, calling the ECCC a "farce."[51] Amidst the 2011 controversy over the failure to investigate Cases 003 and 004, the OCIJ also refused to admit civil party applications for these cases, including Seng's.[52]

These events formed the backdrop of Seng's decision to withdraw as a civil party in November 2011. The press release about her withdrawal noted that she had served as the "'poster child' for the genocide and a strong, articulate voice ... as victim and opinion-maker in supporting the ECCC despite its serious flaws ... No longer. Within recent months, the scale has tipped for her" due to a series of "compounded, viciously intractable, toxic shenanigans" that were "the worst legacy imaginable for [Cambodia's] ... long-suffering people."[53]

For this reason, the statement continued, Seng "no longer wishes to have any legal association with this ECCC which is mocking the dead, her and other victims and embedding impunity." The court, the statement concluded, had become "a political farce, an irreversible sham of extraordinary perversion in denying justice to victims, exploiting their suffering, soiling the memories of their loved ones."

At a November 15 press conference about her decision, Seng added that she had also withdrawn because "I do not have faith in the lead [civil party] co-lawyers."[54] Seng was referring to a change in civil parties representation. In Case 001, which had less than a hundred civil parties, the civil parties were sorted into four groups loosely based on intermediary group affiliation.[55]

This system proved unruly. While she had initially worried about the management of the civil parties, Seng noted that the victims weren't "messing up the process. It's the lawyers who should know better. It's their egos that are competing in the public arena, fighting for space, fighting for the microphone.... It's shameful!"[56]

Given such issues and the challenge of coordinating the almost 4,000 civil parties for Case 002, an ECCC working group recommended a significant modification of civil party participation. The February 2010 revision of the Internal Rules established Civil Party Lead Co-Lawyers who would streamline civil party representation, interests, and claims.[57] A civil party would still retain his or her lawyer, but this civil party

---

[49] Giry 2012; Gillison 2011, 2012.   [50] Titthara and Kozlovski 2011.
[51] Freeman 2012.   [52] PTC 2012; Di Certo 2012.
[53] Khmer Rouge Victims in Cambodia Press Release 2011.   [54] Di Certo 2011.
[55] Thomas and Chy 2009, 250.
[56] Author interview, Theary Seng, Phnom Penh, June 29, 2009.
[57] ECCC Internal Rules (Rev 5), Rule 12, February 9, 2010. See also Jarvis 2014.

lawyer would ultimately be secondary to the Lead Co-Lawyers, who would coordinate civil party participation.

If Seng recognized the need for changes, she was disappointed in the Lead Co-Lawyers appointed. "I decided to withdraw completely because I do not have faith in the court... [and] in the lead [civil party] co-lawyers. One is an incompetent neophyte with no international background who would not allow me—as a victim—to speak with her, and the other is the same."[58] (The co-lead lawyers stated that they were only allowed to meet with civil party lawyers, not the civil parties themselves.) At her press conference, Seng added, "I feel such a relief that I don't have to play a role in that theater anymore."[59]

Instead, she became a strong critic of the court. She announced a "Poetic Justice" campaign featuring dartboards with the faces of different war criminals including the Case 002, 003, and 004 suspects, Pol Pot, and even foreigners like Henry Kissinger and Mao who had a role in the rise of the Khmer Rouge. "Poetic justice is to negate the nefarious legacy of the Khmer Rouge tribunal," Seng stated. "The UN has failed us miserably."[60]

She also spoke out when the Supreme Court Chamber's (SCC) final decision against Duch was announced on February 3, 2012. The SCC overruled the Trial Chamber's sentence of 35 years that—after giving Duch credit for cooperation and time served—effectively amounted to a 19-year sentence.

Many Cambodians had been upset with the Trial Chamber sentence, which raised the possibility Duch might walk free one day. Seng told *Time Magazine*, "If you can kill 14,000 people and serve only 19 years—11 hours per life taken—what is that? It's a joke."[61] But Seng and other human rights activists were similarly upset when the SCC sentenced Duch to life. Seng complained that the decision was politicized since it absolved the government for Duch's unlawful detention and failed to give him credit for mitigating factors. Duch, she said, was being made a "scapegoat" for DK crimes and for the government's attempt to "whitewash its own KR history and crimes."[62]

Meanwhile, the dispute over Cases 003 and 004 was once again emerging. The Cambodian government refused to recognize the person the UN had nominated to take over as International Co-Investigating Judge, Laurent Kasper-Ansermet, who was clear about his intention to push forward with the investigations. His efforts were stymied at every turn. In response, Kasper-Ansermet issued a March 21, 2012 "Note of the International Reserve Co-Investigating Judge to the Parties on the Egregious Dysfunctions within the ECCC Impeding the Proper Conduct of Investigations in Cases 003 and 004."[63] In response, Kasper-Ansermet resigned on May 4, 2012. Kasper-Ansermet's successor was able to relaunch the investigations into Cases 003 and 004, though many were skeptical the cases would come to trial.

---

[58] Di Certo 2011.   [59] Ibid.   [60] Ibid.   [61] Friedman 2010.
[62] Seng 2012. See also Giry 2010, 2012.   [63] OCIJ 2012. See also Giry 2012.

The justice facade

As these controversies illustrate, international courts are placed in an unstable and paradoxical position. On the one hand, they are premised on the aspirations of the transitional justice imaginary, an imagined flow of "international standards" and the "rule of law"—key ingredients of liberal democratic transformation—to post-conflict sites like Cambodia. On the other side, these "international" courts are contrasted with their imagined opposite, the political "show trial" associated with authoritarianism.

Transitional justice imaginary discourses, which assert the rule of law is being enacted and justice delivered, are omnipresent in international tribunals. They can be found in UN statements as well as the "Group of Experts" report that first began to envision the court that would become the ECCC.[64]

When giving his 2010 remarks at the ECCC, Ban Ki-moon similarly stressed the importance of "preventing impunity" as the court delivered "international justice" to the Cambodian people. And, as we have seen, Seng was a critic of the court before and after her engagement with KRT outreach and victim participation, critiquing the court for its politicization and rule of law failures. She also often described the court, and her participation in it, using metaphors of performance.

Indeed, the ECCC, like other courts, is sometimes referred to as "the show." As noted earlier, the courtroom has a "stage" (the courtroom) with curtains that open and close. Participants, like actors, occupy given roles and are enabled and constrained by a structuring "set" (the court as a whole and the broader global justice of which it is a part) and "script" (law and rules of procedure).

The juridical performance takes place within this context, which delimits the parameters of action. If the judges serve as a tangible metonym of justice, the victim, the "injured party," occupies a critical role.[65] It is an affectively loaded position—the "sufferer" who is wounded, bereft, and traumatized—that is critical to the legitimacy of the court since it is on their behalf, and the larger society for which they stand, that justice is being delivered. In this regard, the KID booklet illustrates both the justice facade of pure "global justice" being enacted in Cambodia and the ideal type of person for whom it is rendered—the suffering Uncle San, a "backward" subject acting within the parameters established by the court and thereby being transformed.

As we have seen repeatedly, the facade breaks down in the turbulent and muddy waters of everyday life and practice. Thus, even as the dialogic public sphere is performatively asserted in forums, it is undermined by the translation and vernacularization process due to variation in the knowledge and objectives of the intermediaries and the on-the-ground understandings of Cambodians.

Seng's experience illustrates another fissure in the facade. If she sought to realize democratization goals through the court, she also wanted to transform the role and possibilities of victim voice. Even as she noted she was regarded as the "poster child"

---

[64] See Lallah, Stephen, and Ratner 1999, paragraph 2.
[65] Madlingozi 2011; McEvoy and McConnachie 2013; see also Clarke 2009; Elander 2013; Fassin 2008; Fassin and Rechman 2009.

for the victims, she told me, "I don't act like a victim. I'm not a victim in any sense of the word except legal."[66]

If she had suffered enormously during DK and advocated trauma awareness and healing, she refused the term "victim" as well as one of the naturalized qualities of victimhood, a passivity and docility that comes from injury. And here Seng's actions revealed a key crack in the justice facade, which also asserts the creation of a democratic space of agency and vocality but remains in tension with the ideal type of the victim and the conservative structure of law, which seeks to regulate and control the proceedings. This fissure was accentuated even further when she removed her lawyer, yet another buffer between herself and the alleged source of her injury, the defendant/perpetrator.

An extremely active victim is dangerous in this regard. Seng pushed the boundaries of the limits of civil party participation to the point where she was almost directly speaking to the accused. To her, such a prominent role for victims realized the participatory and agentive possibilities of victim participation; to the judges, her actions had violated the Internal Rules, which, their ruling stated, only gave civil party lawyers "the right to make brief oral observations."[67]

Many people viewed this decision as a key moment when the court began to restrict civil party participation, eventually creating another buffer—the Lead Co-Lawyers. For Seng, the court's denial of her right to speak undercut the purpose of civil party participation, making her a passive part of the "décor," like a "potted flower," someone who had been silenced and used and was unable to "communicate my interest" in a court that had become a "sham."

Eventually, Seng renounced the court as a facade, an inauthentic performance of justice. Her experience highlights the unstable performativity bound up with the justice facade, as it asserts the "rule of law" and associated identity positions like that of victim—even as the performance is destabilized by the fissures in the facade (the agency it simultaneously asserts and diminishes) and behind it (the often very different on-the-ground knowledge and practices mediating combustive encounters with "global justice"). This sort of "Justice Trouble" was also evident when Bou Meng took the stand two days after Vann Nath. His testimony would further highlight the "turbulence" that arises from courtroom disciplines and "justice in translation."

---

[66] Author interview, Theary Seng, Phnom Penh, June 29, 2009.　　　[67] PTC 2008b.

6

Discipline (Uncle Meng and the Trials of the Foreign)

July 1, 2009, ECCC Courtroom

"The scar marks from the beatings, do they still remain to this day, Uncle?"

President Non Nil asked civil party Bou Meng this question on the morning of July 1, two days after Vann Nath had testified. Non Nil leaned forward, "Or are they healed and all gone?"[1]

Like Vann Nath, 68-year-old Uncle Meng had survived S-21 because he could paint, though not before he had been tortured, an experience he had just finished recounting to the court. "[They've] healed already. But there are scars all over my back, Mr. President," Uncle Meng replied, motioning toward different parts of his shoulders and back. "You can even see them on the back of my arms." He continued, "They lashed me with the end of a whip while I lay face down on the ground. They beat me one by one, switching when they got tired." Bou Meng paused and then said, his voice barely audible, "Five of them were there, beating me at the same time."

"Can we please see the scars briefly?" Non Nil asked, motioning to Bou Meng to come forward. "Yes," Uncle Meng replied. "[You] can."

As the court waited, Uncle Meng's international lawyer, Silke Studzinsky rose to intervene. "Mr. President, I would like [us to take a] break now before Mr. Bou Meng shows his scars and to decide if this is appropriate."

It was the second time Studzinsky had intervened on behalf of her client that morning. As the proceedings had commenced, Studzinsky had asked to "make some observations." The previous day, she noted, civil party and S-21 survivor Chum Mey, "was overwhelmed sometimes when he [re]counted his story and he had to cry, and he could not control his emotions any more." Glancing up at the judges as she read from her notes, she continued, "He shares his traumatization" as well with "[Uncle Meng], who is my client."[2]

Accordingly, Studzinsky requested the court assure witnesses "that if they need time to cope with their emotions ... that they can be sure to have this time before they continue with their testimony," perhaps including "a short break" in which

---

[1] Duch Trial, Day 37, 32; Khmer version 25.   [2] Day 37, 1.

The Justice Facade: Trials of Transition in Cambodia. Alexander Laban Hinton. © Alexander Laban Hinton, 2018. Published 2018 by Oxford University Press.

"to recover." In addition, the court should offer assistance from psychological support staff.

Uncle Meng felt "strong" and looked forward to testifying, Studzinsky concluded, but "at some points of his story, [might become] very weak and will be moved very much by his emotions." At such times, it would be appropriate to give him time to "relax" before proceeding.

Studzinsky's intervention was linked to the larger backdrop of civil party representation. She was the international lawyer for civil party Group 2, which included the Khmer Institute of Democracy (KID), the Center for Social Development (CSD), and the Cambodian Human Rights and Development Association (ADHOC). A civil party and human rights lawyer from Germany, Studzinsky also served as the German Development Service (DED)-funded senior legal advisor to ADHOC, where she assisted their Khmer Rouge Tribunal (KRT) outreach program.[3] Bou Meng and Chum Mey had both filed civil party applications through ADHOC and were members of Group 2.

Like CSD and other non-governmental organizations (NGOs) working on KRT outreach, ADHOC also had a partnership with the Transcultural Psychosocial Organization (TPO). TPO helped train ADHOC staff on mental health issues, attended civil party forums, and offered mental health support to witnesses and civil parties.[4] These efforts were part of TPO's larger "Justice & Relief for Survivors of the Khmer Rouge Program," which included counseling services and on-site assistance for distressed witnesses and civil parties.[5] This larger backdrop of mental health services and concern about trauma was behind Studzinky's initial remarks and suggestion that Bou Meng be offered psychosocial support if distressed.

"The Judges," Non Nil replied, were "monitoring and observing the proceedings" and had noted the survivors were "very emotional." Mental health support staff were on hand to assist. The Trial Chamber had also observed that the witnesses were able to compose themselves and get "under control to respond to further questions."[6] The court did not want to "incite the emotions of the witnesses until he or she cries," but if it happened the judges would "take immediate action" to ensure the witness could "control their emotions." Then he called Bou Meng to the stand.

"Uncle," Non Nil instructed, "Could you please tell the court about your experience[s] during the Khmer Rouge regime from April 17, 1975 to January 7, 1979?"[7]

---

[3] "Civil Party Lawyer, Silke Studzinsky," Civil Parties Before the Extraordinary Chambers in the Courts of Cambodia website (http://www.civilparties.org).

[4] Raab and Polunda 2010, 12.

[5] "Justice & Relief for Survivors of the Khmer Rouge Program," TPO website (http://tpocambodia.org).

[6] Day 37, 5.   [7] Duch Trial, Day 37, 9.

Figure 6.1 Bou Meng and his wife blindfolded before the gates of S-21. Painting by Bou Meng. *Image courtesy of DC-Cam/SRI.*

The Testimony of Uncle Meng: A Traumatized Survivor who Painted Pol Pot amidst Screams for Help

In 1977, Uncle Meng and his wife were working, like many Cambodians during Democratic Kampuchea (DK), on a rural cooperative building dams and digging canals. The labor was difficult, pushing him to the limits of his physical abilities.

One day, he was told that he was being sent to the University of Fine Arts in Phnom Penh to teach. He was pleased. When he realized that their car was not headed in the direction of the university, "I felt uneased and I felt a bit scared and I felt I was dizzy." Uncle Meng and his wife were driven to a house by S-21 and suddenly ordered to "put our hands behind our backs and they cuffed our hands. Then my wife started crying and said, 'What did I do wrong?'"[8] Their dehumanization was immediate. A guard replied, "You, the contemptible, you don't have to ask. Angkar [the Organization] has many eyes, like pineapples, and Angkar only arrests those who make mistakes or offence." Uncle Meng thought about his work at the cooperative and "could not think of any mistake that my wife and I made."[9]

They were blindfolded and led into S-21 and registered (see Figure 6.1). "After they photographed my wife," Uncle Meng told the court, "then they photographed

---

[8] Day 37, 11.   [9] Day 37, 17–18.

me." He never saw her again. Today, the only photograph of his wife that he has is a copy of her S-21 mugshot. "I would like to show [it] to the judges," he stated. "Her name was Ma Yoeun alias Thy," Uncle Meng said as her black and white photograph was displayed on the court monitor. Her hair was cropped short, revolutionary style; a white tag with the number "331" was pinned to her black shirt. "She was about 25 years old."[10]

Uncle Meng was taken to a cell "in which about twenty to thirty detainees were placed. They all looked like hell because their hair grew long … I felt dizzy when I entered the room and I was so confused."[11] He was stripped to his underwear and shackled by the ankle. The prisoners' speech and movement was restricted; they had to request permission even to relieve themselves into an old ammunition can or plastic jug. Guards beat prisoners who made too much noise with a stick.[12] Uncle Meng recalled that a guard once stomped on the chest of the prisoner lying next to him. The prisoner coughed blood and died.

Food was minimal. "I was always hungry," Uncle Meng recalled. "When I saw the lizard crawling on the ceiling I would wish that it dropped down so that I could grab it and eat."[13] The prisoners were bathed infrequently and hosed down. "I used to raise pigs," Uncle Meng noted. "When I washed my pigs, then I water-hosed my pigs and I used my hands to clean my pigs. But [at S-21] I was even lower than my pigs or my dog because no soap was used, no scarf was used to change or dry my body."[14] The guards, Uncle Meng recalled, made jokes about the prisoners' naked bodies, mocking the size of their private parts.[15] The prisoners became thin, grew weak, and got "skin rashes and a lot of skin lice. It was so itchy."[16]

Worse was to come. Prisoners disappeared. Uncle Meng had an idea about what happened since the guards threatened that they would "peel my skin." A prisoner who slept next to Uncle Meng explained this meant "you will be beaten during the interrogation and I felt so horrified in my mind. I was so shocked. I thought, what mistake did I make."[17]

Four or five months later, Uncle Meng, in a severely weakened state, was interrogated. He was led, blindfolded and handcuffed to a room where he was ordered to lie, face down, on the floor, his ankle shackled to a bar. His interrogators asked if he was CIA or KGB. "I told them I did not know anything," Uncle Meng told the court.[18] "They had a bunch of sticks and they dropped [the pile] on the floor and it made noise," Uncle Meng continued. "And I was asked to choose which stick I preferred. And I responded, 'Whichever stick I choose, it is still a stick that you will use to beat me up so it is up to you, Brother, to decide.'"

Then Chan, one of Duch's top deputies, "stood up and grabbed a stick and started to beat me.[19] He asked me to count the number of lashes. When I counted up to ten I told him, and he said 'It's not yet ten, I only hit you once.' And I can remember his words … I can always remember his face, the person who mistreated me."[20]

---

[10] Day 37, 45–46.   [11] Day 37, 21.   [12] Day 37, 23.   [13] Day 37, 66.
[14] Day 37, 76.   [15] Day 37, 26.   [16] Day 37, 76.   [17] Day 37, 12.
[18] Day 37, 29.   [19] Day 37, 12.   [20] Day 37, 74.

As many as five interrogators took turns beating Uncle Meng, an experience Vann Nath depicted in a Tuol Sleng painting. "I felt so painful," Uncle Meng recalled. "There were wounds—many wounds on my back and the blood was on the floor flowing from my back. Whips were also used to torture me. I was so shocked and painful."[21] Uncle Meng kept telling his interrogators that he didn't know how to answer their questions: "I could not think of any mistake that I made. I did not know what the CIA or KGB network was; then how could I respond. So they just kept beating me. In my mind, I thought of my mother."[22] His back was covered with wounds, which his captors would sometimes pour gravel into or poke.

Uncle Meng's torture continued for weeks, during which he slept in a tiny individual cell. Uncle Meng was tortured in various ways, including being given electric shocks so severe he lost consciousness. Despite the torture, Uncle Meng claimed he never confessed. "I gave the same response every day," he testified. "I did not know who was the leader or who introduced me into the CIA or KGB." In the end, his interrogators wrote up "a false confession and ordered me to sign. I can not recall the content of that confession," but "inside my heart I of course did not approve."[23]

After signing his confession, Uncle Meng was returned to a communal cell. One day, toward the end of 1977, a young cadre asked, "In this room, who can do the painting?" Uncle Meng was an artist, "So I raised my hand. I said, 'yes, I can do the painting.'"[24] He was unshackled and tested. "They wanted to know whether I was really a painter," Uncle Meng said, so "they gave me a paper and a pencil so that I could draw."[25] After Uncle Meng had proved his ability, he was transferred to a small artisan workshop, where Vann Nath also worked. The artists were given better food and allowed to sleep without chains. And they survived. Almost every other S-21 prisoner, including Uncle Meng's wife, was executed.

Uncle Meng's first assignment was to paint a large portrait of Pol Pot based on a photograph of the Khmer Rouge leader. As Uncle Meng worked, Duch sometimes sat "nearby me, watching me, sitting on a chair with his legs crossed," even offering suggestions.[26]

If he did not personally harm Uncle Meng, Duch made threats, including a warning that, if his portrait of Pol Pot was flawed, Uncle Meng would be used as "human fertilizer."[27] As for the abuse of other prisoners, Uncle Meng recalled an incident involving a Vietnamese man who had claimed he could make wax moulds. The man "was tested and Duch saw that he could not do it. Then he ordered the interrogators to kick him like kick[ing] a ball."[28] The man disappeared. Another time, while painting, Uncle Meng witnessed an incident in which female guards kicked a pregnant woman because she was not walking quickly enough.[29] On another occasion, two guards passed his office carrying a "very thin man" whose arms and legs were tied to a pole like a pig.[30] While Uncle Meng never witnessed torture, "I heard the screams; people crying for help all around the compound."[31]

---

[21] Day 37, 13.   [22] Day 37, 13.   [23] Day 37, 53, 85.   [24] Day 37, 18.
[25] Day 37, 67.   [26] Day 37, 19, 36.   [27] Day 37, 64.   [28] Day 37, 38.
[29] Day 37, 50, 78.   [30] Day 37, 48.   [31] Day 37, 46.

Figure 6.2 Painters and Sculptures in the S-21 artisan workshop. Painting by Bou Meng. *Image courtesy of DC-Cam/SRI.*

After the defense challenged him on this point, Uncle Meng swore "right before the iron genie" that if he was "exaggerating anything, then I would be run over by a bus."[32] The defense also noted there were inconsistencies in Uncle Meng's testimony, a point Uncle Meng acknowledged, explaining "it is because I have been severely tortured ... if I made any mistake in my testimony it is result from the very poor memory of mine; resulted, of course, from such torture."[33] As he finished, he was close to tears.

Indeed, Uncle Meng's suffering, past and present, was a central theme during his testimony, displayed most visibly in his description of his torture, the many times he lost his composure, and his scars. Besides memory problems, Uncle Meng said that his torture and imprisonment had resulted in ailments such as hearing loss, poor eyesight, and premature aging. He had consulted with mental health professionals and was given medication "so that I would not have insomnia, and I take two types of tablets."[34]

In many ways, the emotionality of Uncle Meng's testimony peaked when he posed a question to Duch through President Non Nil near the end of the day. "Mr. President," Uncle Meng requested, "I would like to ask him where did he smash my wife." Uncle Meng explained that he had searched for her after DK to no avail and assumed she had been executed. He just wanted Duch to "tell me where she was

---

[32] Day 37, 93.   [33] Day 37, 94.   [34] Day 37, 74.

killed or smashed. Then I would go to that location and just get the soil … to pray for her soul."[35]

Duch replied that he was particularly moved by Uncle Meng's testimony and wanted "to respond to your desire, but it was beyond my capacity because this work [was] done by my subordinate, but I would like to presume that your wife might have been killed at Boeung Choueng Ek." Duch added, "Please accept my highest assurance of my regards and respects toward the soul of your wife. That's all."[36] Uncle Meng began to cry.[37]

If this brief synopsis provides an overview of Bou Meng's testimony, it is a particular kind as I discuss below. This account is also redactic,[38] editing out information that is less relevant to—or even threatens the integrity of—the juridical articulation in the making. Nevertheless, traces of the editing process remain, both obvious (the juxtaposition of quotations from the trial transcript with my summary indicating the text is truncated) and more indirect (the sometimes odd court translations of Bou Meng's testimony). These traces suggest an excess of meaning that has been elided as well as the juridical disciplines that produce legalistic narratives and subjectivities, ones foregrounded in the justice facade. This productivity was evident at moments such as the deliberations over Bou Meng's scars, Studzinsky's remarks about civil party emotion, and Bou Meng's very entrance into the court, a moment to which I now return.

Translation and the Trials of the Foreign

"Court officer, bring the survivor, Bou Meng, into the courtroom," Non Nil had instructed at the start of the proceedings.[39] A moment later, Uncle Meng, wearing an untucked dress shirt, top buttons unfastened, entered the courtroom. Clasped in both hands, he carried an enlargement of his wife's S-21 mugshot, which he carefully set on the desktop of the witness stand. The court official who had led Uncle Meng into the courtroom helped him put on a headset, which almost everyone in the courtroom wore.

"Uncle, What's your name, Uncle?" Judge Non Nil began.

"[My] name," Bou Meng said, bumping the microphone set on his desk as he rose to his feet. "Bou Meng."

"Uncle, you can sit down, because the proceedings will be really long and we will have a full day to hear your testimony," Non Nil instructed. "The Trial Chamber judges give you permission to sit." As Bou Meng quickly sat down, an illuminated red band at the bottom of the head of his microphone ceased to glow.

"Second. Uncle, before you respond to my questions," continued Non Nil with a slight smile, "Uncle, could you please wait until you see the red light on the head of microphone before Uncle begins speaking. If Uncle speaks when the red light is not on, the sound will not reach the interpreters. As a consequence, the translators

---

[35] Day 37, 88. [36] Day 37, 89. [37] MacDonald 2009. [38] Hinton 2016.
[39] Day 37, 6; Khmer version, 5.

won't be able to translate and thus the international colleagues in the proceedings and public gallery would not hear what you are saying."[40] Finally, Non Nil noted that since Bou Meng had hearing problems, "when you listen to any questions you should be quiet and wait until the red light is on. Then you can respond."

With these words, delivered less than thirty seconds after Uncle Meng had settled into his seat, President Non Nil introduced Uncle Meng to the disciplines of the court. His remarks centered on this issue of translation and a related technology: the microphone. Like other international tribunals, translation is simultaneous at the ECCC. The primary language, projected into the public gallery by a speaker-system, is Khmer. Everything that is said in Khmer is immediately translated into English, then from English into French. All the participants must speak one of these three official languages. Bou Meng's headset included channels for each language.

The words Bou Meng had spoken, "[My] name … [is] Bou Meng," had taken a journey from the microphone on his desk to the headsets of those listening in other languages. Non Nil had quickly summarized this semantic flow as Bou Meng's "message" was sent to the translators who then conveyed it to the international participants, who otherwise "wouldn't hear or understand." The translators sat out of sight in an enclosed second floor room at the back of the public gallery.

For translation to take place, Bou Meng had to act in specific ways. In the aforementioned sequence, Non Nil told Bou Meng that he had to wait until the red band on the head of his microphone illuminated before speaking. If he spoke out of order, his voice would not be heard. Just a few minutes later, Non Nil would repeat these instructions, adding that Bou Meng should "not answer too quickly, Uncle, watch for the light before [responding]. Uncle, speak a bit more slowly. Watch for the light until you see [the red light] on my microphone is off."[41] As Bou Meng's testimony proceeded, he continued to be coached on how to speak and what to say, instructions part of a larger process in which Bou Meng's speech and behavior were regulated by juridical disciplines and technologies.

If this sort of courtroom "translation" refers to the particular "process of turning from one language into another," the term has a more abstract meaning of "transference; removal or conveyance from one person, place, or condition to another," an action that involves "transformation, alternation, change."[42] This general sense of transportation from one state to another is captured by the etymological connection of "translation" to "transfer," which comes from the Latin *transferre*, "to bear, carry, bring" (*transferre*) "across" (*trans-*). The Khmer term Non Nil used, *bok brae*, has a roughly similar sense, suggesting a removal (like peeling bark off a tree) and a transformation into a different form.[43] In both cases, there is a suggestion of something "stripped away" from one context and transformed as it is introduced into another.

In non-literary contexts, such as translation at a tribunal, it is often assumed that, while everyone recognizes a "loss," the task of translation is a more or less

---

[40] Day 37, 6, Khmer, 5–6.   [41] Day 37, 6.   [42] "Translation," *OED On-line* 2014.
[43] Headley et al, 1977, 459, 600.

straightforward technical exercise. Within the field of translation studies, however, there has been much debate about what happens during the "transfer," as "the text" is translated into another language.[44] Even if there are key differences in the translation of a literary text and trial testimony, the two converge in the centrality of translation in the courtroom on both linguistic (translation into a foreign language) and discursive levels (a translation into juridical form). Some of the discussions in translation studies therefore provide a way to reapproach the disciplines that structured Bou Meng's testimony. Accordingly, I now make another return, a re-examination of Bou Meng's testimony as, to use translation theorist Antoine Berman's term, a "trial of the foreign,"[45] involving justice as exile, desire, appropriation, and de/formation.

Justice and Trials of the Foreign

Justice as exile

Justice entails exile. The departure leads to change; change means that there can be no return to the origin. A secondary sense of "exile" captures this fact: exile as "waste" and "ruin." What was familiar becomes strange, but uncannily so since it bears the trace of its origin, the "home" for which the translation longs. The translation is a look alike, a double that can never duplicate the original, a double that is itself further doubled, replicated, parsed, fragmented.

The temporality of the transitional justice imaginary is illustrative as a post-conflict society is imagined as one of transformation whereby, through the transitional justice mechanism, it moves along a linear trajectory from an original state of "ruin" to one of liberal democratic change and "development." Inflecting this trajectory as one of "exile," however, highlights the point that the process is not just one of emancipation but also loss, and perhaps even "ruin"—a lack that infuses the process, a disjuncture between what is seen, desired, and imagined. Bou Meng's testimony also illustrates this point, beginning with the very act of translating his testimony in court.

As Bou Meng speaks into the microphone, his words are converted, first into electrical signals that travel to the translation booth, then into English and from English into French. The glowing red band on the microphone signifies the exile-in-the-making of his testimony; then the light darkens and is gone, like his words that have been carried across to the headsets of those listening in different languages. The words cannot return. Back-translation is impossible even if the trace of the origin remains in the de/formation, awkwardness, and gaps in the translated text.

For instance, when Studzinsky spoke of the "emotional difficulties" of her client, the English term she used was translated as *sâtiarama*, a Khmer term linked to Buddhist mindfulness and the proper focus of consciousness versus the turbulence of a consciousness out of balance. Indeed, idioms of balance are central to understanding Khmer ethnopsychology and have humoral dynamics and somatic

---

[44] Venuti 2012, *passim.*   [45] Berman 2012.

manifestations that are glossed over in a straightforward translation using a bio-medical category like post-traumatic stress disorder (PTSD). In this sense, Bou Meng's emotive disposition is "exiled" in translation, becoming something "other" that points "home" to his emotional disposition but is unable to return to it since it involves a complicated semantic network, the "bushy undergrowth"[46] of a particular context that is masked by the justice facade. *Sâtiarama* becomes "emotion," stripped of its Buddhist connotations and filtered into a Global North biomedical frame suggesting PTSD.

This frame is deeply enmeshed with the transitional justice imaginary, which asserts a traumatized and wounded victim awaiting the healing provided by the transitional justice process. Thus, Uncle San remains suspended in the past, suffering from symptoms of PTSD in his hammock until he (and, through metonymy, Cambodia as a whole) is cured by his participation in the ECCC. Bou Meng was portrayed in a similar manner, as illustrated by Studzinsky's comment that Bou Meng "shares his traumatization" with Chum Mey and other "survivors, victims, civil parties and witnesses" in need of mental health services.

To highlight Bou Meng's traumatization, as part of a larger legalistic frame of "suffering" required for civil party participation, Cambodian civil party lawyer Kong Pisey asked Bou Meng if he had sought "psychological support." Bou Meng replied affirmatively, explaining he previously "had consultation with psychological support" and received "two types of tablets" to help with insomnia,[47] a symptom he shared with Uncle San. This juridical framing of Bou Meng's emotional states glosses over the ways he copes with his suffering, including, as Uncle San is depicted as doing in the booklet, praying for the souls of the dead. Indeed, I have foregrounded contrast between Uncle San and Bou Meng by highlighting how he, like Uncle San, was referred as "Uncle" despite the ways "Uncle Meng's" understanding diverged from the transitional justice imaginary manifest in the KID booklet.

Accordingly, this framing elides key aspects of Cambodian ethnopsychology. In Khmer, for example, Bou Meng explains that he takes three pills, including vitamins. These pills help his "nerves" work (*brâsae brâsat*), a term that is difficult to translate because it refers to internal vessels that help maintain a bodily flow that, if obstructed or disrupted, may result in idioms of distress—ones that again are difficult to translate. In his testimony, Bou Meng mentions two of these somatic manifestations of psychological disruption, "thinking too much" and having difficulty sleeping, which the medicines are meant to help.[48] Of course, Cambodians have a wide variety of non-biomedical ways of treating such conditions and facilitating bodily flow, ranging from using tiger balm to pinching key parts of the body—many of which I observed Bou Meng doing at the ECCC.

This "bushy undergrowth" of his understanding is "clipped away" from Bou Meng's testimony as it is refashioned to accord with juridical order. This sort of justice as exile can be seen throughout Bou Meng's testimony. At times, for example, Bou Meng, like other Cambodians who testified, invoked Cambodian proverbs to

---

[46] Ibid, 244.   [47] Day 37, 74.   [48] Day 37, 58.

highlight a point. Sometimes these proverbs were translated and sometimes—as was frequently the case with trial dialogue and testimony more broadly (indeed, the English-language translations often leave out significant portions of text, especially when the translator considers it repetitious)—they were not.

Even when such idioms were noted and translated, they often didn't make much sense. Thus, when Bou Meng tried to explain why he didn't remember a S-21 episode Vann Nath had recounted about Bou Meng having been taken away, tortured, and then forced to apologize to the other prisoner-artisans, Bou Meng replied, "I cannot recall or maybe I forgot, because I never offered my apologies to anyone … As the Khmer proverb says, 'The elephants with four legs would have collapsed sometime and the wise person would forget anyway.' "[49]

Bou Meng's invocation of this "old Cambodian proverb" also suggests how he, like many Cambodians from rural backgrounds, often invoke agrarian metaphors, idioms, and experiences that are difficult to translate and considered irrelevant in the context of the court, particularly for foreigners unfamiliar with rural life. Bou Meng's testimony was sprinkled with such references, such as his stating that the prisoners were treated worse than the pigs he took care of at home.

When describing how the Khmer Rouge treated his wounds after he was whipped, Bou Meng explained that there was "no medicine, just a bowl of salt water that they poured on my back. I jerked violently. Oh, it was beyond pain, hurting more than even the beating."[50] As an example of the enormity of his pain, Bou Meng referred to what happened when salt was poured on a frog, an analogy difficult to translate into English and for speakers less familiar with rural life. He added that he was also given "rabbit pellet tablets," another term that doesn't translate easily. Bou Meng explained, though it was not translated, that the tablets were called this because they looked like "rabbit feces." Taking them gave Bou Meng a headache and made him feel dizzy, symptoms that again suggest a disruption in proper bodily flow according to Cambodian ethnopsychology. While this "treatment" healed his open wounds, Bou Meng said, invoking a Buddhist idiom, he experienced "enormous suffering" (*vetonea nas*).

Justice as desire

Bou Meng's invocation of "suffering" returns us to that glowing light, a reconsideration of it as the flame of desire. Desire involves a longing as well as unconscious process, something tucked out of sight—like the cord of Bou Meng's microphone that trails away into an underground circuitry carrying the current of his speech to the overhead translation booth that remains largely unseen, where it is transformed again, and transmitted once more, this time via radio waves, into the headsets of those listening to the translation.

If justice as exile focuses on banishment, justice as desire directs us toward the vehicle of that banishment, the circuitry that is glimpsed but then passes out of sight

---

[49] Day 37, 64; Khmer, 51. See also, Day 37, 38.   [50] Day 37, 31; Khmer, 24–25.

as the translation takes place. On one level, desire is on display, foregrounded like the illumination of the microphone's red light. But it is also "unconscious," largely out of sight like the translation booth and the electrical currents that transmit sound underground.

There are many ways to approach this "unconscious" process, including as a psychoanalytic current. Along these lines, one might examine the psychodynamics of testimony in terms of what is said, heard, and repressed. Here I focus on a different and largely unconscious current of justice as desire, translation in terms of juridical order—translation as a disciplinary ordering and classificatory process producing subjectivities.

Bou Meng may recount his DK experiences in a variety of forums: at home, to his children, through his art, to the media, by memoir, during lectures, and so forth. His speech act may vary across these contexts as through time. The court is a particular field in which speech and action are constituted within a terrain of affordances and constraints that canalize what is said and done.

While this process began with legal consultation and socialization long before Bou Meng arrived at the courtroom, the impact of juridical canalization is immediate as Bou Meng enters the court and is subjected to a legal regimen. He is shown where and how to sit and symbolically hooked up to the translation apparatus of the headset and microphone. When he stands and bumps the microphone, Non Nil instructs him on how and when to speak. In doing so, Non Nil invokes the power of the juridical regime, noting that the Trial Chamber authorizes Bou Meng to sit and expects him to watch the light on the President's microphone—indirectly referencing the power of the court to regulate and even cut off the sound from a participant's microphone, one dimension of its regulatory and monitoring role.

The court's canalization of Bou Meng's testimony further emerged in Non Nil's initial background questioning. Soon after instructing Bou Meng on the use of his microphone, Non Nil asked Bou Meng to describe his experiences during the DK period noting, "If you can, describe all those accounts. If you cannot, then the Chamber would put some questions to you" regarding DK and S-21.[51] "My apology if I cannot recall the exact date due to the serious torture that I received," Bou Meng replied, "My memory is not in great shape." He went on to note his hard labor in the reeducation camp, the shock of arrest, and his torture. "[T]hey just kept beating me," he testified. "I had a lot of scars on my back as evidence from that torture."[52] Then he began to cry, at which point Non Nil encouraged him to fortify his consciousness (*sâtiarama*) so he could tell his story.

Soon thereafter, however, the discursive mode shifted, as the judges and then the different parties had the opportunity to question Bou Meng. If Bou Meng emphasized his suffering, the judges asked questions directly linked to the legal facts of the case, ones defined by the criminal allegations and applicable law. In this frame, Bou Meng's replies became much shorter and were "clipped," as illustrated by the following exchange:

---

[51] Day 37, 9; Khmer, 8.   [52] Day 37, 13.

PRESIDENT NON NIL: "Do you think [your wife was] killed at S-21?"[53]

BOU MENG: "Your question reminds me [of] the question that I would like to ask to Mr. Kaing Guek Eav. I want to know whether he asked his subordinates to smash my wife at S-21 or at Choeung Ek [killing field] so that I could collect the ashes or remains so that I can make her soul rest in peace."

JUDGE NON NIL: "You have not answered to my question . . ."

Later, Non Nil would state more directly, "A witness is not supposed to give a kind of presumption because it is not really appropriate . . . [I]f the questions is put to you whether you say that you saw it or you didn't see it, you should just say "yes" or "no" and please try to avoid giving your presumption.[54] Here we catch yet another glimpse of justice as desire, the often unconscious undercurrents that shape "the said" so that it fits into the juridical discursive order.

Indeed, my initial description of Bou Meng's testimony was directly modeled after the summary of Bou Meng's testimony done by a lawyer working as a trial monitor.[55] I even took the first section heading from her account to structure my account according to a legal framing. The legal monitor's remarks, like other juridical accounts including the verdict, which ultimately emerge from such testimony, focus on tropes of victimhood, inhumane treatment, and suffering, which directly tie to his status as a victim and civil party and the larger factual allegations of crimes against humanity.

As the testimony is canalized and later recategorized (as it is summarized and added to the legal databases of the parties), it is pruned and clipped in accordance with juridical "desire." We return to the notion of "exile," as well, as Bou Meng's testimony is "borne across" to another modality of being, words that are no longer his own, but now part of the court record.

Justice as appropriation

"[D]ecide if this is appropriate."[56] Just as Bou Meng was about to remove his shirt and display his scars in the courtroom, Studzinsky intervened and requested the Trial Chamber to reconsider. Studzinsky's actions likely had to do with her earlier remarks about the need for the court to be more attuned to the emotions and trauma of her clients as well as the fact that Bou Meng's scarring was extensive and would require taking off his shirt and publicly revealing his scarred torso.

After the break, President Non Nil announced that the Trial Chamber had cancelled its "request to show the scars on the survivor's back."[57] Non Nil said photos of the scars could be used. "Mr. President, I do not have any photos of the marks," Bou Meng informed him. "I only have the marks on my body." Bou Meng agreed to have photos taken after the hearing.[58]

---

[53] Day 37, 44–45. [54] Day 37, 95. [55] MacDonald 2009. [56] Day 37, 32.
[57] Day 37, 33. [58] Trial Chamber 2010, 85, note 444.

This exchange regarding Bou Meng's scars revealed a moment of what might be called "justice as appropriation." If justice as exile involves a departure from which there is no return and justice as desire an attempt to "carry across" what is being translated in a particular way (to accord with the juridical discursive order), then "justice as appropriation" points toward the culmination of the process, as the translation is relocated to "the other side" to which it has been borne.

This appropriation takes place in at least two ways. To "appropriate" something is to take possession of it, to make that thing, as the etymology of the term suggests, "one's own."[59] As an adjective, "appropriate" suggests that which is proper or suitable to a given person, place, or condition. Justice as appropriation involves both of these senses.

Through its actions related to Bou Meng's scars—as well as its regulation of Bou Meng's emotion and suffering—the court "takes possession" of it, the exile becoming complete. His scars are appropriated in the juridical process, which renders them as "evidence" of his trauma and suffering. This process involves a doubling, as the original "scar" is photographed and then inputted into and redisplayed in the court record. As the trial process proceeds, Bou Meng's scars are recast to fit with juridical desire, eventually finding ultimate re-expression as a piece of evidence supporting Duch's conviction in accordance with the court's legal classificatory order.

Thus, in the Duch verdict, "scars" are listed as one of a number of outcomes of "beatings" that constitute "torture techniques" (each category and sub-category being given a number, in this case "2.4.4.1.1"), which is itself a sub-category of "The use of torture within the S-21 complex" (2.4.4.1) and "Torture, including rape" (2.4.4). The sub-categories are part of the broader criminal category of "Crimes against Humanity" (2.4), which also encompasses "Murder and extermination" (2.4.1), "Enslavement" (2.4.2), "Imprisonment" (2.4.3), "Other inhumane acts" (2.4.5), and "Persecution on political grounds" (2.4.6).

Bou Meng's display of scars is referenced in a footnote and includes a specific court record number for the photographs.[60] His experience is also described in a number of paragraphs illustrating "Specific incidents of torture" (2.4.4.1.2).[61] The inclusion of Vann Nath's sketches and paintings in the court record can similarly be viewed as an instance of justice as appropriation, in this case a work of art undergoing exile.

This appropriation is not a simple, one-sided imposition of power, since Bou Meng has chosen to participate in the trial process. But his agency and actions, as illustrated by micro-interactions such as Non Nil's instructions about the use of the microphone and what can and cannot be said (or found relevant), are constrained by the juridical process and authority.

More broadly, the tribunal itself might be viewed as an illustration of justice as appropriation in the sense that Cambodia's history—and the lived and remembered experiences of Cambodians like Thun Saray, Theary Seng, Nou Va, Vannath Chea, Sophea Im, Bou Meng—and "transition" is in a sense appropriated by "the

---

[59] "Appropriate," *OED* 2015 (accessed June 28, 2015).
[60] Trial Chamber 2010, 85, note 444.   [61] Trial Chamber 2010, 88.

international community." This appropriation is manifest in the aesthetics of justice illustrated in the previous chapter and is also symbolically enacted in the Uncle San booklet.

These exiles and appropriations are naturalized in the juridical process, as the court's work is positively inflected by Public Affairs Section and other people linked to the court to assert that the ECCC provides "justice, national reconciliation, stability, peace, and security in Cambodia" as the KID booklet, echoing the 2003 Agreement, puts it. Interestingly, while the English translation in the booklet uses these words, the Khmer text simply refers to "national unity" and "seeking justice for the victims." If the ECCC provides benefits for Cambodia, it is also an institution enmeshed with power, ranging from the Cambodian government's use of it for legitimacy to the international community's desire to integrate Cambodia into, and thus legitimate the larger project of, the "new world order" of neoliberalism and liberal democratic practices—even as it redacts the international community's complicated history place before, during, and after DK.

This connection to neoliberalism and democracy brings us to the second sense of justice as appropriation, or what is "fitting" or "suitable." In addition to the appropriation of his words and his scars, Bou Meng himself is appropriated as he is transformed into a particular type of subject "suitable" to the courtroom context. Studzinsky's intervention on behalf of Bou Meng and other victims revealed a great deal about the "appropriate" subject position into which people participating in such transitional justice mechanisms are cast. Thus Studzinsky identifies Bou Meng as a "kind" of person (victim and legal client/civil party) characterized by a disposition (emotionality and trauma) and, implicitly, invested with certain rights and status (someone entitled to sensitivity and care).

Studzinsky's questioning of the "appropriateness" of having Bou Meng display his scars likewise involved assumptions about his subjectivity as a liberal democratic participatory being invested with given rights, including the right to privacy and not to be partially exposed in public. Uncle San's journey provides another illustration of this point, as he is depicted as "moving forward through justice" into a subject position in which he is invested by law with participatory rights including the right to truth and the "right to request collective and moral reparations."[62] His symbolic entry into this realm of justice as exile, desire, and appropriation is, as with Bou Meng, linked to his being given a set of headphones, which symbolically render possible a translation of the juridical process.

Justice as (de)formation

Through such appropriations, the legal process produces a facadist articulation of reality according with a broader set of discursive forms and classificatory orders associated with the transitional justice imaginary. All such articulations involve the redactic, an editing out of that which does not accord with the larger discursive

---

[62] KID 2008, 22.

formation in the making.[63] Traces of what has been redacted remain, emerging in given moments of slippage, breakdowns in translation, and sudden eruptions of the uncanny. These traces, threaded throughout Bou Meng's testimony, suggest alternative desires and classificatory orders that have been redacted. If there is justice as formation, in the sense of the creation of a juridical articulation, then there is justice as "deformation" in the sense that there is a surplus of meaning in circulation that is inevitably distorted and elided by this articulation.

What, we therefore need to ask, is "clipped" away in this juridical process of (de)formation? The moments of slippage are usually quickly pushed out of sight. Thus Bou Meng's initial entry into the court and his unease using court technologies and procedures does not appear in the monitor's account. Nor does it appear in documents like the verdict. Instead, the moment passes largely unnoticed, recorded in the official court transcript but otherwise assumed to be unremarkable despite, as we have seen, being imbued with a surplus of meaning that is revealing about the justice facade naturalized at the court.

If there is justice as desire in terms of the discourses and classificatory orders that structure the juridical formation, there is also Bou Meng's desire. This desire, due to his legal socialization, may dovetail to an extent with juridical discourses. Thus, at one point during his initial description of his DK experiences, Bou Meng noted he was happy to be giving testimony at the ECCC, which he hoped "would find justice for me."[64] While testifying, Bou Meng made a number of such statements, as he did during media interviews and meetings with me.

But these juridical framings were basic, reflecting discursive strands linked to the transitional justice imaginary, such as the importance of the tribunal for justice, prevention, reconciliation, and educating the next generation. At the start of the trial, Bou Meng told Non Nil, "I'm not really sure whether I understand your question," and asked the judge to phrase things in more "simplified Khmer."[65] With the exception of Bou Meng's references to "justice," these notions were backgrounded in his Khmer testimony and mixed with other sorts of discourses, particularly those linked to his deep Buddhist belief.

Buddhist and desire

In Buddhism, the very notion of desire is complicated, as desire is linked to the "three poisons" (attachment, ignorance, aversion) and the resulting cravings that lead to suffering. The path to Enlightenment involves recognition of the reality, origins, and path to end suffering. To diminish suffering, then, a Buddhist should let go of craving and act ethically, performing good deeds that would condition one's future being.

From this Buddhist perspective, justice is bound up with this karmic principle of cause and effect. The Khmer term that Bou Meng used and that was translated into English as "justice," as noted earlier, is etymologically linked to Buddhism and

---

[63] See Hinton 2016.   [64] Day 37, 13–14.   [65] Day 37, 8.

religious idioms that are deemed largely irrelevant to secular law and the justice facade.

Thus, when Bou Meng described to the court that, while imprisoned at S-21, he was so hungry that he wanted to eat the lizards crawling on the cell walls, he immediately shifted into a Buddhist frame to describe his plight. "I pondered what sort of bad deeds (*bon*) I had done in my life to end up like this," Bou Meng told the court, speaking slowly and looking down. "I wondered what sort of karma (*kamma*) from my past life was impacting me and linking me to these people. But I couldn't see my mistake, what had led to these karmic consequences (*kamma phal*)."[66] Then Bou Meng, consciously contrasting the Buddhist and juridical discourses on "justice," noted, "This is if we are speaking of the consequences of karma. If we speak we are speaking of law, then I had no fault at all." When he proclaimed his innocence to his captors, they told him "Angkar has the eyes of a pineapple" and didn't arrest people mistakenly.

In this courtroom sequence, Bou Meng's Buddhist understandings suddenly burst forth in a line of juridical questioning about the "inhumane acts." His comments about karmic justice are thinly translated into English, leaving a gap in meaning that is ignored. From a legalistic perspective, the primary significance of this passage is given to the fact that Bou Meng was so hungry he wanted to eat a lizard, a comment noted by the tribunal monitor and referenced indirectly in the verdict in a footnote as one of the "facts" demonstrating the "Deprivation of adequate food" (2.4.5.1) and supporting conviction for "Crimes against Humanity Committed at S-21" (2.4).[67]

If Bou Meng's comments about karma are edited out of the juridical formation, they are central to his conception of justice and story about S-21. During this part of his testimony, Bou Meng interpreted his incarceration in terms of karmic justice, which holds that one's actions in the present condition one's situation in the future. As noted in the previous chapter, the Khmer word that is often glossed as "justice," *yutethoa*, literally means "in accordance with" (*yute*) dhamma (*thoa*). A Cambodian Buddhist monk, Venerable Sovanratana, told me that *yutethoa* is that which "fits into the way of nature ... the consequences of [an act] rebound upon the doer ... Whatever he receives is just because of the consequences of his past actions."[68]

Venerable Sovanratana went on to explain that there is not necessarily a need for an external punishment because the perpetrator's bad deeds naturally condition the future, which is "in accordance with dhamma." When I asked if a tribunal accorded with Buddhism, Venerable Sovanratana replied, "Well, it's difficult to say." If some might say that, regardless of a trial, perpetrators suffer the karmic consequences of their action, others might contend that the tribunal "is part of the result and consequences of [their karma]."

Invoking Buddhist rationalism, which emphasizes the analysis of evidence (*ceak sdaeng*) to discern truth from falsehood (*khos-treuv*) and moral right from wrong

---

[66] Day 37, 66; Khmer, 52.   [67] Trial Chamber 2010a, 95, note 501.
[68] Author interview with Venerable Sovanratana, Phnom Penh, March 13, 2011.

(*bon bap*),[69] Venerable Sovanratana continued, "whatever generates knowledge and awareness about right and wrong," including a tribunal, "is welcome in Buddhism." For him, the trial, as long as it was "just and fair," was in accordance with Buddhism since "it is part of the result [of karma]." Venerable Sovanratana noted that the Buddha did not oppose courts during the time that he lived and that, when a monk violated monastic rules, he might be brought before a monastic court. "So Buddhism does not teach us to wait for the ripening of karma to produce a result ... From that point, [a court] is not contrary to the Buddhist teaching." Venerable Sovanratana explained that he had visited the court with some of his novice monks to learn more about "what happened during the Khmer Rouge regime" and to observe how the court was functioning.[70]

This Buddhist emphasis on correct understanding, which is central both to the Four Noble Truths and Eightfold Noble Path in the sense of understanding the reality of things, was also invoked by Bou Meng during his testimony as he noted the importance of understanding right and wrong and telling the truth. In an interview, he told me "I always tell the truth," explaining "I'm really scared of sinning."[71]

During an interview, Bou Meng also noted the importance of perpetrators learning to distinguish "right from wrong," since, he told me, their actions were the result of "wrong thinking."[72] The court, he said, could help them in this regard. Nevertheless, as Venerable Sovanratana suggested, from a Buddhist perspective there is no absolute need to try perpetrators since they will inevitably suffer the consequences of their actions. To hold perpetrators accountable in a court of law, Venerable Sovanratana pointed out, also ran the risk of promoting vindictiveness: "it must not be done for retribution" but instead to determine what "happened in reality."

Bou Meng sometimes struggled with conflicting emotions about perpetrators. When asked about his feelings toward senior Khmer Rouge leaders, he stated that, according to Buddhism, it was necessary to pity them in their old age. He also sometimes noted the importance of ending the cycle of vindictiveness, telling me, "Buddhists can't hold grudges. If a person sins, they will always receive sin" as a karmic consequence.[73] At the same time, Bou Meng acknowledged that sometimes he "overwhelmingly" desired revenge, a feeling amplified by his scars, which reminded him of the abuses.[74]

Thus, Bou Meng's scars had a range of associations, including ones that strongly diverged from the juridical appropriation that occurred at the court. His scars signified social suffering, memory, somatic distress, anger, and a personal struggle between a desire for revenge and a Buddhist sanction on vindictiveness and emphasis on detachment as a means of ending suffering and cycles of revenge. Such conflicting emotions are edited out of the juridical process, with the Trial Chamber strongly warning parties against expressing hostility, anger, and malice toward defendants,

[69] See Ponchaud 1989, 154, 173.
[70] Author interview with Venerable Sovanratana, Phnom Penh, March 13, 2011.
[71] Author interview with Bou Meng, Phnom Penh, July 2, 2008.
[72] Author interview with Bou Meng, Phnom Penh, July 2, 2008.   [73] Ibid.
[74] Huy 2008, 9, 119f.

emotions that are nowhere mentioned in the judgment that the court renders except to note that its goal "is not revenge."[75]

These Buddhist principles were visually depicted on the walls of Venerable Sovanratana's pagoda, Wat Mongkulvan. Throughout Cambodia, one finds murals that depict the story of the Buddha's life and related legends. In fact, Bou Meng, whose parents sent him to be educated at a pagoda when he was five, developed his love of painting at the pagoda, where he would try to draw pictures depicting such Buddhist tales.[76] Bou Meng's education at the pagoda—barely mentioned in his trial testimony—revolved around Buddhist teachings, including learning about the ten lives of the Buddha and about doctrine related to dhamma, merit, and sin. Indeed, during one of our meetings, Bou Meng referenced the Vessandara story that Thun Saray had related to me.

Bou Meng later learned to paint murals of the Buddha's life that included scenes similar to those on the walls of Mongkulvan pagoda. This Buddhist aesthetic included depictions of the Buddhist hells that illustrate future torments that parallel past sins, such as drunks having their mouths stuffed with flaming torches, gossiping women having their tongues pulled out with tongs, and a perpetrator who used a blade to kill a man being sawed in half.

Venerable Sovanratana explained that the murals symbolized "the concept of rebirth or rebecoming in Buddhism," since what happens in the "next life depends on what men are doing in this life." The paintings suggest what happens when people perform "unwholesome acts, like adultery, drinking alcohol, and telling lies, especially as Buddhism prescribes in the five moral principles."[77]

As we saw, this Buddhist aesthetic put into relief the key Buddhist notion that one is bound by one's im/moral acts. This sense of ethical connection also informs one's relationship to the dead to whom, at least in the lay conceptions, merit may be transmitted through prayers and offerings to monks, who act as conduits between the living and the dead. The dead, particularly those who have died violently and are not yet reborn, are thought to circulate amongst the living, sometimes appearing as apparitions or in dreams. This was especially true of DK victims, including those tortured and killed at S-21.

This belief was also critical to Bou Meng. He had nightmares and dreams about his wife. In one, "my wife appeared leading a large group of prisoners who had been executed [at S-21]. They were dressed in black and she led them in front of my house ... She said, 'Only Bou Meng can help us find justice.' "[78] Another time, when visiting Tuol Sleng, his new wife had seen a door suddenly open and shut. Bou Meng interpreted such visions as evidence that "the spirit of my wife is not calm (*sngop*). Therefore I want reparations to hold a big ceremony and send merit to [the spirit of] my wife."[79]

---

[75] Trial Chamber 2010, 201.
[76] The details in this paragraph follow Huy 2010, 25f; see also Huy 2008.
[77] Author interview with Venerable Sovanratana, Phnom Penh, July 1, 2011.
[78] Author interview with Bou Meng, Phnom Penh, July 2, 2008.   [79] Ibid.

One of the early tensions between the civil parties and the court concerned the desire of some, like Bou Meng, to have individual reparations. The court was only mandated to provide "collective and moral reparations," however, which meant that they would not receive funds to support such commemorations for the souls of the dead.

From the start of Bou Meng's testimony, it was clear that the meaning of his participation was more deeply linked to his Buddhist beliefs and his relationship to his wife's spirit than to any of the ostensible goals naturalized in the ECCC's justice facade. Given this excess of meaning, a number of slippages and translation problems ensued. He entered the courtroom carrying an enlargement of his wife's S-21 mugshot, face-forward so everyone would see her. He began mentioning her as soon as Non Nil commenced his questioning, a pattern that persisted throughout the day regardless of whether Bou Meng was being asked about her. He often stated his desire to ask Duch where his wife had been killed.

At one point, a civil party lawyer asked Bou Meng, "Today how do you feel about the fact that you are a survivor?"[80] Bou Meng replied that he was "so happy" and that telling his story to the court made his body and chest "felt lighter," another ethnopsychological idiom linked to well-being that didn't translate smoothly into English. He then shifted and began to talk about the almost incalculable suffering he had endured. "But it wasn't just that I wasn't able to help save my wife," he continued. "Why did my wife have to die?" It was because of his wife that Bou Meng became a civil party. He explained that he wanted to ask the Accused " 'Where did my wife die?' I want to take earth from that place as a commemorative symbol to be used to hold a ceremony to light incense and send merit to her spirit so that her heart can be calmed." Again invoking an idiom that did not translate easily, Bou Meng noted that ultimately, only the Spirits of the Earth, Wind, and Water knew where the victims were killed and buried.

When Bou Meng was finally given the chance to ask Duch where he had "smashed and discarded" Bou Meng's wife, Duch replied that he didn't know for certain since his subordinates executed her. But given the date of her arrest, Duch continued, he presumed she had been killed at Choeung Ek.

This question and Duch's reply ultimately had little relevance to the court's desire for evidentiary fact and the juridical formation in the making. Such "justice as desire" diverged from Bou Meng's desire to gather soil from the site of his wife's execution so he could transfer merit to help her spirit be calmed and have a better rebirth. These sets of understandings are "clipped" by the court's desire for a particular type of legal formation according with the transitional justice imaginary.

The Lord of the Iron Staff

Yet another rupture occurred near the end of the day when Bou Meng was being questioned by Savuth Kar, Duch's Cambodian defense co-lawyer. Kar suggested

---

[80] Day 37, 85; Khmer 68.

that Bou Meng had contradicted himself by saying that the detainees couldn't speak while also saying that he had heard their screams. Part of Bou Meng's reply was translated in English as "I'm not here to talk or to implicate anyone. I'm talking here, right before the iron genie, and if I talked something exaggerating anything, then I would be run over by a bus."[81]

In Khmer, Bou Meng had referred to the local court guardian spirit, or *neak ta*, known as the "Lord of the Iron Staff." While dropped from the translation, Bou Meng had said, "I am speaking according to justice (*yutethoa*). The spirit (*neak ta*), the Lord of the Iron Staff, if I'm not telling the truth, may he let a car strike and kill me."[82] As he spoke, Bou Meng raised his voice while pointing toward where the shrine of the Lord of the Iron Staff is located on the ECCC compound.

If the "iron genie" translation made little sense in English, some foreigners familiar with the court likely understood the reference to the *neak ta*. For some who did, a reference to such spirit beliefs may have been noticed momentarily but viewed as irrelevant, a local superstition ultimately at odds with the (hyper-rational) juridical enterprise. Thus, while there were exceptions, when I mentioned the *neak ta* to international court personnel, they suggested it was quaint or simply expressed little interest. Some may have even considered having a *neak ta* in a court complex inappropriate but to be tolerated, since all Cambodian courts have *neak ta* before which oaths are sworn.

Most Cambodian observers would have immediately understood the reference to a *neak ta* in Khmer and that Bou Meng was swearing an oath as proof of the truth of his testimony. *Neak ta* are part of a folk cosmology of animistic beings circulating among the living in Cambodia.[83] Almost every village has *neak ta*, local guardian spirits sometimes said to be the spirit of the founding ancestors of the village, who are nevertheless feared and to whom offerings are made. When offended or disrespected, *neak ta*, including the *neak ta* found in Cambodian court complexes, may inflict sickness or hardship. While the depth of belief and knowledge about *neak ta* varies, for many Cambodians *neak ta* are highly significant. This was true for Bou Meng as well as Sambath.

Sambath's strong belief may be why senior ECCC administrators asked him to establish the court's *neak ta*. They told Sambath, "We have to build a spirit house because every court in Cambodia has one." Sambath began by inviting a renowned holy man from Takeo province to the court. "It was a sunny day and very hot. He poured water on every part of the compound," asking how the different buildings would be used. "He asked where the trial would take place," Sambath recalled. "I told him 'over there,'" indicating the courtroom building. When the holy man poured water in an area by the court, smoke began "coming out, powerful, very strong. Then he said 'this is the best place to build.'"

Sambath asked what sort of spirit house they should construct. The holy man closed his eyes and invited the spirits to come. "Because this is a big job he invited many spirits," before informing Sambath that the court's *neak ta* was the Lord of the

[81] Day 37, 93; Khmer, 74.   [82] Day 37, Khmer, 74.
[83] Ang 1987; Ebihara 1968; Guillou 2012.

Iron Staff. "The job is too big," Sambath recalled the holy man saying to him, so they had to have "the strongest one." Having found the court's *neak ta*, Sambath enlisted the services of a well-known professor at the School of Fine Arts to construct the sculpture of the Lord of the Iron Staff. The process began on March 31, 2006 on a day when the moon was full. Sambath organized a large religious ceremony in honor of the Lord of the Iron Staff, including food, prayers, and offerings.

Every witness, Sambath noted, had to swear an oath before the *neak ta*. Sambath had done this. If someone did so and failed to tell the truth, then the *neak ta* might afflict them in some manner, as illustrated by Bou Meng's remark.

Given the resonance of *neak ta* for many Cambodians, especially villagers, it is not surprising that there have been attempts to use the *neak ta* for grafting. The official ECCC booklet includes a photograph of the *neak ta*.

The *neak ta* is also prominently featured on the cover of the Uncle San booklet. When I asked Suon about the inclusion of the Lord of the Iron Staff, he was clear about its importance for the villagers, who immediately recognized and asked about the *neak ta* during outreach sessions. The image in the booklet, he said, was quite realistic. Suon went on to describe the oath-taking process, noting that it was used in Cambodian courts and accompanied by the lighting of incense and swearing to "tell only the truth. I will not lie to anyone. I will tell the court only what I have seen and heard and so forth. If I lie to the people, may the [*neak ta*] kill me." For the villagers, the *neak ta* was associated with "respect," Suon told me, suggesting yet another way in which the booklet sought to legitimate the juridical process using everyday understandings, practices, and aesthetics.

The *neak ta* was clearly of importance to Bou Meng. During an interview shortly after he testified, I asked Bou Meng if he had sworn an oath. Bou Meng replied, "The President didn't have me swear an oath. I don't know why and have wondered about this. All of the witnesses swear oaths. But not me. Perhaps the judges thought that I only tell the truth. It was only different for me."[84] Bou Meng didn't realize that civil parties, like other parties and in contrast to witnesses, did not have to swear an oath before testifying.

At another point, Bou Meng said, "Let me tell you a story that illustrates that if you don't tell the truth the Lord of the Iron Staff will make you have an accident."[85] When Mam Nai, one of Duch's top S-21 deputies, had testified, Mam Nai had proclaimed his ignorance of and lack of involvement in the abuses, including the beating of Bou Meng. It was Mam Nai, Bou Meng had testified, who had asked him to count the lashes he was being given.

After Mam Nai's testimony, Bou Meng told me, Mam Nai's son had picked him up and, perhaps a kilometer from the court, had a car accident. This was, Bou Meng surmised, a result of his swearing an oath to the *neak ta* and then lying in court. Bou Meng then noted the moment when Kar Savuth had suggested that Bou Meng was not being fully honest with the court. "Last month," Bou Meng recalled, "Kar Savuth questioned if my words were true. I replied 'I have the Lord of the Iron

[84] Author interview with Bou Meng, Phnom Penh, August 12, 2009.   [85] Ibid.

Staff as my witness.' If I had not been telling the truth, then I wouldn't have sworn the oath."

The truth of his statements, Bou Meng stated, was demonstrated by the fact that he had sworn to the *neak ta* that if he were lying he should be "hit and struck dead by a car. But I was not hit. Only the car of Mam Nai had a collision because he had not told the truth."[86] Given his deep Buddhist beliefs, Bou Meng told the truth. He feared the karmic consequences of lying. This "bushy undergrowth" of Bou Meng's understanding of the world and testifying in court, one in which Buddhism and animism were both highly salient, erupted for a moment in the "iron genie" translation, a slippage that passed without much notice.

If Bou Meng's invocation of the *neak ta* provides an illustration of a momentary slippage suggesting that something highly meaningful is being edited out of the juridical formation in the making, other slippages were directly in tension with this juridical formation despite being more apparent and interwoven into the proceedings. "Justice as desire" seeks to emplot and order the narrative flow so that it accords with the victim-perpetrator binary naturalized in the transitional justice imaginary.

Within the frame of the court, Bou Meng's subjectivity is appropriated into the category of victim, though one of a particular sort—a rights-invested liberal democratic victim subjectivity. This subjectivity, as noted earlier, was not the only one circulating in the court even if it predominated. There was also a Buddhist subjectivity that emerged at times, such as during Bou Meng's references to how he wondered what bad acts he had done in the past that had led him to suffer so much at S-21. From this Buddhist perspective, the victim also bears a degree of blame since, by implication, one's life is conditioned by one's past acts. This Buddhist view on suffering is different than the liberal democratic one that was part of the juridical formation in-the-making, which assumes a victim's blamelessness and innocence in contrast to the intentionality of the criminal perpetrator.

There is another manner in which Bou Meng's testimony was in tension with this juridical subjectivity. As a legally recognized civil party and S-21 survivor, Bou Meng had victim status. His questioning proceeded along these lines, which constituted the borders of "the appropriate." But his case and that of a number of S-21 victims and civil parties is not so simple since they were themselves Khmer Rouge—cadre and soldiers, perhaps at one time even perpetrators.

Bou Meng, for example, joined the revolution in the early 1970s, but this "grey zone" of his past was barely mentioned in court in keeping with the "clipping" of the complicated geopolitical past. Thus, during his preliminary questioning of Bou Meng, President Non Nil asked, "Before the 17th of April 1975, where did you live and what was your occupation back then?" Bou Meng replied, "I went into the jungle to liberate the country and to save King Norodom Sihanouk." Non Nil then immediately shifted the discussion to the temporal jurisdiction of the court, asking Bou Meng about his experiences from "April 1975 until the 7th of January 1979."[87]

---

[86] Ibid.   [87] Day 37, 9.

Yet, this statement that Bou Meng had been a Khmer Rouge revolutionary passed by largely without comment. Judge Lavernge asked a few related questions, including one about the extent of Bou Meng's devotion. Bou Meng replied, "I wore a black shirt, but my mind was not black. I did what I was instructed."[88]

Yet, if the other parties largely ignored Bou Meng's past, the Defense did not. International Defense Co-Lawyer Canizares ended the day by seeking to establish a parallel between Bou Meng and Duch, whose defense partly centered around the idea that Duch had quickly become disillusioned with the revolution but had to reluctantly carry out his orders or be killed. Thus Canizares asked Bou Meng about his lack of confidence in the regime and the necessity of nevertheless complying. Bou Meng affirmed this was the case. "[Was it] fear that made you follow 100 percent the orders that were given to you?" Canizares asked as she posed the final question of the day. Bou Meng replied, "In fact, that was the case."[89]

Here again we return to a doubleness that pervades the juridical process, as what is asserted as an ideal (the pure innocent victim) comes up against a more complex reality (the victim stained by association with the impure perpetrator category). This doubleness reveals an excess of meaning and a lack in the justice facade being asserted, one suggesting that "justice as deformation" is simultaneously taking place as alternative, complex local realities are clipped away and edited out by the disciplines of the court. The redactic would reappear throughout Duch's trial,[90] including the focus of the next book section, a two-week period devoted to civil party testimony in August 2009 that included a Documentation Center of Cambodia outreach tour and theatrical production, "Breaking the Silence."

---

[88] Day 37, 58.　　　[89] Day 37, 102.　　　[90] See Hinton 2016.

PART III

EDDIES

Preamble III

Breaking the Silence

Evening of August 16, 2009 (Day 1, DC-Cam ECCC Outreach Tour, National Institute of Education, Phnom Penh, Cambodia)

"Speak, speak, speak."[1]

With these words, sung by Yin Vutha, "Breaking the Silence: A New Cambodian Play," draws to a close. Throughout the performance, a collaboration between two local non-governmental organizations (NGOs)—the Documentation Center of Cambodia (DC-Cam) and the Cambodian branch of AMRITA Performing Arts—and the Dutch playwright Annemarie Prins, Vutha, in dark blue shirt with a sash around his waist, has played the part of narrator.

In this final scene, he tells the audience, "This is the story of Breaking the Silence," after which he twice sings the verse: "Transform the River of Blood into a River of Reconciliation. A River of Responsibility."[2]

It is the same verse that the cast, featuring four female actors affiliated with the Royal University of Fine Arts, sings as they walk off the stage in a line. A male monkey dancer, dressed in white, dances around them as they depart and before Vutha sings his final exhortation to "speak."

I sit about ten rows back from the makeshift stage in an auditorium at Cambodia's National Institute of Education. A handful of journalists and foreigners, including an Extraordinary Chambers in the Courts of Cambodia (ECCC) international judge and legal officer, are in the audience, but the hall is primarily filled by hundreds of Cambodians brought to the performance by DC-Cam on the first evening of its August 16–18, 2009 "ECCC Tour and Genocide Education" (ETGE) outreach program.

"Breaking the Silence" is broken into seven scenes related to Democratic Kampuchea (DK). As the four actors tell the audience at the start of the play:

Sovanna
So many stories.
We have to tell our stories.

---

[1] Prins 2009.

[2] Prins 2009, "Epilogue" (*Breaking the Silence* has no pagination so quotations are referenced by script section).

Figure 1 Concluding Scene in "Breaking the Silence," August 8, 2010. Photo by James Mizerski. *Photo courtesy of DC-Cam/SRI.*

Sina
We're telling our stories
Out of a relentless urge.

Sokly
How did it happen
That Khmer killed Khmer?

Theary
You must try
To help us think this through.[3]

After this sequence, the first scene begins. Vutha announces each scene's thematic and assigns roles to the actors, who, when not acting, sit on small stools on the spare stage. Several of the scenes center on the interaction of victims and perpetrators. One deals with survivor guilt, while another focuses on rape, trauma, and stigma. The scenes explore the tensions and complexities of guilt, remorse, apology, and the possibility of forgiveness and reconciliation. The play does not offer clear answers. As its Synopsis states, the play is based on "real stories of people who survived the Khmer Rouge era. / Stories that continue to evolve. / You're invited to imagine their future, which could also be your future."[4]

This evening the message is directed at the participants in the ETGE outreach program. A DC-Cam report on the program notes that, among the 459 Cambodians

---

[3] Prins 2009, "Prologue."   [4] Prins 2009, "Synopsis."

DC-Cam brought to Phnom Penh for the event, there were "350 Cham Musli[m] religious leaders from 396 mosques, 13 Khmer Kampuchea Kraom from Pursat [Province], 30 [Buddhist] nuns from Kampong Speu and Phnom Penh and selected villagers from [various] provinces," many of whom were civil parties.[5]

DC-Cam was among the earliest and most active intermediary organizations working on Khmer Rouge Tribunal (KRT) outreach. As the ECCC began operation, DC-Cam revamped existing programs and established new ones to do outreach, including its "Living Documents" program that brought large groups of Cambodians to learn, discuss, and visit the court.

The ETGE program involved several of these programs and illustrates how DC-Cam adapted to the historical moment. Among the ETGE participants, for example, were thirty civil parties and other complainants assisted by DC-Cam's Victim Participation Project. They and the other ETGE participants were bused to the National Institute for Education for a mid-afternoon educational session followed by dinner and the performance of "Breaking the Silence."

Youk Chhang, the Director of DC-Cam, greeted the group at the start of the proceedings. He emphasized the importance of their upcoming visit to the ECCC and "the crucial role of victims in the process."[6] He noted that they would watch and discuss a play related to apology.

Three DC-Cam staffers next spoke, beginning with Farina So, the leader of DC-Cam's Cham-Muslim Oral History project.[7] The majority of the audience was, like her, Cham, including many religious leaders who, a DC-Cam report on the ETGE states, were "key persons for disseminating information because they are well-respected and educated people in the community" and also serve as religious teachers and judges in their villages. The ETGE report explains that DC-Cam's Cham Oral History project was "launched in 2004" when DC-Cam began "working with mosques throughout the country on a variety of project[s], including interviewing Cham-Muslim religious leaders and Cham-Muslim women about their life experiences under DK in order to ensure that the voice of ethnic minorities is heard."[8]

After offering a greeting in Cham, So gave a brief overview of the project, noting the importance of increasing knowledge about how Cham were targeted and died in large numbers during DK. So further described DC-Cam's plans for the project, including further documentation of the abuse. Through such documentation and making "their voices heard," she noted, Cham-Muslims could "turn community suffering and anger toward educating the younger generation."[9]

The audience also included thirteen members of another ethnic group, Khmer Kampuchea Kraom, targeted during DK. The report notes that the Khmer Kampuchea Kraom "were cruelly abused by the Khmer Rouge and their participation is a powerful means to keep alive their [DK] experiences."[10] More broadly, the report notes the diversity of ETGE, which included both men and women as well as "a range of religious beliefs, age and status under the Khmer Rouge."[11]

---

[5] Sirik 2009.   [6] Ibid, 2.   [7] Ibid, 2.   [8] Ibid, 1.   [9] Ibid, 3.
[10] Ibid, 1–2.   [11] Ibid, 1.

After these introductory remarks, the focus of the forum shifted, as a former S-21 cadre and a child survivor of the prison—both of whom had testified earlier in Duch's trial—spoke to the crowd. The cadre, Him Huy, supervised the transport of S-21 detainees to a killing field outside Phnom Penh. Him Huy described his experiences including "the fear that followed him the whole time he was working at S-21."[12]

Norng Chanphal, the survivor, next told the crowd about how, when he was a young child, he, along with his mother and a brother, were imprisoned at S-21 near the end of DK. After one night, Norng Chanphal and his brother were separated from their mother who, he told the audience, he last saw gazing at him in the distance from a cell window. He told the ETGE participants that he hoped that "the Khmer Rouge tribunal will be able to find justice for him and all Cambodian survivors who suffered from the genocide."[13]

In the Q&A session that followed, audience members described their experiences during DK and asked questions regarding such issues as whether DK leaders felt remorse and were telling the truth, the possibility of compensation, the punishment the defendants might face, why so many people were killed, and why the international community did not intervene during DK.

After dinner, the ETGE participants viewed "Breaking the Silence." Before the performance began, Sayana Ser, who helped coordinate productions of the play, welcomed the group and informed them they would see a drama depicting stories related to DK, ones that might resonate with their own experiences.

DC-Cam's ETGE report states that the play, which had opened in February 2009, depicts "common stories" and was meant to "promote discussion of KR history among survivors and between victims and perpetrators" as well as to "educate and foster communication and knowledge ... [and] contribute to healing, forgiveness and reconciliation."[14]

The specific scenes were described by the next speaker, Suon Bun Rith, the Country Director of Amrita Performing Arts, which had overseen production of the play in partnership with Annemarie Prins and DC-Cam. Bun Rith described the scenes in the play, the first of which was a story of "divided people," in which three Cambodians approach a former perpetrator in different ways. The second part concerned two young girls, one a daughter and one a Khmer Rouge nurse, whose lives were ruined by the revolution, while the third was concerned with the guilt and psychological suffering of a young man who, after being tortured by the Khmer Rouge, implicated others.

Scene Four was concerned with a youth who joined the revolution because he dreamed of a better future but soon found himself obediently carrying out terrible orders, actions that led to estrangement from his mother. The fifth scene told of a little girl who, because she was starving, broke into her family's small stash of rice and forever felt remorse for never apologizing to her mother. In Scene Six, the narrative focuses on a young girl raped by Khmer Rouge soldiers, one of whom is depicted in

---

[12] Ibid, 3.   [13] Ibid, 3.   [14] Ibid, 4–5.

the last scene as he and fellow former comrades reminisce. Rith concluded by noting that the play had been performed in the provinces before he gave the floor to
Chhang for final remarks.

When the play had premiered in February, Chhang had written of how, in
Cambodia, there had been a "long silence" that had "lasted for decades and [been]
kept alive by fear, pain, and politics. In recent years, however, there have been solid
efforts to end this silence in the form of legal justice, outreach ... [and] genocide
education." "Breaking the Silence," he continued, was "the most powerful play since
the collapse of the Khmer Rouge regime in 1979."

The DK victims, Chhang wrote, "are emotionally broken people living in a broken society; a people without souls or with our souls wandering around. I have
found our soul in this play ... It will help restore our dignity and humanity and lift
up our morality" as well as play a part in "the rebuilding of Cambodian society."[15] In
English, at least, his comments seemed to accord with those of the playwright and
the transitional justice imaginary.

In her preface to the play, Prins stated that she wanted the play to help such
Cambodians "find a way out of trauma's silence; contributing to open dialogue as
part of the process of reconciliation."[16] She added during an interview, "The victims don't talk about what happened, neither with their children nor really amongst
themselves. The perpetrators are also reticent and live in a kind of isolation. It is very
difficult for people to talk, and that makes the healing process more difficult."[17] The
subtitle to the article stated, "Dutch theatre director breaks Cambodia's silence," a
sentiment suggested by Prins herself, who said elsewhere, "no one has done this in
Cambodia before."[18] A *New York Times* article about the performance headlined
that the play was, "A Drama for Closure for Victims and Perpetrators of the Khmer
Rouge."[19]

Such characterizations of the play parallel comments frequently made about the
court, which suggest this transitional justice mechanism will enable silenced and
traumatized victims both to tell their stories and engage in dialogue with perpetrators and thereby bring about reconciliation.

These transitional justice imaginary discourses are also manifest in the Khmer
Institute of Democracy booklet, which depicts Uncle San in a static, silenced state
until he is given a voice in the court. Doing so enables him to heal and gain closure
(finally sleeping without "bad dreams"), a seeming realization of the transitional justice imaginary's goal of teleological transformation leading from authoritarianism,
trauma, silence, and violence to democracy, healing, dialogue, and peace.

The chapters in this book section seek to step behind this justice facade and explore
the lived experience of victim participation as well as the ways in which this experience was mediated by another Cambodian intermediary organization, DC-Cam.
The next chapter builds upon the previous chapters by unpacking how the ECCC
sought to produce a certain liberal democratic, right-bearing juridical subjectivity

---

[15] Chhang 2009, 1.   [16] Prins 2009.   [17] Gottlieb 2009.
[18] Chng 2010, 80.   [19] McGrane 2009.

even as alternative subjectivities also mediated the experience of Cambodians in and around the court.

Chapter 7 begins the morning after "Breaking the Silence," when the participants in DC-Cam's ETGE attended the first day of two weeks of civil party testimony in which relatives of victims testified. Three international civil parties—each in many respects exemplary victims embodying the qualities of wound, suffering, helplessness, and emotionality that were being transformed through the transitional justice process into active, speaking liberal democratic subjects—spoke. Even as they did, it was evident that there were cracks in this justice facade revealing underlying complexities obscured and pushed out of sight. Such fissures were also evident when the ETGE participants visited Tuol Sleng and performed a ceremony for the spirits of the dead, highlighting Buddhist subjectivities backgrounded by the juridical process.

In Chapter 8, "Normativity," I follow this line of discussion about the understandings of less educated Cambodian civil parties, including rural villagers. The chapter focuses, in particular, on everyday understandings of "return," which inform transactions with beings ranging from patrons to family members and the spirits of the dead. For many Cambodians, the court provided an opportunity to fulfill their obligations to significant others. Not doing so might lead to a rupturing and disordering of their social world, including angering the dead who might afflict a relative in response. The chapter also explores civil party views of Duch as relations with the defense became increasingly tense.

The last chapter in this section, "Disposition," picks up on this thread while returning to "Breaking the Silence." Beginning with an interview with Youk Chhang, the head of DC-Cam, the chapter explores his path to the NGO and the projects it undertook, including KRT outreach. The second half of the chapter looks at how "Breaking the Silence" emerged from these efforts. A collaboration from the start, the play on the surface reflects the aspirations of the transitional justice imaginary, as illustrated by the title.

Chhang, however, pointed out that this title made little sense in Khmer and therefore that his staff simply referred to it as "Pol Pot Stories." Indeed, Chhang carefully translated the text so that it would make sense in rural Cambodian vernaculars. He noted that transitional justice imaginary ideas of "reconciliation" and "healing" were problematic and did not accord with the complicated on-the-ground understandings of Cambodian villagers. Nevertheless, the tribunal made a positive impact not just by holding former Khmer Rouge leaders accountable, but by potentially catalyzing combustive acts of imagination as Cambodians directly or indirectly engaged with the court.

7

Subjectivity (DC-Cam and the ECCC Outreach Tour)

Morning of August 17, 2009 (Day 2, DC-Cam KRT Outreach Tour, ECCC Courtroom, Phnom Penh, Cambodia)

"Before hearing the statements of the civil parties," Judge Non Nil announced, "the Chamber would like to know if the defense intends to challenge any of the applications of civil parties."[1] As he spoke, the judge glanced toward the defense lawyers and the public gallery behind them, dotted with the white caps of Muslim Cham men.

The gallery was packed with the participants from the Documentation Center of Cambodia (DC-Cam)'s "ECCC Tour and Genocide Education" (ETGE) outreach program. They had arisen early to be bused to the court. I rode in a DC-Cam van along with Him Huy, the former S-21 guard who had spoken at the ETGE. When I asked Him Huy why he was going, he replied in a flat tone, "Youk suggested it." "Are you interested?" I followed up. "Not so much," Him Huy said, "I have been here before," alluding to the testimony he had given earlier in Duch's trial. After we arrived, Him Huy walked over to a fence, squatted, and puffed a hand-rolled cigarette, smoke billowing in the air.

Before the hearing began, Sambath provided a brief overview of the court as well as particular details about what the audience would see. Sambath also instructed them about court protocol. "You need to stand," Sambath informed them, "when the judges enter and leave the courtroom."

I sat in a back row next to Him Huy. It felt awkward to be sitting at an international court beside a former perpetrator who, if not indicted, had admitted killing prisoners. Vann Nath described him as "savage." I thought of how Him Huy had once ridden on Bou Meng's back up the stairs of S-21. When I ask Him Huy if he wanted to move closer to the courtroom, he smiled slightly and, in a barely audible voice, said, "No."

I turned the conversation to his family. He told me he has six boys and three girls, one of whom was in the eleventh grade and would later volunteer at DC-Cam. There she would work on a project alongside Norng Chanphal's daughter, who had also come to the court to assist with the ETGE. At one point, Chhang would assign them to go to a large Phnom Penh pagoda to photograph a *pchum ben* ceremony. They,

---

[1] Day 59, 1, 2.

The Justice Facade: Trials of Transition in Cambodia. Alexander Laban Hinton. © Alexander Laban Hinton, 2018. Published 2018 by Oxford University Press.

like their fathers, appeared to have attained the sort of reconciliation the transitional justice imaginary promises.

It was not a straightforward process. I sensed tension between Norng Chanphal and Him Huy and wondered if it was possible for a child survivor of S-21 whose mother and father had been killed at the prison to get along with, perhaps even forgive, the former cadre who may have overseen the transport when she was executed. At lunch the day before, I had sat at a table next to Him Huy and Norng Chanphal. No one spoke.

Over time, as Him Huy and Norng Chanphal worked together on DC-Cam projects, I observed a noticeable change in their relationship. They would talk and laugh when in each other's presence. When I asked Chhang about their relationship, he noted that now "they share beer and cigarettes and always want to stay in the same room when they travel with us [for projects]." He added, "The Cambodian way of reconciliation is by action, not dialogue,"[2] and is always deeply personal.

On the second day of the trial, Duch had apologized and stated he would cooperate. Duch's actions, however, often appeared to contradict his words. Thus, in response to Non Nil's opening query on August 17, Duch's international lawyer, Marie-Paule Canizares, stated that the defense was challenging roughly half of the Case 001 civil party applications. On the one hand, a number of civil parties had not provided sufficient evidence establishing their ties to a victim. In other cases, there was no proof that an alleged victim had been detained at S-21.

This development was the latest manifestation of the growing tension between Duch and the civil parties. If the court was supposed to produce reconciliation—and Duch's apology meant as a key moment in this regard—the hoped-for rapprochement had not materialized. In part, the tension was linked to a perception that Duch lacked respect for the civil parties despite stating that he sought their forgiveness. One of the first signs of this tension was a petition submitted by twenty-eight civil parties, including Bou Meng, requesting that Duch cease gesturing disrespectfully toward the civil parties.

On other occasions, Duch appeared to show disregard or even scorn for civil party lawyers. This behavior drew a rebuke from President Non Nil, who asked Duch to show "proper gesture and attitude in responding to the questions by the [civil party] lawyers or exercise his right to remain silent rather than laughing."[3] For his part, Duch may have felt slighted by his attempts to engage the civil parties and the sometimes harsh tone of civil party lawyers.

A second source of tension stemmed from the perception Duch was not telling the whole truth. This emerged clearly during the testimony of the S-21 survivors, which diverged from Duch's account. It became apparent that Duch was not simply admitting his guilt but instead following a defense strategy centered on superior orders and duress. This gave the impression that Duch was minimizing his role, agency, and revolutionary fervor.

    [2] Youk Chhang, e-mail communication, December 5, 2016.   [3] Day 14, 76.

To make this argument, Duch was ready to challenge anything that was unsubstantiated and undercut his defense, a position at odds with his assertion he would cooperate and accept his guilt. Earlier in the trial, Duch had contested the claims of witnesses, ranging from S-21 survivors to former staff, who asserted a more incriminating view of S-21. Duch was now challenging the status of civil parties who had been participating in the trial for months.

Finally, some civil parties may have been upset with how Duch was being treated in court. Duch often stood center stage and was also allowed to make observations on witness testimony. Meanwhile, the civil parties were only allowed to speak indirectly through lawyers, who were sometimes given as little as ten minutes to question witnesses.

The Trial Court also made decisions that suggested it was curtailing civil party rights, such as not allowing them to make opening statements. There were also ongoing concerns the civil parties would not be allowed to speak on Duch's character and sentencing, the final part of the trial. The court would render a major decision on this issue at the conclusion of the civil party testimony.

Amidst this backdrop, Judge Non Nil instructed civil party lawyers to guide their clients so that their statements were "framed to the facts"[4] of the case. In addition, the lawyers were to "introduce his or her civil party" by providing identifying information and proving a link to a confirmed S-21 victim.[5]

As civil party lawyers sought clarifications, almost a dozen civil parties sat in two rows behind them. S-21 survivor Chum Mey was among them, headphones on, in the seat closest to the packed public gallery. In front of him sat a middle-aged woman in a black jacket. She would be the first civil party to speak. Her daughter, also dressed in black, sat two seats away. Her testimony would follow.[6]

Martine Lefeuvre, France

Martine Lefeuvre was a 57-year-old French woman who married a Cambodian diplomat, Ouk Ket, in October 1971. Ket, her lawyer informed the court, was "third secretary at the Cambodian embassy in Senegal when he was recalled by the [Democratic Kampuchea (DK)] Foreign Ministry in 1977 ... He returned to Phnom Penh and later on Mrs. Lefeuvre learned that he had been executed [at S-21] on 9 December 1977."[7] His name, Lefeuvre's lawyer continued, could be found on two documents in the case file, the list of prisoners and his S-21 photograph.

"I will first of all give you a chronology of our life," Lefeuvre said as she began her statement, speaking in French and occasionally glancing at notes. Behind her, in the first row of the public gallery, sat a line of white-robed Buddhist nuns from the ETGE program, hands clasped in their laps.

In 1972, she noted, the couple, who had met while Ket was studying engineering in France, moved to Senegal, where he worked at the Cambodian Embassy. They

---

[4] Day 59, 8, 9.   [5] Day 59, 8.
[6] On civil party testimony during Duch's trial, see Carmichael 2015; Cruvellier 2014; Hinton 2016.
[7] Day 59, 14–15.

had two children, a boy, Makara, in 1973, and a girl, Neary, two years later. After the Khmer Rouge took power, Ket told her he wanted to return home "out of love for his country . . . He had skills and he wanted to take part in the reconstruction."[8]

Accordingly, when recalled in 1977, Ket decided to go. Lefeuvre told him she feared he would be killed. In response, "he looked at me and tapped my cheek and said, 'But, honey, Cambodians are not savages.'"[9] He thought that, at worst, he might be required to do agricultural labor. He sent two postcards as he traveled to Cambodia. She heard no more.

As her worry increased, Lefeuvre, who had returned to France, began seeking information about her husband, traveling to the Chinese Embassy and contacting organizations like Amnesty International and the Red Cross. She began to hear awful stories about the DK regime. So, in late 1979, she decided to travel to refugee camps in Thailand to look for her husband.

Conditions there were very difficult, with children dying of malnutrition and dehydration. The experience led her to become a nurse. Eventually she found a friend of her husband who told her he had worked at Tuol Sleng for several months. Lefeuvre asked him, "'What is Tuol Sleng?' And he explained to me that it is an extermination camp and 'I found your husband's name in the Tuol Sleng files.'"[10] She was "crushed, devastated . . . [and] in a rage" and kept asking "why, why, why?"[11]

She had no idea what to tell her children. They kept asking, "Have you seen Daddy? Will we see Daddy again?"[12] She was now a widow; they were fatherless. When she finally told her seven-year-old son what happened, he replied, "I will take revenge."[13] The family was devastated. "We were unable to grieve. No body . . . no tomb . . . there isn't a day I don't think of it."[14] As a single mother, she now had to provide for the family and so obtained her nursing degree, though eventually she began to think of Ket when she saw injured people or drew blood. She considered suicide.

She began to gather information related to Ket's death because she "wanted to find the truth."[15] In 1990, she made contact with Ket's family and traveled to Cambodia with Makara and Neary to "follow Ket's traces."[16] They stayed with her mother-in-law in a house that lacked running water and electricity. Makara almost died of dysentery.

Shortly after arriving, the family visited Tuol Sleng and were "completely overtaken by the horror. And we begin looking through all of the photographs . . . trying to find Ket's face, and we do not find him."[17] They were enraged and it was hard to get Makara and Neary to leave "because their fists are clenched and they're clenching their teeth before such a quantity of terror."[18]

Next they went to Choueng Ek, Lefeuvre told the court. Blinking rapidly to hold back tears, Lefeuvre spoke of their shock at the piles of skulls at the memorial, as "we say to ourselves that Ket's skull is among all those thousands of skulls, and then we look at the pits, which we walk over. There are teeth coming up through the ground, leg bones, radiuses, pieces of shirts, strings, earth, were covering the people who

---

8 Day 59, 17.   9 Day 59, 36.   10 Day 59, 22.   11 Day 59, 38.
12 Day 59, 23.   13 Day 59, 38.   14 Day 59, 40–41.   15 Day 59, 43.
16 Day 59, 24.   17 Day 59, 25.   18 Day 59, 25.

were killed there. And we are completely revulsed."[19] Subsequently, the family began doing research in the Tuol Sleng archive, "set on finding the trace of my husband, the father of my children."[20] Eventually they found his name on a list of 301 prisoners, which notes his name, occupation, date of arrival at S-21 (June 15, 1977) and execution approximately six months later, on December 9.

After seeing the faces of other S-21 victims, she said, "I could imagine how [Ket] himself was terrified and then I decide that his crime will not remain unpunished."[21] Lefeuvre recounted how she began to gather evidence, visiting DC-Cam and unsuccessfully trying to bring suit in France. When she heard about the formation of the Extraordinary Chambers in the Courts of Cambodia (ECCC), she was determined to join because "such atrocities cannot and must not remain unpunished . . . This is why I'm very proud to be before you today."[22]

"But now," she continued, "I would like to speak to you about who [Ket] was." During their seven years together, Lefeuvre came to know Ket as "very kind, well educated, delicate, generous, intellectually brilliant, calm, jovial with a very nice Khmer smile, soft, [and] interested in all technological novelties."[23] He was a good husband and father and liked to play music and volleyball and to cook food from all over the world.

"Life with him was pure happiness," Lefeuvre stated, "We were like the fingers of one single hand." But Ket was taken from her, "kidnapped with his hands tied behind his back, blindfolded and brought in a truck . . . [and then] tied up like a slave to a metal bar, chained up in his filthy cell . . . deprived of his most elementary rights."[24] Now, Lefeuvre continued, she understood "his physical and psychological degradation. I can picture it. He died a slow death at S-21 in the most complete secrecy, in solitude, and on the 9th of December 1977 murderers broke his skull at Choeung Ek and then cut his throat while throwing him into a pit."[25]

The effects of his "absolutely inexcusable murder" on their family were profound and "unbearable." His death, Lefeuvre stated, "is a permanent absence. My children grew up without the presence [comfort, and protection] of their father." Their suffering had not receded over time; it had grown so intense that it "is like a gigantic screen that [is placed] too close to our eyes." No body had been found. No reparations had been received. And, to date, no one had taken into account the suffering of Ket and other victims and survivors. She hoped the ECCC could do so.

She was here, she told the court, "to bring back Ket's dignity that was [stamped out] at S-21." She had also come "to refresh the memory of somebody who seems to be suffering from amnesia . . . an intellectual who could have stopped the extermination machine."[26] Duch, she contended, should have taken his own life instead of participating in the torture and murder of so many people.

"Had this math professor forgotten to reflect, to think?"[27] she asked.

Lefeuvre also had expectations from the court. She thought "the punishment must be commensurate with the crimes committed. In other words, a maximum

---

[19] Day 59, 26. [20] Day 59, 26. [21] Day 59, 27. [22] Day 59, 28.
[23] Day 59, 28. [24] Day 59, 29. [25] Day 59, 29–30. [26] Day 59, 31.
[27] Day 59, 31.

sentence."[28] In terms of collective reparations, she suggested a number of possibilities, such as the improvement of the roads leading to Tuol Sleng or the undertaking of educational initiatives about the genocide.

When her civil party lawyer asked if she could forgive Duch, Lefeuvre replied, "At this moment, no."[29] Forgiveness, she noted, was a process. It required finding, passing judgment on, and punishing the perpetrators, as well as reparation. "What was done to Ket is something that we feel in our own body and in our own minds, and at this point I'm not ready."

She had no questions for Duch.

Duch, however, had observations. Standing, bags under his eyes, Duch began, "I would like to recognize that the biography of your family is historical fact and truth." Such facts, he added, were different from a flower that blossoms and then withers. The truth, in contrast, doesn't change; it lasts forever.[30] Her suffering could not be forgotten. "I will not run away from the crimes I have committed," he told her. "It is inexcusable. The nation of Cambodia can point their finger to me. They can curse me. They can punish me however they wish." Before the court, he concluded, "I do not intend to deny any crimes committed at S-21, and I would like to apologize to Madame Lefeuvre and other people who have lost their loved ones during the regime."[31]

Lefeuvre's eyes were fixed on the ceiling. She had removed her headphones, refusing to listen.

Ouk Neary, France

"Regarding my father, the first memory that I have is his death."[32]

Lefeuvre and Ouk Ket's daughter, Ouk Neary, made this statement to the court as she began her testimony, which included a brief homage to her father. After briefly describing several memories of her father, ranging from the ripping of gift wrap to a strum of the guitar, Ouk requested that the court display several photographs, some of the only traces she had of her father.

In black and white, the photographs flashed on the screen: Ket standing with his arm around his wife, carefully holding an infant by a tree, sitting on a park bench with friends, and celebrating, perhaps at a wedding. In one, he stands, dressed in black and hands sloped at his sides, against a white background. It was a photograph of Ket from S-21.

"I grew up without a father," Ouk told the court. Her French grandmother helped raise her while her mother worked and searched for clues about Ket. After a while, it seemed almost normal. All this changed when, at the age of 16, she traveled with her mother and brother to Cambodia and visited Tuol Sleng.

Entering the building on the compound was "the most tremendous shock of my life," beginning with the detention rooms and photographs of corpses in Building A, which she described as the place "where the truth was the most blatant." She was "traumatized" by the photographs in Building B, which Ouk described to the court,

---

[28] Day 59, 31.   [29] Day 59, 42.   [30] Day 59, 46; Khmer, 33.
[31] Day 59, 47; Khmer, 33.   [32] Day 59, 49.

noting one in which "the detainee was not dead. He raises his hand and he tries to lean up with his beaten-in-face, and I asked myself whom is he asking help from?"[33]

The classroom walls, in turn, seemed "surreal," a corridor of cells created "by breaking open the walls, doors that did not exist before and completely upended the operation of what had previously been a school, and froze it into a barbaric dimension."[34] The classrooms, she continued, showed "the total lack of humanity of which people are capable and which reverses the basic motion that leads to the creation of schools ... [changing] it into a machinery to crush human beings, to crush brains. The sole purpose of S-21 was death."

As she and Makara traversed the rooms filled with prisoner photographs, she suddenly turned to her brother and said, "We have to start all over again and look at each [photograph] because perhaps [our] father is there ... we can't afford to miss him."[35] She remembered coming out into "oppressive heat" and thinking about how the victims must have felt as they struggled to hold on, waiting for help that never arrived. She was also shocked by how the document files in the archive were "under heaps of dust, which in itself is an insult to humanity." The reason she was spending so much time discussing Tuol Sleng, she told the court, was because "that day is the day when a drop of poison came to me, and I have never since that day stopped trying to find out what happened."[36]

She would later consider pursuing a doctorate on the S-21 documents before deciding to "leave the past behind me, as many Cambodians say who don't want to talk about this anymore. And I understand them full well."[37] In 2004, however, she was invited to view Rithy Panh's documentary film, "S-21: The Khmer Rouge Killing Machine," in which Vann Nath appeared. She was shocked, in particular, by three things discussed during the film: the prisoners killed by having their blood drained, a woman who committed suicide, and medical experiments.

"I leave you to imagine the repulsion which rose in me when I discovered all these horrors," Ouk said, noting that, in the case of the medical experiments, "the only possible form of anesthesia was with salt water. And so individuals were taken, tied to a post; the front part of the abdomen was opened up in order that ... a young physician could put his hands into the abdomen of someone who was alive in order to cut the appendix out."[38] She paused and bit her lip, before continuing, "The victim, who was screaming in pain initially, would stare at the young man mute."

These discoveries, Ouk testified, became "an invisible disability, a psychological agony, a journey into hell."[39] She recalled how once, when she had a three-year-old son and was talking to her partner, she could only think of "one thing ... to break away, to extricate myself from reality and jump out the window for reasons I could not fathom myself."[40] Other times she would dissociate, seeing "people's lips moving, but you're completely elsewhere."[41]

She reassured the court that she was "much better now" after having gone into psychotherapy in 2004. Her therapist had helped her "to put into words everything that I had seen" and rebuild her life.[42] Similarly, Ouk noted the healing potential of

---

[33] Day 59, 55. [34] Day 59, 55. [35] Day 59, 56. [36] Day 59, 57.
[37] Day 59, 60. [38] Day 59, 63. [39] Day 59, 64. [40] Day 59, 64.
[41] Day 59, 71. [42] Day 59, 70.

the court. She read a quote from Rithy Panh's preface to Vann Nath's memoir, "The older you become, the more the history of a genocide comes back to you in an insidious way, a bit like a poison that has been distilled into your body bit by bit. The only way to relieve things is to testify."[43]

Forgiveness was another matter. Just months before, Ouk told the court, she had returned to Choueng Ek, which she regarded as "the worst place I've ever been."[44] She noted the pits at the site differed, depending on whether the victim was an adult or infant. "That baby could have been me," she said, pausing. "I could have been grabbed by the foot and had my skull crushed against a tree that was used to destroy all of the children, and sometimes I get the feeling that I'm the only survivor amongst them all."[45] The violence that took place at Choueng Ek was "unforgivable."[46]

On the verge of tears, she looked at Duch and said, "for several months I have been observing you and I know enough at this point to tell the accused I have no interest in him."[47] She turned and looked down and read from a prepared statement, "His obsequiousness is unable to hide in my eyes the cynical … and bloodthirsty brute."

In court, she contended, Duch claimed to be taking "responsibility without ever soiling his hand" or acknowledging his "dirty work." To her, Duch "represents the shame of the human race." There were, she added, "17,000 reasons to inflict [the] maximum penalty."[48] She also hoped that Duch realized he was not "the thinking head of Cambodia" and would stop pontificating.

Ouk concluded her testimony by saying that she wanted to share the insights she had gleaned during her life and therapy with "Cambodian people who might not be able to deal with this subject." She had found that "the only way to face the future is to dissect what happened and by providing an explanation [of] this and when we're able to break down into pieces everything that happened and we try to reconstitute the puzzle … it may improve things of course. We cannot remain in solitude."[49]

Duch had little to say. "Mr. President," he began, "I would like to bow my body and mind to acknowledge the testimony of Ms. Ouk," whose testimony was a "historical document for the next generation not to forget the tragedy."[50] Echoing parts of his remarks to her mother, Duch acknowledged that he was legally and emotionally responsible for the crimes committed at S-21, concluding his remarks as he had begun by addressing the President "with respect" (*ti korop, daoy korop*). They were the words he used to address his superiors in S-21 confession annotations.

Robert Hamill, New Zealand

"This is the story of an innocent man brought to his knees and killed in the prime of his life," stated the next civil party, Robert Hamill, "and the impact his death had on just one family."[51] If both Lefeuvre and Ouk had expressed their anger and suffering, Hamill, a former Olympic rower from New Zealand, would make his claim even more forcefully. Hamill hoped "other families likewise affected by the losses of

---

[43] Day 59, 70; Vann Nath 1998.
[44] Day 59, 65.   [45] Day 59, 65–66.   [46] Day 59, 66.   [47] Day 59, 67.
[48] Day 59, 67.   [49] Day 59, 72.   [50] Day 59, 74.   [51] Day 59, 79.

this barbaric time can somehow relate to my statement and recognize that they are not alone in their grief" and that the trial would provide "justice, acknowledgment, and vindication."[52]

The week before, he noted, marked the 31st anniversary of the day his brother, Kerry Hamill, was captured while sailing off the coast of Cambodia and sent to S-21. There, he was forced to confess and then executed. A former interrogator reported that Kerry was burned alive in car tires, though Duch refuted this claim. "He unquestionably suffered beyond all imagination,"[53] Hamill stated, noting that Kerry's confession was a mix of truth and lies and even some grim humor, as he listed "Colonel Sanders" and "Captain Peppers" as members of his "CIA network."

His family had no idea what had happened to Kerry. "The silence . . . was deafening," a period of "crushing uncertainty."[54] They learned of Kerry's death from a newspaper. After the discovery, Hamill said, choking out the words, "my brother had been captured, tortured and killed . . . [our] family life disintegrated."[55] Their brother John became depressed and jumped off a cliff. "Duch," Hamill said as he turned to him, "when you killed my brother Kerry you killed my brother John as well."[56] Their father wept in the kitchen at night and his business fell apart. His mother became depressed and bedridden. Hamill himself developed an alcohol problem.

"Ultimately I do not know how Kerry finally met his fate," Hamill told the court. "At best, my brother was blindfolded, taken out to the S-21 compound to a pre-dug trench, made to kneel down beside it, hit over the head with a metal bar, his throat slit and then buried. That was the best case scenario."[57] He imagined that, as a "special prisoner," Kerry had suffered greatly before being forced to "sit in the middle of car tires covered in petrol and seared alive."[58] Thinking about it made Hamill "feel sick."

Hamill requested that a black and white photo from S-21 be displayed, which "I imagine illustrates what Kerry suffered." It shows a prisoner, shackled by the leg, lying in a pool of blood. His arm is slightly raised, as if he is trying to push himself up. Hamill noted how the prisoner "is shackled, the way he has been grotesquely beaten, the blood flowing from his gaping wounds, yet the continuing struggle, the resilience."[59] Beginning to sob, Hamill told the court, "[T]his is my gorgeous . . . beautiful brother Kerry Hamill at S-21. This is the sort of image that haunted me when I was 16 and still haunts me today. I have lost so much sleep over this image."[60] Hamill considered himself "tough and determined" but now sat before "this court frail and emotional. I should feel ashamed from behaving so weakly, but I do not. The only person in this Court who should feel shame is that man."[61] Meanwhile, an elderly Cambodian civil party had passed out upon seeing the photograph, which had led her to imagine her husband's fate at S-21.[62]

"Duch," Hamill said, pausing, as he turned to Duch, who suddenly sat upright. "At times I've wanted to smash you—to use your words—in the same way that you smashed so many others. At times, I've imagined you shackled, starved, whipped, and clubbed viciously."[63] He emphasized each verb and then rasped out the word

---

[52] Day 59, 79. [53] Day 59, 84. [54] Day 59, 86. [55] Day 59, 91, 92.
[56] Day 59, 93–94. [57] Day 59, 98. [58] Day 59, 99. [59] Day 59, 100.
[60] Day 59, 100. [61] Day 59, 104. [62] Day 61, 22. [63] Day 59, 104.

"viciously" a second time as he glared at Duch. His statement shaking in his hand, Hamill continued, "I have imagined your scrotum electrified, being forced to eat your own feces, being nearly drowned, and having your throat cut. I have wanted that to be your experience, your reality. I have wanted you to suffer the way you made Kerry and so many others."[64]

Now, however, he was "trying to let go and this [trial] process is part of that." He was giving to Duch, to bear alone, "all the crushing weight of emotion—the anger, the grief, and the sorrow … for it is you who created this burden which no one deserves."[65] As he spoke, Hamill's voice began to lose its edge. "From this day forward," he told Duch, "I feel nothing toward you. To me what you did removed you from the ranks of being human." He repeated the last phrase in almost a whisper before concluding that if anything were to be learned from his statement and the trial, it was that the world must "take notice of the evil that can happen when people do nothing."[66]

Unlike Lefeuvre and Ouk, Hamill questioned the accused. "Duch," Hamill began as he looked at Duch, "I acknowledge you pleading guilty …" Judge Non Nil cut in, "Please hold on, Mr. Hamill … you can put your questions through the Bench but not directly to the accused … as you are a civil party." Non Nil also cautioned Hamill that he should avoid harsh words and instead use those of a legal and ethical character. The Court, he noted, was a place for legal debate.[67]

"I am angry beyond words with you," Hamill continued, "but I acknowledge and respect your guilty plea. Your acknowledgment is a small but significant contribution to addressing the harm that you caused."[68] Noting Duch's good memory, Hamill requested that he tell the truth before posing his first question, "What do you remember of my brother?"

Duch's reply was not helpful. Duch remembered a British man who an interrogator had told him was "very gentle and polite" but he had never met him. Duch also didn't know when Kerry had been killed. After interrogation, Kerry and "the British man" [John Dewhurst] "had to be beaten to death and their bodies … burned to ashes."[69] That was a direct order from his superiors.

When Hamill asked if he knew what had happened to the ashes, Duch replied that the Standing Committee had ordered "S-21 to burn the dead bodies to ashes [to] get rid of evidence."[70] Last, his voice tired and his lips pressed tight, Hamill asked Duch, "what can you do to help the victims, including my family?"[71] Duch replied that he could do little. Then, perhaps thinking of his repeated apologies to the victims, Duch recounted the story of when he went to see a former mentor who had been sent to S-21. In accordance with Cambodian custom, "I had to kneel and pray to him for forgiveness. And [Vorn Vet] pointed his finger at me and scolded me, 'You're a murderer.' "[72]

At the end of the day, Duch acknowledged the suffering of the civil parties, which was "miserable, detailed and deep."[73] If the victims wanted to "point their fingers

---

[64] Day 59, 104.   [65] Day 59, 104.   [66] Day 59, 105.   [67] Day 59, 107.
[68] Day 59, 108.   [69] Day 59, 110.   [70] Day 59, 113.   [71] Day 59, 114.
[72] Day 59, 114.
[73] Day 59, 118; Khmer, 84.

at me," Duch stated, he would not be offended: "That is your right and I accept it with respect." He added, "even if the people throw stones at me and cause my death I would not say anything."[74]

Duch had joined the revolution in order to "liberate the country," but had ended up at S-21. It was up to the victims to decide "whether they forgive me or not." Duch reiterated his acceptance of responsibility and stated, "I am very remorseful for what I did … I bow my head and body before the Cambodian people."[75]

Before sitting down, Duch looked at Hamill and bowed.

Morning, August 18, 2009 (Day 3, DC-Cam KRT Outreach Tour, Tuol Sleng Genocide Museum, Phnom Penh, Cambodia)

Eyes closed and hands clasped, two dozen Buddhist nuns stood in front of "The Victims Graves," a Tuol Sleng Genocide Museum memorial dedicated to the last prisoners killed at S-21. The memorial terrace, near the entrance to Tuol Sleng, consists of fourteen raised white coffins, the concrete bleached from the sun. As the line of white-robed nuns recited scripture for the dead, other participants from the ETGE program gathered behind them, raising their palms in respect. The crowd grew, nearing 100 people.

At "Breaking the Silence," I had asked some of the nuns if they thought the court accorded with Buddhist principles. They all began to speak at once. "Whatever one does," one said, "the result (*phal*) of that action returns. It is the law of karma."

The themes of violence, karma, and rebirth appeared in several of the scenes in "Breaking the Silence," such as Scene 5 about "a little girl who wanted to say sorry but could not" after stealing the last of her family's rice one night during DK. In the scene, the girl recounts how her mother, who later starved to death, "told us once that children should be good. That doing bad things will create bad Karma and that they will come back in the next life as snakes, slugs, or worms."[76] By transferring merit to those who have a disturbed death and may have trouble reincarnating or may be reborn in a lowly form—"The Howling Dead" as one song in the performance is titled—the *bangsokol* ceremony transfers merit to improve their karmic fate.

Similarly, after attending the Duch trial, the ETGE participants had gathered at a Phnom Penh restaurant for dinner. At one point, the audience was invited to share their impressions of the trial. One nun told the story of how she "lost all her family members and how she was forced to work day and night. These sufferings were, however, relieved once she entered into a religious life. The Buddhist teaching has educated her to remain calm and give up the idea of revenge." In terms of the Duch trial, she continued, "I want to see Duch and other Khmer Rouge leaders confess what they committed against the Cambodian people so that survivors can be [relieved] and the souls of the victims can rest in peace."[77]

---

[74] Day 59, 118; Khmer, 84.
[76] Prins 2009, Scene 5.

[75] Day 59, 118: Khmer, 84.
[77] Sirik 2009, 6.

When interviewed by DC-Cam staff, ETGE participants expressed a range of views of Duch. Some said their "suffering and anger were relieved when they saw Duch on trial" and that his "acknowledgement to the relatives of S-21 victims that day helped cool [their] minds and hearts." Others, "especially ones who had relatives executed at the prison," said they found it "very hard to offer forgiveness to Duch."[78]

Halfway through the *bangsokol* ceremony at "The Victims Graves" memorial, I watched as three nuns held out a single plastic water bottle, each holding it with a single hand, and began pouring water onto the terrace. One held a finger over the top of the bottle to make sure the water flowed in a trickle. Meanwhile, a group of white-capped Cham men passed behind the nuns. When the nuns finished, they raised their hands in a *sampeah*, then suddenly stopped the impromptu ceremony, before slowly beginning their tour of Tuol Sleng, the last segment of the DC-Cam ETGE program.

If the museum still asserts the People's Republic of Kampuchea atrocity narrative, many visitors, especially foreigners like those who began to fill Tuol Sleng after the early morning visit of the ETGE participants, have increasingly interpreted the museum in terms of a human rights narrative.[79] While this sort of frame may be relevant to some victims and survivors, their engagement with the complex is often much more about personal experience and memory, as illustrated by the testimony of Lefeuvre, Ouk, and Hamill. Many also viewed the site as haunted.

The photos and Vann Nath paintings were particularly significant. A few of the nuns, for example, had briefly glanced up at the Tuol Sleng signage about "The Victims Grave," but they had been much more interested in the photographs as was the case for many ETGE tour participants. They stared intently at the photographs, searching for the face of a lost friend or relative. One of the villagers participating in the ETGE tour was successful. After walking "slowly back and forth among the photo galleries of [B]uilding B to carefully examine the photographs," the woman "finally found him" and began to cry.[80]

The visit to Tuol Sleng was relatively quick, perhaps because many of the ETGE participants had been there before and were eager to begin the long trip home. As they prepared to board their bus, I asked one of the Buddhist nuns why they had performed the *bangsokol* ceremony at "The Victims Graves" memorial. "To send the result (*phal*) [of the ceremony] to the dead," she replied, "for their karma [and rebirth]." Over the next few days, this concern for the karma and the souls of the dead, as well as the possibility of forgiveness and reconciliation, would emerge repeatedly in the testimony of other ECCC civil parties.

[78] Ibid, 9.
[79] Hinton 2016. See also Caswell 2014; R. Hughes 2008; Schlund-Vials 2012.
[80] Sirik 2009, 8.

8

Normativity (Civil Party Testimony)

August 18, 2009 (ECCC Courtroom, Phnom Penh)

"My Brother, whose spirit remains even if you died at S-21, please brother, know that this trial is being done for you."[1]

As he called out these words from the witness stand, civil party Neth Phally held up a black and white photograph of his elder brother, a Khmer Rouge soldier he had last seen recovering from an injury at a Khmer Rouge hospital. Neth waited for him to return for twenty-five years.

"My hope ended in June 2004" he told the court the day after Lefeuvre, Ouk, and Hamill testified. The Documentation Center of Cambodia (DC-Cam) "brought me a copy of [my brother's] biography. That was the time I realized he died at the Tuol Sleng Prison."[2] His family was devastated. His father soon became ill and subsequently died. Later, while at work chopping rubber trees, Neth had become distracted while thinking of his brother and was hit by a falling tree, which "severed my left arm, so I am now forever handicapped ... My father died, my brother perished and I became an amputee ... So I have been living with this great suffering and hopelessness."[3]

Neth later visited Tuol Sleng. The display of the instruments of torture was particularly terrifying as he imagined his brother's cries of pain. Then he went to his brother's cell, which "was more like a pig pen ... not a place for a human being."[4] Neth later asked Duch, "What did my brother do wrong or what was the mistake that led to [his] death?"[5] Duch replied with a general discussion of the purges that led to his brother's arrest.

When Non Nil asked Neth if he had more questions, Neth responded, "I want to show this photograph of my elder brother." Raising the enlarged photograph to eye level, facing forward so that his brother's boyish face was turned to the judges, Neth continued, "It's like my elder brother is sitting here by me in this court watching as the accused is tried. His spirit can be calmed by the hybrid court."[6] As he spoke, Neth stared into the back of the photograph, now a barrier between him and the judges.

---

[1] Day 60, 109–10; Khmer, 84.   [2] Day 60, 101.   [3] Day 60, 106; Khmer, 81.
[4] Day 60, 104; Khmer, 80.   [5] Day 60, 108.   [6] Day 60, 109; Khmer, 84.

The Justice Facade: Trials of Transition in Cambodia. Alexander Laban Hinton. © Alexander Laban Hinton, 2018. Published 2018 by Oxford University Press.

Then Neth began to address his brother: "Elder brother, when you were brought to Tuol Sleng prison and later executed, they blindfolded you. Now this court has removed the blindfold so you can see the person who caused these savage acts." Pausing every few words, Neth continued, "Please Elder Brother, the spirit of my brother, always remain with me and in this photograph, so that I can pay my respect and perform ceremonies to send merit to you whenever I have the opportunity. Even if I can't find your body, I have this photo to serve as a witness and replacement for your remains."[7] He then bowed his head and looked down, saying "That's all."

Non Nil had the photograph displayed. Neth's brother was dressed in a black shirt buttoned to the collar. The background was divided into panels of light and dark. Neth's brother stands wide-eyed and unsmiling, his face pale. No one spoke as the camera slowly zoomed in on the brother's face. It seemed as if he were moving, approaching the viewer, about to burst out of the frame.

Neth's address to his brother seemed out of place, a sudden intrusion of something familiar yet strange that had been out of sight—all the more so for those not familiar with local spirit beliefs but who sensed much was being lost in translation. Everyone was aware that an unspoken absence, a spirit of the dead, was a presence in the court. The participants brought different frames of knowledge to the court, leading them to act and interpret the proceedings in ways that varied, sometimes dramatically so.

One source of variation was the degree of familiarity with juridical process. At the start of the day, for example, Antonya Tioulong, a 57-year-old woman had testified. Her neat white shirt contrasted starkly with Neth's ill-fitting shirt, a sign of her higher status. Many of the Cambodians were familiar with her name, as her father had been a high-ranking Sihanouk official. She would testify about how her sister Raingsy was killed at S-21.

Before beginning, Tioulong had asked if she could deliver her statement in French since "my Cambodian language is not fluent as I was exiled and [have] lived in France for almost 40 years."[8] The first four civil parties in this trial phase, then, did so in a foreign language. Like Lefeuvre, Ouk, and Hamill, Tioulong was educated and eloquent. Each spoke at length and delivered carefully crafted statements that had a clear narrative structure and invoked legal terms and issues in an "appropriate" manner. If their remarks more or less seamlessly fit with the transitional justice imaginary, the testimony of Neth and other civil parties often did not, thereby highlighting the different normative understandings circulating in court.

These alternative normative circuits of meaning were evident in the testimony of the three other civil parties who testified later that day, including Neth. All were from rural backgrounds and had less formal education than Tioulong, Lefeuvre, Ouk, and Hamill. Their initial testimony was also more brief and uneven.

---

[7] Day 60, 110; Khmer, 84.
[8] Day 60, 7. On the testimony of Tioulong and other civil parties, see Carmichael 2015; Cruvellier 2014.

Hav Sophea (August 18, 2009)

The civil party who spoke after Tioulong, Hav Sophea, was a 33-year-old rice farmer whose father had been killed at S-21. She was born 21 days after her father's arrest. She seemed uneasy in the courtroom. Her civil party lawyer, Alain Werner, informed the court that Hav Sophea would not be giving a statement; instead, he would "ask her questions to go with her through her evidence."[9]

The third civil party, So Soung, who spoke immediately before Neth, was a 55-year-old woman from Sihanoukville who was married to a construction worker. Her statement lasted about two minutes before her civil party lawyer began drawing out her testimony with questions. Like Neth, these civil parties did not seem conversant or familiar with the juridical setting as illustrated by the fact that their stories were not told as narratives but as "clipped" responses to questions focused on "relevant" legal issues. None of them framed their remarks in terms of larger legal principles, historical events, international law and tribunals, or juridical roles as had Hamill, Lefeuvre, Ouk, and Tioulong.

Nevertheless, there were common threads that ran through the testimony of the civil parties, regardless of status and education. Tuol Sleng figured prominently in many of their accounts. Hav Sophea, for example, told the court how she and her mother had traveled to Tuol Sleng in 2007, where they felt "shocked and moved" and tearful.[10] Later, when they saw a display of prisoner clothing, her mother asked if she could look through it to find her husband's belongings.

In contrast to the foreign tourists visiting Tuol Sleng, who often regard Tuol Sleng through a human rights lens (foregrounding humanitarianism, universal suffering, atrocity, and global citizenship),[11] the experience of many Cambodians is more personal as they may search for clues about their lost loved ones. This is even more true for civil parties, who suddenly are confronted with devastating depictions of how their relatives might have suffered, including the images of corpses, rows of prisoner photos, and Vann Nath's paintings. As illustrated by the 2008 Reenactment, Tuol Sleng could be read in yet another way—as a crime scene—from the perspective of the court.

Hav Sophea said that her trip there inspired her to become a civil party. She filed through DC-Cam, which gave her a copy of her father's S-21 photo. After visiting Tuol Sleng, she began to dream of him, "although I had never seen his face . . . I could see him through the photo and I—in my dreams he was holding my hand, running away from the S-21 compound, running for [his] life."[12]

Her remarks underscore a second thread, also evident in outreach tours like DC-Cam's ETGE, which appear in civil party testimony: the salience of photographs. From a juridical perspective, the photographs could serve as evidence supporting a victim's claim to civil party status. Duch, in turn, sometimes contested the authenticity of the photographs. Almost all of the civil parties sought to display a photograph

---

[9] Day 60, 44.   [10] Day 60, 52.
[11] Hinton 2016. See also Caswell 2014; R. Hughes 2008; Schlund-Vials 2012.
[12] Day 60, 53; Khmer, 38.

of their deceased loved one, seeking to give them "a face," "dignity," "a voice," or in the case of Neth, an active presence and witnessing in the court.

Ou Savrith and the spirits of the dead (August 20, 2009)

Neth's testimony highlights a third theme in civil party testimony, one also evident in outreach projects: the importance of the spirits of the dead. As noted earlier, many Cambodians believe the spirits of the dead may have difficulty reincarnating, particularly after violent deaths.

At the end of the week, for example, Ou Savrith, a 53-year-old Cambodian testifying by videoconference from France, told the court about the execution of his brother and the devastating impact it had on his life. A businessman, Ou Savrith spoke in French in a carefully crafted statement that included rhetorical questions, such as "Who was my brother?" "What does he represent to me?" and "Why do I miss him?" In so doing, he kept most of his testimony focused on the juridical concerns of the court, including suffering. "I have been thinking of [my brother] every day," he said, "30 years, 10,950 and some days and nights trying to think about what happened inside the walls of S-21."[13]

These feelings were amplified by a visit to Tuol Sleng in 1992, which he called "absolute horror. I was frozen."[14] At one point, while standing in a former cell, he looked out and was struck by the "beautiful weather, blue sky, sparrows singing, wonderful vegetation, and we were in an island of barbarity in the middle of an ocean of softness. How was it possible?"[15]

The trial, he stated, had provided some answers, making his abstract imaginings more concrete and enabling him to "try to experience what [my brother] experienced, to share in my own way his suffering, his anxiety," even if this meant imagining his brother's torture and "total dehumanization."[16]

During his 1992 trip, a spirit medium made contact with his brother's spirit. "We Cambodians believe in this sort of things," he told the court.[17] The medium informed Ou Savrith that his brother was "sad and terrorized … He had suffered great pain during his life on earth and he did not wish to reincarnate." Eventually, the brother had "sought refuge in a pagoda … [and] placed himself under the protection of a monk. The young woman told me the name of the pagoda. I was totally upset."[18] The next day he went to the pagoda and gazed at the ceiling, searching for his brother's spirit. He does this each time he visits a pagoda.

Like Neth's prayer to his brother, Ou Savrith's anecdote about the medium, given amidst his otherwise more "appropriate" testimony, again suggested a current of surplus meaning—transactions with the spirits of the dead—running just beneath the justice facade, an excess that occasionally burst into view. These sudden invocations of the spirits of the dead were familiar to the Cambodians in the court, resonating with everyday conceptions of social exchange and moral obligation.

---

[13] Day 62, 62.　　[14] Day 62, 65.　　[15] Day 62, 65.　　[16] Day 62, 66.
[17] Day 62, 67.　　[18] Day 62, 67.

Obligation and return

A key concept underlying these everyday understandings of obligation is *sång*, a verb meaning "to return" something. It may refer to the return of an object but is often invoked in the context of paying back debt, monetary or moral.[19] Interestingly, the secondary meaning suggests a "flowing back" due to an obstruction. *Sång* is also a word for subtraction. Related terms include compensation (*samnång*) and revenge (*sångsuk*). *Sång*, therefore, connotes a moral return, repayment of an obligation or debt.

Many civil parties highlighted the good deeds done by their loved ones who had perished at S-21. While describing her sister's "radiant personality," for example, Tioulong noted that she behaved like "an older sister as in the traditional way in [Khmer] society, where the older siblings must take care of the younger ones ... She protected us all the time."[20] Tioulong added, "Her role as a protective elder sister haunts me" and made her fate "particularly unjust."[21]

Phung Sunthary (August 19, 2009)

This notion of having an obligation to those who do good deeds on one's behalf, a norm stressed in Cambodian moral education,[22] also emerged on the third day of civil party testimony when the wife and daughter of Phung Thon, Duch's former teacher and S-21 prisoner, took the stand. His daughter, Phung Sunthary, was a former pedagogical trainer living in Phnom Penh. She wore a stylish dress and read from a lengthy prepared statement.

Her testimony, she said, was dedicated to her father's spirit. To begin, she requested photos of her father be displayed, the last of which was his S-21 photograph. Phung Thon's hair is disheveled, his cheekbones gaunt. He looks hopeless. The ordeal, she stated, "turned him into garbage."[23] Her father, she went on, "always protected us. He was our refuge, sheltering us from the outside world of hatred and difficulties."[24] She told anecdotes highlighting his love and devotion and described his virtuous character. It was her duty "to attest to ... the memory, the dignity, the caring father."[25]

As her remarks suggest, there is a strong emphasis in Cambodia on showing gratitude and respect and repaying the good deeds others have done on one's behalf, particularly parents, siblings, and teachers. The significance of such bonds is illustrated by the extension of kinship idioms to patrons, who may be called "mothers" (*me*) of their subordinate "children" or "grandchildren." Mistreating or showing disrespect toward a person to whom one has such bonds, in turn, is considered a moral breach.

From this perspective, Duch's actions were particularly egregious since many people with whom he had moral ties were killed at S-21. Now he was confronted

---

[19] See Headley et al. 1977, 1039; Hinton 2005.   [20] Day 60, 25.   [21] Day 60, 27.
[22] See Hinton 2005.   [23] Day 61; Khmer, 22.   [24] Day 61, 29; Khmer, 23.
[25] Day 61, 30.

with the execution of a teacher to whom he was even closer, Phung Thon. He also appeared caught in a lie.

Phung Sunthary posed three questions to Duch, asking him who had made the decision to kill her father, how he was tortured, and who had ordered Phung Thon sent to S-21. Duch had replied that he did not know, noting that Phung Thon's documents didn't bear his annotations and therefore Phung Thon must have been arrested while S-21 was under "the chairmanship of [my predecessor] Nat."[26]

When asked to explain how it could be that this was the case when documents list Phung Thon's arrival date at S-21 as December 12, 1976, Duch replied that he would need time to explain. Prior to 1970, he stated, invoking idioms of obligation and respect, he had greatly respected (*tuk chett korop kaot khlach*) six people, one of whom was Phung Thon. Duch claimed he regretted he wasn't aware of "Teacher" Phung Thon's detention. Using two Khmer roots for "return" (*top* and *sâng*), Duch said he would have been unable to save his former teacher but would have aided him in small ways as "repayment for his good deeds" (*topsnong sângkun*).[27]

In Khmer, people are sometimes said to be "tied" (*châng*) through such moral exchanges. As illustrated by Phung Sunthary's and Duch's remarks, a person becomes bound to others in a relationship requiring the person for whom a good deed has been done to respect and repay the benefactor's kindness—though it is often said that the deeds of parents and teachers can never be fully repaid. A person who fails to repay such good deeds is scorned as an ingrate (*romilkun*) as opposed to someone who is grateful and remains aware of such kindness (*doeungkun*).

Such "ties" also may be negative in the sense that one "owes" a return to someone who had done a "bad deed" to you. Prior to posing her questions to Duch, for example, Phung Sunthary had told the court, "I am not here to seek revenge. I'm here to seek the truth."[28] Duch referenced her comment during his observations, saying that he believed that she was after the truth, not repaying a grudge and seeking vengeance (*sâng kumnum sângsoek*).[29] He added that he would work with her to continue seeking "the truth."

Such negative ties provide an emotional current upon which governments try to draw, such as when the Khmer Rouge spoke of "class anger" for the bad deeds done to the poor by the oppressor classes. Similarly, the People's Republic of Kampuchea (PRK) regime spoke of being "tied in anger" (*châng komhoeng*) or seized with "hot anguish" (*chheu chap*) against the Democratic Kampuchea (DK) leaders who had killed so many and turned Cambodia into "the prison without walls."

If such conceptions of proper "return" and moral exchange are idealized, they nevertheless may inform social interactions and evaluation. In the context of S-21, the civil parties were tied to Duch through the bad things he had done to their loved ones, a negative action that morally obligated the civil parties to make a "return." This obligation created the possibility of revenge.

---

[26] Day 61, 64.   [27] Day 61, 69; Khmer, 53. See also Hinton 2005.
[28] Day 61, 59.   [29] Day 61, 70; Khmer, 54.

In juridical forums, there is awareness of this danger, which is one of the reasons for the tight security and glass wall separating the public gallery from the courtroom. Within the courtroom, the civil parties sit on the opposite side of the courtroom from the defense. They are separated by the well of the courtroom, a space through which no one may pass without authorization. The well also signifies, as a metaphor for renewal and transformation, a change in the relationship between the parties (for example, as victims' feelings of anger and vengeance are subordinated to legal process and given new expression by the sentence instead of violence).[30]

The movement of the parties is also highly regulated, as participants sit or, when recognized, are granted "standing" to speak while remaining behind a symbolic "bar." The Trial Chamber judges, in turn, are positioned between the prosecution and civil parties, on one side of the room, and the defense on the other. This placement, along with their elevated seating and authority, signify that "something higher"—law and the pursuit of justice rather than emotion—inform courtroom dynamics. The "well" symbolically connotes the "currents" running below the surface, including powerful emotions "driven back" and controlled by the Trial Chamber, the guardians of law.

From afar, one sees only the surface of a well; even when one gazes below, there is only shadow and darkness. In these respects, "the well" is a symbol of what has been pushed out of sight, the uncanny, and the haunting of what might suddenly burst forth in courtroom moments like Neth's invocation of his brother, Hamill's outburst at Duch, or Phung Thon's wife, after possibly glimpsing her husband's spirit, fainting in court.[31] Legal proceedings, predicated upon rationality, are uneasy with emotion, as illustrated by perceived insensitivity of the Trial Chamber to civil parties upset.

At times, the issue of civil party anger and vengeance came more directly into focus. President Non Nil might issue a warning, such as when he instructed Hamill to "refrain from using strong words that are abusive ... Instead, we should use words of a legalistic nature that are endowed with morality and virtue ... [not for] revenge."[32]

Such comments highlight how juridical mechanisms seek to transform the moral exchange between victims and perpetrators, shifting their relation from the realm of emotion to the rationality of law. This legal context provided a different sort of "return," providing civil parties with the opportunity to seek truth and justice, to restore the voice of their loved ones, and to provide evidence contributing to possible conviction. Some civil parties viewed their testimony and participation as a form of "return" to the dead, a connection they sometimes stated directly such as when Touch Monin noted, "My intention is to pay my gratitude (*tob snong sângkun*) to the spirit of my Elder [cousin], Chea Khan, alias Chin, who did good deeds (*kun bomnach*) of great significance for my family."[33] The court also allowed the civil parties to make a claim for reparations (*samnâng*), a Khmer word related to "return" (*sâng*).

---

[30] Hinton 2016.   [31] Day 61, 10.   [32] Day 59, 107; Khmer, 76.
[33] Day 63, 98; Khmer, 84.

The legalistic "return" provided by the court, however, had limitations with regard to the spirits of the dead, to whom there is an obligation to make a "return." To not do so would be to fail to "know the good deeds of others" and, through this disrespect and ungratefulness, potentially incur their anger and lead them to afflict the living.

Each year, as Chea Vannath had noted, Cambodians celebrate *pchum ben*, traveling to pagodas to make offerings to the spirits of the dead, including relatives who perished during DK.[34] But, as illustrated by the Khmer Institute of Democracy (KID) booklet frame of Uncle San praying, Cambodian Buddhists attend to the spirits of the dead at other times, sometimes lighting incense before a photograph or the cremated remains of relatives. On other occasions, they may pray for the dead at the pagoda and perform ceremonies to transfer merit to the spirits of the dead to facilitate and enhance their reincarnation. This is part of the reason so many civil parties, like Bou Meng, asked Duch to confirm where their loved ones were killed; they wanted to gather soil to perform such ceremonies.

This obligation to the dead complicated civil party response to Duch's apology. In the framework of moral exchange, an apology is a return, something given to partly "pay back" for past wrongs. The problem, which paralleled the issue of sentencing, was the magnitude of what Duch had done since some deeds are perceived as so harmful they cannot be repaid.

Touch Monin discussed a related anecdote moments after stating his desire to make a "return" to his cousin. When Touch Monin's family had arrived in the countryside at the start of DK, he testified, the "old people" had said that, because his family was rich and bourgeoisie, they could not be forgiven, literally "make a return" (*tob snong*) for the bad deeds (oppression) their class had perpetrated upon the poor.[35]

Chum Neou and Chum Sirath (August 20, 2009)

Civil party Chum Neou noted the difficulty of forgiving Duch. She had joined the revolution in 1971 and was stationed in Phnom Penh after the war. Shortly after her husband was sent to S-21, Chum Neou was sent to a work camp. She was pregnant and eventually gave birth there. "I have never talked about this experience,"[36] she said as she described how her baby became sick and died. After DK, she returned to her village but found that only one member of her family had survived. Other villagers provided her with emotional support, telling her to forget about the past.[37]

Duch's lawyer, François Roux, tried to draw a parallel between Chum Neou and Duch. "Do the villagers still consider you [to be] a member of the Khmer Rouge?" Roux asked. "This question is truly difficult to answer," Chum Neou replied. She explained that, after DK, her aunt was furious with her, saying "It's the fault of you, despicable one (*haeng*), and your group that so many of our children died."

She related her experience to Duch's apologies. When, after DK, she first met her aunt in public while traveling along the road, Chum Neou recounted, "I fell to my

---

[34] Davis 2015; Ledgerwood 2012.   [35] Day 63, 98; Khmer, 84.
[36] Day 62, 86; Khmer, 69.   [37] Day 63, 19; Khmer, 16.

knees and genuflected, offering my apology." Her aunt would not accept it. "And this was my aunt by blood," Chum Neou said. She contrasted her apology with Duch's "one word of apology in the court, which I can't accept."

In response to Roux's question, Chum Neou explained that part of the reason she had filed a complaint was so that her relatives and neighbors would not "look down on me ... The Khmer Rouge were savage. The truth is that I joined [the revolution] out of love of my country, not realizing that this despicable group would act so abusively and do bad deeds to me."[38]

"I have no further questions," Roux replied.

Like Chum Neou, many civil parties refused to forgive Duch. Their motivations were complex and varied. For some, the enormity of what Duch had done made forgiveness impossible. Ou Savrith had stated this clearly when he said, "on behalf of my entire family I must say we will not forgive [Duch] because forgiveness is beyond the death camps, and today all that remains is despair."[39]

Such comments highlight the predicament Duch's apology created. To accept it might suggest his crimes, and the claims of the victims, were less serious. Their response to Duch's apology was also self-implicating since honor and face were at stake in the exchanges. Many civil parties felt they had the "duty" to restore dignity to the spirits of the dead. Not making this "return" to the dead could be dangerous, inhibiting their rebirth and incurring their wrath.

Chum Neou's contrast between her apology to her aunt and Duch's apology suggested a second key factor in the refusal of the civil parties to accept Duch's apology: the belief he was insincere. This perspective was perhaps shown most directly by another civil party, Chum Sirath, whose two brothers were executed at S-21.

"In the beginning when I heard the apology made by the accused," Chum Sirath testified, "I was happy." This feeling soon "dissipated" and now "I believe [his apology] is not genuine." Chum Sirath noted Duch's claim to pray to the spirits of the dead on his own birthday, which suggested he did this "to make himself feel better." When Chum Sirath wrote a letter to Duch asking for information about his brother, who Duch had known, Duch replied that "he didn't know anything about this. So that's why I said his expressions [of remorse are] not genuine." He continued, "I will not be able to accept [Duch's] apology that is impure."[40]

Chhin Navy and Buddhist return (August 24, 2009)

If most civil parties said they could not forgive Duch, this was not always the case, as illustrated by the testimony of 70-year-old Chhin Navy. During DK, while living in the countryside, her sister had told the Khmer Rouge who her husband, a well-connected civil servant, had been CIA. He was taken away shortly thereafter.[41]

Chhin Navy blamed her sister for her husband's arrest and was angry with her. After DK, however, her anger had abated and eventually ceased. She even looked

[38] Day 63, 43; Khmer, 35.   [39] Day 62, 76.   [40] Day 62, 36; Khmer, 27.
[41] Day 63, 55.

after her sister's children. She came to understand that her sister "was indoctrinated" by communist ideology and had been trying to prove her loyalty to the revolution.

This understanding was part of the larger Buddhist lens through which Chhin Navy viewed her sister's actions. Ultimately, she noted, people reap what they sow. To illustrate this point, Chhin Navy invoked a related Buddhist saying, "If you plant a hot chili pepper, you'll get a hot chili pepper; if you plant sweet sugarcane, you'll receive sweet sugarcane; if you plan bitter *sdauv* [a plant], your yield will be bitter *sdauv*. Thus, after continuing reflection, I stopped being angry. Whatever a person does—that person will receive the result."[42]

Her sister, she continued, would receive the yield from having reported on Chhin Navy's husband. "Maybe she was stupid," she noted, "but she'll get the result of her action. I'm not angry with her."[43] She added, "If I did not study Buddhist discipline then the anger would still be burning in my heart." Relatedly, Chhin Navy said, "I really want to tell Mr. Duch, as well, that I pity him." Like her sister, Duch would receive the result of what he had done at S-21.

Chhin Navy's testimony was filled with references to Buddhism, ranging from her use of prayer to her invocation of Buddhist precepts and principles to interpret the DK past and the juridical present. Her testimony foregrounded a Buddhist approach to forgiveness, yet another moral articulation that was used to interpret Duch's behavior.

To hold onto anger, from this perspective, is to hold onto an attachment that can negatively impact one's own future. Instead, one should reflect upon the causes of past actions, seeking to distinguish right from wrong. Anger is pointless since the person who did the bad deed will suffer the consequences, since bad actions negatively condition rebirth—as was the case for Chhin Navy's sister and Duch.

At one point, Chhin Navy stated, "[My sister] will receive the results [of her actions]. I'm not angry with her. I have calmed (*sgnop*) my heart and extinguished the fire [of my anger]."[44] This comment asserted Buddhist ideals of calmness and detachment, which go along with proper understanding that is reflected by Chhin Navy's repeated remarks that she had overcome her anger through sustained reflection or analysis (*picharana*).

This conception of act and result is also suggestive of some of the differences between the Cambodian Buddhist and legal conceptions of justice. Both seek to discover truth and discern right from wrong. If legal justice focuses on accountability and punishment, however, these objectives are not primary from a Buddhist perspective since karmic justice will play out regardless of any juridical mechanism.

This point was highlighted during a March 2011 visit to Tuol Sleng. I saw S-21 survivor Chum Mey sitting on a bench. He asked me to sit by him and we began to chat. Eventually, our conversation turned to the court. After he had noted the importance of seeking justice for and transferring merit to the spirits of the dead,

---

[42] Day 63, 76; Khmer, 65. [43] Day 63, 76; Khmer, 66.
[44] Day 63, 76; Khmer, 66.

I asked him if Buddhism and the law were connected. "The law takes everything from Buddhism," he told me.[45]

"For example," Chum Mey continued, "Both the law and the dharma of the Buddha forbid killing. According to Buddhism, a person is not supposed to do this [kill] or oppress or be abusive toward others. The laws that have been created are like this, not allowing the violation of human rights or the abuse, killing, or torture of other people." Human rights, he concluded, "forbid us from doing things that are against the Buddha and his dharma ... so we must really respect human rights."

But the relationship between Buddhism and legal justice is uneasy. If they share a concern for moral behavior and "right understanding," other Buddhist principles are potentially at odds with legal justice. In a series of interviews about justice that DC-Cam conducted with leading Cambodian monks during the early 2000s, for example, the topic of vindictiveness repeatedly arose. As one of the vices, anger leads to attachment and bad action, which negatively affect karma and rebirth. Accordingly, it is imperative to let go of one's anger.

This was perhaps most clearly expressed by Venerable Bour Kry, who, in response to a question about whether teaching about the past might stir up hot anguish (*chheu chap*) noted, "Buddha advised, 'The past should be forgotten, focus on the present and don't anticipate the future.' Why? Because the past is like a dead body. If we don't bury it but keep it at home, it stinks and no one will live near us. Therefore we should bury the past."[46] When the DC-Cam interviewer, invoking the global citizenship trope of "never forget," responded, "Nonetheless, I think that if we forget a past event, sooner or later it will happen again," Venerable Bour Kry told her, "Buddha did not think that way. Things that are finished are forever finished. Nothing happens twice."

This Buddhist notion of forgetting is sometimes invoked by those, including older Cambodians focused on Buddhist practice as they near the end of their life, who show less interest in or choose not to participate in the trials. This moral emphasis on forgetting sometimes circulated at court, even if it was potentially at odds with the legalism of the proceedings and notion that healing requires verbal testimony. Some civil parties noted their ambivalence about testifying, which could stir up difficult feelings, even if they decided to participate nevertheless for the spirits of the dead, to seek the truth, or to educate future generations.[47]

This tension was at times evident during civil party testimony, as illustrated by Chhin Navy's frequent invocation of the Buddhist emphasis on letting go of one's anger. She also mentioned the imperative of forgetting during an anecdote about how, during PRK, she became dizzy and fainted at Tuol Sleng after being given documents about her husband's imprisonment. The following day, she remained visibly upset. At work, a colleague "comforted me, [saying] that I should ... try to forget (*kat chett*) what happened ... that I should only think of the prosperous future time and forget what happened in the past."[48]

[45] Author interview with Chum Mey, Phnom Penh, March 15, 2011.
[46] Sann and Em 2002, 39.
[47] Personal communication, Samphors Huy, September 17, 2013.   [48] Day 63, 74.

If Chhin Navy had become a civil party to find out more information and to seek justice, many other Cambodians did not choose this path. Some did not know about the trial or how to go about joining as a civil party, despite Khmer Rouge Tribunal (KRT) outreach efforts. Still others simply decided not to engage with the trial.

For example, when I asked Yum, a Buddhist nun in the countryside who had suffered greatly during DK and now spent much of her time at the local pagoda,[49] if she was interested in Duch's trial, she answered indirectly, saying that those who commit offenses should be tried. As for Duch's apology, she noted that previously she had been really angry but had calmed her emotions as she sought to lead a moral life as a nun.

According to Buddhism, Yum explained, one should let go of one's anger and not be vindictive. She added, "It's not necessary to kill that person [who has done a bad deed]. Because that person will receive [back the karmic return for the action]. If one kills others, in a later life one will be killed in return . . . For those who sin, their karma is like this." A person like Duch who had killed a lot, she added, "likely won't be reborn as a person. They'll be reborn in the [Buddhist] Hells."[50] While Yum did not oppose the ECCC, then, she did not view it as critical due to her strong Buddhist belief that emphasized letting go of anger, ending the cycle of violence, forgetting, and karmic justice.

Protest

As Duch's trial proceeded, the tensions between Duch and the civil parties continued to heighten, creating an atmosphere in which forgiveness became increasingly difficult. These tensions came to a head when the defense challenged the legitimacy of several civil parties and the court ruled that the civil parties did not have the right to participate in the next phases of the trial on character and sentencing.

If they were silenced inside the court, the civil parties were vocal outside it. At a press conference, the civil parties voiced their complaints, also laid out in a letter addressed to the Trial Chamber. The twenty-eight civil parties who signed the letter complained about the decision on sentencing and character, which had "diminished" their role. They viewed it as part of a larger pattern of "many unbalanced treatments between the accused and the victims."[51]

Two weeks later, in direct response to the court's decision denying them the right to participate in the proceedings on character, thirty-three civil parties created a Victim's Association. The civil parties also made media appearances. Chum Mey and Bou Meng, for example, appeared on the weekly television show, "Duch on Trial," to discuss their boycott. Sitting on a bench, the waters of the Mekong behind their backs, the two civil parties complained about being silenced by the court.

---

[49] Hinton 2005.

[50] Author interview with Yum [pseudonym], Banyan village, June 28, 2009.

[51] "Letter of Civil Parties in Case 001 to the President of the Trial Chamber," August 30, 2009 (http://www.civilparties.org).

Chum Mey, his voice rising, stated, "This is about our rights. Under the Khmer Rouge we had no rights at all. The UN and the whole world is now involved in this court. This is why we are protesting." Pointing his index finger for emphasis, Bou Meng added, "I'm a victim of the Pol Pot regime and genocide. Now I'm a victim of the court."

Judgment

During the remainder of Duch's trial, most civil parties remained upset about what they perceived as unfair treatment and Duch's failure to show proper remorse. During closing arguments in late November 2009, civil party lawyers stated this clearly.

While the civil parties appreciated the opportunity to speak, international defense co-lawyer Silke Studzinsky stated, some felt unwelcome and that the Trial Chamber "was not very receptive to their sufferings." The civil parties had not even been thanked. "Thank you," Studzinsky said, "are two small, little words, but they mean a lot. [Civil Parties] were treated as standby witnesses, mere fill-ins."[52] Noting that civil parties had been excluded from speaking on character and sentencing, Studzinsky added that her clients "felt they were deprived from their participation rights."[53] Her national co-civil party lawyer spoke next, stating that the clients felt Duch "was neither sincere nor truthful," his responses "half-hearted," and his apologies and pleas for forgiveness "unctuous" and characterized by "crocodile tears."[54]

On July 26, 2010, the Trial Chamber delivered its "disposition," finding Duch guilty of crimes against humanity and war crimes.[55] Due to mitigating factors, including his cooperation and illegal detention by the Cambodian government prior to the trial, they sentenced Duch to thirty-five years, less credit for cooperation (five years) and time served (eleven years). This meant Duch could effectively walk free in nineteen years. In addition, the Trial Chamber accepted only sixty-six of the ninety civil parties.

Many civil parties were angered and appealed to the Supreme Court Chamber (SCC). On February 3, 2012, the SCC sentenced Duch to life—exceeding the forty-five years the prosecution requested. In addition, the SCC approved ten of the civil parties rejected by the Trial Chamber. Many civil parties were pleased. "It is the absolute justice [for which] I had hoped," Chum Mey told a reporter. "I am at ease now."[56] Meanwhile, and as noted earlier, Seng and members of the human rights community complained the decision scapegoated Duch and whitewashed the government's illegal detention of Duch while seeking to legitimate its rule.[57]

---

[52] Day 73, 50–51. [53] Day 73, 53. [54] Day 73, 68, 70.
[55] Trial Chamber 2010. [56] Naren and Foster 2012.
[57] Giry 2012; Seng 2012; see also Hinton 2016, 257f. and Hinton 2017.

9

Disposition (Youk Chhang, Documenter and Survivor)

March 22, 2014 (Bopha Phnom Penh Titanic Restaurant)

"Win a little bit, lose a little bit."

Youk Chhang, Director of the Documentation Center of Cambodia (DC-Cam), sits across from me at an outdoor riverside restaurant in Phnom Penh, describing the origin of the play "Breaking the Silence." The Tonle Sap's muddy waters trail behind him. Fishing boats crisscross the river, its waters low. A cruise ship docks city center. I wonder if the tourists will gamble or visit Tuol Sleng.

We had met at DC-Cam, located in a three-story building near Cambodia's Independence Monument and fronted by a black gate with a peephole, a security precaution from the 1990s. "Let's eat at the river," Chhang had said. "It's more beautiful."

I have known Chhang for years, first as a researcher in the early 2000s and later as an Academic Advisor to DC-Cam. I'm familiar with his love of aesthetics and the arts. He has worked with visual artists, including Sera, the Franco-Khmer painter and cartoonist who participated in memory workshops with Vann Nath. A Sera painting adorns one of DC-Cam's walls. Other art as well as Buddha images are scattered throughout the compound, including an antique pagoda painting of the Buddha that Chhang said was an inspiration for the figure depicted in the Extraordinary Chambers in the Courts of Cambodia (ECCC) logo.

As we chatted, he pointed to a wooden structure. "It's the hull of a fishing boat," he told me. "I have been purchasing them from villagers who have had to give up fishing due to the low water levels on Mekong. It's because of global warming and the dams." There were several boat hulls in DC-Cam's courtyard. One was filled with plants; another had been fitted with shelves that held DC-Cam publications.

While Chhang had devoted much of his life to documenting the Cambodian genocide, he was interested in topics related to reconstruction and peace-building. He helped produce "A River Changes Course," an award-winning film on environmental destruction in the country as well as "Don't Think I've Forgotten: Cambodia's Lost Rock & Roll." On the side, he worked on a cookbook on Cambodian cuisine.

I was aware of parts of his story from past conversations and articles written about or by him. Duplicates of documentation DC-Cam had gathered over the years

The Justice Facade: Trials of Transition in Cambodia. Alexander Laban Hinton. © Alexander Laban Hinton, 2018. Published 2018 by Oxford University Press.

had been transferred to the ECCC, constituting a significant part of the case file. Defense lawyers had contested the reliability of some of this material, leading Chhang to testify about it in Case 002.

At the time, just days before the 2012 final decision in Duch's case, Chhang explained the origins of DC-Cam and how he had come to run it. Chhang was impeccably dressed. On the first day, he wore a black traditional jacket, which accented light streaks of grey in his hair.[1] He spoke in Khmer, switching at times to English and French. In addition, he told the court, he spoke a little Lao and Thai, a legacy of his time in a refugee camp on the Thai border.

His path to the camp was related by his experiences as a teenager during Democratic Kampuchea (DK). These experiences also shaped his vision for DC-Cam and informed the Khmer Rouge Tribunal (KRT) outreach initiatives the non-governmental organization (NGO) would undertake, including its work on "Breaking the Silence," its "Living Documents" program, and the mid-August 2009 "ECCC Tour and Genocide Education" (ETGE) initiative.

The Documentation Center of Cambodia

Youk Chhang's path to DC-Cam

Raised in Phnom Penh, Chhang was just 14 when the Khmer Rouge came to power. Several themes stand out in his recollections of DK, all linked to the struggle to retain a sense of humanity amidst the violence and suffering.

The first is loneliness.[2] Even during the 1970–1975 civil war, Chhang recalls becoming increasingly self-reliant and independent as his school closed and his parents focused on the safety of the family. His father, a cadaster drafted into the army, died during this period.

When the Khmer Rouge entered Phnom Penh, Chhang was alone at home. Chhang was forced out of the house and city as part of the Khmer Rouge rustication of the urban population. Chhang had no idea where to go but overheard some people say they were returning to their home villages. He decided to travel to his mother's birth village in Takeo province, a journey that took several weeks. Months later his mother and siblings arrived.

Youk's family was soon broken apart. They were relocated to Battambang province in 1976 as part of a second wave of Khmer Rouge population movements meant to increase rice production in less populated areas. There he was assigned to a mobile brigade youth unit tasked with digging canals. At night he would often sneak back to the village to see his family, but later his unit was sent to work further way. "I was alone more and more," he recalled.[3]

Besides loneliness, hunger is also an important part of Chhang's recollections of DK. "Food became my god during the regime," he has said.[4] During DK, when

---

[1] Youk Chhang Testimony, Case 002.1, Day 25 (February 1, 2012).
[2] The following material on loneliness is based on Chhang 2005a.   [3] Ibid, 6.
[4] See, for example, Ibid, 6.

people were often forced to work long hours on minimal rations, survival depended upon the ability to procure enough food. "Hunger can make you learn a lot of things," Chhang states. "I taught myself how to swim, for example, so I could dive down and cut the sweet sugarcane growing in the flooded rice fields. And I learned how to steal food, how to kill and eat snakes and rats, and how to find edible leaves in the jungle."[5] Food became an obsession, something he dreamed about "all the time. It would help me fall asleep and gave me the strength I needed to return to the fields to work each day."

The lack of food also resulted in suffering and death, another theme in Chhang's recollections. One day he was caught stealing rice for his starving and pregnant sister, a "crime" for which he was beaten with an axe, tortured, and imprisoned for two weeks.

In 1977, another sister, whose infant son had starved to death, was accused of stealing rice. To prove her guilt, a Khmer Rouge cadre "slashed her belly open. Her stomach was empty. And then she died a slow, horrible death."[6] All of his mother's siblings and many of her relatives died or were killed during this time. Chhang only has one family photo left, a black and white photo taken in 1968 at his sister's wedding. There are eight people in the photo, including the young Chhang, kneeling on the ground in shorts. Every other person in the photo died during DK.[7]

Amidst this violence, Cambodians faced an ongoing struggle to retain their humanity. It was a time when it was expedient to turn one's back on the suffering of others. One's survival could depend upon it.

Moral struggles took place daily as people made life-and-death decisions. When Chhang was imprisoned, for example, a man from his mother's village successfully sought Chhang's release.[8] The man later disappeared. Another base person provided Chhang's family with food at a dire time. Such acts by family, friends, acquaintances, and "even total strangers may have saved my life more than one time. These were people who saw the value of life and did their best to assert their humanity during a time when it was difficult to do so."

Chhang's DK experiences raised questions that would lead him to DC-Cam. His first stop was Thailand. At his mother's urging, Chhang slipped across the border and sought refuge at the largest camp, Khao-I-Dang.

He began learning English by playing scrabble.[9] Chhang later worked for a humanitarian organization and learned to type.[10] When he was offered the chance to relocate to the United States (U.S.), he chose Texas because it was the place where John F. Kennedy, whose civil rights work he admired, had been assassinated.

After a stay at the Philippines Refugee Processing Center, Chhang arrived in Texas in 1987 at the age of 25. He enrolled at the University of Dallas, majoring in political science. While he enjoyed his new life, he felt "broken inside."[11] And he kept returning to DK. Upon arriving in the U.S., an English teacher had given him a copy of a book, *How Pol Pot Came to Power*, and inscribed a note saying that

---

[5] Ibid, 6–7. [6] Chhang 2002, 3. [7] Eads n.d.
[8] The material in this paragraph is based on Chhang 2005a, 7. [9] Eads n.d.
[10] Chhang Testimony, Case 002.1, Day 25, 6, 8. [11] Mydans 2006.

she hoped he would one day find the truth about the past.[12] Chhang began to correspond with the author, Ben Kiernan, and other scholars. He later translated the thesis of Khieu Samphan and worked on the Campaign to Oppose the Return of the Khmer Rouge.

In 1992, Chhang returned to Cambodia to work for the United Nations Transitional Authority in Cambodia (UNTAC), another step toward DC-Cam. In April 1994, the U.S. had passed the "Cambodian Genocide Justice Act" which, glossing over U.S. policy in Cambodia from 1979 until the Paris Peace Agreement, stated: "Consistent with international law, it is the policy of the United States to support efforts to bring to justice members of the Khmer Rouge for their crimes against humanity committed in Cambodia between April 17, 1975 and January 7, 1979."[13] To this end, the Act urged the President to call for the creation of a Khmer Rouge tribunal and to provide funds to assist with the collection of evidence.

A small group of U.S. scholars and activists had already begun collecting such documentation to lay the groundwork for a trial.[14] One of them, Greg Stanton, had established the Cambodian Genocide Project in 1981 after visiting Cambodia. He would later push for passage of the Cambodian Genocide Justice Act while at the State Department. David Hawk, with whom Kassie Neou had worked closely, had run another program in the 1980s focused on documentation.

The passage of the 1994 Act enabled these documentation efforts to expand dramatically. In December 1994, Yale University's Cambodian Genocide Program was awarded $499,000 by the U.S. Department of State to carry out research, funds later supplemented by other sources. The objectives of the Cambodian Genocide Program were to (a) "collect, study, and preserve" documentation about DK; (b) "make this information available to a court or tribunal" willing to prosecute the Khmer Rouge; and (c) "generate a critical, analytical understanding of genocide" to help prevent atrocities from taking place elsewhere in the world.[15]

Yale immediately established a Phnom Penh field office, which would become DC-Cam. Kiernan, the director of the Cambodian Genocide Program, recruited Chhang to be the Cambodian head of this office, which became an independent, local NGO in January 1997.

Documentation

During the next decade, DC-Cam gathered an enormous amount of documentation while launching a number of projects. Like other intermediary organizations, DC-Cam's eventual KRT outreach activities were grafted onto these existing programmatic strengths repurposed for the new historical moment as a Khmer Rouge

---

[12] Chhang Testimony, Case 002.1, Day 25, 12.
[13] "The Cambodian Genocide Justice Act" (22 U.S.C. 2656, Part D, Sections 571–574), 1994 (http://www.dccam.org).
[14] Chhang Testimony, Case 002.1, Day 25, 11–12.
[15] "Introduction," Cambodian Genocide Program (http://www.yale.edu/cgp).

tribunal became a reality. These institutional strengths, as well as Chhang's vision, shaped outreach activities such as the mid-August 2009 ETGE program, its involvement in "Breaking the Silence," and its focal ECCC outreach initiative, "Living Documents."

The "Living Documents" program was directly related to DC-Cam's initial primary focus, documentation, though the purview of the NGO expanded after Chhang took over to include issues related to "memory and justice." The early documentation phase, which began in 1995 and continues, is directly linked to the original mandate of the Cambodian Genocide Program.

If the object of DC-Cam's core "Documentation Project" was to gather material to help hold DK "leaders responsible for their decisions while ensuring that the past is not forgotten," it also did so as "a starting point for reeducation, justice, and national reconciliation" and to create a "foundation for justice and lasting peace."[16] These efforts began with a sense of urgency given that many documents related to DK had already disappeared.

Almost immediately, DC-Cam uncovered troves of documents, including, in March 1996, more than 100,000 pages of records of the Khmer Rouge security police, or the Santebal archive. These security police records, including confessions, meeting minutes, correspondence, videos, and biographies, provided key evidence on DK crimes.[17]

Many of these documents had been collected by the Ministry of Interior as part of the People's Republic of Kampuchea (PRK) efforts to chronicle DK atrocities, including the evidence gathering by people like Thun Saray for the People's Revolutionary Tribunal (PRT). PRT materials ranging from field investigation reports to Communist Party of Kampuchea documents, were given in duplicate to DC-Cam in 1996.[18]

As part of its "first transition" efforts, the PRK regime also gathered over a million handwritten "Renakse petitions" from all over Cambodia, which detail death and suffering during DK. These were given to DC-Cam in 1997 and later used for DC-Cam's Victims Participation project.[19]

As part of its documentation, DC-Cam also launched a "Mapping Project" in 1995. Combining field research with new satellite technologies, DC-Cam staff scoured the countryside counting DK mass graves (19,733 in 388 clusters), security centers (196), and genocide memorials (81).

Other documents, including thousands of S-21 confessions and photos were the basis for the creation of the "Tuol Sleng Archive."[20] DC-Cam's collection includes a duplicate copy of much of this archive.[21] In total, DC-Cam has gathered almost a million pages of documentation related to DK, the largest such archive in the world.

---

[16] "Documentation," DC-Cam webpage (http://www.d.dccam.org).
[17] Ciorciari and Chhang 2005, 228; Chhang Testimony, Case 002.1, Day 25, 43.
[18] Ciorciari and Chhang 2005, 232.   [19] Ibid.
[20] Chhang Testimony, Case 002.1, Day 25, 67.
[21] Chhang Testimony, Case, 002.1, Day 25, 67.

Memory and justice

Over time, DC-Cam increasingly focused on issues related to memory and justice. While Chhang had received extensive training from Cambodian Genocide Program, which had an academic and legal orientation, he decided to shift the emphasis in 1997 when he took over and renamed the institution DC-Cam. If DC-Cam retains an academic ethos, Chhang wanted to position himself as a survivor and DC-Cam more broadly as an institution devoted to the "voice of survivors."[22]

This key shift in emphasis was marked by a new slogan, "searching for a truth." Chhang explained that his idea "was that everyone holds their own piece of their own truth. And each of us must search for our own truth."[23] To catalyze this vision, Chhang wanted to start a magazine. However, he found it difficult to procure funding, perhaps donors were "reluctant to support [an initiative that might] stir up discussion of the Khmer Rouge at the grassroots level and upset the government of Cambodia. So no support! ... Then one night I got a fax from Norway. A human rights office [in the Norwegian Ministry of Foreign Affairs] had decided to give $30,000" to start the magazine, *Searching for the Truth*. So, Chhang added, "the turning point from CGP to DC-Cam is that slogan," which is linked to the idea that each person had to "search for [their own] story and history."[24]

This shift was evident in the structure of *Searching for the Truth*, launched in January 2000. Three magazine sections, "Documentation," "History," and "Legal," were related to the DC-Cam's original concerns. However, the magazine included sections on "Public Debate" and "Family Tracing" as well as letters from readers and material related to the arts.[25] As this structure suggests, "searching for the truth" operated on two levels, described in Chhang's lead editorial for the first issue, "For the Truth." On the one hand, he offered a vision for the magazine that dovetailed with notions of global justice, democratization, and human rights, noting goals such as combatting "impunity," building a "strong democratic society" premised on "the rule of law," and "seeking justice."[26]

But, he continued, the magazine would also assist Cambodians in their own search for truth. To seek justice, it was necessary for people to be informed and participate in the judicial process. DC-Cam would be a "messenger" in this regard as it launched "an educational campaign with the objective of disseminating information on the tribunals and the history of [DK]." *Searching for the Truth* was the "end result" of this initiative, one that would also be part of a "truth-telling mechanism" in Cambodia since survivors have "a right to know the truth about what happened" as part of their own truth-seeking process.

Often, Chhang's editorial continued, survivors stated, "I want to know what happened, who ordered the killing, and why." *Searching for the Truth*, and DC-Cam more broadly, would help them answer such questions while playing a role somewhat similar to a truth commission.[27]

---

[22] Skype interview with Youk Chhang, December 15, 2016.   [23] Ibid.   [24] Ibid.
[25] Chhang 2000a.   [26] Ibid.   [27] Ibid, 2.

Chhang also identified with the new focus on truth, memory, and justice, as illustrated by editorials in which he recounted his own efforts in this regard. In his second editorial, "Memory,"[28] Chhang wrote of how, during his childhood prior to DK, he served as a messenger for his mother, who sold gems.

Since she was illiterate, Chhang's mother would give him verbal directions so that he could "go collect messages or money from her clients." Using notes or his memory, he would then seek out the clients, often stopping to ask people directions. Twenty years later, Chhang would use this skill again as he traveled around the Cambodian countryside with the Mapping Project team. "Now I must ask people again for directions," he noted, "this time to the genocide sites and the home villages of witnesses . . . so that the [precious] memory of their experiences can be recorded."

Many of the stories became part of the DC-Cam archive. If DC-Cam initially sought DK-era primary documentation, it began to undertake new field initiatives focused on collecting post-DK materials, particularly field interviews with victims, survivors, witnesses, and perpetrators.

Some of these were linked to DC-Cam's "Promoting Accountability" project, which also began in 2000. Drawing on the biographical information found in documentary sources, DC-Cam staffers interviewed former Khmer Rouge as well as survivors. By 2007, they had conducted over 10,000 interviews.[29] Like *Searching for the Truth*, the Accountability project was meant to serve a truth-seeking function, as people on the local level told their DK experiences.

Such stories increasingly became central to DC-Cam's work. In his editorial, Chhang stated that he is still his mother's "messenger." Instead of gathering a payment or communication related to her gem business, he now collects "the truth of genocide history" for her and other survivors.[30]

Chhang says that he was changed by such encounters, just as his life was transformed by DK. His DK experiences left him with unanswered questions echoing those asked by other Cambodians. Why did his sister die such a horrible death? Why was he tortured? Why did his family suffer so much? They are the same sorts of questions Cambodians ask him today. Chhang regards the "need to find answers"—for himself, for his mother, and for Cambodian survivors—as his "calling."[31]

His experiences also left him angry and desiring revenge. In 1995, he recalls being enraged as he drove to his DK village.[32] "I could hear nothing but the wind," he recalls.[33] He found the man and others who had been in charge and revealed that he lived there during DK. The man, Chhoung, didn't remember him. Chhoung, who had seemed so powerful, was old, thin, and poor. He acknowledged that many people had died, while contending, like the ECCC accused, that "Decisions came from the top down and I obeyed."

---

[28] The following draws on Chhang 2000b.

[29] Documentation Center of Cambodia, "Promoting Accountability," undated (http://www.d.dccam.org).

[30] Chhang 2000b, 2.   [31] Chhang 2008, 2.

[32] This story is recounted in Eads n.d. On Youk's anger and desire for revenge, see also Chhang 2005c, 5; Chhang 2005a, 7.

[33] Youk Chhang, e-mail correspondence, Monday, July 23, 2012.

Chhang has returned to the village several times. He now views both Chhoung and himself differently. He found, to his surprise, that Chhoung "was actually not a bad man; he was simply a man who did bad things because the revolution promised him a better life and society. And it also helped me to learn that revenge was not the answer, as it would not bring back what I or anyone else had lost."[34]

He has found happiness in "doing research and seeking answers ... research sets me free when I suddenly discover a piece of truth." It also helps "heal my anger by moving me toward an understanding of how Cambodians [like Chhoung] could commit so many atrocities." In some respects, DC-Cam's work is premised upon a similar assumption: it is only by "searching for the truth" that one may be able to move on.

After meeting many people like Chhoung, Chhang realized the line between the lower-level perpetrators and victims is often thin. "They are us, and we are them," he has stated.[35] This is not the case, however, for Khmer Rouge leaders who he believes must be held accountable.

The ability to forgive varies from person to person, depending on their perspective and experiences. Several years ago, for example, Chhoung and his DK deputy Choap biked to Phnom Penh to ask forgiveness from Chhang's family. He brought meat and bananas as a gift. No one in his family, except his mother, was able to forgive Chhoung. Now a devout Buddhist, she "said it was enough ... and his act put her heart to rest."[36] While Chhang no longer bears malice toward Chhoung, he has not yet forgiven him. For Chhang, it is necessary to have "prosecution before we can ever reach the point of true forgiveness."

Nevertheless, Chhang has continued to return to Chhoung's village where, as in many places in Cambodia today, perpetrators like Chhoung live side by side with their former victims. Recently, Chhang returned to the village to celebrate the completion of a small DC-Cam infrastructure project, which involved building 200 meters of road.[37]

"I built the road there for my mother," Chhang explains, just as much of the work he is "doing at DC-Cam is also for my mother,"[38] even though she had no desire to return to this place where so many family members perished. "She never asked for a road" specifically, he explained, but asked him to somehow "help the villagers. She has two friends still living there and they were base people ... Both of them are [in their] late 70s and go to the pagoda. So I built the road linking their village to the pagoda and ... the rice fields where others can also use the road to go to work."[39]

Chhang said that if the road was dedicated to the members of Chhang's family and others who died during DK, including 300 people in Chhoung's village alone,[40] it was also meant as a symbol of and step toward reconciliation. On the one hand, the road serves to help build up infrastructure in a war-torn community. On the other hand, it is meant to help "rebuild trust and repair wounded communities"

---

[34] Chhang 2005c, 5.   [35] Chhang, "A Survivor Documents Cambodia's Nightmare".
[36] Chhang 2007, 4.   [37] VOA Staff Report 2010.
[38] Youk Chhang, e-mail communication, August 1, 2012.   [39] Ibid.
[40] VOA Staff Report 2010.

and to symbolically bring together former Khmer Rouge like Chhoung and their victims, who will walk together daily on this path, which is called "Reconciliation Road."[41] This sort of conjoining of former victims and perpetrators, or "putting the broken pieces back together," as Chhang sometimes says, was evident in a number of DC-Cam projects.

Indeed, reconciliation became an increasing focus of DC-Cam's activities. It also is linked to DC-Cam's key focus on "justice and memory," which Chhang called the NGO's "twin approach," and one that again operated on two levels, one linked to global justice and human rights, the other to Cambodians on the ground.

Thus, in the preface to a DC-Cam book on reconciliation, Thomas Hammarberg, a key participant in the tribunal negotiations and the United Nations (U.N.) official depicted signing the 2003 Agreement in the Khmer Institute of Democracy (KID) booklet, states that "memory and justice" reflect "the whole purpose of the Documentation Center of Cambodia." It was also part of the broader process of Cambodia "striving toward justice" and to "build a society ruled by law."[42]

If his reading of this DC-Cam "purpose" captured a dimension of the NGO's efforts in this regard, ones that accorded with the transitional justice imaginary, Hammarberg did not discuss the second key aspect: the personal search for the truth that Chhang introduced when he took over DC-Cam in 1997. Chhang stressed the duality of DC-Cam's "twin approach" and how it operated "in parallel" to the tribunal.

As illustrated by his second *Searching for the Truth* editorial, "Memory," Chhang viewed this local dimension of memory as deeply personal. "In the Cambodian context," he said, discussing his many conversations with survivors, "memory is like a shadow. It's with you, it belongs to you. It's part of you though you can't see it. Sometimes it's in front, sometimes it's behind you."[43] This notion of the shadow and memory has Buddhist connotations, such as a well-known saying that "the shadow follows the body" (*sramaol antul tam bran*) in the sense that one's past actions condition the future. Chhang also viewed memory as critical to "restoring the power of imagination among the survivors," a critical endeavor linked both to "Breaking the Silence" and the Living Documents Project.[44]

Living Documents and KRT outreach

DC-Cam's KRT outreach work emerged as the NGO was entering a new phase that increasingly emphasized community engagement, one that started in 2000 with the launch of the magazine and Promoting Accountability project that accelerated in 2003 after the agreement to hold the tribunal had been reached. In contrast to the past-orientation of the initial documentation phase, this new phase was more present-oriented, emphasizing a more direct connection with the population as the tribunal became a reality.

---

[41] Nelson 2010, 59.   [42] Hammarberg, in Linton 2004, i–ii.
[43] Skype interview with Youk Chhang, December 15, 2016.   [44] Ibid.

It also reflected DC-Cam's independence from the Cambodia Genocide Project and attunement to local concerns and ways of understanding that diverged transitional justice imaginary discourses regarding justice, democratization, accountability, human rights, and rule of law. If these ideas can still be found in DC-Cam texts, especially in English, DC-Cam often reframes and vernacularizes these concepts in ways that have more resonance with the Cambodian population, particularly those in the countryside. "Breaking the Silence," as we shall see, illustrates this point.

DC-Cam staffers, even more than staff at CSD, KID, and other KRT intermediary organizations, have received foreign degrees and trained abroad, interfacing frequently with international civil society, legal personnel, diplomats, and scholars. Like Chhang, these staffers were well-positioned to translate juridical notions into terms villagers may understand, a goal of DC-Cam's main KRT outreach project, "Living Documents."

In 2005, as preparations for the tribunal were commencing, Chhang wrote a *Searching for the Truth* article outlining three DC-Cam initiatives related to outreach.[45] The first, the "Victims of Torture" project (2003–2009), sought both to document the experience of and assess the mental health of victims and perpetrators living near rural security centers. The Living Documents Project (2004–present) began the following year. That same year, DC-Cam opened its Public Information Room, to facilitate access to their holdings. DC-Cam's Genocide Education Project (2004–present), in turn, sought to reintroduce education about DK, which had begun to be largely erased from Cambodia's school texts during the second transition.

As the ECCC commenced, DC-Cam revamped pre-existing programs and established new ones to do outreach activities. The Living Documents program began bringing large groups of Cambodians to learn about and discuss the court, a process that often included visits to the ECCC, Tuol Sleng, and Choeung Ek. DC-Cam also established Response Team (2007–present) and Cambodia Tribunal Monitoring projects starting in 2008.

The origins of the Living Documents Project (LDP) dates to 2002, when the U.N. was threatening to pull out of negotiations to hold a tribunal. Chhang was dismayed that the voice of survivors was being left out of the process, so he decided to launch an initiative foregrounding survivors. "So I thought that besides the millions of documents I have collected," Chhang said, "I need the living documents, the people themselves. That's how the [LDP] was named. It aligned with our [documentation mission]."[46]

Meanwhile, reporters, researchers, and U.N. officials kept asking if DC-Cam had sufficient documentation for a tribunal. He began to respond, "In this country, everyone wants to be a witness. There's plenty besides all the hundreds of thousands of pages of paper documents. There are millions of living documents."[47] Even before the project was named, Chhang criss-crossed Canada in the midst of winter to generate interest. While successful in raising awareness, the Canadian government ultimately

---

[45] Chhang 2005b. For a list of DC-Cam projects see: DC-Cam, "Projects," undated (http://www.d.dccam.org).
[46] Skype interview with Youk Chhang, December 14, 2016.   [47] Ibid.

did not provide hoped-for funding for outreach. Instead, DC-Cam received a grant of $800,000 from the Patrick J. Leahy War Victims Fund.[48]

This funding enabled DC-Cam to launch the LDP in February 2006. Few Cambodians, Chhang explained in an essay, had "the means to obtain information on the forthcoming Khmer Rouge tribunal," especially DK "survivors, who are often poor and illiterate, and whose educations were interrupted by the regime."[49] Despite the importance of justice for healing, Chhang's essay states, there were no significant "plans to keep the public informed." The LDP would fill this gap by bringing community representatives to Phnom Penh to attend the trials. In doing so, the LDP would "build momentum for democracy in Cambodia by allowing participants to serve as surrogate witnesses and 'judges' at the tribunals; hold open, participatory discussions; [and make] people aware of their 'right to know.'"[50]

If the first LDP tours commenced in 2006, the project itself was modified in response to events at the court, funding, and institutional priorities. The first phase of the LDP focused on raising awareness about and understanding of the tribunal and involved bringing groups of up to 500 people to Phnom Penh. Over 5,500 people participated in Phase 1, which concluded in March 2009.[51] DC-Cam targeted over 1,000 commune chiefs as well as minority groups such as Muslim Chams and Kampuchea Kraom. In late 2007, LDP participants were also offered assistance in filing complaints, an initiative that would become part of DC-Cam's parallel "Victims Participation Project" (2008–present).[52]

Phase 2 of the LDP commenced in April 2008 with the aim of bringing smaller groups of up to fifty Phase 1 participants, especially respected figures such as commune and village chiefs, to Phnom Penh to attend trial proceedings. If the first phase was focused more on awareness-raising, Phase 2 sought to build on this basis to increase knowledge and situate the participants, as local leaders, to disseminate information about the ECCC in their communities.[53] To support these activities, the LDP began to conduct village outreach forums in 2009. These forums would become the focus of a third phase of the project in which ECCC verdicts were screened and discussed in villages.[54]

The LDP outreach programs had a roughly similar sequence, one that other NGOs and the Public Affairs Section (PAS) would use as a model. A typical tour would begin with legal training "on how to monitor a hearing, witness protection, defense, the legal terms likely to be heard, legal concepts ... a summation of the arguments that will likely be put forward, and a profile of the person on trial [whose hearing they would attend],"[55] and Q&A sessions. During the next two days, participants visited Tuol Sleng and Choueng Ek and attended an ECCC session. The LDP team then selected the homes of some participants for follow-up village forums.[56]

---

[48] Ibid.   [49] Chhang 2005b, 3.   [50] Ibid, 4.

[51] DeFalco 2010, 3; Pentelovitch 2009, 1.

[52] Pentelovitch 2009, 1. See also "Victim Participation Project (VPA)," Documentation Center of Cambodia website (http://www.d.dccam.org).

[53] DeFalco 2010, 3; Pentelovitch 2009, 1.   [54] DeFalco 2010, 3.

[55] Pentelovitch 2009, 3.   [56] Ibid, 4.

If, in contrast to the PAS inreach tours, the DC-Cam ECCC outreach initiative involved more preparation and engagement, LDP participants sometimes also had trouble understanding the complexities of law—though this was often less true of officials like commune chiefs than rural villagers with less formal education. LDP staff had to mediate this divide, translating juridical discourses in terms more comprehensible.

The two main project leaders, Savina Sirik and Ly Sok-Kheang, both of whom had graduate degrees from abroad and extensive international training,[57] noted the challenges in explaining complicated legal concepts to villagers. Like other NGOs, the DC-Cam staffers also used simplification even as they tried to adhere to the legal sense of the concepts in question.[58] Ly told me that he often used comparison. The role of a judge, he might tell them, was like a third-party mediator, such as a highly respected person who is well educated "so they can see what is right and what is wrong."[59] As noted in the last chapter, this idea of discerning right and wrong is in keeping with Buddhist notions of clear sight and right understanding. DC-Cam also sought to create outreach materials, such as informational booklets, that were easy to read and films about villagers and everyday life.

This was also part of the reason that the LDP tried to integrate performances of "Breaking the Silence" into their outreach program. When I met Chhang in 2014, he discussed at length the efforts to create a drama that would appeal to such rural villagers.

Whereas DC-Cam had long focused on the tribunal, the organization more recently began looking beyond the ECCC. DC-Cam's documentation and outreach work continue but the NGO is increasingly concerned with its memory and education efforts, including the creation of an academic program, as well as public policy and transnational issues such as genocide and human rights in Southeast Asia, justice legacy, sustainability, environment, and reconstruction.

To do so, DC-Cam has begun transforming into the Sleuk Rith Institute (SRI), which aims to become the leading genocide museum, research, and public policy institute in Asia.[60] The establishment of Sleuk Rith reflects DC-Cam's increasing engagement with regional and global concerns even as it retains its longstanding focus on research and documentation as well as its "twin approach" of "justice and memory" in the Cambodian context. As part of these efforts, DC-Cam has also recently launched the Anlong Veng Peace Center, a community reconciliation, education, and human rights initiative located in the heart of a major former Khmer Rouge zone. It was amidst the backdrop of change at DC-Cam and at the ECCC that Chhang and I met at the restaurant on the banks of the Tonle Sap river in 2014.

---

[57] DeFalco 2010, 7.   [58] Ibid, 13–14.
[59] Interview with Ly Sok-Kheang, Phnom Penh, August 14, 2009.
[60] "About," Sleuk Rith website (http://www.cambodiasri.org).

Breaking the Silence

Origins and hybridity

"I lost that one," Chhang told me as he finished explaining the origin of the title "Breaking the Silence." "You have to lose a little bit, win a little bit," he continued, before ending with a chuckle, "But the villagers never call it "Breaking the Silence." They call it Pol Pot stories![61]

Chhang had worked closely with Director Annemarie Prins throughout the creative and production process. Prins had originally decided to write the play after being invited by Amrita to give a 2004 workshop in Phnom Penh, one focused on the work of Samuel Beckett and in which performers from "Breaking the Silence" participated.[62] During the workshop, which sought to "introduce six actors/teachers ... to the world of western contemporary theater,"[63] actors recounted personal stories about DK, which formed the basis of a first play, "3 Years, 8 Months, 20 Days." Because of the 2006 play's limited run and audience, Prins explained, "I realized I had to make a second play. This new production would need to be made to tour throughout the country and deal not only with history, but also with the question of how to go on."[64]

In partnership with Amrita and DC-Cam, Prins returned to Cambodia in January 2008 to do research. Among other things, she interviewed Chhang several times, who helped arrange for her and her Dutch dramaturge to conduct interviews with victims and perpetrators in the countryside. The seven stories in "Breaking the Silence" are a composite, even if at times they reflect particular stories.

The first scene, "A Story about Divided People," which focuses on a former Khmer Rouge perpetrator, is loosely based on an interview Prins did in Takeo with the former deputy head of the Kraing Ta Chan prison camp, a focus of Case 002.[65] Centered on the experiences of actor Chhon Sina, the second scene, "Nurse," tells the story of a young girl who witnessed her sick father die after receiving an injection from a callous teenage nurse at a Khmer Rouge hospital.[66] Other scenes mix the details of different stories to a greater extent, including two (Scenes 4 and 5) touching on Chhang's experiences.[67]

"Breaking the Silence" was a fusion from its inception. Prins and her small team from the Netherlands brought understandings of contemporary theater. Her Brechtian approach was illustrated by the play's economy, such as its spare set and costume design, open stage, gender-crossing acting, and restricted movements amplifying the importance of text and symbolism.[68]

---

[61] Author interview, Youk Chhang, Phnom Penh, March 22, 2014.
[62] Prins 2009, "A Note from the Director." For an overview of the origins and production of "Breaking the Silence," see Chng 2010.
[63] Prins 2009, "A Note from the Director."   [64] Ibid.
[65] Author interview, Suon Bun Rith, Phnom Penh, March 22, 2014.
[66] Men Kimseng 2010.
[67] Author interview, Youk Chhang, Phnom Penh, March 22, 2014.   [68] Chng 2010, 68.

Figure 9.1 Scene from "Breaking the Silence," August 8, 2010. Photo by James Mizerski, *courtesy of DC-Cam/SRI.*

From the start, however, these contemporary theater techniques and concepts were blended with Cambodian theatrical conventions. Amrita provided expertise in this regard. Founded in 2003, Amrita seeks both to "help revive and preserve the wide spectrum of Cambodia's traditional performing arts," which had been greatly diminished due to the DK deaths of many artists, and to be a "pioneer" by "creating Cambodian contemporary dance and theater" and "ushering their country's ancient performing arts heritage into the future."[69]

This attempt to blend traditional Cambodian and contemporary performing arts was evident in almost every aspect of the play, ranging from the incorporation of traditional Khmer music and dance to the use of a monkey dancer (though without a mask).[70] To this end, the production team bore in mind throughout its goal of creating a play that would be presented to a broad Cambodian audience, including rural villagers. Accordingly, there were many attempts to make what was—given the influence of modern theater and Brechtian economy—inevitably going to be a somewhat strange performance, also appear familiar. The set, for example, was simple and included everyday objects and images, such as a back stage "wall" made from rice sacks sewn together. The minimal feel was also supposed to suggest the rice fields during DK, an effect amplified by a background of "grass" (made out of plastic twine).[71]

---

[69] "About us," Amrita Performing Arts website (http://amritaperformingarts.org).
[70] See Chng 2010.
[71] Author interview, Suon Bun Rith, Phnom Penh, March 22, 2014.

DC-Cam contributed to the project in many ways, such as by providing Prins with research materials and helping to arrange interviews in the countryside, including meetings with roughly a hundred Khmer Rouge child soldiers.[72] Once the play was completed, DC-Cam was directly involved in coordinating the community outreach, audience dialogues, and performances, the first of which took place on February 21 and 22, 2009 in Phnom Penh followed by eight performances in the countryside over the next two weeks (February 25 to March 11).[73] Eventually, DC-Cam wove the performance into its KRT outreach, as illustrated by the ETGE program. DC-Cam also subsequently helped arrange for "Breaking the Silence" to be broadcast on radio.

"Pol Pot stories"

DC-Cam also played a central role in the translation of the script into Khmer. If Sok Kunty was officially listed as the translator, Chhang was heavily involved in the process, interacting intensively with Prins. They were both in agreement that the play needed to be presented in a manner that would appeal to rural Cambodians, though they nevertheless had different understandings that had to be negotiated. "You win a little bit," he repeated several times during our meeting. "You lose a little." But, ultimately, if "Breaking the Silence" is usually read in one way in English, one that dovetails with a number of assumptions of the transitional justice imaginary, it had quite different connotations in Khmer.

As someone who had grown up in Cambodia but spent part of his youth abroad, Chhang was well aware of these two "flows" of meaning in "Breaking the Silence," and he himself switched between them at times. But, with Prins's general agreement, he remained intent on rendering dialogue and action that would resonate in the countryside. "I deleted all of the English thinking!" Chhang told me. "I wanted it very simple so the people would have their own drama. And [Prins] agreed. I edited all the language to make sure it was Khmer language, Khmer tone, Khmer story. Everything's just so Khmer," reflecting the Khmer "spirit and soul."[74] He added, "For every word, I used local [terms], the old farmer language."

This process led to points of disagreement, particularly because for Prins the play was ultimately about "breaking the silence"—in the teleological sense of the transitional justice imaginary—to bring about reconciliation and healing in both the individual (coping, trauma) and social senses (rebuilding and transforming shattered communities). While Chhang understood Prins's position, the title did not make much sense in Khmer. " 'Breaking the Silence' is English. It's not Khmer," Chhang told me. "If you translate the words 'breaking the silence' it doesn't fit. The Khmer is Pol Pot stories. That's what people call it."[75]

Almost all the Khmer speakers I asked about the title agreed. Some, like Chhang, noted that the term used to translate "silence" (*sngnop sngat*) even had Buddhist

---

72 Youk Chhang, e-mail communication, December 5, 2016.   73 Ibid; Chng 2010, 61.
74 Author interview, Youk Chhang, Phnom Penh, March 22, 2014.   75 Ibid.

valences, suggesting the positive state of calm that comes from meditation and letting go of anger. Civil party Chhin Navy had highlighted this sought-after state
when she testified about how she "calmed" (*sngnop*) her heart and extinguished the
"fire [of my anger]" toward her sister. This positive valence stands in opposition to
the title's English-language connotation of a traumatic post-conflict "silence" that
represses and impedes healing—as illustrated by the KID booklet's depiction of
Uncle San.

Ultimately, Chhang relented due to Prins's insistence on sticking to this English
phrase linked to the transitional justice imaginary. "So I lose," Chhang said. "I gave
it to Annemarie Prins. But I told her, 'you will lose to me when you go to the village.'"[76] Consequently, during the performances, the official title "Breaking the
Silence" (*tomleay pheap sngop sngat*) was used. "But the people don't pay attention
because they don't get it."

Similarly, Chhang added, the dramatic ending (at least in English) of the play,
where Vutha intones, "Speak, speak, speak" (*niyeay, niyeay, niyeay*) also didn't make
much sense in Khmer. "That's [another] one I lost," Chhang said with a chuckle.
"That phrase is foreign. I told her, 'people won't get it.' She said, 'no, it has to be
there.' I said, 'Okay. Fine.'"[77] Illustrating by humming the Khmer, Chhang
explained that Cambodians focused on the ring-like sound made by enunciating
the Khmer term for "speak" (*niyeay*) three times in a row. "She didn't believe me,"
Chhang continued, chuckling again as he noted that Cambodians focused on the
sound of these words, not the meaning suggested by the English.

Disposition

These sorts of misunderstandings continued even as the play commenced production in February 2009. On February 21 and 22, the opening performances were held
in a more traditional performance space and attended by a broad audience, including Sambath. Chhang said that, on the first night, he was "so touched I couldn't
even speak" afterward.[78] Then the plays moved to the countryside, beginning with
a performance in Kompong Cham. Amrita sent an advance team to liaise with local
officials and prepare for the performance.[79]

If the organizers had hoped for 300 people to attend the first performance on the
evening of February 25, 2009, they were pleased that over 500 attended, including "about 100 children seated on woven mats, 250 adults seated in chairs, and
another 200 adults standing to watch the play" as well as thirty-five Norwegian
students.[80] In contrast to the Phnom Penh performances, which accorded with protocols of audience silence and applause, the Kompong Cham staging was much
looser as people brought candy and other food and were eating and chatting during
the performance.[81]

---

[76] Ibid.   [77] Ibid.   [78] Youk Chhang, e-mail communication, December 6, 2016.
[79] Author interview, Youk Chhang, Phnom Penh, March 22, 2014.
[80] Ser 2009, 49–50. See also author interview, Suon Bun Rith, Phnom Penh, March 22, 2014.
[81] Author interview, Youk Chhang, Phnom Penh, March 22, 2014.

Not familiar with rural Cambodian conventions, Prins, who also didn't receive flowers as customary in modern performance protocols, was upset afterward. Chhang spoke with her, explaining that the "people had embraced your performance, the people took over," which was what she sought.[82] As subsequent performances were held, Prins became more comfortable with the rural performance conventions and appreciated the engagement. "So she broke the silence herself,"[83] Chhang said, noting how this experience in the countryside increased her cultural sensitivity—even if she retained her ideas about the need to "break the silence" to help people deal with trauma and reconcile.

Indeed, these two interpretive tracks—one global and reflecting the teleological assumptions of the transitional justice imaginary, the other local and enmeshed with the "bushy undergrowth" of the Cambodian context to use Antoine Berman's phrase—resulted in often divergent readings of "Breaking the Silence." This point is illustrated by the English-language focus on a disposition, the reconciliation (and interlinked ideas of "closure" and "healing") that are assumed to result from "breaking the silence."

The term "disposition" suggests both arrangement and inclination, including an orientation toward the other. The term also connotes order and, as illustrated by its Latin etymological root *disponere*, a root it shares with the word "dispose," the "action of getting rid of or making over."[84] Along these lines, in the transitional justice imaginary discourses reflected by Prins's insistence on keeping the title and ending of the play, reconciliation suggests a new arrangement in which post-conflict interpersonal tensions are "disposed of" through the creation of a new arrangement, a liberal democratic society characterized by, to invoke the often-repeated goals of the ECCC, justice, national reconciliation, stability, peace, and healing.

Reconciliation

During our 2014 meeting, Chhang discussed the idea of reconciliation at length, and it became apparent that everyday Cambodian understandings of "reconciliation," and the relationship of talk and silence to it, diverged from the model asserted by the justice facade. In contrast to Judeo-Christian confession discourses and related contemporary therapeutic assumptions about the importance of verbal speech to heal psychic trauma and interpersonal rupture—ones highlighted at the South African Truth and Reconciliation Commission[85]—Cambodians place more emphasis on non-verbal behaviors and may positively value silence. Indeed, for some, dialogue is even viewed as dangerous in the sense that it may antagonize others, lead to loss of face and shame, and be at odds with Buddhist norms of forgetting and non-self.

Chhang often highlighted such differences through real-life stories or by pointing to scenes in "Breaking the Silence." For Cambodians, Chhang noted, non-verbal

---

[82] Ibid.   [83] Ibid.   [84] "Disposition," *Shorter OED* 2007.
[85] Moon 2009; Ross 2003; Wilson 2001.

behaviors were more important than spoken behaviors. He pointed to Scene 6, the story about Chea, a thirteen-year-old girl who was raped by Khmer Rouge soldiers and subsequently ostracized in her community, as an example. "Now, thirty years later," one of Chea's neighbors states, "A silent woman./Nobody comes near her./Nobody talks to her./People turn away when she passes." Then the woman sees Chea and the scene concludes,

My heart races, I sweat.
I have to soothe my heart. I cannot bear the guilt (*aramm khos chkong*) anymore.
Slowly I take one step toward her. Two steps.
"Chea, will you forgive (*soum toas*) me, please.
Will you hold my heart and forgive me.
Please come with me so we can drink a cup of tea together."
Maybe I am too late.
Tomorrow I will try again.[86]

For English speakers, this scene reads as if, filled with guilt, the neighbor apologizes and seeks forgiveness. Parts of the sequence don't translate well, including the emphasis on "guilt" (the concept of "guilt" [*aram khos chkong*] is difficult to translate and is here rendered as something along the lines of "very improper feeling") and the idea that "guilt" is unbearable and drives a person to apologize, a confessional act ideally leading to forgiveness and reconciliation.

In this scene, as in two other scenes where a direct apology is made, non-verbal behaviors are, for the Cambodian village audience, more important than formal verbal apology. All three of these scenes feature body language in which the people offering the apology respectfully place their hands together (*sampeah*) and bend their head and bodies (*aon*), sometimes even prostrating on their knees, while making an apology (*at toas, soum toas*) with eyes lowered.

The people receiving the apology, in turn, convey their openness and willingness to forgive not by saying, "apology accepted" or "I forgive you," but through subtle actions, such as looking at or away from the person offering the apology or by accepting or not accepting small gifts proffered, such as the tea the neighbor presents to Chea. Such actions are also influenced by relative social standing, including age, gender, and status.

"In Khmer," Chhang told me as we discussed the scene, we "don't use the word 'forgiveness.'"[87] Instead, the idea of apology and forgiveness was translated with terms like *soum toas* ("forgive me" or "excuse me," literally "please guilt"). "The moment you use the word 'forgiveness,'" Chhang added, "the moment you use the word "'apology,' you're already disconnected from the original meaning in Khmer," which is linked to body language and culturally appropriate behavior. Indeed, in rural Cambodian villages, apologies are sometimes considered inappropriate and even threatening, exposing the parties to a loss of face and possibly stirring old

---

[86] Prins 2009, Scene 6.
[87] Author interview, Youk Chhang, Phnom Penh, March 22, 2014.

grievances. Instead, remorse was better expressed through polite behavior, bodily posture, and the performance of good deeds contributing to a community.[88]

As illustrated by the ending of Chea's story, none of the scenes in "Breaking the Silence" conclude with clear resolution. Prins, Chhang explained, sought to leave the ending open to provoke thought. "Prins challenges us in a good way in that we don't tell the answer to the audience. They have to think," Chhang said. "In Khmer performance, they usually give the answer … You don't have a monkey [dancer] without a face. You don't have women performing a man's role. You don't have the same actors in all the stories." He continued, "It's a challenge. It's a provocation to allow people to break the silence, to ask questions … It's a blend between the two cultures."[89]

For Chhang, then, "breaking the silence" referred to a questioning or consideration of ruptured social relationships, not a straightforward movement from trauma and social dysfunction to healing and reconciliation as suggested by the justice facade. Indeed, Chhang was critical of this foreign assumption that reconciliation proceeds in "an absolute direction and that [there] is the only one way to forgive and apologize. It's not an absolute" and one could "do more harm than good when you say, 'You have to meet. Please talk and forgive.'"[90] Thus, if an English speaker assumed that "breaking the silence" and reconciliation would occur once Chea or the other characters being supplicated dialogued and then accepted the proffered apology, Khmer speakers understood apology and forgiveness differently.

On the one hand, silence was not just a negative state, but a culturally-appropriate disposition toward others, especially in situations where talk could further aggravate social relations and lead to conflict and even violence. On the other hand, when someone chose to "break the silence," their path forward could lead in a number of directions, including coming full circle back to a state of non-reconciled silence or a silence that accorded with Buddhist notions of forgiveness and "letting go" of negative effects like vindictiveness, malice, and anger.

Based on his years of research in Cambodia as well as his own experience, Chhang observed a pattern in which "breaking the silence," when chosen, could lead in two key directions after a period of "testing." In such situations, he said, "there are two ways to reconcile. One is to be reconnected, one is to be silent." Even when there was "reconnection," the "broken pieces" no longer fit together the same way. It was always hard, he said, more so for the victims.

For example, Prak Khan, a S-21 interrogator who testified during the Duch trial, apologized to the family of Nae Non, a female prisoner whose confessions he had extracted, perhaps sexually abusing her. After his apology, Nae Non's parents walked away without saying anything. Later, they told Chhang they didn't know how to respond: "If they say, 'Yes, I forgive you,' then they feel as if they insult the death of their own daughter. If they don't say anything, then they are very greedy. They're

---

[88] See, for example, Ly 2014, 236.
[89] Author interview, Youk Chhang, Phnom Penh, March 22, 2014.   [90] Ibid.

Buddhist. They must forgive those who apologize, who want to do good."[91] Prak Khan, in contrast, was thereafter "free now to move on with his life. He's happy."

For Chhang, this situation illustrated how victims had to sacrifice more when an apology was given. In this case, a reconciliation of a sort took place, but it was one that involved not forgiveness and the acceptance of an apology but a "letting go" and "being apart." This was not the same as being silent but a breaking of the silence and testing that leads back to silence. "It's like a full circle," Chhang said. "You test it. You break the silence. Then you realize one must sacrifice. Who? Should [the parents] sacrifice for the sake of Prak Khan? He may apologize. But then the one who is most reconciled is Prak Khan."[92] Such situations were not simple moments of forgiveness and reconciliation, but "very, very demanding" processes in which the parties should be given "more than one choice rather than just giving an apology. It's too absolute."

Chhang viewed his disposition towards Chhoung similarly. "I have been doing this for my mother," Chhang said about his work in his former DK village. "I don't go there with anger. I don't go with revenge. Because my mother would not want that to happen. So I have 'let go' for a long time, sacrificing my own reconciliation approach for the sake of my mother."[93]

If he had "let go"—especially after finally returning to the site of the DK prison where he was held—Chhang had not reconciled with Chhoung. "They tortured me. They put me in prison. They made me suffer," Chhang explained. "Even though they apologize, would it be enough? If I'm honest with myself, it won't be enough. Because the scars are still with me ... and his words of apology won't take away the scars of genocide."[94] Doing so would require a sacrifice he was not willing to make. Instead, he came "full circle," returning to a position of silence after breaking the silence and "testing."

As these examples illustrate, Chhang saw the reconciliation process in Cambodia as something that rarely proceeded in a straightforward manner, instead often being circular and even going backwards to a state of silence. In part, the difficulty of reconciling was related to the different sets of expectations of perpetrators and victims, with victims desiring, as we saw in the last chapter, a proper "return." On the perpetrator side, Chhang said, moving his hands closer and further apart to illustrate, "a very low bar" is set in such situations while the victims have high expectations about "how much the perpetrator should do to compensate or pay back [for] what they did ... Because the perpetrator sets the bar so low, they usually met expectations,"[95] in contrast to the victims who were left dissatisfied.

A person like Chhoung or Prak Khan therefore might use an apology "as a way to bring some closure to himself," creating a boundary of a sort since the apology marked a new moment upon which they now focused—instead of the original acts for which they had apologized and that were, in a sense, masked or even erased from view by the apology. In this sense, the sorts of teleological apologies linked to the transitional justice imaginary could mask both the complexities of reconciliation and the acts committed.

---

[91] Ibid.　　[92] Ibid.　　[93] Ibid.　　[94] Ibid.　　[95] Ibid.

Given the difficulty of reconciliation and the different expectations of victims and perpetrators, Chhang viewed legal justice as an important way to help address victim expectations, even if it had shortcomings. On the positive side, a court provided the victims with recognition both during the legal process itself and through the verdict, which, like the perpetrator's apology, could serve as a sort of symbolic boundary to which they could at times return instead of always going back to their suffering.

For Chhang, this was particularly important given the amount of time that had passed. Justice might help victims "deal with the past" and bring some relief, even if it only "helped a little bit" due to the brutality of genocide. "A final judgement doesn't bring full closure," Chhang said, though "it helps deal with the past, ... contributes in a small way so people can move on."[96]

But, in contrast to the grandiose claims often made about courts like the ECCC, the justice provided was limited. Part of the problem, Chhang said with an ironic laugh, was that "justice is always late, the lawyers late. They always arrive after the crimes have been committed ... The victims feel it is unjust that they suffered and people were killed and nobody cared."[97]

Even when justice finally did arrive, it always fell short. "It can never be a full justice in terms of what the victim expected," Chhang said. And, critically—and in contrast to the claims of the transitional justice imaginary—justice got in the way of reconciliation. "Someone wins, someone loses," Chhang stated. "It's completely wrong to say that the court is a place to reconcile." Instead, it created a barrier between perpetrators and victims.

The Duch case illustrated this point as the legal proceedings hindered the building of trust between Duch and the victims. As we saw in previous chapters, many civil parties believed that Duch was insincere, saying only what was needed to reduce his sentence. This perception was amplified in part because of his perceived arrogance and manner of apology,[98] as Duch offered words of remorse not matched by the non-verbal conventions of prostration that should accompany apologies and that were enacted in "Breaking the Silence."

If, in Cambodia, Buddhist norms emphasize letting go, the court did not allow for a process of communication and trust-building because the legal proceedings had created "a barrier between Duch and his victims. Clearly the court is not a place to reconcile. Otherwise trust would have been built between Duch and his victims." Chhang added, "Duch may be sincere, but the people just don't believe it. Why? Because the legal proceedings limit communication."[99]

If many victims found it difficult to accept Duch's apology, others were able to do so, often because of Buddhist faith. This was evident in Chhin Navy's testimony. She pitied Duch but believed he, like her sister, would ultimately receive karmic justice. This Buddhist attitude had also influenced Chhang's mother's acceptance of Chhoung's apology. As was the case in the scene with Chea, Chhoung slightly prostrated his body and made an offering. "He apologized to her," Chhang said.

---

[96] Ibid.   [97] Ibid.   [98] See also Ledgerwood 2009.
[99] Author interview, Youk Chhang, Phnom Penh, March 22, 2014.

"Her body language showed that she accepted it. She smiled and held his hand. They bowed."[100] However, he noted that she had never returned to Chhoung's village.[101]

Such interactions not only occur among the living, but also between the living and the dead. Ghosts and the spirits of the dead, for example, are a presence throughout "Breaking the Silence." In Scene 3, a story of the "betrayal and eternal guilt" of "Mr. Rithy" (who gave names while being tortured), Mr. Rithy states, "I think of the dead every day. I pray to the gods that if I denounced them, their spirits will not suffer the consequence." When asked what he would say if one of the dead came back to life, Mr. Rithy replies, "I would bow deep down and ask for forgiveness."[102]

The next scene ends with a song about "The Howling Dead," while Scene 7 includes a song about supernatural witches (*ap*) who at night send their head flying about "with their intestines dangling behind./Their tongues lick blood and pus./They eat the flesh of dead bodies."[103]

This scene ends with a former Khmer Rouge child soldier encouraging his former comrade to join him in praying to the dead at Tuol Sleng, where "I make offerings and ask their spirits to forgive me (*apay toas*)." Chhang said that such references to the spirits of the dead were one of the ways he sought to translate the play in terms with which rural villagers would be familiar.[104]

Such transactions with the dead were a constant presence in the background of the court, ones that, as we have seen, at times burst into the foreground. If perpetrators might make offerings to appease the spirits of the dead and seek their forgiveness, the relatives of those who had been killed, like Nae Non's parents, might also fear that, if they accepted apologies offered by perpetrators, the spirits of their loved ones would be angered, perhaps becoming restless and even afflicting them in dreams, through sickness, or with bad fortune.

Currents and eddies

Transform the River of Blood into a River of Reconciliation.
A River of Responsibility.[105]

For Chhang, these lines, sung just before the last line of "Breaking the Silence" in which the audience is told to "speak, speak, speak," formed the critical ending of the play. In Cambodia, rivers, and the water they contain, are critical to everyday life and survival and sometimes provide the basis for powerful metaphors, including the idea of "crossing the river" to describe childbirth. Khmer Rouge art and song, in turn, were filled with symbolism and references to blood.

This call for transformation at the end of "Breaking the Silence" played into both of these understandings. The "river of blood," Chhang explained, referred to "those

[100] Ibid.   [101] Skype interview with Youk Chhang, December 15, 2016.
[102] Prins 2009, Scene 3.   [103] Ibid, Scene 7.
[104] Author interview, Youk Chhang, Phnom Penh, March 22, 2014.
[105] Prins 2009, Epilogue.

who spilled the blood. I want them to be responsible and then to reconcile. So it comes back to justice and memory ... It's just put in an artistic way."[106] He liked the song so much that he introduced it into the DC-Cam Genocide Education Project. He hoped that it would one day become a national song.

If justice and memory offered a path to reconciliation, it was just one of many paths that might be taken in post-conflict Cambodia, ones that led some to inter-act with former perpetrators and adversaries, others to move forward in a semi-reconciled state of "letting go," still more to remain in, or come full circle and return to, a state of silence. While Chhang wanted people to "break the silence" and test these possible outcomes, he was well aware that, for many Cambodians, especially those deeply Buddhist, calmness and quiet were positively valued dispositions that also offered a legitimate orientation toward others, including the spirits of the dead. Indeed, some Cambodians viewed overt speech, including apology, as threatening to the social order and status. And when chosen, rapprochement was better under-taken through non-verbal cues and positive social actions.

These kinds of everyday understandings were largely pushed out of sight in the English-language rendering of "Breaking the Silence," where the highlighted end-ing was "speak, speak, speak." For rural Cambodian audiences, these words were insignificant and made little sense, appreciated more for the ringing sound made by intoning the word "speak" three times. In English-language discourse, in contrast, this word was critical, linked to justice facade assumptions that the path from con-flict and trauma to reconciliation is paved by the transformative power of speech operative in the court.

The problem, Chhang noted, is that this view assumes that reconciliation proceeds in a singular "absolute direction," thereby occluding complex local understandings that may operate in very different ways from the linear teleology naturalized in the transitional justice imaginary. Just as the phrase "speak, speak, speak" is heard as a meaningless ringing sound to rural Cambodians, so too do many English speakers fail to understand or even see these "countercurrents" and "eddies" underlying the seeming "justice cascade," ones that pass by unnoticed or are viewed as insignificant background noise of the sort that Chhang made to illustrate how Cambodians hear the ring-like sounds of the last words (*"niyeay, niyeay, niyeay"* / *"speak, speak, speak"*) of "Breaking the Silence": "nnnnnnnyyyyyyyeeeeee".

---

[106] Author interview, Youk Chhang, Phnom Penh, March 22, 2014.

Conclusion

Justice in Translation

Neth Phally (February 28, 2015)

What does international justice mean in Cambodia?

In 2015, I interviewed Neth Phally, the civil party who had prayed to his brother's spirit in court, to ask about his experience of victim participation and understand how he might answer such a question. We met at the Documentation Center of Cambodia (DC-Cam), which had, as part of its Victims Participation Project, assisted with his application. Neth arrived dressed in a worn dress shirt, unbuttoned at the top and bottom, his prosthetic left arm hanging limply at his side.

The injury was the result of being struck by a tree while working at a rubber plantation. When a co-worker told Neth that nearby ditches were used for Democratic Kampuchea executions, Neth thought to himself, "My elder [brother], at Tuol Sleng they killed him and buried him in a mass grave like this, though we don't know how. They also bashed [babies] against tree trunks like the trees in this rubber plantation," an image Vann Nath depicted in a Tuol Sleng painting. "I was distracted, pitying my brother," Neth continued, "so I didn't hear them call out that a tree was falling in time to get out of the way. That's how I had my accident [and injured my arm]."[1]

We ascended a set of stairs to an empty office and sat at a small table. On a wall hung a painting by the well-known Cambodian artist Svay Ken, based on photos Chhang had taken in Northeastern Cambodia and featuring Cambodia's ethnic minority hill tribe groups. I noticed an ECCC (Extraordinary Chambers in the Courts of Cambodia) logo affixed to a bag Neth carried, a gift from the court.

During the Duch case, Neth had been a member of the "DC-Cam group" of civil parties. Neth had also joined as a civil party in Case 002. By this time, the new civil party system was in place, with civil parties representation coordinated by Co-Lead Lawyers. Certain civil parties, including Neth, had been designated as "focal points" who were to assist, explain, and update civil parties living in their area about the court.

This new system of representation solved problems that emerged in Case 001, including repetitiveness and disorganization. Some people, including Chhang, saw the necessity of the new system while lamenting that it distanced civil party participation.[2] Theary Seng was more skeptical, viewing the change as part of the ECCC "farce."

---

[1] Author interview with Neth Phally, Phnom Penh, February 28, 2015.
[2] Skype interview with Youk Chhang, December 15, 2016.

The Justice Facade: Trials of Transition in Cambodia. Alexander Laban Hinton. © Alexander Laban Hinton, 2018. Published 2018 by Oxford University Press.

Still others suggested, usually off the record, that the new scheme, in combination with the Cambodian oversight of the Victims Support Section, enabled the government to regulate civil party voice as part of its efforts to control the tribunal. This use of the tribunal suggests how multiple actors within the transitional justice assemblage may seek to appropriate or reframe the proceedings: not just "the international community," foreign states, and the Cambodian government but also local officials, non-governmental organizations (NGOs), their intermediaries, and victims—as well as opposition figures like Seng who deemed the ECCC a show trial.

When I asked how he felt when he testified, Neth replied that, having never before spoken so publically, he was quite scared. His lawyer had reassured him, telling him he had a brave heart and to focus on telling his story. But he was shocked upon entering the courtroom. "I had never before seen a court room, with the judges wearing robes, the seats all arranged for different parties, and the accused person … I was terrified. But I sought to put my thoughts, my fear, my feelings in order."[3]

Upon seeing Duch, Neth said he became furious, but told himself to "calm my heart (*sngop chhett*) and let the court seek justice for us." For Neth, justice consisted of two key things: first, Duch's acknowledgement of the crime he committed against Neth's brother; and second, finding justice on behalf of his brother. It was for this reason that Neth had invited his brother's spirit to enter the photograph so that his brother, who had been killed blindfolded, could see the person responsible for his death and see justice. "I wanted his spirit to know that his younger [brother] was seeking justice on behalf of, and to send to, his elder [brother]."[4]

If this moment at the court was important, Neth's "dark world" interactions with the spirit of his dead brother had begun long ago and would continue afterward, often through *bangsokol* and other Buddhist ceremonies. The day before the Trial Chamber had delivered its Case 001 verdict in 2010, for example, the Khmer Rouge Victims Association, headed by Chum Mey and Bou Meng, organized a ceremony to commemorate the dead in a large Tuol Sleng courtyard. Perhaps a hundred Cambodians, as well as Lefeuvre, Ouk, and Hamill, sat on mats facing five monks and surrounded by the media and tourist observers. Chhang, wearing a black tie, prayed with them, sitting close to the front row along with many of the civil parties, including Neth.

The participants moved forward on their knees to make offerings to the monks, such as cases of water and other drinks, present boxes, incense, flowers, and money. During the ceremony, the monks chanted, tossed lotus petals, and sprinkled holy water on the participants, while transmitting merit to the spirits of the dead. Some civil parties wept. At one point, a woman presented the monks with an enlarged S-21 photograph of her loved one, presumably, like Neth, to help conjure his spirit. Afterward, it started to rain. I spoke briefly to Theary Seng, who said, "I guess the tears are falling."

Civil party Chum Sirath, another leader of the Victims Association, explained that the ceremony had been held to call the spirits of the dead "to please come back

---

[3] Author interview with Neth Phally, Phnom Penh, February 28, 2015.   [4] Ibid.

and to listen to the verdict. When you have heard the verdict, we ardently pray for your souls to enjoy peace and happiness with words denied to you during your time on this earth."[5] Neth recalled, "I lit incense and prayed for my brother's soul. And I offered money so the result would be sent to him through the monks."[6]

After his testimony, as before, Neth interacted with the spirits of the dead in other ways. Shortly after testifying, Neth said, his brother appeared in his dreams, standing before Neth for a moment, saying nothing, then disappearing.[7] Neth had also set up a small memorial where the portrait of his brother—the same one he held up in court—hung near a painting of the Buddha and incense bowls.[8] He would go there, light incense, and pray for the souls of his brother along with his parents and other relatives—just as Uncle San is depicted as doing in the Khmer Institute of Democracy (KID) booklet. Before testifying, Neth had also lit incense and prayed that the spirit of his brother would enter the photograph when Neth raised it in court.[9] By doing so, Neth stated, "I felt this would help release his soul from wandering and help him find peace so he could be reborn."[10]

This concern with Buddhism and the spirits of the dead dominated the discussion during my interview with Neth. While he had a basic understanding of legal process, he found it difficult to comprehend.[11] Like many civil parties, Neth needed assistance filling out his civil party application and struggled to understand terms like "testimony" and "prosecutor" or even what exactly the lawyers did.

With help from DC-Cam staff and his lawyer, who used simplification, short summaries, and analogy, Neth was able to understand somewhat better. Like Neth, Hav Sophea, another DC-Cam civil party who had testified and participated in the Tuol Sleng ceremony, told me that she had difficulty understanding the proceedings, comprehending perhaps half of what happened.[12] This was not uncommon.[13]

Even if Neth had been selected to serve as a civil party focal point, he noted he could only answer basic questions. "I did this in Case 001 and now 002, before these other [newer civil parties]," Neth said. "I have been to Phnom Penh. I know the court. And I have testified and know what happens and can tell [the Case 002 civil parties from my area] about my experience ... so they won't be afraid."[14]

As Sambath noted about his conversations with villagers, Neth said that, when meeting civil parties from his area, he was often asked why it took so long to reach a verdict. He would reply that justice was not as fast as they might wish because the judges and prosecutors had to discuss and crosscheck things. "It's not like television," Neth would tell them, "where a verdict is quickly reached—or how it was during the Khmer Rouge period."[15]

[5] Leitsinger 2010.
[6] Author interview with Neth Phally, Phnom Penh, February 28, 2015.
[7] Ibid.
[8] Stover, Balthazard, and Koenig 2011, 505.
[9] Author interview with Neth Phally, Phnom Penh, February 28, 2015.
[10] Stover, Balthazard, and Koenig 2011, 505.
[11] Author interview with Neth Phally, Phnom Penh, February 28, 2015.
[12] Author interview with Hav Sophea, Phnom Penh, February 25, 2010.
[13] See also Pham et al. 2011, 284.
[14] Author interview with Neth Phally, Phnom Penh, February 28, 2015.
[15] Ibid.

If Neth had a rudimentary comprehension of legal process, he primarily understood it in terms of knowledge and practices that are part of everyday life in Cambodia. Though the court involved foreigners, he told me, it was "just like Buddhism. Those who do wrong things have guilt. Those who do good, receive good." Thus Duch "did a bad thing and received a bad result, his life imprisonment."[16] Similarly, he interpreted the meaning of the sword in the hand of the Angkorean official in the ECCC logo in a Buddhist fashion as symbolizing the discernment of right and wrong.

His view of Duch followed along these lines. If Neth believed Duch had not told the entire truth, Duch had acknowledged that Neth's brother was killed at S-21 and had accepted responsibility for the crimes at the prison. Accordingly, Neth was willing to accept Duch's apology—from a Buddhist perspective—since Duch, Neth believed, was seeking to discern right and wrong and improve himself.

"I can accept his apology," Neth told me. "I'm not offended. It's a good thing when a person acknowledges fault and bad actions. But that person is still guilty."[17] For this reason, Neth could not pardon (*at aon toas*) Duch, whose guilt was enormous. Reconciliation ultimately was not possible. Neth added, sadly, that if his brother had lived the two of them could jointly have taken care of their parents.

Neth's use of the phrase "taken care of" (*chenhchouem*) here also highlighted everyday understandings of reciprocity and return that were a strong undercurrent of civil party testimony and broader conceptions of family relationships, including those with the dead. Throughout his testimony, Neth signaled his bond to his brother by referring to him as "elder [brother]" (*bâng*) and implicitly suggesting the gratitude owed to him.

Overall, Neth was pleased with his experience at the court. In fact, he said his testimony was a highlight of his life, a time when he was able to speak before many people. Overall, Neth said that he was 80 percent satisfied with the court, his 20 percent dissatisfaction due to the death of Ieng Sary and Ieng Thirith. His overall satisfaction was echoed by Hav Sophea and other civil parties, particularly after Duch received a life sentence.

However, as illustrated by twists and turns of victim participation during the Duch trial, there was variation in civil party experience as well as the degree and temporal expression of their satisfaction as has been the case in other tribunals.[18] Echoing other civil parties, for example, Neth expressed frustration that he was unable to tell the full story about what happened to him and his brother, particularly, he said, invoking another Buddhist idiom, their "suffering" (*tukkha*).[19]

Responding to this civil party dissatisfaction, the Transcultural Psychosocial Organization (TPO) began offering ECCC civil parties "testimonial therapy." Originally developed in Chile as a therapeutic method for victims of torture, testimonial therapy holds that narrative expression can transform negative emotions and help survivors better cope with trauma.[20] The method was later adapted in a variety of post-conflict contexts, including Cambodia.

---

[16] Ibid.   [17] Ibid.
[18] Kirchenbauer, Balthazard, Ky, Vinck, and Pham 2013; Stover, Balthazard, and Koenig 2011; Pham, Vinck, Balthazard, Hean, and Stover 2009. See also Stover and Weinstein 2004.
[19] Author interview with Neth Phally, Phnom Penh, February 28, 2015.
[20] Agger, Igreja, Kiehle, and Polatin 2012.

TPO's version of testimonial therapy fused this Western therapeutic assumption about the efficacy of verbal and narrative expression to treat trauma—one highlighted by the title of "Breaking the Silence" and part of the justice facade—with local Buddhist understandings and the *bangsokol* ceremony.[21] Working with a TPO counselor, civil parties would "restore their painful memories and convert them into a written testimony." Subsequently, this narrative would be "read aloud and delivered to the survivors by monks from a local pagoda in a Buddhist ceremony ... in [the] presence of other survivors, relatives, community members, local authorities, government officials, NGO representatives, youth and others." TPO's website explains that the ceremony "promotes acknowledgement of suffering, the destigmatization of survivors[,] and restores their dignity. It also allows the survivors to ease the suffering of the spirits of ancestors and pay respect to deceased relatives."[22]

Neth Phally was among those who participated in this treatment. Like many civil parties, he suffered from various somatic symptoms, including feelings of anger (when thinking about the past), difficulty sleeping, frequently needing to relieve himself at night, and the lack of "calm" (*sngeam*) sleep. These symptoms were often linked to "thinking too much."[23] He used a variety of traditional practices to deal with this psychological distress, including distracting himself by thinking of other things or talking to neighbors, visiting a local healer (*krou khmaer*), taking traditional medicines, applying tiger balm to alter the disturbed humoral "wind" in his body, making offerings to monks, being sprinkled with holy water, lighting incense, and praying.

He had also sought treatment from TPO, which gave him medication and helped him learn to "lighten" (*tuu sral*) his tension, "ease" (*somruol*) his mind, and "kill"/control (*romnoap*) disruptive emotions. Testimonial therapy also helped. "We made offerings to the monks," he recalled, "and the story of me and my brother was read. The monks took the book [with my story] and recited scripture," which helped ease his heart and also, via the *bangsokol* ceremony, transfer merit to his brother's spirit. He kept the ceremonial book in his desk at home.

Discourses surrounding international trials assert that the desire for Justice is universal, a uniform norm everyone shares and that leads to peace, healing, and reconciliation. And indeed, surveys of Cambodian perceptions of the ECCC show that legal justice is valued.[24] Neth spoke of justice and wanted Duch to be sentenced to life for his bad deeds. But, as we have seen, his encounter with "global justice" was mediated by everyday understandings of Buddhism, obligation, and transactions with the dead. Indeed, Neth said that Duch's sentence was important to him because the justice it provided would calm (*sngop*) the restless spirit of his brother.[25]

[21] "Justice & Relief for Survivors of the Khmer Rouge," TPO website www.tpocambodia.org. See also Agger, Igreja, Kiehle, and Polatin 2012; Kijewski 2017.

[22] "Justice & Relief for Survivors of the Khmer Rouge," TPO website.

[23] Author interview with Neth Phally, Phnom Penh, February 28, 2015.

[24] Kirchenbauer et al. 2013; Pham et al. 2011.

[25] Author interview with Neth Phally, Phnom Penh, February 28, 2015.

Likewise, Neth's experience with TPO illustrates how "healing" does not flow in a straightforward manner from "justice," but is linked to complex understandings about health, treatment, equanimity, and the ideal mental state, one that is "calm" and "at ease," notions that are directly linked to Cambodian Buddhist understandings of mind, body, and, as Chea Vannath emphasized, equanimity. Thus one study reported that, while having positive attitudes regarding the tribunal, not a single Case 001 civil party reported gaining a sense of "closure" or "healing" from their participation, a finding not unusual in transitional justice; many were also more negative about the impact of the tribunal than the general population of survivors.[26]

The justice facade largely masks these sorts of local understandings that—even if they may suddenly dehisce at moments such as when Neth held up the photo of his brother—circulate and flow behind this surface-level exterior, largely unseen and unrecognized by outside observers. This "bushy undergrowth" of normative meaning, to use Berman's term again, provides a key local texture that mediates the experience and understanding of Cambodians encountering "global justice" and the ECCC, one that often stands at odds with the normativity of the justice facade and the transitional justice imaginary that informs it.

Justice in Translation

What, then, does the experience of Neth Phally and other people discussed in this book tell us about whether or not there is a point to international justice in places like Cambodia? Their engagements with the ECCC illustrate that answering such a question demands attention to translation, an issue that has been largely overlooked in the literature on transitional justice in general and international criminal justice in particular.

Kassie Neou highlighted this point when he critiqued colleagues who translated notions of law and human rights in a literal manner. Instead, he emphasized the need for thick translation. Translation, Neou told me, can't be word for word "because the concepts are [too] different." Instead, a translator needed to take a word or concept and "explain the meaning of it and then sometimes add some analogy to make sure all of them understand."[27]

Neou emphasized the importance of eye contact. "If I see the eyes of my audience," he emphasized, "I can tell if they understand." This attunement to audience was so important that he had incorporated the method into his pedagogy for training human rights trainers. Neou also learned that, as opposed to assuming he and his staff knew the best way to translate human rights concepts, translation needed to be

---

[26] Pham et al. 2011, 284. On transitional justice more broadly, see Weinstein 2011.
[27] Author interview with Kassie Neou, Phnom Penh, March 18, 2016.

a more open and on the ground process, one in which those who had been trained would innovate in ways that could not have been imagined.

His experience working with monks, who incorporated human rights ideas into Buddhist stories familiar to Cambodian villagers, was illustrative in this regard.

As the monks, who were highly attuned to their lay congregations, did this thick translation, Neou noted, the idea of human rights was reworked and reframed, thickly translated in terms of the Buddhist moral precepts and related concepts and then again as part of Buddha stories, ending up as something somewhat resonant with if quite different from "international [human rights] norms and standards."

The same sort of translation process took place at the ECCC, with "international norms and standards" related to justice translated more or less thickly. In some cases, like courtroom translation, the translations were more thin and "one to one." An ECCC translator, for example, told me that, when he accompanied the ECCC to the field, he would adhere closely to the legal terms.

At NGO civil party outreach sessions in the countryside, which involved rural villagers who might be illiterate or have minimal formal education and literacy skills, translation had to be thicker, though the extent varied. While recognizing the need to frame things in ways villagers could understand, for example, Theary Seng noted that at the end of the day, "we have to use legal terms." Within the same NGO, however, there was variation. Thus her Center for Social Development staffers, like Sopheap Im, more frequently used analogy and Buddhism to reframe legal idioms in terms villagers could understand.

However, as with Neou's discussion of the deep translation of human rights, the "international norms and standards" related to the ECCC were sometimes translated in ways that were distant from their formal legal sense. Im's discussion of rural villager "light world" and "dark world" understandings of the legal process highlighted this point. So too did Neth's view of the judicial process, which drew on both sets of understanding even if he ultimately didn't comprehend much of the legal process and "dark world" understandings and practices, such as the *bangsokol* ceremony, were primary for him.

Such understandings are largely masked by the justice facade. Instead of a global "cascade" of justice and accountability, the Cambodian case illustrates that what takes place is far more complex as ideas like "justice" land in different terrains of knowledge, power, and practice. The interstitial NGO "vortices" and "eddies" I have discussed illustrate this point. So, too, does the fact that it is difficult to even translate the word "justice" in Khmer, a term that has Buddhist resonances and is understood by many Cambodians in terms of ideas like karma. Even in English, however, the concept of "justice" may be fluid. Karnavas highlighted this point when he noted how variable the idea of "international standards" could be in international courts.

The global-local binary, so central to the transitional justice imaginary and often invoked in transitional justice and international law, collapses amidst this fluidity and variation.[28] This point was evident in my earlier discussion of the interstitial spaces of the transitional justice assemblage in which local NGOs operated, ones that didn't fit with this binary.

NGO leaders had often lived abroad and fused concepts in creative and non-predictable ways—as did their staff members who traveled abroad and received training in law, human rights, and transitional justice. This binary likewise broke down in civil party testimony, which included people born in other countries and members of the Cambodian diaspora. To understand the meaning of a tribunal like the ECCC, then, we must shift from universalizing invocations of "international justice" and "justice cascades" to a focus on phenomenology—lived experience, the interstitial spaces in which "justice" is "translated," and the on-the-ground understandings and practices in which it is enacted.

To date, there has been too little attention to "justice in translation" in transitional justice and international law. As with the peacebuilding and development literatures, there is an increasing recognition of the importance of "the local" and "the everyday" in transitional justice even if less so in international law.[29] While transitional justice scholars from a number of disciplines have sought to more closely attend to the "local," the more phenomenological work has come from anthropologists. However, the issue of translation remains underexamined.

Within anthropology, perhaps the most detailed work on "justice in translation" has been done by Sally Merry, particularly her discussions of "vernacularization."[30] Many of the issues explored in this book, ranging from thick and thin translation to the key role of intermediaries, resonate with dynamics Merry has discussed, including the ways in which the flow of "international norms and standards" lands and is reframed given the affordances of "particular geographies rutted by history and culture" as well as power.[31] My earlier discussion of "affordances" and use of the riverine metaphor—emphasizing the contours of complex on-the-ground "ecosystems" including NGO "eddies"—parallel this idea even if it is inflected in terms of phenomenology.

Other anthropologists, like a growing number of transitional justice scholars,[32] have similarly emphasized how transitional justice and international tribunals are linked to discourse and power, including structural violence and neoliberalism. Examples include Richard Wilson's groundbreaking work on the South African Truth and Reconciliation Commission, Kimberly Theidon's study of Peru, and Kamari Clarke's discussion of the International Criminal Court and Sub-Saharan Africa.[33]

---

[28] Merry 2006b. See also Goodale 2007; Ullrich 2016.

[29] Riaño-Alcalá and Baines 2012; Eltringham 2008, 2009; Hinton 2016; Kelsall 2013; Meierhenrich and Pendas 2017.

[30] Merry 2006b; Levitt and Merry 2009.   [31] Levitt and Merry 2009, 455.

[32] See, e.g., Dembour and Kelly 2007, *passim*; Eltringham 2009, 2012; Hinton 2016; Wilson 2011. On "Fourth Generation" transitional justice, see Sharp 2013.

[33] Theidon 2014; Wilson 2001, 2011; Clarke 2009; see also Sanford 2003.

My use of the justice facade metaphor highlights the ways in which transitional justice and international law may mask power, such as through place-making discourse related to time and space, the ways the court's jurisdiction precluded a discussion of history and structural violence, how the court was used by the Cambodian government to buttress its legitimacy even as it provided a veneer that deflected attention away from economic and political issues including judicial corruption, political intimidation of the sort that led Saray to flee the country, and controversies over land appropriation and environmental degradation. With regard to translation in particular, my discussion of Bou Meng's testimony focused on juridical disciplines, which structure, "clip," and appropriate testimony, a process that is a sort of "exile."[34]

To acknowledge such masking effects of transitional justice and international law is not to argue that, in the end, such measures are simply externally imposed neocolonial interventions that lack fit with and meaning that accords with on-the-ground realities. As is the case with peacebuilding and development, such initiatives may miss the mark in this regard, often to a great extent, while asserting place-making discourses that are bound up with power as suggested above.[35] In such cases, the question posed at the beginning of this book about whether or not international justice has meaning in a place like Cambodia would seemingly have a simple answer: "No."

But this sort of an answer fails to pay adequate attention to the second dimension of transitional justice, the complex ways it lands and is translated within different local "ecosystems," dynamics to which a phenomenology of transitional justice attends. As Neou's remarks suggest, if informed by discourse and power, the process of "justice in translation" cannot be fully predetermined and unfolds in unpredictable ways. It also points to the combustive dimensions of transitional justice, the way this assemblage may catalyze the imagination even if in ways that diverge sharply from the transitional justice imaginary.

Transitional Justice, Combustion, and the Imagination

Accordingly, the title of this book is not meant to dismiss global justice as mere "facade" in the sense of a deception, even as it is a call to recognize that the transitional justice imaginary is performatively asserted in sites of "transition" like Cambodia. This book has been a sustained argument for the need to step behind this justice facade—which is porous and unstable—to understand what international justice means on the ground in such contexts.

A "closure" of a sort may take place, but it is not simply the closure naturalized in the transitional justice imaginary, which asserts the need for therapeutic voice, apology, and forgiveness. Instead, it is the "everyday closure" of people on the ground

---

[34] On translation and power, see also Das 2002.
[35] Gupta and Ferguson 1997; Ferguson 1990; Escobar 1995.

who are positioned in the midst of local realities, power, and the transitional justice assemblage, creatively navigating the encounter in some cases, more or less ignoring it in others.

This is not to say that these encounters are completely open spaces of creativity. It is to argue that they are interstitial moments of combustion, points of conjuncture (and "friction" to use Tsing's term) that fizzle, spark, and fire. They are also spaces of "heat" in the sense that they involve taken-for-granted understandings as well as structures of power ranging from political organization to flows of capital. However, the conjuncture with difference and the new (including flows associated with the place-making discourse of "global justice") may also provide a spark to the imagination, opening the possibility of creative engagement and thinking in new ways—but not simply the ways asserted by the justice facade and the transitional justice imaginary from which it springs.

Thus Neth did not simply "localize" the normative current of a "justice cascade." Instead, he stood amidst the conjunction of a variety of discourses and flows—not just international law but also his engagement with outreach initiatives and NGO intermediaries, his past experience and understandings, and the affordances of the court. Indeed, we might think of international tribunals like the ECCC in terms of "affordances" that may (or may not) spark the imagination in combustive encounters with the transitional justice assemblage. This recognition moves us away from the teleological and transformative assumptions of the transitional justice imaginary and "justice cascade" metaphor—as well as related discourses about globalization and locality—to focus on more phenomenological concerns, including agency, creativity, imagination, and individual paths of engagement with "global justice" amidst complicated histories, geopolitics, discourses, and structural power.

This book is filled with examples of combustive moments that emerge from such transitional justice affordances, set in the backdrop of Cambodian history and earlier transitions, ranging from the creation of the KID booklet to "Breaking the Silence." Each person I interviewed brought their own history and perspective to this imaginative encounter—just like Neth used the affordances of civil party participation, TPO mental health services and testimonial therapy, and testimony to forge his own meaning from "global justice," one that diverged in important ways from the assumptions of the transitional justice imaginary.

For Chhang, who could articulate discourses associated with the transitional justice imaginary when necessary in more formal and international contexts, justice was not just about accountability—though this was important for Chhang as it was for Neth and others—but about imagination. "Imagination," Chhang said, is necessary "to make you a complete person" by facing the past and considering the future in new ways, something that could restore "humanity, taking away insecurity" as people considered "what if" questions.[36]

---

[36] Skype interview with Youk Chhang, December 15, 2016.

"Breaking the Silence," like the trial itself, could help catalyze the imagination and therefore bring about healing of a sort—just not that asserted by the teleology of the transitional justice imaginary. Relatedly, DC-Cam's slogan "justice and memory" diverged from this imaginary in important ways, particularly in terms of the connection of justice and memory to imagination and the sorts of (non-teleological) healing it might enable, including a return to a position of unforgiving and unreconciled silence (as opposed to the transitional justice imaginary's teleological assumptions about voiced apology, forgiveness, and reconciliation).

It is precisely these sorts of combustive encounters with and understandings of transitional justice that are masked by the justice facade and so often missed by the "international community," including many (but not all) working in the field of transitional justice and human rights, who see a surface facade that reflects their idealized imaginaries of transitional justice, human rights, globalization, and democratization. In the extreme, such projections may instantiate Orientalist binary essentialisms and mask power.

Most commonly, such projections of the transitional justice imaginary obscure the complexities lying behind the justice facade, including the imaginative and often combustive encounters that take place amidst the multiple flows and affordances of the transitional justice assemblage. If we want to effectively acknowledge "the local," as the 2004 report of the U.N. Secretary-General suggests, we need to unpack our own imaginaries and reflect on the assumptions naturalized therein.

To unpack the assumptions of the transitional justice is not to simply dismiss it. It is to engage in a "critical transitional justice studies"[37] that allows us to recognize what has been naturalized. Doing so is crucial since the justice facade masks complicated histories, politics, organizational structures, and other flows that co-constitute the everyday experience and understanding of transitional justice. Only by stepping behind the justice facade may we assess whether international justice has a point in transitional justice and peacebuilding contexts like Cambodia. This book has shown that transitional justice may have meaning, but a meaning that often diverges strongly from the naturalized assumptions of the justice facade. To fail to unpack these assumptions and take account of "justice in translation," then, is to risk remaining suspended, like Uncle San, in the webs of the transitional justice imaginary.

---

[37] See Hinton 2010b.

ECCC Timeline

1953	Cambodian independence from France
	Prince Sihanouk dominates Kingdom of Cambodia until 1970
1967	Khmer Rouge begin armed struggle against Prince Sihanouk
1973	U.S. carpet-bombing of Cambodian countryside spikes
1975	Khmer Rouge, led by Pol Pot, topple Khmer Republic
	Democratic Kampuchea (DK) established
1979	Vietnamese-backed army overthrows DK regime
	People's Republic of Kampuchea (PRK) established
	New Cambodian civil war begins
1989	Vietnamese troops withdraw from Cambodia
1991	Paris Peace Agreement
1993	UNTAC elections
	Royal Government of Cambodia formed
	Proliferation of democracy and human rights NGOs begins
1997	Discussions to hold a tribunal commence
1999	Khmer Rouge movement ends following Pol Pot's 1998 death
2003	UN and Cambodia sign agreement to hold tribunal
2006	ECCC commences operation
2007	Case 001 and 002 suspects detained by ECCC
2009	Case 001 Trial Proceedings held
2010	Case 001 Trial Chamber Judgment
2011	Case 002/1 begins
	Ieng Thirith deemed unfit to stand trial due to dementia
2012	C001 Supreme Court Chamber Final Decision
	Duch sentenced to life
2013	Ieng Sary dies
2014	Case Trial Chamber 002/1 Judgment
	Khieu Samphan and Nuon Chea sentenced to life
2015	Case 002/2 commences
	Case 003 defendants charged
2016	Supreme Court Chamber Final Decision in Case 002/1
	Life sentence for Khieu Samphan and Nuon Chea upheld
2017	Case 002/2 Trial Proceedings conclude
2018	Case 002/2 Trial Chamber Judgment expected

References Cited

Acharya, Amitav. 2004. "How Ideas Spread: Whose Norms Matter? Norm Localization and Institutional Change in Asian Regionalism." *International Organization* 58: 239–75.

Adams, William Yewdale. 1998. *The Philosophical Roots of Anthropology*. Stanford: CSLI Publications.

Agger, Inger. 2015. "Calming the Mind: Healing after Mass Atrocity in Cambodia." *Transcultural Psychiatry* 52(4): 543–60.

Agger, Inger, Victor Igreja, Rachel Kiehle, and Peter Polatin. 2012. "Testimony Ceremonies in Asia: Integrating Spirituality in Testimonial Therapy for Torture Survivors in India, Sri Lanka, Cambodia and the Philippines." *Transcultural Psychiatry* 49(3–4): 568–89.

Allen, Tim. 2006. *Trial Justice: The International Criminal Court and the Lord's Resistance Army*. London: Zed.

American Psychiatric Association. 2000. *Diagnostic and Statistical Manual of Mental Disorders*, 4th Edition. Washington: American Psychiatric Association.

Amnesty International. 2002. "Cambodia: Cambodians deserve international standards of justice." Press Release, 19 November.

Amnesty International. 2003. "Cambodia: Fair trial and due process are not up for negotiation." Press Release, 25 April.

An-Na'im, Adullahi Ahmed. 2013. "Editorial Note: From the Neocolonial 'Transitional' to Indigenous Formations of Justice." *International Journal for Transitional Justice* 7(2): 197–204.

Anderson, Benedict. 2006. *Imagined Communities: Reflections on the Origin and Spread of Nationalism*. New York: Verso.

Ang Choulean. 1987. *Les Êtres Surnaturels dans la Religion Populaire Khmère*. Paris: Cedoreck.

Appadurai, Arjun. 1996. *Modernity at Large: Cultural Dimensions of Globalization*. Minneapolis: University of Minnesota Press.

Arendt, Hannah. 1994. *Eichmann in Jerusalem: A Report on the Banality of Evil*. New York: Penguin.

Arendt, Hannah. 1973. *Origins of Totalitarianism*. New York: Harcourt, Brace, Jovanovich.

Arthur, Paige. 2009. "How 'Transitions' Reshaped Human Rights: A Conceptual History of Transitional Justice." *Human Rights Quarterly* 31(2): 321–67.

Autesserre, Séverine. 2014. *Peaceland: Conflict Resolution and the Everyday Politics of International Intervention*. New York: Cambridge University Press.

Ayeni, Victor O. 2014. "Ombudsmen as Human Rights Institutions." *Journal of Human Rights* 13(4): 498–511.

Balthazard, Mychelle. 2013. "Khmer Rouge Tribunal Justice Project Evaluation Report, ADHOC Project, 2010–2012." Project Evaluation. Phnom Penh: ADHOC.

Balthazard, Mychelle. 2010. "Making an Impact: Guidance on Designing Effective Outreach Programs, Cambodian Case Report." Unpublished report.

Ban Ki-moon. 2010. "Secretary-General's Remarks to Pledging Conference for the Extraordinary Chambers in the Courts of Cambodia." 25 May. New York: Office of United Nations Secretary General Ban Ki-Moon.

Barthes, Roland. 1972. *Mythologies*. New York: Farrar, Straus and Giroux.

Bass, Gary J. 2001. *Stay the Hand of Vengeance: The Politics of War Crimes Tribunals.* Princeton: Princeton University Press.

Bauman, Zygmunt. 1989. *Modernity and the Holocaust.* Cambridge: Polity.

Baylis, Elena. 2008. "Tribunal-Hopping with the Post-Conflict Justice Junkies." *Oregon Review of International Law* 10: 361–90.

Berman, Antoine. 2012. "Translation and the Trials of the Foreign." In *The Translation Studies Reader*, 3rd Edition, edited by Lawrence Venuti, 240–53. New York: Routledge.

Bhaba, Homi K. 2004. *The Location of Culture.* New York: Routledge.

Boellstorff, Tom. 2003. "Dubbing Culture: Indonesian *gay* and *lesbi* Subjectivities and Ethnography in an already Globalized World." *American Ethnologist* 30(2): 225–42.

Bopha, Chheang. 2008. "Vann Nath, Survivor of the Khmer Rouge S-21 Prison, Determined to stand up for Remembrance." Ka-set website. 28 August.

Bourdieu, Pierre. 1987. "The Force of Law: Toward a Sociology of the Juridical Field." *The Hastings Law Journal* 38: 814–53.

Bourdieu, Pierre. 1977. *Outline of a Theory of Practice.* New York: Cambridge University Press.

Boutros Boutros-Ghali. 1992. "An Agenda for Peace: Preventive Diplomacy, Peacemaking and Peace-keeping." United Nations A/47/277-S/24111. New York: United Nations, 21 January.

Boutros Boutros-Ghali. 1991. "Report of the Secretary-General on Cambodia." New York: United Nations Security Council, S/23613, 19 February.

Burnet, Jennie E. 2012. *Genocide Lives in Us: Women, Memory, and Silence in Rwanda.* Madison: University of Wisconsin Press.

Butler, Judith. 2006. *Gender Trouble: Feminism and the Subversion of Identity.* New York: Routledge.

The Cambodia Daily Staff. 2007. "CSD Chief Files 1st Civil Party Application to ECCC." *The Cambodian Daily Weekly Review*, 23–29 September, 3.

The Cambodia Daily Staff. 2017. "Hugs, Tears, and Uncertainty after Adhoc 5's Surprise Release." *The Cambodian Daily*, 30 June.

Cambodia Defenders Project. N.d. "Gender-Based Violence under the Khmer Rouge." Phnom Penh. Cambodia Defenders Project website.

Carmichael, Robert. 2015. *When Clouds Fell from the Sky: A Disappearance, A Daughter's Search and Cambodia's First War Criminal.* Bangkok: Asia Horizons Books.

Castoriadis, Cornelius. 1987. *The Imaginary Institution of Society.* Cambridge, MA: MIT Press.

Caswell, Michelle. 2014. *Archiving the Unspeakable: Silence, Memory, and the Photographic Record in Cambodia.* Madison: University of Wisconsin Press.

Center for Social Development (CSD). 2007. *Booklet of Public Forum on Justice & National Reconciliation.* Phnom Penh: Center for Social Development.

Center for Social Development (CSD). 2006. *The Khmer Rouge and National Reconciliation— Opinions from the Cambodians.* Phnom Penh: Center for Social Development.

Center for Social Development (CSD). 1998. *National Survey on Public Attitudes toward Corruption.* Phnom Penh: Center for Social Development.

Chandara, Lor. 2006. "CSD President Chea Vannath to Step Down." *The Cambodia Daily*, 27 January.

Chandler, David P. 2007. *A History of Cambodia.* Boulder, CO: Westview.

Chandler, David P. 1991. *The Tragedy of Cambodian History: Politics, War and Revolution since 1945.* New Haven: Yale University Press.

Chandler, David P. 1999. *Voices from S-21: Terror and History in Pol Pot's Secret Prison.* Berkeley: University of California Press.

Chea, Vannath. 2016. *A Cambodian Survivor's Odyssey*. Self-published memoir, Phnom Penh, Cambodia.

Chea, Vannath. 1999. "Anti-Corruption Activities: Case of Cambodia (Working with Reform Willing Government)." Paper given at the 9th International Anti-Corruption Conference, Durban, South Africa, 11 October.

Chea, Vannath. 2002. "Khmer Rouge and National Reconciliation." *Peace Review* 14(3): 303–07.

Chea, Vannath. 1996. "Let Ieng Sary's Karma Decide his Future." *The Phnom Penh Post*, 6 September.

Chea, Vannath. 2003. "Untitled." Paper presented at the Second Regional Conference on Poverty Reduction Strategies, Phnom Penh, Cambodia, 16–18 October.

Chhang, Youk. 2000a. "For the Truth." *Searching for the Truth* 1 (January): 1–3.

Chhang, Youk. 2005a. "How Did I Survive the Khmer Rouge?" *Searching for the Truth*, Special English Edition, Second Quarter: 7.

Chhang, Youk. 2000b. "Memory." *Searching for the Truth* 2 (February): 1–2.

Chhang, Youk. 2005c. "Research and Healing." *Searching for the Truth*, Special English Edition, Fourth Quarter: 5.

Chhang, Youk. 2009. "Restoring Cambodian Community and Way of Life: Breaking the Silence." *Searching for the Truth*, Special English Edition, 1st Quarter: 1.

Chhang, Youk. 2002. "The Right to Life." *Searching for the Truth* 28 (April): 3.

Chhang, Youk. 2008. "The Thief of History." *Searching for the Truth*, Special English Edition, Third Quarter: 2.

Chhang, Youk. 2005b. "Three Projects to Help Survivors of Democratic Kampuchea See Justice Done and Encourage the Public to Increase their Participation in the Khmer Rouge Tribunal." *Searching for the Truth*, Special English Edition, Third Quarter: 2–4.

Chhang, Youk. 2007. "Why the Khmer Rouge Tribunal Matters to the Cambodian Community: Justice for the Future, Not the Victims." *Searching for the Truth*, Special English Edition, Third Quarter: 4–7.

Chng Chin Ying, Jocelyn. 2010. "Disturbing the Silence: A Study of Performance and Collective Memory in Cambodia." MA Thesis, University of Tampere and University of Amsterdam.

Christie, Ryerson. 2013. *Peacebuilding and NGOs: State-Civil Society Interactions*. New York: Routledge.

Christodoulidis, Emilios. 2009. "Strategies of Rupture." *Law and Critique* 20(1): 3–26.

Chum Mey. 2012. *Survivor: The Triumph of an Ordinary Man in the Khmer Rouge Genocide*. Phnom Penh: Documentation Center of Cambodia.

Chy, Terith. 2009. *A Thousand Voices*. Phnom Penh: Documentation Center of Cambodia.

Ciorciari, John D. and Youk Chhang. 2005. "Documenting the Crimes of Democratic Kampuchea." In *Bringing the Khmer Rouge to Justice: Prosecuting Mass Violence Before the Cambodian Courts*, edited by Jaya Ramji and Beth Van Schaak, 226–27. Lewiston, NY: Edwin Mellen Press.

Ciorciari, John D. and Anne Heindel, eds. 2014. *Hybrid Justice: The Extraordinary Chambers in the Courts of Cambodia*. Ann Arbor: University of Michigan Press.

Clark, Phil. 2012. "Creeks of Justice: Debating Post-Atrocity Accountability and Amnesty in Rwanda and Uganda." In *Amnesty in the Age of Human Rights Accountability: Comparative and International Perspectives*, edited by Francesca Lessa and Leigh A. Payne, 210–37. New York: Cambridge University Press.

Clark, Phil. 2011. *The Gacaca Courts, Post-Genocide Justice and Reconciliation in Rwanda*. New York: Cambridge University Press.

Clarke, Kamari Maxine. 2009. *Fictions of Justice: The International Criminal Court and the Challenge of Legal Pluralism in Sub-Saharan Africa.* New York: Cambridge University Press.

Clarke, Kamari Maxine and Mark Goodale. 2010. *Mirrors of Justice: Law and Power in the Post-Cold War Era.* New York: Cambridge University Press.

Clarke, Karmari Maxine, Abel S. Knotterus, and Eefje de Volder, eds. 2016. *Africa and the ICC: Perceptions of Justice.* New York: Cambridge University Press.

Collier, Stephen J. and Aihwa Ong, eds. 2005. *Global Assemblages: Technology, Politics and Ethics as Anthropological Problems.* Malden, MA: Blackwell.

Cruvellier, Thierry. 2014. *The Master of Confessions: The Making of a Khmer Rouge Torturer.* New York: Ecco.

Curtis, Dennis E. and Judith Resnik. 1987. "Images of Justice." *The Yale Law Journal* 96(8): 1727–72.

Das, Veena. 2002. "Violence and Translation." *Anthropological Quarterly* 75(1): 105–12.

Davis, Erik W. 2015. *Deathpower: Buddhism's Ritual Imagination in Cambodia.* New York: Columbia University Press.

DeFalco, Randle C. 2010. "Project Evaluation: Living Documents Project, Phase 2, Stage 1." Phnom Penh: Documentation Center of Cambodia.

Deleuze, Gilles and Félix Guattari. 1987. *A Thousand Plateaus.* Minneapolis: University of Minnesota Press.

Dembour, Marie-Bénédicte and Tobias Kelly, eds. 2007. *Paths to International Justice: Social and Legal Perspectives.* New York: Cambridge University Press.

Democratic Kampuchea. 1978. *Black Paper: Facts and Evidences of the Acts of Aggression and Annexation of Vietnam against Kampuchea.* Phnom Penh: Department of Press and Information of the Ministry of Foreign Affairs.

De Nike, Howard J., John Quigley, and Kenneth J. Robinson, eds. 2000. *Genocide in Cambodia: Documents from the Trial of Pol Pot and Ieng Sary.* Philadelphia: University of Pennsylvania Press.

Derrida, Jacques. 1992. "The Force of Law." In *Deconstruction and the Possibility of Justice,* edited by Drucilla Cornell, Michel Rosenfeld, and David Gray Carlson, 3–67. New York: Routledge.

Desjarlais, Robert and C. Jason Throop. 2011. "Phenomenological Approaches in Anthropology." *Annual Review of Anthropology* 40: 87–102.

Di Certo, Bridget. 2011. "KRT critic offers 'Poetic Justice'." *The Phnom Penh Post,* 1 March.

Di Certo, Bridget. 2012. "Theary Seng out as civil party." *The Phnom Penh Post,* 1 March.

Dobbs, Leo. 1992. "Comics, Monks Spread Human Rights Message." *The Phnom Penh Post,* 25 September.

Donovan, Dolores A. 1993. "The Cambodian Legal System: An Overview." In *Rebuilding Cambodia: Human Resources, Human Rights, and Law,* edited by Frederick Z. Brown. Baltimore: Johns Hopkins University Foreign Policy Institute.

Doughty, Kirsten Connor. 2016. *Remediation in Rwanda: Grassroots Legal Forums.* Philadelphia: University of Pennsylvania Press.

Douglas, Lawrence. 2001. *The Memory of Judgment: Making Law and History in the Trials of the Holocaust.* New Haven: Yale University Press.

Drexler, Elizabeth F. 2013. "Fatal Knowledges: The Social and Political Legacies of Collaboration and Betrayal in Timor-Leste." *International Journal of Transitional Justice* 7(1): 74–94.

Drumbl, Marc. 2007. *Atrocity, Punishment, and International Law.* Cambridge: Cambridge University Press.

Duthie, Roger and Paul Seils, eds. 2017. *Justice Mosaics: How Context Shapes Transitional Justice in Fractured Societies*. New York: International Center for Transitional Justice.

Dwyer, Leslie. 2015. "Reimagining Transitional Justice in Bali." AllegraLab, 22 January.

Dy, Khamboly. 2007. *A History of Democratic Kampuchea (1975–1979)*. Phnom Penh: Documentation Center of Cambodia.

Dy, Khamboly. 2013. "Challenges of Teaching Genocide in Cambodian Secondary Schools." Policy and Practice: Pedagogy about the Holocaust and Genocide Papers. Working Paper 4. Worcester, MA: Clark University.

Eads, Brian. N.d. "Youk Chhang's Journey to Justice." *Reader's Digest Asia*.

Ebihara, May Mayko. 1968. "Svay, A Khmer Village in Cambodia." PhD Dissertation, Department of Anthropology, Columbia University.

ECCC. 2003. "Agreement between the United Nations and the Royal Government of Cambodia Concerning the Prosecution under Cambodian Law of Crimes Committed during the Period of Democratic Kampuchea." 6 June. Phnom Penh: Extraordinary Chambers in the Courts of Cambodia.

ECCC. 2012. "Compilation of Statements of Apology Made by Kaing Guek Eav alias Duch during the Proceedings." ECCC Doc. F28.1.

ECCC. 2010. "Internal Rules (Rev. 5)." 9 February. Phnom Penh: Extraordinary Chambers in the Courts of Cambodia.

ECCC. 2008. "Practice Direction on Victim Participation (Revision 1)." Practice Direction 02/2007/Rev. 1, 27 October.

ECCC. 2009. "Transcript of Proceedings—'Duch' Trial Public." Case file no. 001/18–07–2007-ECCC/TC.

ECCC Press Release. 2010. "Germany contributes 1.2 million Euro to the Cambodian side of the ECCC." 21 December. Phnom Penh: ECCC.

ECCC Public Affairs Section. Undated. *An Introduction to the Khmer Rouge Tribunal*, 5th Edition. Phnom Penh: ECCC.

ECCC Public Affairs Section Staff. 2009a. "Reaction by Mr. Pen Vuth, Chief of Chheu Teal commune, Kandal." *The Court Report* 15 (July): 1–10.

ECCC Public Affairs Staff. 2009b. "The New Chief of Public Affairs: Reach Sambath." *The Court Report* 14 (June): 1–12.

ECCC Public Affairs Staff. 2009c. "The Khmer Institute of Democracy (KID): Outreach Update—May 2009." *The Court Report* 13 (May): 1–12.

Edelman, Marc and Angelique Haugerud, eds. 2005. *The Anthropology of Development and Globalization: From Classical Political Economy to Contemporary Neoliberalism*. Malden, MA: Blackwell.

Edwards, Penny. 2007. *Cambodge: The Cultivation of a Nation, 1860–1945*. Honolulu: University of Hawaii Press.

Elander, Maria. 2013. "The Victim's Address: Expressivism and the Victim at the Extraordinary Chambers in the Courts of Cambodia." *International Journal of Transitional Justice* 7(1): 95–115.

Elster, Jon. 2004. *Closing the Books: Transitional Justice in Historical Perspective*. New York: Cambridge University Press.

Eltringham, Nigel. 2008. "'A War Crimes Community?': The Legacy of the International Criminal Tribunal for Rwanda Beyond Jurisprudence." *New England Journal of International and Comparative Law* 14(2): 309–18.

Eltringham, Nigel. 2015. "Rescuing (Cosmopolitan) Locals at the International Criminal Tribunal for Rwanda." *Allegra: A Visual Lab of Legal Anthropology* [weblog article], 21 January.

Eltringham, Nigel. 2012. "Spectators to the Spectacle of Law: The Formation of a 'Validating Public' at the International Criminal Tribunal for Rwanda." *Ethnos* 77(3): 425–45.

Eltringham, Nigel. 2009. "'We are not a Truth Commission': Fragmented Narratives and the Historical Record at the International Criminal Tribunal for Rwanda." *Journal of Genocide Research* 11(1): 55–79.

Escobar, Arturo. 1995. *Encountering Development: The Making and Unmaking of the Third World.* Princeton: Princeton University Press.

Etcheson, Craig. 2006. "A 'Fair and Public Trial': A Political History of the Extraordinary Chambers." In *The Extraordinary Chambers*, edited by Stephen Humphries and David Berry. 8–24. New York: Open Society Justice Initiative.

Etcheson, Craig. 2005. *After the Killing Fields: Lessons from the Cambodian Genocide.* Westport, CT: Praeger.

Evans, Matthew. 2016. "Structural Violence, Socioeconomic Rights, and Transformative Justice." *Journal of Human Rights* 15(1): 1–20.

Fassin, Didier. 2008. "The Humanitarian Politics of Testimony: Subjectification through Trauma in the Israeli-Palestinian Conflict." *Cultural Anthropology* 23(3): 531–58.

Fassin, Didier and Richard Rechtman. 2009. *The Empire of Trauma: An Inquiry into the Condition of Victimhood.* Princeton: Princeton University Press.

Fawthrop, Tom and Helen Jarvis. 2004. *Getting Away with Genocide: Cambodia's Long Struggle Against the Khmer Rouge.* London: Pluto.

Ferguson, James. 1994. "The Anti-Politics Machine: 'Development' and Bureaucratic Power in Lesotho." *The Ecologist* 24(5, September/October): 176–81.

Ferguson, James. 1990. *The Anti-Politics Machine: "Development," Depoliticization, and Bureaucratic Power in Lesotho.* Minneapolis: University of Minnesota Press.

Fetcher, Anne-Meike and Heather Hindman, eds. 2011. *Inside the Everyday Lives of Development Workers.* Sterling, VA: Kumarian.

Fichtelberg, Aaron. 2015. *Hybrid Tribunals: A Comparative Examination.* New York: Springer.

Finnemore, Martha and Kathryn Sikkink. 1998. "International Norm Dynamics and Political Change." *International Organization* 52(4): 887–917.

Fletcher, Laurel E. and Harvey M. Weinstein. 2002. "Violence and Social Repair: Rethinking the Contribution of Justice to Reconciliation." *Human Rights Quarterly* 24: 573–639.

Foucault, Michel. 1990. *A History of Sexuality, Volume 1: An Introduction.* New York: Vintage.

Foucault, Michel. 1995. *Discipline & Punish: The Birth of the Prison.* New York: Vintage.

Frank, Bernard. 1970. "The Ombudsman and Human Rights." *Administrative Law Review* 22(3): 467–92.

Franzki, Hannah and Maria Carolina Olarte. 2014. "Understanding the Political Economy of Transitional Justice: A Critical Theory Perspective." In *Transitional Justice Theories*, edited by Susanne Bukley-Zistel, Teresa Koloma Beck, Christian Braun, and Friederike Mieth, 201–21. New York: Routledge.

Freeman, Joe. 2012. "Pau, Pestman and Ianuzzi leave Khmer Rouge court 'farce' behind." *The Phnom Penh Post*, 21 December.

Friedman, Megan. 2010. "Quotes: Senior Khmer Rouge Official's Prison Sentence." *Time*, 26 July.

Fukuyama, Francis. 1989. "The End of History?" *The National Interest.* 16(Summer): 3–18.

Geertz, Clifford. 1985. *Local Knowledge: Further Essays in Interpretive Anthropology.* New York: Basic.

Geertz, Clifford. 1973. *The Interpretation of Cultures: Selected Essays.* New York: Basic Books.

Gillison, Douglas. 2012. "Extraordinary Injustice." *The Investigative Fund*, 27 February.

Gillison, Douglas. 2011. "Justice Denied." *Foreign Policy*, 23 November.

Giry, Stéphanie. 2009. "Against the Law." *The National*, 14 August.

Giry, Stéphanie. 2010. "Cambodia's Perfect War Criminal." *The New York Review of Books* Blog, 25 October.

Giry, Stéphanie. 2012. "Necessary Scapegoats? The Making of the Khmer Rouge Tribunal." *The New York Review of Books* Blog, 23 July.

Goldston, James. 2007. "Letter to the Editor on Corruption Charges at Khmer Rouge Court." *Cambodia Daily*, 7 March.

Goodale, Mark. 2007. "Locating Rights, Envisioning Law between the Global and the Local." In *The Practice of Human Rights: Tracking Law between the Global and the Local*. Edited by Mark Goodale and Salley Engle Merry. 1–38. New York: Cambridge University Press.

Goodale, Mark and Sally Engle Merry, eds. 2007. *The Practice of Human Rights: Tracking Law between the Global and the Local*. New York: Cambridge University Press.

Gottesman, Evan. 2003. *Cambodia after the Khmer Rouge: Inside the Politics of Nation Building*. New Haven: Yale University Press.

Gottlieb, Sebastiaan. 2009. "'The First time I've Cried for Thirty Years' Dutch theatre Director breaks Cambodia's Silence." Radio Netherlands, 23 February.

Guilhot, Nicolas. 2002. "The Transition to the Human World of Democracy: Notes for a History of the Concept of Transition, from Early Marxism to 1989." *European Journal of Social Theory* 5(2): 219–42.

Guillou, Anne Yvonne. 2012. "An Alternative Memory of the Khmer Rouge Genocide: The Dead of the Mass Graves and the Land Guardian Spirits (*neak ta*)." *South East Asia Research* 20(2): 207–26.

Gupta, Akhil and James Ferguson, eds. 1997. *Culture, Power, Place: Explorations in Critical Anthropology*. Durham, NC: Duke University Press.

Gurd, Tracey. 2006. "Outreach: A Key to Success." In *The Extraordinary Chambers*, 117–29. New York: Open Society Justice Initiative.

Habermas, Jürgen. 1991. *The Structural Transformation of the Public Sphere: An Inquiry into a Category of Bourgeois Society*. Cambridge, MA: MIT Press.

Hall, John A. 2008. "A Tribunal Worth Paying For." *Wall Street Journal Online*, 16 July.

Hammer, Joshua. 2015. "The Very Tricky Trial of the Khmer Rouge." *The New York Review of Books*, 21 May, 42–44.

Harris, Ian. 2005. *Cambodian Buddhism: History and Practice*. Honolulu: University of Hawaii Press.

Hayes, Michael. 1993. "Good Ideas on Human Rights." *The Phnom Penh Post*, 30 July.

Hayner, Priscilla B. 1994. "Fifteen Truth Commissions—1974–1994: A Comparative Study." *Human Rights Quarterly* 16: 597–655.

Hayner, Priscilla B. 2002. *Unspeakable Truths: Facing the Challenge of Truth Commissions*. New York: Taylor & Francis.

Hazan, Pierre. 2017. "Beyond Borders: The New Architecture of Transitional Justice." *International Journal of Transitional Justice* 11(1): 1–8.

Hazan, Pierre. 2010. *Judging War, Judging History: Behind Truth and Reconciliation*. Stanford: Stanford University Press.

Headley, Robert K., Jr, Kylin Chhor, Lam Kheng Lim, Lim Hak Kheang, and Chen Chun. 1977. *Cambodian-English Dictionary*, Vols. 1 and 2. Washington, DC: Catholic University of America Press.

Heder, Steve and Judy Ledgerwood, eds. 1996. *Propaganda, Politics, and Violence in Cambodia: Democratic Transition under United Nations Peace-Keeping*. Armonk, NY: ME Sharpe.

Heder, Steve and Brian D. Tittemore. 2004. *Seven Candidates for Prosecution: Accountability for the Crimes of the Khmer Rouge*. Phnom Penh: Documentation Center of Cambodia.

Helman, Gerald B. and Steven R. Ratner. 1993. "Saving Failed States." *Foreign Policy* Winter.

Hinton, Alexander Laban. 2018. "Justice, Temporality, and Shame at the Khmer Rouge Tribunal." In *Temporality and Shame: Perspectives from Psychoanalysis and Philosophy*, edited by Ladson Hinton and Hessel Willemsen, 186–213. New York: Routledge.

Hinton, Alexander Laban. 2016. *Man or Monster? The Trial of a Khmer Rouge Torturer*. Durham, NC: Duke University Press.

Hinton, Alexander Laban. 2017. "The Tribunal." *Mekong Review* 3(1): 15–16.

Hinton, Alexander Laban. 2013. "Transitional Justice Time: Uncle San, Aunty Yan, and Outreach at the Khmer Rouge Tribunal." In *Genocide and Mass Atrocities in Asia: Legacies and Prevention*, edited by Deborah Meyersen and Annie Pohlman, 86–98. New York: Routledge.

Hinton, Alexander Laban. 2008. "Truth, Representation and the Politics of Memory after Genocide." In *People of Virtue: Reconfiguring Religion, Power and Morality in Cambodia Today*, edited by Alexandra Kent and David Chander, 62–81. Copenhagen: NIAS Press.

Hinton, Alexander Laban. 2005. *Why Did They Kill? Cambodia in the Shadow of Genocide*. Berkeley: University of California Press.

Hinton, Alexander Laban, ed. 2010a. *Transitional Justice: Global Mechanisms and Local Realities after Genocide and Mass Violence*. Piscataway, NJ: Rutgers University Press.

Hinton, Alexander Laban, ed. 2010b. "Introduction." In *Transitional Justice: Global Mechanisms and Local Realities after Genocide and Mass Violence*, edited by Alexander Laban Hinton, 1–22. Piscataway, NJ: Rutgers University Press.

Hinton, Devon E. and Alexander L. Hinton, eds. 2014. *Genocide and Mass Violence: Memory, Symptom, and Recovery*. New York: Cambridge University Press.

Hinton, Ladson and Hessel Willemsen, eds. 2018. *Temporality and Shame: Perspectives from Psychoanalysis and Philosophy*. New York: Routledge.

Hirsch, Marianne. 2012. *The Generation of Postmemory: Writing and Visual Culture After the Holocaust*. New York: Columbia University Press.

Hughes, Caroline. 2009. *Dependent Communities: Aid and Politics in Cambodia and East Timor*. Ithaca: Cornell Southeast Asia Program.

Hughes, Caroline. 1998. *Human Rights in Cambodia: International Intervention and National Response*. Doctoral Dissertation, University of Hull.

Hughes, Caroline. 2001. "Mystics and Militants: Democratic Reform in Cambodia." *International Politics* 38: 47–64.

Hughes, Caroline. 2003. *The Political Economy of Cambodia's Transition, 1991–2001*. London: RoutledgeCurzon.

Hughes, Caroline. 1996. *UNTAC in Cambodia: The Impact of Human Rights*. Singapore: Institute for Southeast Asian Studies.

Hughes, Caroline, Joakim Ojendal, and Isabell Schierenbeck. 2015. "The Struggle versus the Song —The Local Turn in Peacebuilding: An Introduction." *Third World Quarterly* 36(5): 817–24.

Hughes, Rachael. 2008. "Dutiful Tourism: Encountering the Cambodian Genocide." *Asia Pacific Viewpoint* 49(3): 318–30.

Hughes, Rachel. 2006. "Fielding Genocide: Post-1979 Cambodia and the Geopolitics of Memory." PhD dissertation, The University of Melbourne.

Human Resources Management. 2008. "Results of the Special Review Made Public: ECCC Human Resource Management Passes Scrutiny Test Successfully." ECCC, 27 March.

Human Rights Watch. 2002. "Cambodia: Khmer Rouge Tribunal Must Meet International Standards." Press Release, 19 December.

Huntington, Samuel P. 1991. "Democracy's Third Wave." *Journal of Democracy* 2(2): 12–34.

Huy, Vannak. 2010. *Bou Meng: A Khmer Rouge Survivor of S-21*. Phnom Penh: Documentation Center of Cambodia.

Huy, Vannak. 2008. "Bou Meng: A Khmer Rouge Survivor of S-21, Memory and Justice after the Khmer Rouge Genocide." MA Thesis, Division of Global Affairs, Rutgers University, Newark.

Igreja, Victor. 2012. "Multiple Temporalities in Indigenous Justice and Healing Practices in Mozambique." *International Journal of Transitional Justice* 6: 404–22.

Inda, Jonathan Xavier and Renato Rosaldo, eds. 2007. *The Anthropology of Globalization*. Malden, MA: Oxford University Press.

Jacobson, Trudy. 2006. "'Punishing' the perpetrators of Cambodian genocide." *NIASNytt* 3 (October-November): 6–7.

Jarvis, Helen. 2014. "'Justice for the Deceased': Victims' Participation in the Extraordinary Chambers in the Courts of Cambodia." *Genocide Studies and Prevention* 8(2): 19–27.

Johnson, Barbara. 1978. "The Critical Difference." *Diacritics* 8(2): 2–9.

Karwande, Maya. 2014. "Implementing an Engagement Model: Outreach at the Special Court for Sierra Leone." In *Transitional Justice, Culture, and Society: Beyond Outreach*, edited by Clara Ramírez-Barat, 49–95. New York: Social Science Research Council.

Kdei Karuna. N.d. "Our Programs." Phnom Penh: Kdei Karuna webpage (http://www.kdei-karuna.org).

Kelsall, Tim. 2013. *Culture under Cross-Examination: International Justice and the Special Court for Sierra Leone*. New York: Cambridge University Press.

Kersten, Mark. 2013. "Meeting the Devil's Advocate—An Interview with Jacques Vergès." Justiceinconflict.org, 26 August.

Khmer Institute of Democracy (KID). 2004. *Survey on the Khmer Rouge Regime and Khmer Rouge Tribunal*. Phnom Penh: Khmer Institute of Democracy.

Khmer Institute of Democracy (KID). 2008. *Uncle San, Aunty Yan, and the KRT*. Khmer Institute of Democracy. Phnom Penh, Cambodia.

Khmer Rouge Victims in Cambodia Press Release. 2011. "ECCC 1st-Recognized Civil Party and Representative of the Orphans Class, Theary Seng, Withdraws Her Civil Party Status and Denounces ECCC as 'Irredeemable Political Farce' that is Negating Justice, Soiling Memory, Embodying Cynicism." 15 November. Phnom Penh: Khmer Rouge Victims in Cambodia.

Khy, Sovuthy. 2016. "Adhoc President Wins Human Rights Award." *The Cambodian Daily*, December 3.

Kiernan, Ben. 2004. *How Pol Pot Came to Power: Colonialism, Nationalism, and Communism in Cambodia, 1930–1975*. New Haven: Yale University Press.

Kiernan, Ben. 2008. *The Pol Pot Regime: Race, Power, and Genocide in Cambodia under the Khmer Rouge, 1975–79*. New Haven: Yale University Press.

Kijewski, Leonie. 2017. "For survivors, even short 'testimony therapy' helps." *The Phnom Penh Post*, 20 January.

Kinetz, Erika. 2008. "Khmer Rouge Victims' Revolving Door Opens." *International Justice Tribune*, 18 February.

Kirchenbauer, Nadine, Mychelle Balthazard, Latt Ky, Patrick Vinck, and Phuong Pham. 2013. *Victim Participation before the Extraordinary Chambers in the Courts of Cambodia: Baseline Study of the Cambodian Human Rights and Development Association's*

Civil Party Scheme for Case 002. Phnom Penh and Cambridge, MA: Cambodian Human Rights and Development Association and Harvard Humanitarian Initiative.

Kleinman, Arthur, Veena Das, and Margaret M. Lock, eds. 1997. *Violence and Subjectivity.* Berkeley: University of California Press.

Korah, Susan. 2010. "Peacemaker from the 'Killing Fields'." Initiatives of Change International, 4 January.

Koskenniemi, Martti. 2002. "Between Impunity and Show Trials." *Max Planck Yearbook of United Nations Law* 6: 1–35.

Kritz, Neil, ed. 1995. *Transitional Justice: How Emerging Democracies Reckon with Former Regimes*, Volumes 1. General Considerations. Washington, DC: United States Institute of Peace.

Lacan, Jacques. 2007. *Écrits.* New York: WW Norton.

Lallah, Rajsoomer, Ninian Stephen, and Steven R. Ratner. 1999. "Report of the Group of Experts for Cambodia established pursuant to General Assembly Resolution 52/135." UN General Assembly Security Council, 53rd session, UN Doc A/53/850, 8 February.

Lambourne, Wendy. 2012. "Outreach, Inreach and Civil Society Participation in Transitional Justice." In *Critical Perspectives in Transitional Justice*, edited by Nicola Palmer, Phil Clark, and Danielle Granville, 235–61. Cambridge: Intersentia.

Lao, Mong Hay. 1998. "Building Democracy in Cambodia: Problems and Prospect." In *Cambodia and the International Community: The Quest for Peace, Development, and Democracy*, edited by Frederick Z. Brown and David G. Timberman. New York: Asia Society.

Lao, Mong Hay. 1999a. "Comment: The Agonizing Quest of Cambodia." *The Phnom Penh Post*, 5 February.

Lao, Mong Hay. 1999b. "Comment: The Development of Democracy in Cambodia." *The Phnom Penh Post*, 24 December.

Laqueur, Thomas. 1989. "Bodies, Details and the Humanitarian Narrative." In *The New Cultural History*, edited by Lynn Hunt, 176–204. Berkeley: University of California Press.

Latt, Ky, Nadine Kirchenbauer, and Melanie Wünsche. 2014. "Outreach Mapping." Phnom Penh: ADHOC Khmer Rouge Tribunal Project.

Lawther, Cheryl, Luke Moffett, and Dov Jacobs, eds. 2017. *Research Handbook on Transitional Justice.* Cheltenham: Edward Elgar.

Ledgerwood, Judy. 2012. "Buddhist Ritual and the Reordering of Social Relations in Cambodia." *South East Asia Research* 20(2): 175–90.

Ledgerwood, Judy. 1997. "The Cambodian Tuol Sleng Museum of Genocidal Crimes National Narrative." *Museum Anthropology* 21(1): 82–98.

Ledgerwood, Judy. 2009. "The Other Day I Saw a Monster." *Searching for the Truth*, August.

Ledgerwood, Judy. 1994. "UN Peacekeeping Missions: The Lessons from Cambodia." *Asia-Pacific Issues*, No 11 (March): 1–10.

Ledgerwood, Judy and Kheang Un. 2003. "Global Concepts and Local Meaning: Human Rights and Buddhism in Cambodia." *Journal of Human Rights* 2(4): 531–49.

Leitsinger, Miranda. 2010. "Cambodia Prepares for Historic Verdict from Genocide Tribunal." CNN, 25 July.

Leitsinger, Miranda. 2009. "First ex-Khmer Rouge Member faces Genocide Court." CNN, 16 February.

Lesley-Rozen, Elena. 2014. "Memory at the Site: Witnessing, education and the repurposing of Tuol Sleng and Choeung Ek in Cambodia." In *Remembering Genocide*, edited by Nigel Eltringham and Pam Maclean, 130–51. London: Routledge.

Leung, Wendy. 2004a. "Development Center Explains Irregularities." *The Cambodia Daily*, 25 November.

Leung, Wendy. 2004b. "Donors Cut Funds for Development Center." *The Cambodia Daily*, 24 November.

Levitt, Peggy and Sally Merry. 2009. "Vernacularization on the Ground: Local Uses of Global Women's Rights in Peru, China, India and the United States." *Global Networks* 9(4): 441–61.

Levy, Daniel and Natan Sznaider. 2006. *The Holocaust and Memory in the Global Age*. Philadelphia: Temple University Press.

Linton, Suzannah. 2004. *Reconciliation in Cambodia*. Phnom Penh: Documentation Center of Cambodia.

Luco, Fabienne. 2002. *Between a Tiger and a Crocodile: Management of Local Conflicts in Cambodia: An Anthropological Approach to Traditional and New Practices*. Phnom Penh: UNESCO.

Lutz, Ellen and Kathryn Sikkink. 2001. "The Justice Cascade: The Evolution and Impact of Foreign Human Rights Trials in Latin America." *Chicago Journal of International Law* 2(1): 1–34.

Ly, Sok-Kheang. 2014. "The Dynamics of Cambodia's Reconciliation Process, 1979 to 2007." PhD Dissertation, Coventry University.

MacDonald, Laura. 2009. "Traumatized Survivor Painted Pol Pot Amidst Screams for Help." *Cambodia Tribunal Monitor*, 1 July.

Mac Ginty, Roger and Oliver P. Richmond. 2013. "The Local Turn in Peace Building: A Critical Agenda for Peace." *Third World Quarterly* 34(5): 763–83.

Macau Daily Times Staff. 2008. "Chief of Personnel Removed from KRouge Court." *Macau Daily Times*, 13 August.

Madlingozi, Tshepo. 2011. "On Transitional Justice Entrepreneurs and the Production of Victims." *Journal of Human Rights Practice* 2(2): 208–28.

Madra, Ek. 2009. "Cambodian PM rejects wider Khmer Rouge trials." *Reuters*, 31 March.

Malkki, Liisa. 1995. *Purity and Exile: Violence, Memory, and National Cosmology among Hutu Refugees in Tanzania*. Chicago: University of Chicago Press.

Malkki, Liisa. 2015. *The Need to Help: The Domestic Arts of International Humanitarianism*. Durham, NC: Duke University Press.

Mani, Rama. 2002. *Beyond Retribution: Seeking Justice in the Shadows of War*. Cambridge: Polity.

Manning, Peter. 2011. "Governing Memory: Justice, Reconciliation and Outreach at the Extraordinary Chambers in the Courts of Cambodia." *Memory Studies* 5(2): 165–81.

Marcucci, John. 1994. "Sharing the Pain: Critical Values and Behaviors in Khmer Culture." In *Cambodian Culture since 1975: Homeland and Exile*, edited by May M. Ebihara, Carol A. Mortland, and Judy Ledgerwood, 129–40. Ithaca: Cornell University Press.

Marks, Stephen P. 2005. "Creating a Human Rights Culture: The Role of Local Knowledge in Cambodia's Difficult Transition." In *Global Justice and the Bulwarks of Localism: Human Rights in Context*, edited by Christopher L. Eisgruber and András Sajó, 257–90. Leiden: Martinus Nijhoff Publishers.

Marston, John. 1997. "Cambodia 1991–94: Hierarchy, Neutrality and Etiquettes of Discourse." PhD dissertation, University of Washington.

McCloud, Scott. 1993. *Understanding Comics: The Invisible Art*. New York: HarperCollins.

McDermid, Charles. 2007. "Looking Back at the 1979 People's Revolutionary Tribunal." *The Phnom Penh Post*, 26 January, 8–9.

McEvoy, Kieran. 2007. "Beyond Legalism: Towards a Thicker Understanding of Transitional Justice." *Journal of Law and Society* 34(4): 411–40.

McEvoy, Kieran and Mirsten McConnachie. 2013. "Victims and Transitional Justice: Voice, Agency and Blame." *Social and Legal Studies* 22(4): 489–513.

McEvoy, Kieran and Lorna McGregor. 2008. *Transitional Justice from Below: Grassroots Activism and the Struggle for Change.* Oxford: Hart Publishing.

McGrane, Sally. 2009. "A Drama of Closure for Victims and Perpetrators of the Khmer Rouge." *The New York Times*, 14 March.

Meierhenrich, Jens and Devin O. Pendas. 2017. "'The Justice of My Cause is Clear, but There's Politics to Fear': Political Trials in Theory and History." In *Political Trials in Theory and History*, edited by Jens Meierhenrich and Devin O. Pendas, 1–64. New York: Cambridge University Press.

Meisenberg, Simon M. and Ignaz Stegmiller, eds. 2016. *The Extraordinary Chambers in the Courts of Cambodia: Assessing their Contribution to International Criminal Law.* The Hague: TMC Asser Press.

Men Kimseng. 2010. "'Breaking the Silence' Takes Courage: Actress." VOA Khmer. 3 May.

Merry, Sally Engle. 2006a. "Anthropology and International Law." *Annual Review of Anthropology* (23): 99–116.

Merry, Sally Engle. 2006b. *Human Rights and Gender Violence: Translating International Law into Local Justice.* Chicago: University of Chicago Press.

Merry, Sally Engle. 2016. *The Seductions of Quantification: Measuring Human Rights, Gender Violence, and Sex Trafficking.* New York: Cambridge University Press.

Merry, Sally Engle. 2010. "What is Legal Culture: An Anthropological Perspective." *Journal of Comparative Law* 5(2): 40–58.

Miller, Zinaida. 2008. "Effects of Invisibility: In Search of the 'Economic' in Transitional Justice." *International Journal of Transitional Justice* 2(3): 266–91.

Minow, Martha. 1998. *Between Vengeance and Forgiveness: Facing History after Genocide and Mass Violence.* Boston: Beacon.

Moon, Claire. 2009. "Healing Past Violence: Traumatic Assumptions and Therapeutic Interventions in War and Reconciliation." *Journal of Human Rights* 8: 71–91.

More, Thomas. 2003. *Utopia.* New York: Penguin.

Morris, Steven J. 1999. *Why Vietnam Invaded Cambodia: Political Culture and the Causes of War.* Stanford: Stanford University Press.

Mosse, David. 2013. "The Anthropology of International Development." *Annual Review of Anthropology* 42: 227–46.

Mosse, David, ed. 2011. *Adventures in Aidland: The Anthropology of Professionals in International Development.* New York: Berghahn.

Moyn, Samuel. 2012. *The Last Utopia: Human Rights in History.* Cambridge, MA: Harvard University Press.

Mueller-Hirth, Natascha. 2017. "Temporalities of Victimhood: Time in the Study of Postconflict Societies." *Sociological Forum* 32(1): 186–206.

Munthit, Ker. 2008a. "Cambodian Genocide Tribunal Faces Allegations." *Associated Press*, 6 August.

Munthit, Ker. 2008b. "Khmer Rouge Defendant Visits Grave Site." *Associated Press*, 26 February.

Munthit, Ker. 1992. "Rights group opens offices in Kandal." *The Phnom Penh Post*, 4 December.

Münyas, Burcu. 2008. "Genocide in the minds of Cambodian youth: Transmitting (hi)stories of genocide to second and third generations in Cambodia." *Journal of Genocide Research* 10(3): 413–39.

Mutua, Makau. 2001. "Savages, Victims, and Saviors: The Metaphor of Human Rights." *Harvard International Law Journal* 42(1): 210–45.

Mutua, Makau. 2015. "What is the Future of Transitional Justice?" *International Journal of Transitional Justice* 9: 1–9.

Mydans, Seth. 2006. "A Survivor Documents Cambodia's Nightmare." *International Herald Tribune*, 4 September.

Mydans, Seth. 1997. "Cambodian Aesop Tells A Fable of Forgiveness." *The New York Times*, 28 June.

Mydans, Seth. 1998b. "Cambodian Leader Resists Punishing Top Khmer Rouge." *The New York Times*, 29 December.

Mydans, Seth. 2007. "Former Khmer Rouge Leader Arrested." *The New York Times*, 20 September.

Mydans, Seth. 1998a. "Under Prodding, 2 Apologize for Cambodian Anguish." *The New York Times*, 30 December.

Myers, Bill and Matt Reed. 2002. "Institute Disowns Ex-Director." *The Cambodia Daily*, 26 June.

Nagy, Rosemary. 2008. "Transitional Justice as a Global Project: Critical Reflections." *Third World Quarterly* 29(2): 275–89.

Naren, Kuch and Alice Foster. 2012. "Ten Duch Victims Celebrate Civil Party Status." *Cambodian Daily*, 4–5 February.

Nelson, Krista. 2010. "Reconciliation Road: Bridging Communities, Rebuilding Trust." *Searching for the Truth*, 59.

Neth, Pheaktra and Sebastian Strangio. 2009. "A Visionary Behind the Scenes." *The Phnom Penh Post*, 2 March.

Neou, Kassie and Jeffrey C. Gallup. 1997. "Teaching Human Rights in Cambodia." *Journal of Democracy* 8(4): 154–64.

Neuman, A. Lin. 2006. "Spokesperson for Ghosts." *Asia Sentinel*, 6 October.

NIMH Press Release. 2005. "PTSD, Depression Epidemic among Cambodian Immigrants." National Institute of Mental Health, 2 August.

Nissen, Christine J. 2005. *Living Under the Rule of Corruption: An Analysis of Everyday Forms of Corrupt Practices in Cambodia*. Phnom Penh, Center for Social Development.

Nuon Chea Defense Team. 2012. "Ieng Sary's application to disqualify Judge Nil Nonn due to his purported admission that he has accepted bribes & request for a public hearing or in the alternative for leave to reply to any submissions presented by Judge Nil Nonn in response to this application." Phnom Penh: ECCC, 14 January.

Nuon Chea Defense Team. 2017. Nuon Chea's Closing Brief in Case 002/02. Phnom Penh: ECCC.

Nuon Chea Defense Team. 2013. Nuon Chea's Closing Submission in Case 002/01. Phnom Penh: ECCC.

Nov, Ann and Jody McPhillips. 2000. "The Poster Boy for Democracy." *The Cambodia Daily*, 11 November.

O'Donnell, Guillermo and Philippe C. Schmitter 1986. *Transitions from Authoritarian Rule: Tentative Conclusions about Uncertain Democracies*. Baltimore: The Johns Hopkins University Press.

Office of the Co-Investigating Judges (OCIJ). 2010. "Closing Order [Case 002]." Phnom Penh, ECCC, 15 September.

Office of the Co-Investigating Judges (OCIJ). 2012. "Note of the International Reserve Co-Investigating Judge to the Parties on the Egregious Dysfunctions within the ECCC Impeding the Proper Conduct of Investigations in Cases 003 and 004." Phnom Penh: ECCC, 21 March.

Office of the Co-Investigating Judges (OCIJ). 2008a. "OCIJ Statement on Reconstruction Recording." Phnom Penh: ECCC, 3 March.

Office of the Co-Investigating Judges (OCIJ). 2007. "Provisional Detention Order (Ieng Sary)." Phnom Penh, ECCC, C22, 14 November.

Office of the Co-Investigating Judges (OCIJ). 2008c. "Report on Reconstruction [Choueng Ek]." Phnom Penh: ECCC, E3/242, 11 April.

Office of the Co-Investigating Judges (OCIJ). 2008b. "Report on Reconstruction [Tuol Sleng]." Phnom Penh: ECCC, E3/244, 11 April.

Office of the Co-Prosecutors (OCP). 2011b. "Statement by the National Co-Prosecutor regarding Case File 003." Phnom Penh: ECCC, 10 May.

Office of the Co-Prosecutors (OCP). 2011a. "Statement from the International Co-Prosecutor regarding Case File 003." Phnom Penh, ECCC, 9 May.

Office of the Co-Prosecutors (OCP). 2017. "Co-Prosecutors' Closing Brief." Phnom Penh: ECCC.

Office of the Co-Prosecutors (OCP). 2009. "Statement of the Co-Prosecutors." Phnom Penh: ECCC. 5 January.

Ong, Aihwa and Stephen J. Collier, eds. 2008. *Global Assemblages: Technology, Politics, and Ethics as Anthropological Problems*. Malden, MA: Wiley.

Open Society Justice Initiative. 2007. "Corruption Allegations at Khmer Rouge Court Must Be Investigated Thoroughly." Press Release, New York: Open Society Justice Initiative, 14 February.

Ortner, Sherry B. 1984. "Theory in Anthropology since the Sixties." *Comparative Studies in Society and History* 26(1): 126–66.

Osborne, Lawrence. 2009. "The Goya of the Cambodian Genocide." *Forbes*, 20 March.

Oxford English Dictionary. 2015. Oxford: Oxford University Press.

Palan, Anugraha. 1994. "NGO in first Khmer criticism of UNTAC." *The Phnom Penh Post*, 23 September.

Panh, Rithy. 2011. "Tribute for Vann Nath." 14 September. E-mail from Association le Cercle des Amis de Vann Nath.

Payne, Leigh. 2008. *Unsettling Accounts: Neither Truth nor Reconciliation in Confessions of State Violence*. Durham, NC: Duke University Press.

Pentelovitch, Norman Henry. 2009. "Project Evaluation: Living Documents Project." Phnom Penh: Documentation Center of Cambodia.

Pentelovitch, Norman Henry. 2008. "Seeing Justice Done: The Importance of Prioritizing Outreach Efforts at International Criminal Tribunals." *Georgetown Journal of International Law* 39(3): 445–94.

Peskin, Victor. 2005. "Courting Rwanda: The Promises and Pitfalls of the ICTR Outreach Programme." *Journal of International Criminal Justice* 3: 950–61.

Peskin, Victor. 2008. *International Justice in Rwanda and the Balkans*. New York: Cambridge University Press.

Pham, Phuong, Patrick Vinck, Mychelle Balthazard, and Sokhom Hean. 2011. *After the First Trial: A Population-Based Survey of Knowledge and Perception of Justice and the Extraordinary Chambers in the Courts of Cambodia*. Berkeley: Human Rights Center, University of California, Berkeley.

Pham, Phuong, Patrick Vinck, Mychelle Balthazard, Sokhom Hean, and Eric Stover. 2009. *So We Will Never Forget: A Population-Based Survey on Attitudes about Social Reconstruction and the Extraordinary Chambers in the Courts of Cambodia.* Berkeley: University of California Human Rights Center.

Pham, Phuong, Patrick Vinck, Mychelle Balthazard, Judith Strasser, and Chariya Om. 2011. "Victim Participation and the Trial of Duch at the Extraordinary Chambers in the Courts of Cambodia." *Journal of Human Rights Practice* 3(3): 264–87.

Phay-Vakalis, Soko, ed. 2010a. *Cambodge: L'Atelier de la Mémoire.* Phnom Penh: Éditions Sonleuk Thmey.

Phay-Vakalis, Soko. 2010b. "Confronting the Cambodian Tragedy with Art." In *Cambodge: L'Atelier de la Mémoire*, edited by Soko Phay-Vakalis, 208–17. Phnom Penh: Éditions Sonleuk Thmey.

Phnom Penh Domestic Service. 1976b. "Khieu Samphan Report," Foreign Broadcast Information Services, Asia & Pacific, 6 January.

Phnom Penh Domestic Service. 1976a. "The Constitution of Democratic Kampuchea," Foreign Broadcast Information Services, Asia & Pacific, 5 January.

Phnom Penh Post Staff. 2007. "1979 Trial Revisited." *The Phnom Penh Post*, 26 January.

Phnom Penh Post Staff. 2014. "Architecture of Justice: Sketches of a Historic Day." *The Phnom Penh Post*, 9 August, 15.

Phnom Penh Post Staff. 2000. "Cambodians Talk about the Khmer Rouge Trial." *The Phnom Penh Post*, 4–17 February.

Picq, Laurence. 1989. *Beyond the Horizon: Five Years with the Khmer Rouge.* New York: St. Martin's.

Pike, Amanda. 2002. "Battambang: The Judge." *PBS Frontline World*, October.

Plato. 2013. *The Republic.* New York: Penguin.

Ponchaud, François. 1989. "Social Change in the Vortex of Revolution." In *Cambodia 1975–1978: Rendezvous with Death*, edited by Karl D. Jackson, 151–78. Princeton: Princeton University Press.

Pre-Trial Chamber. 2008f. "Application for Declarative Relief for Civil Party to Speak in Person, not for Re-Hearing." Phnom Penh: ECCC, 17 July.

Pre-Trial Chamber. 2008b. "Decision on Civil Party Participation in Provisional Detention Appeals." Phnom Penh: ECCC, 20 March.

Pre-Trial Chamber. 2008c. "Directions on Civil Party Oral Submission during the Hearing of the Appeal against Provisional Detention Order." Phnom Penh, ECCC, 20 May.

Pre-Trial Chamber. 2008a. "Joint and Several Submissions on Civil-Party Participation in Appeals Related to Provisional Detention." Phnom Penh: ECCC, 22 February.

Pre-Trial Chamber 2008e. "Public Decision on the Co-Lawyers' Urgent Application for Disqualification of Judge Ney Thol Pending the Appeal against the Provisional Detention Order in the Case of Nuon Chea." Phnom Penh: ECCC, Case File 002/10-09-2007-ECCC/OCIJ (PTC 01), 4 February.

Pre-Trial Chamber (PTC). 2012. "Public Redacted Considerations of the Pre-Trial Chamber Regarding the Appeal against Order on the Admissibility of Civil Party Applicant [redacted]." Phnom Penh: ECCC, 28 February.

Pre-Trial Chamber. 2008d. "Written Version of Oral Decision of 1 July 2008 on the Civil Party's Request to Address the Court in Person." Phnom Penh: ECCC.

Prins, Annemarie. 2009. *Breaking the Silence: A New Cambodian Play.* Phnom Penh: Documentation Center of Cambodia.

Public Affairs Section (PAS). 2014. "Annex 2: PAS Outreach Figures 2009–2014 As of 30 June 2014." Phnom Penh: ECCC.

Public Affairs Section (PAS). 2010. "Press Release – 32,633 Persons Visited the ECCC in 2010." Phnom Penh: ECCC, 30 December.

Public Affairs Section (PAS). 2009. "Press Release: More than 12,000 visitors have attended the Duch Trial." Phnom Penh: ECCC, 22 July.

Raab, Michaela and Julian Polunda. 2010. "Justice for the Survivors and for Future Generations: ADHOC's ECCC/ICC Justice Project, December 2006–March 2010." Project Evaluation. Phnom Penh: ADHOC.

Ramírez-Barat, Clara. 2011. *Making an Impact: Guidelines on Designing and Implementing Outreach Programs for Transitional Justice*. New York: International Center for Transitional Justice.

Ramírez-Barat, Clara, ed. 2014a. *Transitional Justice, Culture, and Society: Beyond Outreach*. New York: Social Science Research Council.

Ramírez-Barat, Clara. 2014b. "Transitional Justice and the Public Sphere." In *Transitional Justice, Culture, and Society: Beyond Outreach*, edited by Clara Ramírez-Barat, 27–45. New York: Social Science Research Council.

Ramírez-Barat, Clara and Maya Karwande. 2010. *Outreach Strategies in International and Hybrid Courts: Report of the ICTJ-ECCC Workshop, Phnom Penh, Cambodia, March 3–5, 2010*. New York: International Center for Transitional Justice.

Ramji, Jaya and Beth Van Schaack, eds. 2005. *Bringing the Khmer Rouge to Justice: Prosecuting Mass Violence Before the Cambodian Courts*. Lewiston, NY: Edward Mellen.

Riaño Acalá, Pila and Erin Baines. 2012. "Editorial Note." *International Journal of Transitional Justice* 6(3): 385–93.

Richmond, Oliver P. and Audra Mitchell, eds. 2012. *Hybrid Forms of Peace: From Everyday Agency to Post-Liberalism*. New York: Palgrave.

Riles, Annelise. 2001. *The Network Inside Out*. Ann Arbor, MI: University of Michigan Press.

Roberts, David W. 2001. *Political Transition in Cambodia 1991–99: Power, Elitism and Democracy*. New York: St. Martin's Press.

Rojas-Perez, Isaias. 2017. *Mourning Remains: State Atrocity, Exhumations, and Governing the Disappeared in Peru's Postwar Andes*. Stanford: Stanford University Press.

Ross, Fiona. 2003. *Bearing Witness: Women and the Truth and Reconciliation Commission in South Africa*. London: Pluto.

Said, Edward. 1989. *Orientalism*. New York: Vintage.

Sanford, Victoria. 2003. *Buried Secrets: Truth and Human Rights in Guatemala*. New York: Palgrave.

Sann, Kalyan and Sokhym Em. 2002. "Interview with Samdech Preah Sokunthea Thibdei Bour Kry, Supreme Head of the Sangha of the Thommayut Nikay (Buddhism Theravada) of the Kingdom of Cambodia." *Searching for the Truth*, 34 (October): 39.

Saray, Thun. 2006. "'No Perfect Justice': Interviews with Thun Saray, Son Chhay, and Ou Vannath." In *The Extraordinary Chambers*, 109–12. New York: Open Society Justice Initiative.

Savelsberg, Joachim J. 2015. *Representing Mass Violence: Conflicting Responses to Human Rights Violations in Darfur*. Berkeley: University of California Press.

Scheffer, David. 2011. *All the Missing Souls: A Personal History of the War Crimes Tribunals*. Princeton: Princeton University Press.

Schlund-Vials, Cathy J. 2012. *War, Genocide, and Justice: Cambodian American Memory Work*. Minneapolis: University of Minnesota Press.

Scott, James C. 1998. *Seeing Like a State: How Certain Schemes to Improve the Human Condition Have Failed.* New Haven: Yale University Press.

Seidel, Katrin. 2015. "In the Name of the 'Rule of Law'." AllegraLab, 23 January.

Seng, Theary C. 2008. "[4 February] Statement of Civil Party Theary Seng to Pre-Trial Chamber: Nuon Chea's Appeal of Provisional Detention." *The Phnom Penh Post*, 20 March.

Seng, Theary C. 2005. *Daughter of the Killing Fields: Asrei's Story.* London: Fusion Press.

Seng, Theary C. 2012. "Duch Final Pronouncement." Theary C. Seng website, 3 February.

Seng, Theary C. 2010. "The Extraordinary Chambers in the Courts of Cambodia: The Issues and Challenges of Prosecuting the Senior Leaders of the Khmer Rouge Regime." Rutgers School of Law Symposium, 2 April.

Seng, Theary C. 2007. "Understanding Trauma in Cambodia." *The Phnom Penh Post*, 14 December.

Ser, Sayana. 2009. "Breaking the Silence: Hope Regained." *Searching for the Truth*, First Quarter (Special English Edition): 48–50.

Sharp, Dustin N. 2014. "Addressing Dilemmas of the Global and the Local in Transitional Justice." *Emory International Law* 29: 71–117.

Sharp, Dustin N. 2015. "Emancipating Transitional Justice from the Bonds of the Paradigmatic Transition." *International Journal of Transitional Justice* 9(1): 150–69.

Sharp, Dustin N. 2013. "Interrogating the Peripheries: The Preoccupations of Fourth Generation Transitional Justice." *Harvard Human Rights Journal* 26: 149–78.

Shaw, Rosalind. 2007. "Memory Frictions: Localizing the Truth and Reconciliation Commission in Sierra Leone." *International Journal of Transitional Justice* 1: 183–207.

Shaw, Rosalind and Lars Waldorf, eds. 2010. *Localizing Transitional Justice: Interventions and Priorities after Mass Violence.* Stanford: Stanford University Press.

Sikkink, Kathryn. 2011. *The Justice Cascade: How Human Rights Prosecutions are Changing World Politics.* New York: WW Norton.

Sikkink, Kathryn and Hun Joon Kim. 2013. "The Justice Cascade: The Origins and Effectiveness of Prosecutions of Human Rights Violations." *Annual Review of Law and Social Science* 9: 269–85.

Simic, Olivera, ed. 2017. *An Introduction to Transitional Justice.* New York: Routledge.

Sirik, Savina. 2009. "Report on the ECCC Tour and Genocide Education, August 16–18, 2009." Phnom Penh: Documentation Center of Cambodia.

So, Farina. 2011. *The Hijab of Cambodia: Memories of Cham Muslim Women after the Khmer Rouge.* Phnom Penh: Documentation Center of Cambodia.

Sokha, Cheang and James O'Toole. 2010. "Hun Sen to Ban Ki-moon: Case 002 last trial at the ECCC." *The Phnom Penh Post*, 27 October.

Sonis, Jeffrey, James L. Gibson, Joop TVM de Jong, Nigel P. Field, Sokhom Hean, and Ivan Komproe. 2009. "Probable Posttraumatic Stress Disorder and Disability in Cambodia: Associations with Perceived Justice, Desire for Revenge, and Attitudes Toward the Khmer Rouge Trials." *JAMA* 302(50): 527–36.

Sperfeldt, Christoph. 2012a. "Cambodian Civil Society and the Khmer Rouge Tribunal." *International Journal of Transitional Justice.* 6: 149–60.

Sperfeldt, Christoph. 2012b. "Collective Reparations at the Extraordinary Chambers in the Courts of Cambodia." *International Criminal Law Review* 12: 457–89.

Sperfeldt, Christoph. 2013. "The Role of Cambodian Civil Society in the Victim Participation Scheme of the Extraordinary Chambers in the Courts of Cambodia." In

Victims of International Crimes: An Interdisciplinary Discourse, edited by T. Bonacker and C. Safferling, 345–72. The Hague: TMC Asser Press.

Spivak, Gayatri C. 1994. "Can the Subaltern Speak." In *Colonial Discourse and Post-Colonial Theory: A Reader*, edited by Patrick Williams and Laura Chrisman, 66–111. New York: Columbia University Press.

Springer, Simon. 2015. *Violent Neoliberalism: Development, Discourse and Dispossession in Cambodia*. New York: Palgrave Macmillan.

Stanton, Gregory H. Undated. "Perfection is the Enemy of Justice: A Response to Amnesty International's Critique of the Draft Agreement Between the U.N. and Cambodia," Genocide Watch (http://www.genocidewatch.org).

Stover, Eric, Mychelle Balthazard, and K. Alexa Koenig. 2011. "Confronting Duch: Civil Party Participation in Case 001 at the Extraordinary Chambers in the Courts of Cambodia." *International Review of the Red Cross* 93(882): 503–46.

Stover, Eric and Harvey M. Weinstein, eds. 2004. *My Neighbor, My Enemy: Justice and Community in the Aftermath of Mass Atrocity*. New York: Cambridge University Press.

Subotic, Jelena. 2009. *Hijacked Justice: Dealing with the Past in the Balkans*. Ithaca, NY: Cornell University Press.

Taylor, Charles. 2004. *Modern Social Imaginaries*, Durham, NC: Duke University Press.

Teitel, Ruti G. 2015. *Globalizing Transitional Justice: Contemporary Essays*. New York: Oxford University Press.

Teitel, Ruti G. 2003. "Transitional Justice Genealogy." *Harvard Human Rights Journal* 16: 69–94.

Thayer, Nate. 1999. "Death in Detail." *Far Eastern Economic Review* 162(18), 13 May.

The War Cry Staff. 2005. "Killing Fields daughter wants justice." *The War Cry*, October 2005.

Theidon, Kimberly. 2014. *Intimate Enemies: Violence and Reconciliation in Peru*. Philadelphia: University of Pennsylvania Press.

Thomas, Sarah and Terith Chy. 2009. "Including the Survivors in the Tribunal Process." In *On Trial: The Khmer Rouge Accountability Process*, edited by John D Ciorciari and Anne Heindel, 214–93. Phnom Penh: Documentation Center of Cambodia.

Titthara, May and Mary Kozlovski. 2011. "KRT interference alleged." *The Phnom Penh Post*, 25 October.

Trial Chamber. 2008. "Decision on the Request of the Co-Lawyers for Civil Party Group 2 to make an Opening Statement during the Substantive Hearing." Phnom Penh: ECCC, 27 March.

Trial Chamber. 2010. "Trial Chamber Judgment, Announced on 26 July 2010, Case 001, Kaing Guek Eav alias Duch." Phnom Penh: ECCC, 26 July.

Tsing, Anna. 2005. *Friction: An Ethnography of Global Connection*. Princeton: Princeton University Press.

Ullrich, Leila. 2016. "Beyond the 'Global-Local Divide': Local Intermediaries, Victims and the Justice Contestations of the International Criminal Court." *Journal of International Criminal Justice* 14: 543–68.

Un, Kheang. 2004. "Democratization without Consolidation: The Case of Cambodia, 1993–2004." PhD Dissertation, Northern Illinois University.

Un, Kheang. 2009. "The Judicial System and Democratization in Post-Conflict Cambodia." In *Beyond Democracy in Cambodia: Political Reconstruction in a Post-Conflict Society*, edited by Joakim Öjendal and Mona Lilja, 70–100. Copenhagen: Nordic Institute of Asian Studies.

United Nations. 1997. "Report of the Special Representative of the Secretary-General for Human Rights in Cambodia, Mr. Thomas Hammarberg, Submitted in Accordance with Commission Resolution 1996/54." UN Economic and Security Council. E/CN.4/1997/85, 31 January.

United Nations. 2008. "What is Transitional Justice: A Backgrounder." 20 February.

United Nations Commission on Human Rights. 1997. "Situation of Human Rights in Cambodia." UN Commission on Human Rights Resolution 1997/49, 11 April.

United Nations Secretary-General. 2004. *The Rule of Law and Transitional Justice in Post-Conflict Societies*. New York: United Nations Security Council (UN Doc S/2004/616), 23 August.

UNTAC Human Rights Component (UNTAC HRC). 1993. "Final Report." Phnom Penh: United Nations Transitional Authority in Cambodia, September.

Urs, Tara. 2007. "Imagining Locally-motivated Accountability for Mass Atrocities: Voices from Cambodia." *Sur: International Journal of Human Rights* 7: 61–100.

Urs, Tara. 2006. *Memorandum on Outreach Strategies for the Extraordinary Chambers in the Courts of Cambodia*. New York: Open Society Justice Initiative.

Vann, Nath. 1998. *A Cambodian Prison Portrait: One year in the Khmer Rouge's S-21*. Bangkok: White Lotus.

Veasna, Mean. 2008. "UNDP: Government Won't Probe Tribunal Allegations." *Voice of America*, 21 February.

Venuti, Lawrence, ed. 2012. *The Translation Studies Reader*. New York: Routledge.

Vickery, Michael. 2000. *Cambodia 1975–1982*. Bangkok: Silkworm.

Victims Support Section. N.d. "Statistics: Civil Party applicants per Case File." Phnom Penh: ECCC.

Victims Support Section. 2010a. "250 Civil Parties Meet ECCC Officials and Lawyers at the Regional Forum for Case 002 Civil Parties." 30–31 August. Phnom Penh: ECCC.

Victims Support Section. 2010b. "Report of the Kratie Forum—Regional Public Forum at Hor Bunny Conference Room, Kratie Provincial Town, Monday, 20 December 2010." Phnom Penh: ECCC.

Victims Unit. 2008. "Historic Achievement in international criminal law: Victims of Khmer Rouge crimes fully involved in proceedings of the ECCC." Statement by the Victims Unit, 4 February. Phnom Penh: ECCC.

VOA Staff Report. 2010. "Breaking Ground on 'Reconciliation Road'." *Voice of America Khmer*, 10 March.

Wagner, Sarah. 2008. *To Know Where He Lies: DNA Technology and the Search for Srebrenica's Missing*. Berkeley: University of California Press.

Watson, James L. ed. 1997. *Golden Arches East: McDonalds in East Asia*. Stanford: Stanford University Press.

Weinstein, Harvey M. 2011. "The Myth of Closure, the Illusion of Reconciliation: Final Thoughts on Five Years as Co-editor-in-Chief." *International Journal of Transitional Justice* 5(1): 1–10.

Williams, Raymond. 1980. "Ideas of Nature." In *Problems in Materialism and Culture, selected essays by Raymond Williams*, 67–85. London: Verso.

Wilson, Richard Asbury. 2001. *The Politics of Truth and Reconciliation in South Africa*. New York: Cambridge University Press.

Wilson, Richard Asbury. 2011. *Writing History in International Courts*. New York: Cambridge University Press.

Witzel, Matthias. 2007. *Understanding Trauma in Cambodia: Basic Concepts*. Phnom Penh: Center for Social Development.

World People's Blog Staff. 2007. "Chea Vannath—Cambodia." *World People's Blog*, 19 December.

Yonekura, Yukiko. 1999. "The Role of Civil Society in Cambodia: Its Role in the Democratisation Process." PhD Dissertation, University of Sussex.

Zigon, Jarrett. 2009. "Phenomenological Anthropology and Morality: A Reply to Robbins." *Ethnos* 74(2): 286–88.

Zigon, Jarrett. 2014. "What is a Situation? An Assemblic Ethnography of the War on Terror." *Cultural Anthropology* 30(3): 501–24.

Index